Giuseppe Veltri
A Mirror of Rabbinic Hermeneutics

Studia Judaica

Forschungen zur Wissenschaft des Judentums

Begründet von
Ernst Ludwig Ehrlich

Herausgegeben von
Günter Stemberger, Charlotte Fonrobert
und Alexander Samely

Band 82

Giuseppe Veltri
A Mirror of Rabbinic Hermeneutics

―

Studies in Religion, Magic and Language Theory
in Ancient Judaism

DE GRUYTER

ISBN 978-3-11-055276-8
e-ISBN (PDF) 978-3-11-036641-9
e-ISBN (EPUB) 978-3-11-043778-2
ISSN 0585-5306

Library of Congress Cataloging-in-Publication Data
A CIP catalog record for this book has been applied for at the Library of Congress.

Bibliographic information published by the Deutsche Nationalbibliothek
The Deutsche Nationalbibliothek lists this publication in the Deutsche Nationalbibliografie;
detailed bibliographic data are available on the Internet at http://dnb.dnb.de.

© 2017 Walter de Gruyter GmbH, Berlin/Boston
This volume is text- and page-identical with the hardback published in 2015.
Typesetting: Meta Systems Publishing & Printservices GmbH, Wustermark
Printing and Binding: CPI books GmbH, Leck
♾ Printed on acid-free paper
Printed in Germany

www.degruyter.com

To my daughter
Livia Filomena Ina

The craft of the word created the universe
ταύτῃ καὶ ὁ τῶν Ἰουδαίων θεσμοθέτης, οὐχ ὁ τυχὼν ἀνήρ, ἐπειδὴ τὴν τοῦ θείου δύναμιν κατὰ τὴν ἀξίαν ἐχώρησε κἀξέφηνεν, εὐθὺς ἐν τῇ εἰσβολῇ γράψας τῶν νόμων "εἶπεν ὁ Θεός", φησί, – τί; "γενέσθω φῶς, καὶ ἐγένετο· γενέσθω γῆ, καὶ ἐγένετο."
(Ps-Longinus, *Perì hýpsous* 8:9).

A missing letter can destroy the entire world
אמר לי בני הוי זהיר במלאכתך שמלאכתך
מלאכת שמים היא שמא אתה מחסר אות אחת או
מייתר אות אחת נמצאת מחריב את כל העולם
כולו
(*Babylonian Talmud Eruvin* 13a)

The intelligent word is universal
כל האומר דברי חכמה אפי' באומות העולם
נקרא חכם
(*Babylonian Talmud Megillah* 16a)

Contents

Introduction —— 1

Documentation style, transliteration and references —— 11

Part I: Officina rabbinica

1 Impertinent Students vs. Sagacious Rabbis: The Art of Learning —— 15
1.1 The Student —— 18
1.2 He Who Always Asks —— 20
1.3 Impertinence is the Beginning of Wisdom —— 21

2 Ezra as "Reformer" in Classical Jewish Literature —— 25
2.1 The Reformation in the 16th century —— 25
2.2 Ezra the Reformer —— 29
2.3 Conclusion —— 38

Part II: Reflecting Roman Religion

3 Roman Religion at the Periphery of the Empire —— 43
3.1 Religious Customs: The Rhetoric of Ethics —— 47
3.1.1 "Roman" Sources for the "Rabbinic" Romans —— 47
3.1.2 Political and Popular "Religiosity" or Culture: Theatre and the Circenses —— 49
3.1.3 The Rhetoric of Ethics —— 64
3.2 Holidays: Religion, Politics, and Social Life —— 64
3.2.1 On the History of Research —— 65
3.2.2 The Calendar —— 66
3.2.3 The Typology of the Festivals —— 68
3.2.4 Day of Rest, pollutio, and Permissions of Commerce —— 69
3.2.5 The Day of Rain: A Judeo-Roman Festival? —— 73
3.2.6 Kalendae —— 75
3.2.7 Elements: Wishes and Presents —— 77
3.2.8 The Rabbinic Explanations of the Origin of the Kalendae —— 79
3.2.8.1 Topos 1: Yanubris and the Calendar —— 82
3.2.8.2 Topos 2: A Black Day —— 82

3.2.8.3	Topos 3: The Voluntary Death of a King —— **83**	
3.2.8.4	The Kalendae: A Detail? —— **84**	
3.2.9	Saturnalia and Sigillaria —— **85**	
3.2.10	Κράτησις —— **89**	
3.2.11	Feriae Imperatoris —— **91**	
3.2.12	Birthday and Day of Death —— **91**	
3.2.13	Apotheosis —— **92**	
3.3	Conclusion —— **94**	

Part III: Performing the Craft of Science & Magic

4	**The Science(s) and "Greek Wisdom"** —— **99**	
4.1	Greek Wisdom and Everyday Sciences —— **101**	
4.2	Empirical Science: Medicine —— **106**	
4.3	Theoretical Science: Astrology —— **110**	
4.4	Conclusion —— **114**	

5	**On Magic: Past and Present Research** —— **115**	
5.1	Magic in Past and Present Scholarship —— **115**	
5.1.1	The Polemic-Apologetic Approach —— **115**	
5.1.2	Archaeological and Philological Research —— **118**	
5.1.3	Folklore and Folk Life Studies —— **121**	
5.1.4	Mysticism, Kabbalah, and Jewish Magic —— **121**	
5.1.5	The Halakhic-Theological Approach —— **123**	
5.2	Magic and Methods in Studying Magic —— **124**	

6	**"Ways of the Amorite" and Hellenism in Jewish Palestine** —— **129**
6.1	The *darkhe ha-emori* —— **132**
6.2	Halakhic Attitudes to Magic and Science —— **144**
6.2.1	Good Manners —— **146**
6.2.2	Common Sense —— **146**
6.2.3	Established and Deep-Rooted Convictions —— **147**
6.2.4	Empirical Observation —— **147**
6.3	Pliny and the "Foreign" Customs of the Magi —— **148** Appendix: A Comparison between Pliny and Tosefta Shabbat —— **154**

7	**The Magician/Magush in Rabbinic Judaism** —— **159**
7.1	Magus & Physician —— **160**

| 7.2 | Magician and Illusionist —— **165** |
| 7.3 | Medieval Developments —— **170** |

8 **"Watermarks" in the MS *Munich, Hebr.* 95 —— 173**
8.1	Notes on the Manuscript —— **174**
8.2	A Page, or Fragments of a Handbook? —— **174**
8.3	Water, Waters, Creation, and other Mirabilia —— **179**
8.4	A Veritable "Watermark" —— **182**

9 **The Meal of the Spirits, the Three *Parcae* and Lilith —— 185**
9.1	A Decree by Burkhard, Bishop of Worms: The Table Set for the Three *Parcae* —— **188**
9.2	The Prepared Table —— **190**
9.3	Sideros (Iron), Lilith, and the Name of God —— **196**
9.4	Concluding Thoughts —— **200**

10 **Evidence and Plausibility: on Magic and Ariel Toaff's *Pasque di Sangue* —— 203**
10.1	Ariel Toaff's *Pasque di Sangue* —— **203**
10.2	The Geographic Limits of the Phenomenon "Magic" —— **206**
10.3	The Use of "Blood" – The Word and the Code —— **208**
10.4	Defining "Magic" —— **209**
10.5	Conclusion —— **213**

Part IV: **Reflecting on Languages and Texts**

11 **Reflecting on Languages and Texts —— 217**
11.1	Holy, Rabbinic and Common language —— **220**
11.1.1	Leshon ha-qodesh —— **221**
11.1.2	Leshon ḥakhamim —— **223**
11.1.3	Common language —— **224**
11.2	Dialect or different pronunciation? —— **224**
11.3	Language, text transmission and exegesis —— **226**
11.4	Conclusion —— **231**

12 **On Editing Rabbinic Texts —— 233**
12.1	The Quest for the Ur-Text —— **233**
12.2	Editions are a Product of Time and Authority —— **237**
12.3	Editions as Interpretations of Texts —— **241**

12.4   The Pragmatic Edition: Midrash Tehillim —— **244**
12.5   Conclusion —— **246**

13   **On Some Greek Loanwords in Aquila's Translation of the Bible —— 247**
13.1   Leviticus 23:24 and the Feast of Tabernacles —— **247**
13.2   Ezekiel 16:10 on Dressing —— **248**
13.3   Ezekiel 23:43 on Prostitution —— **249**
13.4   Psalm 48 (47):15 and the Eternal World —— **250**
13.5   Proverbs 18:21 and Rhetorical Figures —— **251**
13.6   Proverbs 25:11 on Rhetoric —— **251**
13.7   Esther 1:6 on Colours —— **252**

14   **The Septuagint in Disgrace —— 253**
14.1   Talmudic Stories and Post-Talmudic Developments —— **253**
14.2   Medieval reception and the Megillat Ta'anit Batra —— **261**

15   **In Lieu of a Conclusion: Pleasure and Desire of Learning —— 267**
15.1   The Song of Songs in Discussions —— **268**
15.2   The Pleasure of Sin —— **277**

Selected Bibliography —— 281

Index of Primary Sources —— 295

Introduction

In considering the multifarious world of theoretical and empirical sciences, a Venetian rabbi of the XVII century, Simḥah (Simone) Luzzatto, wondered about the reliability of the images projected by the mirror. According to him, although mirrors are constructed on the basis of the same material, they reflect the images in different ways in their shapes.[1] The reason for the different *reflection* cannot be due to the object, because they reflect the *same* object; therefore one has to infer that the perceived difference depends on the receiver, i.e. the eyes (or the reflective surfaces of the mirrors). The different visions of reality and hence also the fallacy of "realities," depend on the receiver.

Jerusalem Talmud, Shabbat 6,1 (7d) contains an interesting tradition:

> Three things were allowed to the members of the House of Rabbi: that they look at oneself in the mirror; that they trim one's *qomi*, and they teach Greek to their sons. For they were close to the (Roman) government.

To look in one's mirror has nothing to do with hair trimming. It was a mantic practice ascribed to kings and emperors called *specularia*. The author of the *Historia Augusta* tells us that Didius Iulianus

> was mad enough to perform a number of rites with the aid of magicians, such as were calculated either to lessen the hate of the people or to restrain the arms of the soldiers. For the magicians sacrificed certain victims that are foreign to the Roman ritual and chanted unholy songs, *so we are told, before a mirror, into which boys are said to gaze, after bandages have been bound over their eyes and charms muttered over their heads.*[2]

---

1 Simone Luzzatto. *Scritti politici e filosofici di un ebreo scettico nella Venezia del Seicento.* Introduced, commented, and edited by Giuseppe Veltri in cooperation with Anna Lissa & Paola Ferruta (Milan: Bompiani, 2013), 97: "... che se bene della istessa material construtti siano un poco do varietà che nella loro figura accade diuersificano non poco l'imagini da essi riflesse".
2 *Historia Augusta, Didius Iulianus* VII: 9-11: "Nam et quasdam non convenientes Romanis sacris hostias immolaverunt et carmina profana incantaverunt et ea, quae ad speculum dicunt fieri, in quod pueri praeligatis oculis incantato vertice respicere dicuntur, Iulianus fecit. Tuncquem puer vidisse dicitur et adventum Severi et Iuliani decessionem." English translation quoted from *Historia Augusta, Volume I: Hadrian. Aelius. Antoninus Pius. Marcus Aurelius. L. Verus. Avidius Cassius. Commodus. Pertinax. Didius Julianus. Septimius Severus. Pescennius Niger. Clodius Albinus*, Transl. David Magie (Loeb Library, 1921), from internet address http://penelope.uchicago.edu/Thayer/E/Roman/Texts/Historia_Augusta/Didius_Julianus*.html,
June, 2013; emphasis added). See also Judas Bergmann, "Die Schicksalserforschung der römischen Kaiser in der Agada," *Monatsschrift für Geschichte und Wissenschaft des Judentums* 81 (1937): 478–481.

Divination through a mirror is also considered here as a kind of art or science to be attributed to the structure of power. To look into the mirror is the expression of a structure of power strung between magic and politics, directed toward interpreting reality as it is, should be or as is politically convenient. The mirror is thus an instrument of power to act upon reality and world(s) of reference.

Both the mirror of multifarious hermeneutic reflections or epistemological imagination and the (magic) instrument of power are the main topic of this study. Rabbinic hermeneutics reflects this multifaceted world of the text and of reality, seen as a world of reference worth commentary. As a mirror, it includes this world but perhaps also falsifies reality, that is, adapting it to one's own aims and necessities.

The present study is the product of my research on ancient Judaism in the last 15 years. It consists of four parts: Part I, considered as introduction, is the description of the "Rabbinic Workshop" (I: *Officina Rabbinica*), the rabbinic world where the student plays a role and a reformation always takes place, the world where the mirror was created and manufactured. Part II deals with the historical environment, the world of reference of rabbinic Judaism in Palestine and in the Hellenistic Diaspora (II: *Reflecting Roman Religion*); Part III focuses on magic and the sciences, as ancient (political and empirical) activities of influence in the double meaning of receiving and adopting something and of attempt to producing an effect on persons and objects (III. *Performing the Craft of Sciences and Magic*). Part IV addresses the rabbinic concern with texts (IV: *Reflecting on Languages and Texts*) as the main area of "influence" of the rabbinic academy in a space between the texts of the past and the real world of the present.

* * *

Part I: Officina Rabbinica
Rabbinical texts are but fragments of past discussions and debates without fixed starting points or fixed termini. Talmudic texts are often a riddle to students as there is no consistent structure, no inherent style, and an apparent lack of methodology. This is rather surprising considering the centrality of teaching and learning, and the fact that instruction was the essence of these texts.

In order to understand the teachings of the rabbis – these cryptic texts of rabbinic academies – the student needs to resort to impertinent means and a certain degree of *chutzpah*. Only then, as I outline in this chapter, is the student able to access the texts. To "raise up many disciples" (Mishnah Avot 1:1), as the main aim of the teachers, sought to equip the students with the necessary skills to pose questions and thus to absorb the lesson by means of indirect education.

Hermeneutics is a perpetual method of "reforming," i.e. of re-shaping the idea, the concepts, the "imaginative grammar"[3] of the past (tradition) as mirrored by the transmitted texts. Martin Luther's Reformation garnered interest among Jews as well – especially in the periphery of European Jewry where the later Lutheran anti-Jewish tractates never had an impact. However, the Reformation also sparked interest in Jewish reforms, such as those of the Karaites, whose understanding of Judaism bore similarities to the thinking of the Christian reformers. One of the most apparent reforms in Judaism before the nineteenth century was Ezra's (re-)creation of the Jewish traditional literature as described in the bible and through the legend of the Septuagint. It was Ezra's work which marked the transition from the creation of the Hebrew text to its interpretation, that is, to the realm of the rabbis.

Utilizing several instances of historical "reforms" concerning Judaism – with an emphasis on Ezra – I discuss in this chapter the nature of the reforms themselves. I explore the structures of reforming, and the strategy to promote new developments while standing firmly on the ground of tradition. Reforms are more than a mere challenge to existing texts by "re-canonizing" them. They supposedly constitute a mode of recourse to a "Golden Age," with the explicit aim of justifying political and cultural changes. The reforms are manifestations of political changes sought through canonical change. Ezra's story is the perfect example of this.

Part II: Reflecting Roman Religion

Discussing the Roman occupation of *Palaestina* in antiquity, and the Jewish sources mirroring it, solely through the prism of military repression is too simplistic. Discussing it in a political-historical way or through the prism of a clash of civilisations likewise falls short. Judea had been a province of Rome (or Byzantium) for the better part of a millennium until the Muslim conquest. Thus, cultural-historical elements of Roman life – customs and religious practices – were a fact in the province, yet under the conditions of the military as the main representative in this part of Rome's periphery. The cultural transfer from the Greco-Roman occupiers to the occupied Jews is a crucial aspect for understanding Jewish society in ancient *Palaestina* and the rabbinic texts reflecting it.

---

[3] On the concept of "imaginative grammar," see the introduction to my study *Language of Conformity and Dissent: On the Imaginative Grammar of Jewish Intellectuals in the Nineteenth and Twentieth Centuries* (Boston: Academic Studies Press, 2013), 11–13.

In this second section, I discuss the representation of Greco-Roman customs in rabbinic sources through the examples of the so-called *darkhe ha-emori*, the "ways of the Amorites," and the Roman festivals as they were celebrated in the periphery of the empire. By doing so, I argue that these cultural aspects were not merely noted to present the "follies" of the Romans, or to draw a clear boundary between the Jews and the imperial occupiers. The representation often served the purpose of separating oneself from the Other, but also of absorbing new customs and mores into the armature of Jewish identity and culture – such as the sphere of one's own holidays – by a transformative process, giving them a new background and meaning. Yet that absorption and adaptation were always carried out under the condition of compatibility with one's own traditions. The cultural aspects of the Greco-Roman world as they are noted in the rabbinic sources were religious, social, and political reactions to the on-going process of common, everyday interaction between Jews and Greco-Romans, direct daily contact with their culture and identity. Essentially, the rabbinic sources provide proof of a crisis in culture and identity, and the struggle to preserve both under one's own conditions of Jewish tradition.

Part III: Performing the craft of science and magic
The presentation of magic and healing as reflected in rabbinic sources is as multi-faceted and widely accessible as the modern conception of what constitutes magic and sciences in the ancient world. Magic – and its intertwining with sciences such as medicine – had penetrated society. The scholar who researches and discusses the contemporary conception of magic in ancient Judaism often misses the forest for the trees, and for a simple reason: there is not one forest. Not even the classification of "magic" provides solid ground for studying it. This chapter is dedicated to the discussion of magic from the scholarly perspective, since it evokes a multitude of intellectual, religious, and social connotations.

In this chapter, I present an overview of research and suggested topics for future inquiry. This is intended to serve as a map for the various "forests" of magic as represented in the rabbinic texts. I operate on the premise that magic as represented in the sources was likely a subject discussed at home in the sphere between lived existential practice and academic, that is, rabbinic views and thinking. Magic was always more than simply its developments within the context of a single people or nation. It should be understood and approached holistically. I begin with an overview of the trends in scholarship over the past two centuries and in the various fields of research, followed by an outline of how to approach magic analytically and conceptually as an object of study.

One of the most valuable Jewish manuscripts in Germany is the Munich Cod. Hebr. 95, a complete copy of the Babylonian Talmud dating back to

France in 1342. This late medieval copy is associated with an interesting fact beyond the realm of the Talmud, constituting evidence for magic's infusion into the process of editing sacred texts. In his reproduction of the manuscript in 1912, Hermann Strack dismissively notes that on fol. 157b "there is no text [of the Gemara]." However, transcribed there are magical recipes focusing on water, and supposedly safeguarding the manuscript against damage that might be caused by water. Using precious parchment for writing down spells was not the result of mere doodling by the scribe. Neither was it proof of the infusion of superstition into the text itself. It was done for the simple reason that magical and non-magical life formed a single entity in late antiquity and the Middle Ages. The editors deemed the magical recipes and formulae important for the physical manuscript itself, not its content. They were considered important features for protecting and preserving the product of editing against existing and expected threats, a kind of "security system."

Few topics are as mysterious and riddling as magic practices and beliefs as a focus for academic inquiry. Yet magic itself is far from marginal for the social sciences, since it is an empirical science par excellence, especially through its correlation with medicine and healing. When following examples of magic (concerning birth anxieties and child mortality in this chapter), it is possible to follow the tradition from Greco-Roman and Jewish antiquity well down into the Middle Ages among Christians and Jews. In this example, it is magic that allows the projection and addressing of fears for the unborn or recently born child, problems concerning fertility, and magical explanations for anatomical/medical issues in respect to conception, nativity, and mortality of child and mother. These are everyday concerns for health in the bosom of the family. As such, magic is the psychological strategy for preparation and coping with the most essential aspects of human life, the cycle of birth and death. I do not wish to expound on magic through an extensive discussion of various aspects. In this chapter, however, I attempt to offer tools to cope with the seemingly overwhelming nature of magic as a focus for future research.

When the Italian-Israeli historian Ariel Toaff published *Blood Passover: The Jews of Europe and Ritual Murder* (*Pasque di sangue: Ebrei d'Europa e omicidi rituali*) in 2007, an outcry was heard among the scholars of Jewish history. Based on his research of medieval and early modern Jewish texts, and the protocols of inquisitorial trials, Toaff's findings seemingly proved that Ashkenazic Jews had exercised a cult based on blood. Thus, he argued, the blood libel accusations, the gravest anti-Jewish charge haunting every Jewish community, were not based on libel but on fact. Human blood allegedly played an essential role for Ashkenazic Passover, and especially magical practices. As such, at least Jews in Ashkenaz were guilty of certain practices as charged by the Inquisition.

Toaff would not have produced this gem for anti-Semites all over the world had he properly grasped the nature of his magical sources. In this chapter, I do not argue the pros and cons of *Blood Passover*, its anti-Jewish and anti-Ashkenazic leitmotif, or the historian's basic armamentarium (others have done so sufficiently). I do, however, use *Blood Passover* as a starting point for presenting and discussing the nature, universality, codes and terminology of magical practices. By doing so, I argue that Toaff is merely one of the latest victims of magic's essence, its seclusion from plain view by misleading encryption.

Part IV: Reflecting on Languages and Texts
Babylonian Talmud, Rosh Ha-Shanah 26a–26b, narrates a tale of the rabbis' puzzlement over several biblical and rabbinic expressions in the tradition. It tells the story of finding explanations of incomprehensible phrases by listening to the people on the streets, and is but one example for such *vox populi vox traditionis*. It points to one of the most important, yet most underestimated facets of tradition: the ignorance that supplements knowledge. It is ignorance that secures the transmission of the "original text," as only the ignorant will refrain from mending/altering/updating the text. As such, it is evidence for a "fluidity" of text tradition. Although the rabbis were quite distant from developing viable theories of philology, these examples hint at their concepts of the nature of language.

In this section, I outline the fact that the canonisation process of texts essentially crystallises linguistic changes, snapshots, and interventions. It gives proof of the necessity of adaptation of the text, and the historical discussions of finding the one "best" variant reading which might become standard. Through the canonisation of texts in individual rabbinic schools, text variants, as I demonstrate, served two purposes: setting a standard, and promoting the individual school.

Editing ancient and modern texts is a titanic task. Provided that the text was produced by one author, the main question remains whether to document all the different variant readings, or to privilege the "original" text – the so-called *ur*-text. An edition can approach a text as being either the absolute beginning of the text's tradition or of the final redaction. Quite interestingly, editors of the nineteenth and twentieth centuries were preoccupied with their quest of establishing "final editions" of texts according to the original author's purported intention. Discussing the futility of these undertakings takes us deep into the core of the nature of what is an edition. I present three questions in investigating and editing rabbinic manuscripts: 1. what exactly is the nature of an edition in antiquity? 2. is it possible to edit a text without its interpretation?

Phrased differently, to what extent can editions reproduce texts free from editorial interference? and 3. what is a pragmatic edition? What are the advantages of a pragmatic edition over other previous editions? In my concluding remarks, I offer an example of a pragmatic redaction by briefly introducing the reader to our edition project of Midrash Tehillim at the Universities of Halle and Münster in Germany.

One very important aspect of text tradition is that of translations. The Jerusalem Talmud, for instance, dedicates some room to explanations of why Aquila of Sinope chose a particular Greek word for the original in his translation of the Hebrew text. It is a field of rabbinic exegesis in itself and is introduced by the formula *tirgem 'aqilas*, "Aquilas translates (as targum)." These midrashic elements essentially served the purpose of making sense of otherwise meaningless passages. They are, however, inaccessible if the rhetorical art, the images and wordplays these loanwords evoke, are not taken into consideration. Drawing on examples from Ezekiel, Psalms, Proverbs, and Esther, I introduce some of Aquila's Greek "targumata" in this chapter. Although I will offer possible meanings of Greek loanwords in the translation, I do not engage here in philological and text-critical analysis.

From a Christian perspective, the Septuagint, the Greek translation of the Torah, was supposedly the common bond between the ancient Christians and Jews. At the core stood the conviction that the Greek Torah had been divinely inspired twice: for Moses to write down, and the translators to render into Greek in Alexandria. For rabbinic Judaism, however, the Greek Torah was of little importance in the beginning. The Hebrew "translations" were noteworthy; the Greek "Torah for the King Ptolemy [Talmai, in Hebrew]" was of little interest. In the post-Talmudic tractates of Sefer Torah and Soferim we have the earliest proof of direct criticism of the Septuagint. Yet it was one of the most important translations based on an alteration of the original Torah in writing. The discussion of the Septuagint in rabbinic sources also presents evidence of traditions that evolved around the concept of translation itself. In this chapter, I analyse the Talmudic stories on the Septuagint, as well as the medieval sources, in regard to their origin and its context. I then discuss the purpose of the translation itself.

In Lieu of a Conclusion: Desire and Learning
None of the twenty-four books of the Tanakh has been discussed as controversially in Jewish and Christian tradition as שיר השירים, the Song of Songs, or the Song of Solomon. With its artful poetry, its vivid and metaphorical homage to sensuality, and its seemingly overly human content – God is never mentioned – scholars had condemned it as utterly profane; a divine indecency

albeit divinely inspired. In essence, the Song of Songs references the human experience. It refers to the tantalizing agony of human love, guilt, and longing. As such, it is the epitome of human life itself: sensuality and sexuality. Ancient Judaism had indeed been infused with elements of Greek culture and its emphasis on the human body and, yes, aspects of hedonism. As such, the Song of Songs brings to life this period in which love poems flourished.

I discuss here the dimension(s) of love and desire in ancient Judaism, its relation to the mitzvoth and the ancient world. The song, however, is more. It is also a perfect example of the canonisation of texts for tradition. Despite its rather explicitly human content, tradition created here a book of the *Tanakh* describing intimate contact with divinity. Love, and the sexual language telling it, is used to describe the divinity. The result is the union of humankind and God through inseminating the human soul. The Song of Songs is a remarkable example of de-contextualisation and the disentanglement of the original, historical, and cultural context from the text which tradition seeks to canonise.

* * *

I wish to note that some of the following chapters have been published before in German, English, or Italian. They appeared in the following publications:

Part I
- "Freche Schüler vs. gescheite Rabbinen: Die Kunst des Lernens im antiken Judentum." In *Meister und Schüler in Geschichte und Gegenwart: Von Religionen der Antike bis zur modernen Esoterik*, edited by Almut-Barbara Renger, 123–133. Göttingen: V&R Unipress, 2012.
- "Esra als 'Reformator' in der klassischen Literatur des Judentums." In *Reformen im Alten Orient und der Antike. Programme, Darstellungen und Deutungen*, edited by Ernst-Joachim Waschke in cooperation with Johannes Thon, 175–186. Tübingen: Mohr Siebeck, 2009.

Part II
- "Römische Religion an der Peripherie des Reiches: Ein Kapitel rabbinischer Rhetorik." In *The Talmud Yerushalmi and Graeco-Roman Culture* Vol. 2, edited by Peter Schäfer and Cathrine Hezser, 81–138. Tübingen: Mohr Siebeck, 2000 and Magic, Sex and Politics: The Media Power of Theatre Amusements in the Mirror of Rabbinic Literature, in *The Words of a Wise Mouth are Gracious. Divre Pi-Hakam Hen. Festschrift for Günter Stemberger on his 65th Birthday*, ed. Mauro Perani (Berlin: De Gruyter, 2005): 243–256.

Part III
- "On the Influence of "Greek Wisdom": Theoretical and Empirical Sciences in Rabbinic Judaism." In *Jewish Studies Quarterly* 5, No. 4 (1998): 300–317.
- "Magic and Healing." In *The Oxford Handbook of Jewish Daily Life in Roman Palestine*, edited by Catherine Hezser, 586–602. Oxford: Oxford University Press, 2010.
- "The Rabbis and Pliny the Elder: Jewish and Greco-Roman Attitudes to Magic and Empirical Knowledge." *Poetics Today* 19 (1998): 63–89
- "The Figure of the Magician in Rabbinical Judaism: From Empirical Science to Theology." *Jerusalem Studies in Arabic and Islam* 26 (2002): 187–204.
- "'Watermarks' in the Manuscript Munich Hebr. 95: Magical Traditions in Historical Context." In *Jewish Studies Between the Disciplines: Papers in Honor of Peter Schäfer on the Occasion of His 60th Birthday*, edited by Klaus Herrmann, Margarete Schlüter, and Giuseppe Veltri, 243–256. Leiden: Brill, 2003.
- "The Meal of the Spirits, the Three Parcae and Lilith: Apotropaic Strategies for Coping with Birth Anxieties and Child Mortality." *Henoch* 23 (2001): 343–359.
- "Preuve et plausibilité: Réflexions sur la magie à partir du livre de Ariel Toaff." *Cahiers du Centre de Recherches Historiques* 45 (2010): 129–138.

Part IV
- "Sprachauffassungen und Textüberlieferung im rabbinischen Judentum." In *Sprachbewusstsein und Sprachkonzepte im Alten Orient, Alten Testament und rabbinischen Judentum*, edited by Johannes Thon, Giuseppe Veltri and Ernst-Joachim Waschke, 143–162. Halle: Zentrum für Interdisziplinäre Regionalstudien – Vorderer Orient, Afrika, Asien, 2012.
- "From the Search for the Best Text to the Pragmatic Edition: On editing Rabbinic Texts." In *The New Testament and Rabbinic Literature*, edited by Reimund Bieringer, Florentino García Martinez, Didier Pollefeyt, and Peter J. Tomson, 68–73. Boston and Leiden: Brill, 2010.
- Greek Loanwords in the Palestinian Talmud: Some New Suggestions." *Journal of Semitic Studies* 48 (2002): 237–240.
- "The Septuagint in Disgrace. Some Notes on the Stories on Ptolemy in Rabbinic and Medieval Judaism." In *Jewish Reception of Greek Bible Versions*, edited by Nicholas de Lange, Julia Krivoruchko and Cameron Boyd-Taylor, 142–154. Tübingen: Mohr Siebeck, 2008.

Conclusion

The conclusion "Pleasure and Desire of Learning" has not been published before and was first translated from Italian by Dr. Anna Lissa and then revised by Anton Hieke.

My thanks are due to Dr. Anton Hieke for the translation of the three first chapters from the German original and to William Templer for the revision of the book as a whole, and language editing. I also am indebted to the editors of the series for their helpful advice. I wish to dedicate the book to my daughter Livia, as an allusion to a sea of knowledge from a world of texts, traditions and reflection on them.

Halle & Hamburg, January 2015

Documentation style, transliteration and references

The documentation system follows in the main the *Chicago Manual of Style* (humanities style) with exception of the format for subsequent references to the same work, for which I preferred adding one or two words from the title of the book, article, or part of the book. The transliteration of Hebrew works follows the *Encyclopaedia Judaica* (1972), while the transliteration of Greek words retains the common rules of classicists (where, for example υ in the diphthong is "au," "ou" and standing alone "y") with exception of the tonic accents, which are not necessary for the reproduction of Greek letters.

- Quotations from the Biblical text are taken from the *New International Version* unless I expressly quote from an English translation of a rabbinic text. Slight changes to the quotation of biblical texts are not mentioned provided there is no distortion of the original meaning. No abbreviation of biblical, rabbinic, Jewish-Hellenistic or other Jewish or Christian literature is adopted.
- English translations of Josephus are taken from Henry St. John Thackeray, et al., *Josephus*, 2nd edition, vols. 1–9 (Cambridge, Mass., London: Harvard University Press, 1966–1969, 1st edition 1926–1965).
- English translations of Philo follow as a rule F. H. Colson and G. H. Whitaker, eds., *The Works of Philo* (Cambridge, Mass: Loeb Classical Library, Harvard University Press; London: William Heinemann, 1929–1953), vols. 1–10, Ralph Marcus, ed., vols. 10–12.
- If not expressly quoted, all other translations of rabbinic or Christian as well as Jewish and Christian medieval authors are my own.

Part I: **Officina rabbinica**

1 Impertinent Students vs. Sagacious Rabbis: The Art of Learning

The argumentation of Talmudic texts appears somewhat peculiar for the modern reader. There are no premises, no discussions of methodology, and especially no consistent chapters or books which eventually might reveal a characteristic style.[4] The styles delivered to posterity in its brevity sometimes overwhelm or even anger the students of Jewish Studies. The transmitted sentences and fragments of speech are sayings and statements which likely had evolved in the framework of a discussion whose historic and geographic context is not known to us (any longer) – if they had ever entered into the awareness of the tradition. They are, perhaps, merely condensed teachings that are, at best, exemplified through stories. Sometimes, there is not any reference detectible – neither to the contemporary context nor to the text on which the discussion is based.

To the uninformed student, the reading of rabbinic texts might appear like a stage play by Eugène Ionesco: as a seemingly absurd composition of assertion following assertion, formulae following formulae, styles following styles. In the end, there is only an assertion.[5] The unfamiliar reader thus is overwhelmed and the rabbis certainly were not unaware of this. They referred to the secrets of the Torah they were not willing to reveal as is explicitly mentioned in the rabbinic commentary *Pesiqta Rabbati* § 5. There, it is asserted that the Torah is now also available to the non-Jews, the *ummot ha-'olam*, in the form of the Greek translation. Only the oral Torah, the *Torah she-be-'al peh*, remained God's secret he shared exclusively with his people, as a special characteristic of his unique relationship with his son Israel.[6] Even if this text of the *Pesiqta* is a polemic stroke targeted both against Christians as well as the Karai-

---

[4] The lapidary style of Talmudic schools was one of the first topics addressed by the scholars of the so-called *Wissenschaft des Judentums*, as noted in one of the most influential journals of the 19th century, the *Monatsschrift*, see Zacharias Frankel, "Über den Lapidarstyl der talmudischen Historik," *Monatsschrift zur Geschichte und Wissenschaft des Judentums* 1/6 (1851–52): 203–220.

[5] On the rabbinical literary and tradition-historical logic, see Martin S. Jaffee, "Rabbinic Authorship as a Collective Enterprise," in *The Cambridge Companion to the Talmud and Rabbinic Literature*, eds. Charlotte E. Fonrobert and Martin S. Jaffee (Cambridge and New York: Cambridge University Press, 2007), 17–37.

[6] On this text, see G. Veltri, *Eine Tora für den König Talmai: Untersuchungen zum Übersetzungsverständnis in der jüdisch-hellenistischen und rabbinischen Literatur* (Tübingen: Mohr, 1994), 17, 122.

te movement,⁷ it can be emphasised that the structure of Talmudic styles required a form of esoteric approach known only to insiders. Bearing that in mind makes understandable the following Orthodox joke in which a rabbi explains the afterlife: There is no purgatory or hell, but only paradise. After their deaths, the righteous ones (*Ṣadiqqim*) as well as the evildoers (*Resha'im*) get to go to paradise. Moses awaits both groups with the Talmud in hand, which will be a joy and blessing for the righteous ones, but the true and tormenting hell for the unrighteous ones and the evildoers.⁸

Perhaps not because of this prospective end of their ignorance of the Talmudic joy, many non-rabbis turned to the study of rabbinic texts. For some these texts constitute religious customs and beliefs, for others a challenge that is only manageable through studying and the love of hermeneutical tradition. The teachings of the rabbis are an intellectual impertinence that is only accessible by impertinent means. This is my hypothesis as outlined in the following discussion.

The rabbis have handed down to us sketches or fragments of discussions – a literary form like the *canovaccio* of the *commedia dell'arte* – in which only the key points are noted. The redactor, who had chosen the binding assertions and had noted them as anonymous maxims, offers the authoritative reader the opportunity for further debate. The argument is the driving engine of the tradition. Without discussion's soulful impetus it is impossible to hand down the tradition.

Effective learning does not consist of repetition – despite the fact that the word "Mishnah," the name for the canonic work that had developed in the earliest phase of rabbinic literature, means precisely that: "repetition." According to the Babylonian Talmud, Soṭah, fol. 22a, the student/teacher⁹ of a rabbinic academy (a *Tanna'*) is not dissimilar to a *Magush*,¹⁰ since both mnemonically

---

7 The Karaites are a Jewish sect dating from the early medieval period who rejected the rabbinical teachings and other non-biblical texts and traditions as non-authoritative. On the Karaites and their Literature, see Leon Nemoy, *Karaite Anthology: Excerpts from the Early Literature, Translated from Arybic, Aramaic, and Hebrew Sources with Notes* (New Haven: Yale University Press, 1952); Nathan Shur, *History of the Karaites* (Frankfurt am Main: Peter Lang, 1992); Avraham Qanai *An Introduction to Karaite Judaism: History, Theology, Practice, and Culture* (Albany, NY: Qirqisani Center, 2003).
8 Moshe Halbertal, *People of the Book: Canon, Meaning, and Authority* (Cambridge, Mass.: Harvard University Press, 1997), 1.
9 Tanna means "repeater," "transmitter" of the entire "tannatic" tradition. As a rule, the term is translated with "teacher," but it can also include the pupil who is a transmitter of the teaching.
10 A Magush was originally a Zoroastrian priest, and later become tantamount to a magician. On the magician in Judaism, see further details below, pp. 159–172.

repeat what they do not comprehend (or, in Aramaic, *raṭen magusha we-la' yada' ma'y amar tane tanna we-la' yada' ma'y amar*).[11] In essence, teaching is learning, not repeating.

The concept of the master in the understanding of rabbinic interpretation is not what we understand today.[12] The master is not a mercantile "service contractor"[13] of society, but the one who helps formulate questions. The master's maieutic function is unique and prominent. He has no past he is expected to share, but is only supposed to use one method with which the past and the present might be brought into harmony. The learning of the word "how" instead of "what" is important, even crucial as we learn from the *Ernst des Einsatzes* ("earnest character of engaged effort") as defined by Reinhard Neudecker.[14] Even the marital obligations might be ignored for a while (up to three years!) in order to pursue one's studies.[15] The reason for this is that one does not learn contents which might be repeated, but rather methodology, the hermeneutics of life itself. The master does not sell goods but transmits the ways and means of how to "move" in life (and, yes, Halakhah does philologically mean "the way of walking"). Because of this idea, the rabbinic quote from *Pirqe Avot* 6:4 is extremely important: "This is the way of the Torah. Eat a morsel of bread with salt, and drink a measured amount of water. Sleep on the ground and live a life of hardship and labour in the study of the Torah."[16]

In addition to the physical effort, which already contains a goodly portion of asceticism, the student is supposed to be nourished by what is really "tasty" and stimulating; salt and labour. We also have to understand Jesus's word in this context, saying that his disciples were the "salt of the earth" (Matthew 5:13). It is not a coincidence that the Hebrew word *ṭa'am* refers to "taste" as well as "reason," and that *ṭa'ame ha-miṣvot* ("reasons for the commandments") might also refer to a sensual perception of the commandments. Thus, one has to taste the wisdom of the Torah by putting effort in it. The result of such training is not an examination of knowledge – not a final exam – but the certificate that one is capable of "walking" on their own. The aim of training is to "make wise one's master" (Mishnah, Pirqe Avot 6:6).

---

11 On this text and its tradition, see below, p. 161.
12 On the ancient and modern interpretations, see Almut-Barbara, "Das Wissen des 'Meisters': zur Geschichte eines Begriffs im Feld und Umfeld von Religion und Spiritualität," *Gegenworte* 24 (2010): 68–72.
13 See *ibidem*, 70–72.
14 Reinhard Neudecker, "Meister und Jünger im rabbinischen Judentum," *Dialog der Religionen* 6 (1997): 47.
15 See *ibidem*, and Shulḥan 'Arukh, Hilkhot Talmud Torah 3:1,2.
16 Translation from Martin Sicker, *The Moral Maxims of the Sages of Israel: Pirke Avot* (Lincoln, NE: iUniverse, 2004), 325.

1.1 The Student

To understand the criticism of rote memorisation, let us try to place ourselves back in the times of the disciples, the *talmidim*, the sages or teachers, and the *ḥakhamim*. Surprisingly little literature is available on the students in the Talmudic era.[17] It has to do with the fact that students generally were only briefly noted in the tractates on the teacher. It also has to do with the core of rabbinic assertions that the whole body of the halakhic and aggadic literature of Talmud and bible exegesis was quintessentially concerned with education.

I would like to emphasise in this context a contribution in the secondary literature. In 1924, an article appeared by the Hungarian rabbi Isidor Goldberger, who had thoroughly researched the matter, entitled "Der Talmid Chacham."[18] The article is structured according to the classic method of philological/cultural-historical scholarship, and only describes the texts in which the word or the concept of "student" (*talmid*) appears. The article is a treasure trove for future readers, since it is deeply imbued with and characterised by a period of scholarship that still awaits the appreciation it deserves. The student is generally addressed by the word talmid as well as the common *ben* (son) or *na'ar* (young man). It is contrasted with the expression *av* (father), which might be understood as "rabbi," as the exegetic work Sifre Devarim § 34 explains: "The teacher is called father." There are still some differences between *rav* (rabbi) and *av* (father), as we learn from Tosefta Megillah 4:41 (see Babylonian Talmud, Qiddushin 49a):

> R. Yehudah says: He who translates a verse according to its literal meaning is a liar; he who adds is a blasphemer. The translator (*meturgeman*) who stands before the *ḥakham* (sage) is not allowed to leave out, add, or to change unless he is his *av* (father) or his *rav*.

The *meturgeman* (translator/the one who explains) at the school of the sages has to follow in his rendition the guidelines of the sages. The prohibition of alteration is, of course, not valid, if the *meturgeman* is the father of the sage or his rabbi. The student cannot alter the text according to his own will because he cannot harmonise the past and the present.[19]

The aim of a rabbinic school is to have students, as the maxim of the Men of the Great Assembly reads in Pirqe Avot 1:1: to "raise up many disciples" is one of the obligations of the rabbi and stands alongside the thoughtfulness of

---

[17] An exception is, of course, Reinhard Neudecker's work that I have just referred to.
[18] Isidor Goldberger, "Der Talmid Chacham," *Monatsschrift für Geschichte und Wissenschaft des Judentums* 68 (1924): 211–225; 291–307.
[19] See Veltri, *Eine Tora für den König Talmai*, 210.

speech and adding fences around the Torah (*ibidem*). There are no specific numbers referring to students: Rabbi Hillel was said to have 80 students; Rabbi Yoḥanan ben Zakkai only five.[20] It is speculative whether or not this small number indeed included only the exceptional students as Goldberger concluded. Yet it is a fact that Rabbi Yoḥanan praised (or reprimanded) his sons for the virtues just like the patriarch Jacob had done when Yohanan said: "Hyrkanos is a sealed cistern that does not spill one drop; Yosi ha-Kohen is a righteous one, etc." (*ibidem*) The rabbinic literature not only contained praise for the virtues which were supposed to develop in the students, but also (and this to my mind especially) the intellectual acuity that developed through engaged discussion.[21] The student was praised who made his teacher a wise man.

The curriculum of the student was oriented toward the chain of tradition, which clearly formed a kind of trivium and quadrivium of rabbinic origin: Sifre Devarim § 161 presents a circle of thought which is supposed to lead from the fear of God through the Bible, Targum, Mishnah, Talmud and *maʿaseh* (activity/work) back to the fear of God. The post-Talmudic tractate Soferim 16:6 uses the same chain of tradition that is described in Sifre Devarim § 161 for a curriculum vitae of Rabbi Yoḥanan ben Zakkai, as do Avot de-Rabbi Natan, Version B § 28 and Babylonian Talmud, Sukkah 28a. The fear of God stands at the beginning and at the end of learning in order to preclude the student's self-interest (Babylonian Talmud, Nedarim 62a) and his arrogance (Midrash Tanḥuma Yitro 15). "The purpose of scholarship is repentance and the doing of charitable works" (Babylonian Talmud, Berakhot 17a).

One could extend almost without limits the list of virtues, or moral rules for the students and the disciples of the rabbis. Goldberger's article is a treasure trove of quotes and allusions, ethical rules and everything connected with them. One cannot resist the impression that the rabbinical literature is simply rabbinical and marks the end of a process which only one group had managed to survive: the rabbis. Other groups which used to have some influence clearly moved into the background and allowed the rabbis to celebrate themselves. The costs of teaching in relation to the priesthood stands out, as is noted in Mishnah, Avot 6:6. The passage is worth quoting it in its entirety:

> Torah is greater than priesthood or kingship. For kingship has thirty characteristics and priesthood twenty-four, but Torah is acquired through forty-eight things. These are: study, attentive listening, orderly speech, an understanding heart, discernment of the heart,

---

[20] On Hillel, see Babylonian Talmud, Sukkah 28a and Baba Batra 134a; on R. Yoḥanan ben Zakkai, see Mishnah, Avot 2:10.
[21] Babylonian Talmud, Shabbat 63a.

awe, reverence, humility, cheerfulness, purity, attendance on the wise, attaching oneself to colleagues, argumentation with students, sedateness, [knowledge of] Mishnah, moderation in commerce, moderation in *derekh eretz*, moderation in pleasure, moderation in sleep, moderation in conversation, moderation in laughter, patience, a good heart, faith in the wise, acceptance of sufferings, that knows his place, that rejoices in his portion, that makes a fence to his words, that claims no merit for himself, beloved, loves the Omnipresent, loves mankind, loves justice, loves rectitude, loves reproof, and keeps aloof from honor, and does not boast of his learning, and does not delight in making rulings, shares the burden of one's colleagues, and assesses him favorably, and leads him to truth, and leads him to peace, and who is composed in his study, asks and answers, hears and adds, that studies in order to teach, that learns in order to practice, that makes his master wiser, accurately channels what he hears, that sites something in the name of the one who said it. You have learned that everyone who cites something in the name of the one who said it brings redemption to the world, as it is said, *and Esther reported it to the king in Mordecai's name* [Esther 2:22].[22]

Comparable lists of the advantage of teaching are to be found, of course, in the parallel schools of Stoicism and Christianity, especially in the styles of the *Apophthegmata Patrum* of the Christian-Coptic anchorites.[23] Despite all similarities there are also great differences inherent such as the absence of the rabbis' *contemplatio*,[24] and especially the Christians' appreciation of chastity as a virtue. Both groups, however, strongly emphasised teaching and learning as the main task of students as well as teachers.

1.2 He Who Always Asks

The art of learning is predominantly the joy of thinking, the joy of transmitting knowledge. This neither refers to rote memorisation nor to the repetition of the teacher's utterances. The Talmud had fought such concepts. In Midrash Mekhilta de Rabbi Yishma'el, pisḥa, bo' 18, it is transmitted: "You will find that there are four sons: the one who is wise, the other evil [*rasha'*], the third dull, and the fourth is the one who does not ask."

The aim of learning is to beat the teacher by finding the weak spot in his "lecturing around." To ask questions is the essence of learning. In Bereshit Rabbah 8:9 (see also Babylonian Talmud, Bava Meṣia 59b) it is written:

---

[22] Martin Sicker, *The Moral Maxims*, 329. Translation, additions and emphasis are Sicker's.
[23] Martin Dibelius attempted a first comparison between the two genres in 1933. See Martin Dibelius, *Die Formgeschichte des Evangeliums* (Tübingen: Mohr, 1933), 173 et seq.
[24] I exclude here the study of mystical texts as for example the literature of the Hekhalot, a topic which cannot sic et simpliciter be compared with the *contemplatio* of the Church Fathers.

> R. Simlai said: Wherever you find a point [apparently] supporting the heretics [*minim*], you find the refutation at its side. They [the *minim*] asked him again: 'What is meant by, *And God said: Let us make man*?' 'Read what follows,' replied he: 'not, "And gods created (*wa-yivre'u*) man" is written here, but "*And God created – wa-yivra*"' (Genesis 1,27). When they went out his disciples said to him: 'Them you have dismissed with a mere makeshift, but how will you answer us?' Said he to them: 'In the past Adam was created from dust and Eve was created from Adam; but henceforth it shall be *In our image, after our likeness* (*ib.* 26); neither man without woman nor woman without man, and neither of them without the Divine Spirit [*Shekhina*].'[25]

The students illustrate the weakness of the response to the *minim* which was based on the polytheistic difficulty. The rabbi has solved the problem of the plural, as is mentioned in "Let us make man" with Genesis 1:27a "And God created man." Yet, he does not give the *minim* a plausible answer to the question of the plural in "In our image, after our likeness." The suffixes still stand for a plural and thus the problem remains unsolved: Who was involved in the creation of man? Now the answer is: the dust when Adam was created, and Adam when Eve was created. After the creation of the first couple, the chain of the generations begins in which neither Adam nor Eve are mentioned but *ish* (man) and *ishah* (woman), whose element of existence-creating is the Divine Spirit (*Shekhinah*). There is no man without woman, and no woman without man. Neither can exist ontologically without *Shekhinah*. Every man and every woman is created according to the image and likeliness of the first human couple.

The two steps of response as demonstrated in this example show the pedagogical virtue of the students who are not satisfied with an answer and pose a further and more subtle question in order to allow the rabbi to sharpen his knowledge.

1.3 Impertinence is the Beginning of Wisdom

The art of learning is also the evolution of impertinence, to draw from the most absurd situation, a lesson which corners the rabbi. We read in Babylonian Talmud, Berakhot 62a:

---

[25] Harry Freedman and Maurice Simon, trans. *Midrash Rabbah in Ten Volumes* vol. 1: Genesis (London: Soncino Press, 1961), 60. Translation, emphasis, and additions marked by * are Freedman's and Simon's. Other additions are mine. See also Babylonian Talmud, Bava Meşia 59b.

> [The student] R. Kahana once went in and hid under Rav's bed.
> He heard him chatting [with his wife] and joking and doing what he needed to do.
> He said to him [loudly]: It appears that Abba's mouth had never tasted the dish before! [When he discovered his student under the bed Rav] said to him: Kahana, are you here? Get out! That is the limit of impertinence! [Kahana] replied: It is Torah [too], and I need to learn.

Spaces which the reader would perceive as private then, as they would be seen today, are particularly chosen in this text to focus on the principle of learning the Torah. The word of the Torah is supposed to reign everywhere. This is not a paradox and is not only valid for the Jewish Halakhah of the Talmudic period. In the Middle Ages, but especially in the modern period, the debate concerned with sexual pleasure as well as allowed and prohibited positions for intercourse has developed further. Norms were accepted which went beyond the Talmudic Halakhah: not everything the rabbi permitted was indeed allowed to be practiced.[26] This is not the place to discuss the rabbinic ethical and moral debates at the time of *pilpul* ("hair-splitting").[27] Allow me but one comment: it had a lot in common with the contemporary Christian casuistry. It is more important in our context to understand that the principle of learning was superior to the private sphere. In the medieval period also, morality and sexual taboos were subordinate to other principles – at least in the interpretation by Rabbi Yehudah ben Samuel he-Ḥasid of the German-Jewish medieval era. He preferred (and allowed) unfaithfulness over the "chemical," i.e., medicinal, castration in case of a pathologic craving for sex. Otherwise, he argued, the sacrosanct principle of marital sexual life would be in danger.[28] The concentration on sexuality – which dates back to the dichotomous vision of life according to Augustine of Hippo and his disciples in the West – almost automatically resulted in the extension of a sexual morality that occupies today a prominent place in modern society. According to the Talmudic rabbis, the field of sexuality is one among many ploughed by the *talmid ḥakham* with his practical knowledge. What the *talmid* does with his knowledge on those fields of sexuality, however, is not explained.

The relationship between teacher and student is – and will always remain – a dialectical one. This is inherent to its nature. It depends on the time in which teacher and student live. This is doubtless a truism, but it is also

---

26 David Biale, *Eros and the Jews: From Biblical Israel to Contemporary America* (New York: Basic Books, 1992), 79; see also the final chapter, pp. 267–280.
27 On this, see Ruth Berger, *Sexualität, Ehe und Familienleben in der jüdischen Moralliteratur (900–1900)* (Wiesbaden: Harrassowitz, 2003).
28 Biale, *Eros and the Jews*, 79.

quite often an ignored truism. Also ignored is the fact that many methods of education *en vogue* today have been tried and tested before. Even tuitions were common in rabbinic schools,[29] and the technique of rote memorisation is both used and severely criticised today as it was used and criticised then. The method of education that is supposed to support creativity and imagination in the student is what I have referred to by the term "the impertinence of asking." It is commonly said that there are no stupid questions but only stupid answers. This is simply not true. It is only by the questions that we can learn if the one who asks them has understood the matter. Only by the questions can we learn if those who ask them are serious, witty, playful, childish or impertinent. Impertinence – the classic Yiddish *chutzpah* – is an art of learning which cannot be replaced if one does not possess it. *Chutzpah* does not only require knowledge and know-how, but also the wit to express facts in such a way that the listener will understand it better as though it was addressed explicitly.

Chutzpah is typically translated as impertinence. It is an inexplicable attitude. The episode concerning Xanthippe – which is probably invented but nevertheless circulated through the medium of art – can serve to illustrate this attitude: Xanthippe was so angered by her husband Socrates that she cursed him and eventually emptied a bucket of dirty water over his head. To this, Socrates replied coolly that "rain is bound to follow the thunder."[30] He is still seen as a philosopher and she as a brash woman. Such an understanding is, however, unjustified as we still do not know what angered Xanthippe in the first place.

I will conclude my discussion with a popular Yiddish story which illustrates many of the aspects I have referred to here:[31]

> A Jew has been sued for libel. He had supposedly charged somebody with "*chutzpah*." The judge, however, is unaware of this word and asks the Jew to explain it to him. The Jew declares outright that it is impossible to explain the word. Finally, he accepts to translate "chutzpah" as "brashness."
> "But," he adds, "it is not a common brashness, but brashness with *gvure*."
> "What is 'gvure'?," the judge requests to know.
> "Gvure – that is 'strength.'"
> "Thus, chutzpah is a strong brashness?"
> "Well, yes and no. Gvure is not only strength, but strength with *ssekhel*."

---

[29] As discussed by Avtayon in Babylonian Talmud, Yoma 35b.
[30] John Lemprière, Lorenzo da Ponte, and John David Ogilby, *Bibliotheca classica: Or a Dictionary of all the Principal Names and Terms Relating to the Geography, Topography, History, Literature, and Mythology of Antiquy and of the Ancients* (New York: W. C. Dean, 1851), 654. See also the sources there.
[31] An English translation and adaptation of a text itself translated into German.

"What is 'ssekhel'?"
"Ssekhel – that's 'mind, or brains.'"
"So, chutzpah is a strong, clever brashness?"
"Yes and no. Ssekhel is not merely brains, but brains with *ta'am*."
"All right, but what is 'ta'am'?"
"Your Honor, how am I supposed to explain to you what 'chutzpah' is if you do not understand basic English?"

2 Ezra as "Reformer" in Classical Jewish Literature

To "reform," as the term is used today, contains a political connotation which had not developed as late as the French Revolution. "Reform," as used in the Middle Ages, had already invoked the concepts of *restauratio* and *renovatio*. Thus, it had invoked the utopian understanding that was projected into the future, and at the same time the historical understanding that was projected into the past. The idea might be expressed through the paradox that especially those who wish to reform the tradition politically refer to valid structures and seek their identity in the past. In this sense, *re-formatio* is connected to shape and matter, to Platonic archetypes and the organisation of the primary substance. *Re-formatio* refers to an organisation that is used in a political sense in order to justify one's own vision. As such, the category of reform/-ation should be understood as a heuristic, pragmatic, but also ideological tool for the understanding of socio-religious and socio-political events in antiquity, the Middle Ages, and modern period. My following contribution to the discussion is intended to raise the question of how a novelty is presented in the garb of, and especially how reforms have an effect on political-religious processes. I will refer largely to my own research dedicated to understanding "reformation" in its historical development.[32]

2.1 The Reformation in the 16th century

In 1585–1586, the scholar Avraham ibn Migash of Constantinople, former physician at the court of Suleiman the Magnificent (1520–1566),[33] wrote that Maimonides would have danced with joy had he lived to witness Luther's Reformation. According to ibn Migash, the new movement that had originated in the midst of Christianity was willed by God to destroy the old Christianity that was plagued by its internal fragmentation. It was to destroy the old Christianity by

---

[32] I refer in particular to my article, "'… in einigen Glaubensartikeln neigt die jüdische Nation eher zur römischen Kirche': Jüdische Gelehrte über Reformation und Gegenreformation," in *Katholizismus und Judentum: Gemeinsamkeiten und Verwerfungen vom 16. bis zum 20. Jahrhundert*, ed. Hubert Wolf and Giuseppe Veltri (Regensburg: Pustet, 2005), 15–29; and Veltri, *Gegenwart der Tradition* (Leiden: Brill 2002).

[33] On the (idealised) image of this Sultan in Jewish chronicles, see especially Martin Jacobs, *Islamische Geschichte in jüdischen Chroniken* (Tübingen: Mohr Siebeck, 2004), 52–55, 178–184 (Eliyahu Capsali); 253–257 (Yosef Sambari).

using its own weaponry: disunity. God had summoned the spirits of the Lutherans to smash the altars, images of God, and the old heretic beliefs. According to Ibn Migash, the Lutherans had taken back the Christian religion to its original form; they had remodeled and "re-created" it. The reason for that was that Christianity supposedly existed as a shapeless entity yearning for a "reconstruction." One should note the philosophical interpretation of *reformatio* as a "reconstruction" of matter. It has to be seen, of course, in the Jewish context of a return to the Jewish monotheistic faith.[34]

Reform is the recreation of the original status. It is a mythical understanding that has its own origin in the idea of a past *aetas aurea*, Golden Age, in order to justify contemporary political and cultural upheaval. Avraham ibn Migash's excitement about the Protestant turns could only develop in a region distant from the Reformation. It could only develop in a region remote from the truth, one might say, which Jews in Europe had to suffer from at the hands of Luther and the Lutherans. By then, their initial positive attitude toward Jews had already changed for the worse. Luther distanced himself from his earlier statements because he was likely disappointed that Jews did not convert in large numbers. In *Dass Jesus Christus ein geborener Jude sei* ("That Jesus Christ was a born Jew," 1523), Luther had more or less absolved Jews of deicide. The aim of this treatise, however, was clear: "to tempt Jews to the Christian faith," as he himself had announced in the introduction.[35] Twenty years later, in 1543, Luther published another treatise: *Von den Juden und ihren Lügen* ("On Jews and their Lies"). It was full of hatred and animosities. Jewish scholars who had transcribed Luther's name into Hebrew characters as "Lauter," a German word for "sincere," had to find that he was no longer "pure." Luther was reinterpreted in Hebrew as "impure" because the Lutherans had expelled the Jews of Saxony, Alsace and other German states and provinces, and had handed them over to the mob.[36]

---

34 See Avraham Ibn Migash, *Kevod Elohim* (Constantinople, 1585–1586), fol. 128r–v, according to the reprint by Haim Hillel Ben-Sasson, *Sefer Kevod Elohim* (Jerusalem and Haifa: Bet ha-sefarim ha-le'umi yeha-universiṭa'i; Pinat ha-sefer, 1976). An English translation of relevant passages is available in Ben-Sasson, "The Reformation in Contemporary Jewish Eyes," *Proceedings of the Israel Academy of Sciences and Humanities* 4 (1971): 239–327.

35 See Ernst L. Ehrlich, "Luther und die Juden," in *Antisemitismus: Von der Judenfeindschaft zum Holocaust*, ed. Herbert A. Strauss and Norbert Kampe (Frankfurt am Main: Campus, 1988), 50.

36 There is proof of the Jewish reaction in Ben-Sasson, "The Reformation," 292 et seq. See also Chava Fraenkel-Goldschmidt, *Sefer ha-Miqnah* (Jerusalem: Meḳitse Nirdamim, 1970); Fraenkel-Goldschmidt, *The Historical Writings of Joseph of Rosheim: Leader of Jewry in Early Modern Germany* (Leiden: Brill, 2006).

The promise of a new era on the stage of history was unfortunately, at least for the Jews, a false prophecy and as such could only bring harm. This Jewish rejection of the Protestants did not remain unnoticed. The reformer Martin Bucer in 1539 authored the treatise *Von den jude ob un wie die unde den Christe zu halten sind* ("On the Jew/if and how they are to be kept among the Christians"). In this treatise, Bucer noted among other ideas

> It should not seem strange to you that they [Jews] favor the popish stories of atrocities at one time and our pure teachings and management of the churches at another. With the exception that the papists worship paintings and idols and pray to them as well whilst paying lip service to Christ, the papist and Jewish faith and religion are one and the same in the end.[37]

Some years later, in 1545, Luther in a sermon in Leipzig compared the Temple of Jerusalem (which he referred to as a "den of murderers") to Rome, and the Jewish priests to the Roman clerics who had "murdered the soul."[38]

At the end of the 16th century, when ibn Migash recorded his admiration for the Lutherans, there evolved a new Protestant discovery of Judaism, or, to be more precise, the discovery of the Karaites, a Jewish sect. Theologian Jean Morin (1591–1659) and the bible critic and Orientalist Richard Simon (1638–1712) were the first to see the analogy between Protestants and Karaites. They defended the *scriptura* as *intepretes sui* whereas they considered *traditio* as *interpretatio hominis*. The German theologian Johannes Christoph Wolf (1683–1739) commented on this that "Richardum Simonium in *Epistolis selectis* protestantes karraeos vocare."[39] Thus, the reform movement in Christianity had found an identity in Judaism which embodied everything the Reformation

---

[37] Original German text: "Das sie dann den päpstlichen grewlen mär günstigen dann unser reinen lere und haushaltung der kirchen solle euch auch nit seltzam sein. Dann ausgenommen, das die Päpstler bilder und götzen verehren und zuo anbetten fürstellen und Christum ... mit dem mund bekennen, so is der Päpstler und Juden glaube und Religion eben ein ding." Quoted from Ben-Sasson, "The Reformation," 292, note 157.

[38] "... das da sollte ein Bethaus sein (wie Christus aus Jesaja lvi. sagt), machen sie zu einem schendlichen kauffhaus, ja zur Mordgruben der Seelen " (page 31); "... Aber sie trieben allein auffs opffer on die lere und anruffen, Darüber ward das Haus zu nichts anderes denn zu einer Mördergruben. Denn damit verderbten sie die armen seelen ..." (33); "... dann sie nichts sind denn Seelenmörder (weil sie nichts recht leren, wie man gleuben und beten sol) ..." (36) All quotes from *D. Martin Luthers Werke: Kritische Gesamtausgabe* vol. 51 (Weimar: Böhlau, 1914), 22–41.

[39] Quoted in Valerio Marchetti, "The Lutheran Discovery of Karaite Hermeneutics," in *Una Manna Buona per Mantova: Man tov le-Man Tovah – Studi in onore di Vittore Colorni per il suo 92° compleanno*, ed. Mauro Perani (Florence: Olschki, 2004), 433–459.

sought: a return to the origins – *ad fontes*. The Karaites had indeed initiated a turn in the religion from the 9th century onward as they had demanded the supersession of rabbinic Judaism, since in their view it was man-made.

The Karaites had entered history by din of their literal and rationalist exegesis of the Bible text, and their strong criticism of the rabbinic understanding of the oral Torah. The Karaite reform, however, is first and foremost an attack on the position of the established elite in rabbinic Judaism. This elite had held the sole authority over the Jews in Diaspora – in Babylonia in particular – and had identified the rabbinic teachings with the authoritative text. We know the Babylonian sermon in which the Rabbi lectures in Hebrew while his Interpreter (*meturgeman*) renders the lecture into Aramaic.[40] It is a liturgical procedure we know from the Torah reading in the synagogue. This, in a way, personifies Moses, and his *meturgeman* Aaron, the "voice of Moses." The Karaite movement attacked the very same authoritative identity in order to return to the traditional text. This attitude was not a new one, as the quarrels between the Sadducees and Pharisees show. The so-called First Schism of the Samaritans was in particular grounded on the Samaritan belief that they had based their religion on the traditional text.

All reforms constitute a challenge to the existing authoritative texts and/or traditions by attempting to push through a selection of documents and literary compositions within the valid canon of texts. This is the theory. In reality, however, the process of reform works the other way round: a political or religious-political change is justified through recourse to texts which form the foundation of political change or present changes as prophesised. A political change is, *nolens volens*, a canonical one, as the existing authority always points to the validity of *traditio* when learning and executing the law. The valid law is presented and politically executed as the eternally binding one simply by regularly reading and thus publishing it. The public reading was, in a way, the copyrighting of the text and established control over it as changes would be noted. The Arabist Stefan Leder, for instance, has concluded that this practice existed within the institution of the *Riwāya* in the Arabic literary history.[41] But, how could the authorities promote new texts as old traditions? There are several biblical and post-biblical examples that best demonstrate this procedure.

---

[40] For talmudic sources see my *Eine Tora für den König Talmai* (Tübingen: Mohr Siebeck 1994), 194.
[41] See Stefan Leder, *Spoken Word and Written Text: Meaning and Social Significance of the Institution of Riwāya* (Tokyo: Islamic Area Studies Project, 2002).

2.2 Ezra the Reformer

According to the book of Deuteronomy 31:9, the written Torah was given to the priests, Levites, and elders of Israel together with the task of arranging for it to be read aloud to the assembled Israelites every seventh year. This was done "that they may hear, and that they may learn, and fear the Lord our God, and observe to do all the words of this law" (Deuteronomy 31:12). Such a procedure refers to the publication and declaration of a text which had to be read every seventh year because of the lack of printed texts and the low literacy rate of the people.

The (re-)discovery of the book of laws at the time of King Josiah's religious reforms in the 7th century BCE presents a historic "ascertainment" of this commandment found in Deuteronomy. In this case, however, it seems to have been the king and not the priests/Levites who ordered the reading/passage of the laws after the book had been found, written down, or simply composed and then publicised. This book was read before the assembled Israelites in order to be understood by all – and in accordance with the commandment of Deuteronomy. Then the king invoked the covenant with God that they may keep "His commandments, and His testimonies, and his statutes ... to confirm the words of this covenant that were written in this book" (2 Kings 23:3).

According to Ezra 7:12–26, it had been a foreign king, Artaxerxes of Persia, who had ordered the introduction, inauguration or validation of the Torah.[42] His order was met with the acceptance and support of the Jews whose political vision was the reconstruction of the wall, the temple, and the city, as well as the restoration of the public reading of the Torah. This law is now in Ezra's hands (Ezra 7:14) as the king's order had emphasised. The reading of the Torah at the water gate is one of the fundamental texts not only of the classical Jewish literature, but also takes a position that is more elevated than the Ezra redactor had perhaps intended, i.e. it goes beyond the mere story of 'reading and hearing' of a text. It is in this case as well that we see that the reconstruction of a text which was read and explained is the *deus ex machina* of a *political reform*. The same constellation was repeated several centuries later in Egyptian Alexandria.

---

[42] See Abraham Berliner, *Targum Onkelos: Einleitung und Register* (Frankfurt am Main: Kauffmann, 1884), 74; Hans H. Schaeder, *Esra der Schreiber* (Tübingen: Mohr, 1930), 39–59; Antonius H. J. Gunneweg, "Zur Interpretation der Bücher Ezra-Nehemia. Zugleich ein Beitrag zur Methode der Exegese," *Vetus Testamentum Supplement* 32 (1981): 146–161; Klaus Koch, "Ezra and the Origins of Judaism," *Journal of Semitic Studies* 19 (1974): 173–197; Luis Díez Merino, "Philological Aspects in the Research of the Targums," in *Proceedings of the Ninth World Congress of Jewish Studies (Jerusalem 1985) – Panel Sessions: Bible Studies and Ancient Near East*, ed. Moshe H. Goshen-Gottstein (Jerusalem: World Union of Jewish Studies, 1988), 87–97.

After Demetrios of Phaleros had read the Greek text of the Torah in Alexandria, the priests proclaimed together with the eldest of the translators, the representatives of the *politeuma*, as well as the people, that the translation had been carried out in great piety and thoroughness. For that reason, later changes were strictly prohibited. The people agreed to this order and "according to their customs," condemned everybody who would seek to alter the body of the text, either through additions, omissions, or any other form of alteration.[43]

The fact that the translators themselves were present at the proclamation might indicate that this translation was to be understood as being extraordinary (divine inspiration?). This aspect is emphasised by the liturgy-like procedure which refers to the religious sphere.[44] The presence of Demetrios, however, points to the fact that the reading of the text also has a political dimension. According to Aristeas's propaganda, God and the King had jointly worked for the creation of a text for the heathens and Jews. In Aristeas's description, this idea is followed by a formula concerning the unalterability of the text. It is connected to a curse which has no parallel in its application to the text of the Torah – despite the fact that there is a reference to such a Jewish custom in the bible. The rendering "according to their customs" may have recourse to the curses and blessings of the Deuteronomic traditions.[45] Aristeas had likely read Deuteronomy 4:2 and its parallel Deuteronomy 13:1 from this perspective.

The vocabulary of Deuteronomy 4:2 in the language of the LXX deserves some closer attention as the Jewish-Hellenistic scribe had not altered the wording and the implication of this passage to a larger degree. The verb *phylassein* (Deuteronomy 4:2 and Aristeas § 311) in connection with *nomos, rhema*, or, as in Deuteronomy 4:2, with the object *tas entolas* means "guard," "observe," or "watch." Aristeas refers to a written text whose words needed to be "safeguarded." The verb does not invoke the observation of a law anymore, but – through this alteration of meaning – to the safeguarding of a text. In this context, we do not deal with a formula establishing the unalterability of the text, but with a formula prohibiting the alteration of the texts' translation.

---

[43] For the text of the so-called Aristeas 'letter' see *Aristeas ad Philocratem epistula*, ed. Paul Wendland (Leipzig: Teubner 1900); *Aristeas to Philocrates*, ed. Moses Hads (New York: Harper, & Brothers 1962); *Lettera di Aristea*, ed. Francesca Calabi (Milan: Biblioteca universale Rizzoli, 1995). For bibliographic references and secondary literature, see my *Gegenwart der Tradition. Studien zur jüdischen Literatur und Kulturgeschichte* (Leiden: Brill, 2001), 14–16.

[44] See Harry M. Orlinsky, "The Septuagint as Holy Writ and the Philosophy of the Translators," *Hebrew Union College Annual* 46 (1975): 110–113; Daniel R. Schwartz, "The Priests in Ep. Arist. 310," *Journal of Biblical Literature* 97 (1978): 567–571.

[45] See F. Charles Fensham, "Malediction and Benediction an Ancient Near Eastern Vassal-Treatises and the Old Testament," *Zeitschrift für die Alttestamentliche Wissenschaft* 74 (1962): 1–9.

Let us briefly summarise what we have discussed this far: 2 Kings 23, Ezra 7, and the legend of the LXX as transmitted by Aristeas have one aspect in common: they tell stories of recovered/reconstructed texts which are read before the community. They tell stories of texts that are to be treated as binding legal texts from then on. The royal authority – be it Jewish or not – is a decisive factor of the "reform" of the text, and functions as the initiator for "reform," guaranty for the text coming into effect, and finally as the supervisory body of its "eternal" unalterability. There is no doubt that the Book of Ezra had influenced the legend of Aristeas. I believe there are also some references to Ezra-Nehemiah in the reform of Josiah in 2 Kings 23:3.

In any event, Jewish as well as Christian sources concur in the notion that Ezra was the great restorer and "reformer" of Judaism. The reconstruction of the Temple, the restoration of the cult, the supremacy of the Torah, the construction of a community that opted for ethnic seclusion under foreign rule, and the political and religious dissociation of the Samaritans: these are merits attributed to Ezra (and Nehemiah) in the bible. These are also elements that affected the lives of later Jews in Palestine and the Diaspora – the Temple of course excluded. The attitude of Ezra-Nehemiah to foreign rule would also strongly characterise and shape the later Jewish community in a political way.

The most surprising fact is that these were not the reasons Ezra had earned his reputation as the great reformer in classical Judaism. He was indeed seen as the author of a reform as part of the re-creation of Jewish traditional literature. According to rabbinic convictions, he might have even received the Torah, had Moses not been before him. In this way, the rabbis expressed an understanding of what Ezra represents: the end of a process of creating the Hebrew text, as well as the beginning of interpretation, a hermeneutics that occurred largely beyond the realm of direct interference in the text. The rabbis beheld in Ezra the archetype of their elitist and intellectual caste, as is evident in the pithy manifesto of rabbinic Judaism, the treatise Mishnah Avot where the name of Ezra is notoriously not mentioned:

> Moses received the Torah from Sinai and transmitted it to Joshua, Joshua to the elders, the elders to the prophets, and the prophets transmtted it to the Men of the Great Assembly. They used to say three things: Be thorough in judgment; raise up many disciples; and make a fence around the Torah.

The *anshe kneset ha-gedolah* (Men of the Great Assembly) was an institution after the exile and at the time of Ezra. The *kneset* functioned to help constitute rabbinic Judaism and concluded the development of tradition as it was handed down from Moses. One should note the semantic difference between the verbs *limsor* (transmit) and *le-qabbel* or *le-lammed* (preserve or learn). Whereas the first is used for the tradition from Moses to the *kneset ha-gedolah*, the latter is employed from that time onward. Thus, there is a clear break between the tradition from Moses through Ezra, to the *anshe kneset ha-gedolah,* and the "others" who had only received the Torah. Despite the fact that *limsor* and *leqabbel* can be seen as synonymous, one should note the nuances. Even in his apologetic treatise *Contra Apionem* Flavius Josephus (37–c. 100) referred to a more thorough transmission of the Holy Scriptures only until the time of Artaxerxes. Josephus stated that "from the times of Artaxerxes until today the entire story was composed but it does not enjoy the same credibility because of the lack of the prophets' exact tradition [*dia to mē genesthai tēn prophetōn akribē diadochēn*]."[46] Contrary to common belief, Josephus does not discuss the history of the canon at this point. He discusses the imprecision of the Homeric historiography and Homeric tradition, and contrasts this with Jewish historiography, which was more exact by far. He thus refers to 22 books which ought to represent a counter-number to the Homeric poems. Yet, one has to add: according to Josephus, the Jewish tradition is more exact only until Artaxerxes.

The element of exactness, the person of Ezra, and the number of books form the bases for legends which were also known in that period. The 14th chapter of the 4th Book of Ezra – an apocryphal text which was believed to be "canonical" among Christians up to the 16th century, and added to the edition of the *Vulgata* – tells the story of how the holy books were destroyed with the destruction of the Temple. Ezra had begged God to re-create the books. Ezra writes 94 books with the help of five men. The 24 books of the Holy Scriptures were to be released to the public – be they worthy or unworthy – whereas the 70 remaining books were to be kept secret and given to the wisest men alone. A Christian text summarises this tradition the following way:

> Now when the people had gone up [to Jerusalem] they had no Books of the Prophets. And Ezra the scribe went down into that pit [wherein Simeon had cast the Books], and he found a censer full of fire, and the perfume of the incense which rose up from it. And thrice he took some of the dust of those Books, and cast it into his mouth, and straightaway God made to abide in him the spirit of prophecy, and he renewed all the Books of the Prophets.[47]

Thus, reads the so-called *Spelunca Thesaurorum* (*m'arrat gazzē*), which had been ascribed to Ephrem the Syrian.[48] The text is a typical Christian rewrite of

---

46 Josephus, *Contra Apionem* I: 41.
47 English translation from Ernest A. Wallis Budge, ed. *The Book of the Cave of Treasures. A History of the Patriarchs and the Kings their Successors from the Creation to the Crucifixion of Christ* (London: The Religious Tract Society, 1927), 192. See also the *Book of Adam* IV:2.
48 It was first translated into German and published by Carl Bezold, ed. *Die Schatzhöhle aus dem syrischen Texte dreier uneditirten Handschriften in's Deutsche übersetzt und mit Anmerkungen versehen* (Leipzig: J. C. Hinrisch'sche Buchhandlung, 1883), see there p. 51 et seq.

several Jewish traditions which mention Ezra the Scribe. It was typically Christian in as much as Ezra is brought into relation with the prophets. The rabbis would not have agreed to this idea since they saw in Ezra a redactor of the Torah. We will return to this idea later.

It is surprising that the following is hardly recognised in scholarship: namely that in the first century BCE, the scholarship on Homer's texts was, for reasons yet to be determined, also supported by a legend that knew of a pre-Alexandrinian redaction of the Homeric poems. It was said that Peisistratos, the tyrant of Athens, initiated a council edition of Homer's scattered poems. At the same time, this legend evolved, and likely influenced by it, the idea developed in Judaism that Ezra the Scribe had edited the Pentateuch after the Torah had been burnt with Nebuchadnezzar's destruction of the First Temple.[49] The three legends (the legend of the LXX, the restauratio of the biblical books through Ezra, and the legend of Homer's poems) experienced a peculiar interdependency as elements of one intermingled with the other, and the one was perceived as proof of the other.[50] Thus, the idea spread of a council for the edition, constituted by 72 grammarians. It may have arisen in the school of the grammarian Choiroboskos (9th century CE). The 72 grammarians allegedly recreated a text that had been corrupted, dispersed, and even destroyed earlier and again after the days of Homer.[51] Despite the fact that this story stands exposed as fictitious since John Tzetzes (12th century C.E.), it continued to

---

49 See Johann G. Eichhorn, *Einleitung in das alte Testament*, Vierte Original-Ausgabe (Göttingen: Rosenbusch, 1823), 210 et seq.; also Emil Schürer, *The History of the Jewish People in the Age of Jesus Christ (175 B.C.–A.D. 135)*, vol. 3.1, New English version, ed. by Geza Vermes et al. (Edinburgh: Clarke, 1986), 301.
50 On this, see my article, "Tolomeo Filadelfo, emulo di Pisistrato': Alcune note su leggende antiche di biblioteche, edizioni e traduzioni," *Laurentianum* 32 (1991): 144–166.
51 On this aspect, see Friedrich A. Wolf, *Prolegomena ad Homerum sive de operum Homericorum prisca et genuina forma variisque mutationibus et probabili ratione emendandi* (Halis Saxonum: E Libraria Orphanotrophei, 1795); Rpr. Hildesheim, 1963, 109–14; Homeros [Homer], *Odyssa editit Guilielmus Dindorf. Praemittitur Maximilani Sengenbusch Homerica Dissertatio Posterior. Edition Quarta Correctior* (Leipzig: Teubner, 1856); Karl Lehrs, "Zur Homerischen Interpolation," *Rheinisches Museum für Philologie* 17 (1862): 481 et seq.; Fridericus Ritschl, *Friderici Ritschelii opvscvla philologica* (Lipsiae: Teubner, 1866); Victor Bérard, "Pisistrate, rédacteurs des poèmes homériques," *Revue de philologie, de littérature et d'histoire anciennes* 45, no. 3 (1921): 194–233; Thomas W. Allen, *Homer: The Origins and the Transmission* (Oxford: Clarendon Press, 1924); Repr. 1969, 225–248; Reinhold Merkelbach, "Die pisistratische Redaktion der homerischen Gedichte," *Rheinisches Museum für Philologie* 95 (1952): 23–47; John A. Davison, "Peisistratos and Homer," *Transactions and Proceedings of the American Philological Association* 86 (1955): 1–21; John L. Myres and Dorothea Gray, *Homer and his Critics* (London: Routledge & Paul, 1958), 290–291.

flourish. The Humanist Giannozzo Manetti (15th century C.E.), for instance, chose Peisistratos' edition of Homer's poems as support for the truth of the Septuagint.[52] The scholarly critiques from Justus Scaliger (1606) to Humphrey Hody (1705) left no room for doubting the factuality of the legends of the LXX (or LXXII) and Peisistratos.[53]

There is, however, a pivotal element in the legend of Peseistratos. It is outspoken propaganda targeting the edited Homeric texts at the school in Alexandria by postulating an even more authoritative era in which a canonic text was "re-recreated." Texts are known that have been altered to justify a specific status quo. Dieuchides of Megara (4th century BCE) and Apollodoros (2nd century BCE) report of an alteration of Ilias B, 557 in favor of Athens – an alteration that was ascribed to Solon or Peiseistratos. It was a catalogue of ships whose authenticity is still questioned.

> Αἴας δ' ἐκ Σαλαμῖνος ἄγεν δυοκαίδεκα νῆας,
> στῆσε δ' ἄγων ἵν' Ἀθηναίων ἵσταντο φάλαγγες.

(English)
Ajax led twelve ships from Salamis;
Leading them, he stationed his troops where the phalanxes
  of the Athenian stood.[54]

---

[52] Giannozzo Manetti, *Apologeticum adversus suae novae Psalterii traductionis obtrectatores libri 5* (MS), mentioned in Charles Trinkaus, *In our Image and Likeness: Humanity and Divinity in Italiaen Humanist Thought*, vol. 2 (Chicago: Constable, 1970), 588–589; Note 75 (p. 821). Manetti's opinion was adopted by the Jewish scholar Azaria de' Rossi. See his *Me'or 'Enayim*, chapter 7, edition: Azaria de' Rossi, *Sefer Me'or 'Enayim*, ed. David Cassel, 3 vols. (Vilnius: Romm, 1864–1866, reprint, Jerusalem: Makor, 1970).

[53] Justus Scaliger, "Animadversiones in chronologia Eusebii" in *Thesaurus Temporum Eusebii Pamphili Caesareae Palaestinae Episcopi*, ed. Joseph J. Scaliger (Leiden, 1606), 122–125; see also Jürgen C. Lebram, "Ein Streit um die hebräische Bibel und die Septuaginta," in *Leiden University in the Seventeenth Century: An Exchange of Learning*, ed. Theodoor H. Lunsingh Scheurleer (Leiden: Brill, 1975), 36 et seq. (21–63); Humphrey Hody, "Contra historiam LXX interpretum Aeristeae nomine inscriptum dissertation," in Hody, *De Bibliorum textibus originalibus versionibus graecis et latina vulgata* (Oxonii: Scheldoniano, 1705), 1–89. There existed, of course, criticism targeted against a reduction of the story to a fairy tale. See my book, *Eine Tora für den König Talmai: Untersuchungen zum Übersetzungsverständnis in der jüdisch–hellenistischen und rabbinischen Literatur* (Tübingen: Mohr, 1994), 5–6; Veltri, *Libraries, Translations, and 'Canonic' Texts. The Septuagint, Aquila and Ben Sira in the Jewish and Christian Traditions* (Leiden: Brill, 2006): 26–99.

[54] Ernst Heitsch, *Gesammelte Schriften* vol 1: *Zum frühgriechischen Epos* (Munich and Leipzig: Saur, 2001), 131–150. The English translation is taken from Benjamin Sammons, *The Art and Rhetoric of the Homeric Catalogue* (Oxford: Oxford University Press, 2010), 170.

The fact that authoritative redactors may have also altered valid texts was a common one in the antiquity. This may not necessarily be viewed as forgery. Often, such alterations were actually accepted if they were done for political purposes. According to Deuteronomy 17:18, the king was supposed to receive a "copy of this law" (וְכָתַב לוֹ אֶת-מִשְׁנֵה הַתּוֹרָה הַזֹּאת). Today, it would be called an annotated abridged version of the law. Rabbinic Judaism referred to it as an "altered" version of the Torah which the king might listen to or read, since he lacked the time to read the full version.[55] Instead of מִשְׁנֵה הַתּוֹרָה (*mishneh ha-torah*) it was clearly read as *meshanneh torah* ("he changes the Torah") or even *meshunnah torah* ("an altered Torah").

Let us summarise: new or old texts were rediscovered, restored or adjusted to new challenges of the present time. They were altered. The alteration of these texts has to be seen as politically motivated, since they reformed the current situation motivated by an agenda of returning to old ways. Today, we would refer to that as consciously interfering with the text in order to justify political decisions. We would refer to forgery and would, perhaps naïvely, believe we had an original and a secondary version of the text. In the ancient world, however, the text was believed to be an *instrumentum regni*.

The Talmud reports on an alteration of the Torah at the time of Ezra. We read in the Babylonian Talmud, Sanhedrin 21b–22a:

> Mar Zutra, or according to others Mar Uqba, said: "Originally, the Torah was given to Israel in Hebrew characters (*'Ivrit*) and in the holy language (or: language of the holy ones). At the time of Ezra, it was given to Israel in Assyrian letters (*Ashshurit*) and in the Aramaic language. [Finally,] it was transcribed[56] into the Assyrian letters and the holy language. The *'Ivrit* letters and the Aramaic language were left to the common people. Who were the common people? Rabbi Hisda said: The Cutheans (Samaritans). What is (meant) by *'Ivrit* letters: Rabbi Hisda said: The *Libnu'ah* letters.
>
> It was taught: Rabbi Jose said: If Moses had not been born before him, Ezra had been worthy of receiving the Torah (...) And although the Torah was not received through him, it was changed through him as it is written: "And the Torah was written in Aramaic letters, and interpreted in Aramaic (Ezra 4:7)." And again it is written that "... they could neither read the letters nor tell the interpretation to the king" (Daniel 5:8). And it is written further "He is supposed to write a copy for the king" (Deuteronomy 17:18). A scripture which is supposed to be altered.[57]

---

55 Leqaḥ Ṭov on Bereshit 1:1.
56 The translation of this verb is rather difficult. Marcus Jastrow translated it as "select."
57 Jacob Shachter and H. Freedman, eds., *The Soncino Babylonian Talmud*, transl. with Notes, Glossary and Indices under the Editorship of Rabbi Dr. I. Epstein (London: Soncino Press, 1948), http://www.come-and-hear.com/sanhedrin/sanhedrin_0.html (accessed February 20, 2013).

One should not read this text as a description of a turn in text history. One should rather interpret the tale as a rhetorical description of a process which surely had not begun at the time of Ezra but was definitely concluded in the era of the Babylonian Talmud. The letters/characters in question are the old Hebrew writ which can be seen in the scrolls of Qumran and coins dating from the Bar Kokhba era. The Hebrew characters were substituted by the square script – the characters that are still in use today and that are better to be referred to as Ashshurit or Assyrian script. The period was probably not only marked by a shift in the text in relation to script, but also by a standardisation of certain text forms, pronunciation, etc. We also deal with the vocalisation of the text introduced at the time (although not according to common standards).

The reform of the text crystallised at the time and represents a process and especially a class of people (like the writer) that had definitely influenced the text history. It is no accident that the legends of Ezra and Homer are quoted side by side since both deal with the question of text edition and thus with traditions which had been clearly used against other classes and schools: Jerusalem versus Alexandria; Alexandria versus Athens and Pergamon, etc. Thus, an attempt was made to project the undertaking back into mythical times. Everything that is included in the text – or is supposed to be included – is specified. For this reason, the rabbinic literature attributed the origin of the Targum to Ezra.

One rabbinic source that recurs to the story of origin of this Targum is included in the Babylonian Talmud Megillah 3a, Nedarim 37b–38a. According to the redactor, Nehemiah 8:8 reports a *Miqra* (Tanakh) reading with the corresponding Targum. The bible verse states: "And they read in the book, in the Law of God, distinctly; and they gave the sense [of the words], and caused them to understand the reading." The Babylonian Talmud, Megillah 3a, interprets this verse through an exegetic word-by-word explanation by Rabbi Iqa bar Abin, tradent of Rabbi Ḥanan'el, the tradent of Rav:

> *They read from the Book of the Law of God:*
> That is the Mikra (i.e. the consonantic text)
> *In detail (meforash)*
> That is the Targum
> *Giving the meaning (of the words)*
> That is the division in verses
> *So that the people could understand*
> That are signs of meaning (accents?)
> They say to him: That is the Masorah.[58]

---

58 See also Babylonian Talmud, Nedarim 37b und Zevaḥim 37b.

As is clear from the context of this passage, the redactor is faced with the following problem: the Targum to the Prophets by Jonathan ben Uzziel is attributed to the prophets Haggai, Zechariah and Malachi. The Targum to the Torah by Onkelos, however, is attibuted to rabbis Eli'ezer and Yehoshua', and thus later figures. In order not to create the impression that the Targum to the Torah was younger than the one to the prophets, the redactor of the passage of the Talmud interprets Nehemiah 8:8 as proof that Ezra had already had this Targum at hand.[59]

The redactor, however, does not dispute that Nehemiah 8:8 speaks of the origin of this Targum – as medieval and modern scholars had interpreted this passage of the Talmud. No, Ezra and the Levites *read in the book*. They had not created something new on their own initiative, but had rather followed a procedure that was outlined by the text to be read. The redactor clearly ascribed the Masoretic text to Moses. Thus, Ezra had only brought the text to contemporary standards. The Talmud therefore projects the entire Masorah of the bible to the revelation at Mount Sinai – together with Miqra (reading through the help of the character vocalisation), accents, and the separation of the text into verses. The parallel in Babylonian Talmud, Nedarim 37b–38a, explicitly mentions *'iṭṭur, qere* and *ketiv* as *halakhah mi-sinai*. The redactor thus sees the Targum, i.e., the explanation of the words, as fixed as the letters that had transmitted the Torah in its written form. This suggests that the Babylonian Talmud considered the Targum (the halakhic and haggadic explanation of the words) as *torah mi-sinai* which likely was available in its written form at the time.

The fidelity the redactor shows in the text does not allow any recursions to possible other authorities. We read in Avot de Rabbi Natan:

> Wherefore are the dots (in the biblical text)? Nay, thus said Ezra: If Elijah will come and say, why didst thou write them? I shall say unto him: I have already put dots over them. And if he will say: Thou hast written well, I shall remove the dots from over them.[60]

The perfect redactor would thus not hesitate to question the text of the Torah if the prophet Elijah agreed to his changes of the Masora. Prophecy is thus

---

[59] The idea that the Targum is not supposed to be transmitted in the written form like the oral law (see PesiqtaRabbati § 5 and parallels) apparently contradicts this Talmudic concept. The redactor most probably had access to a written form of these Targums (Onkelos and Jonathan).

[60] Midrash Ba-Midbar Rabbah 3:3 in the English translation of Moses H. Segal, "The Promulgation of the Authoritative Text of the Hebrew Bible," *Journal of BiblicalLiterature* 72 (1953): 42. See also my *Libraries, Translations, and Canonic Text*, 17–19.

clearly juxtaposed to tradition. Or, in other words, the authority of the scripture is self-referential and does not allow any other authority.

Therefore, we might summarise again: rabbinic Judaism sees Ezra as the founder who justifies the rabbinic tradition. In this sense, Ezra is not only the founder of Judaism but the *ur*-character of rabbinic Judaism.

2.3 Conclusion

Josephus reported that Ezra had died and been buried in Jerusalem.[61] According to the legend, Ezra died at the noteworthy age of 120. Jewish medieval tradition states he died on Tevet 9th.[62] This is the date the so-called 'Additions' to the Scroll of Fasts (Megillat Ta'anit Batra) offers. There it is written: "On the 9th Tevet, our rabbis did not ask why [one had to fast]. On this day, Ezra the Priest died." The Muslim chronographer Abū L-Rayḥān al-Bīrūnī (d. 440/1048) mentions the Jewish day of fasting – there is no reference to the date of Ezra's death, though.[63] This seems to have been a story that had developed later in order to mask another date which might have been connected to the birth of Christ. That the position of Jesus and Ezra were equal in the respective faiths of Christians and Jews is an idea that exists in Islam. One passage in the Qu'ran mentions that Jews revered Ezra as the son of Allah, like the Christians revere the Messiah.[64] According to Jewish tradition, it is the person of Ezra in whom Jews and Muslims converge as believers, as the medieval traveller Benjamin of Tudela (1130–1173) had claimed (Tudela had supposedly identified Ezra's sepulchre). Tudela writes:

> Thence [from Basra] it is two days to the river Samara [Dijala], which is the commencement of the land of Persia. 1,500 Jews live near the sepulchre of Ezra, the priest, who went forth from Jerusalem to King Artaxerxes and died there. In front of his sepulchre is a large synagogue. And at the side thereof the Mohammedans erected a house of prayer out of their great love and veneration for him, and they like the Jews on that account. And the Mohammedans come hither to pray.[65]

---

61 Josephus, *Antiquitates* XI, 5, § 5.
62 As transmitted in the *Megillat Ta'anit Batra*. On this day of fast, see, however, Sid Z. Leiman, "The Scroll of Fasts: The Ninth of Teveth," *Jewish Quarterly Review* 74.2 (1983): 174–195; see also below, pp. 264–265.
63 See below, p. 265.
64 Sure 9, At-Tauba, Verse 29–30.
65 Marcus Adler, ed. and trans., *The Itinerary of Benjamin of Tudela: Critical Text, Translation and Commentary* (London: Henry Frowde, 1907), 51. It is available online. See http://www.teachittome.com/seforim2/seforim/masaos_binyomin_mitudela_with_english.pdf (accessed 6 June 2013).

If one was to speak of the love and prayer between Jews and Muslims, one might rather expect a reference to Moses. And, if Ezra was buried in Babylonia rather than in Jerusalem, this is indicative for the self-understanding of contemporary Jewry as living under foreign rule (then Persian). Moses could not have been the common heritage as it contradicted the Muslim claim of the final prophecy through Muhammad. The acceptance of the Jews' status in Muslim countries is reached through the legend of Ezra's tomb between the Euphrates and the Tigris – a tomb that unites Jews and Muslims, and the tomb of Ezra the priest, the great reformer and prophet.

Legends should not be misused for historical questions. They are, however, an internal indication of the fact that the great reformer Ezra did not play a larger role for the Christians. Yet for Jews and Muslims, he was a topic for discussion concerning the foundations of the understanding of antiquity.

Part II: **Reflecting Roman Religion**

Part I Collecting Roman Reliefs

3 Roman Religion at the Periphery of the Empire

Mentioning the words "Roman" and "Jews" typically brings to mind, one might even say subconsciously, the military and imperialist aspects of the Roman rule of the Caesars.[66] It also brings to mind the anti-Jewish (or anti-Semitic) tendencies of the *scriptores latini*, who had more or less thoroughly occupied themselves with Jewish conceptions, traditions, and mores.[67] This association of thought is already brought up by the Jewish sources themselves, and is sufficiently justified by the events of ancient history. There are very few Jewish sources one might characterise as 'philo-Roman.' The only exception might be the historiography of the Maccabees, which is outlined in the first and second book of the homonymous work (1 and 2 Maccabees). There are few negative references to the Romans there, since the Maccabees probably could not yet foresee the results of the Roman policy of expansion. The Jewish historiographer Josephus (ca. 37–ca. 100 CE), on the other hand, had defended the Romans and their 'policies,' and had even praised the politics of Emperor Vespa-

---

[66] See, for instance, Karl L. Noethlichs, *Das Judentum und der römische Staat* (Darmstadt: Wissenschaftliche Buchgesellschaft, 1996).
[67] On customs, mores, etc., see Shaye J. D. Cohen, "Anti-Semitism in Antiquity: the Problem of Definition," in *History and Hate. The Dimension of Anti-Semitism*, ed. David Berger (Philadelphia, New York, and Jerusalem: Jewish Publication Society, 1986), 43–47; Louis H. Feldman, *Jew and Gentile in the Ancient World: Attitudes and Interactions from Alexander to Justinian* (Princeton: Princeton University Press, 1993); Peter Schäfer, *Judeophobia: Attitudes Toward the Jews in the Ancient World* (Cambridge and London: Harvard University Press, 1997); Noethlichs, *Das Judentum und der römische Staat*, 125 et seq.; Lucia Raspe, "Manetho on the Exodus: A Reappraisal," *Jewish Studies Quarterly* 5 (1998): 124–155. On the attitude of the Greco-Roman literature to Jews, see the collection of sources in Menahem Stern, ed. and trans., *Greek and Latin Authors on Jews and Judaism* vol 1–2 (Jerusalem: The Israel Academy of Sciences and Humanities, 1974–1980); on the legal sources, see Amnon Linder, *The Jews in Roman Imperial Legislation* [Hebrew] (Jerusalem: The Israel Academy of Sciences and Humanities, 1983); Ammon Linder, *The Jews in the Legal Sources of the Early Middle Ages* (Detroit and Jerusalem: Wayne State University Press 1997). As helpful as these collections of sources are, they should be treated with caution. Without further knowledge of the context, the reader might conclude that the Romans had an entirely negative idea of Judaism. When bearing in mind, however, that other "non-enlightened" peoples – as Pliny calls them – like the Britanni, Galli, etc., held comparable attitudes, the image is put in its proper place. I have attempted to present how stereotypes had been able to influence the historical image of the consequences of the first Jewish war; see my "Enteignung des Landes oder pax romana? Zur politischen Geschichte der Juden nach 70 (Josephus, Bell 7, 216–218)," *Frankfurter judaistische Beiträge* 16 (1988): 1–22. On criticism on my article, see Benjamin H. Isaac, *The Near East Under Roman Rule: Selected Papers* (Boston, Leiden: Brill, 1998), 120–121. I am still not convinced by his arguments against my approach.

sian (9–79 CE). Yet his description of the historical events is too biased to allow full credibility. Josephus' justification of the Roman intervention into Jewish politics has to be understood as an expression of gratitude at best: gratitude for the lenient treatment of his own person.[68] It is not a *communis opinio* of the Jewish community on Rome. Still, it might be possible to discern critical under tones against Roman rule even in the writings of this 'traitor' if a person were willing to supplement the study of his *Bellum Judaicum* by Josephus' later work *Antiquitates Judaicae*.[69] When working on the *Bellum*, Josephus's own recollections of the events of war and post-war were still too vivid and traumatising to be historiographically objective.

Whenever the rabbinic tradition refers to an "evil rule," it is the Roman (or Byzantine)[70] empire. Titus had destroyed the Temple and thus the centre of the Jewish cult and official religion. Hadrian violently ended the last noteworthy Jewish insurrection against foreign rule which – at least by some nonetheless still important rabbis – was considered to be the beginning of the Messianic age. Over the course of time, however, the rabbis did not demonise Roman rule. The rabbis even present Roman rule over the Jewish people to be the will of God.[71] This hermeneutic-religious "U-turn" is not just an expression of accepting the *status quo* which cannot be changed anyway. It is, first and foremost, an expression of the rabbis' reflection on the political and historical consequences of the Temple's destruction: to succeed in reaching national unity was now projected to the eschaton, as the Diaspora of Jews had the grave consequence that any attempt was now futile right from the start.

The reference to the Romans in Jewish sources is not confined to the aspect of military repression. It also touches on cultural-historical elements like Roman customs and religious life. It is a facet of the subject that has yet to spark any great interest among scholars in the field. This is not necessarily rooted in the fact that Judaism, also in later antiquity, is generally researched from the political-historical viewpoint, where preferred topics are 'anti-Semitism,' 'anti-Judaism,' or the istory of minorities. The lack of interest is not even rooted in a religious or religious-historical perspective through which the comparison to the daughter-religion Christianity necessarily moves into the foreground. No,

---

[68] On a positive image of the Romans, see Josephus, *De bello Iudaico* 5:407, and Günter Stemberger, *Die römische Herrschaft im Urteil der Juden* (Darmstadt: Wissenschaftliche Buchgesellschaft, 1983), 35.
[69] Stemberger, *Die römische Herrschaft*, 36–37.
[70] It is difficult for the modern reader of rabbinic texts to ascertain whether the author/redactor is dealing with the Roman or with the Byzantine (Christian) empire when speaking of *Romi*.
[71] On this, see *Ibidem*, 59 et seq.

the lack of interest is rooted in a saddening general lack of interest in the *realia* the rabbinic literature give proof of.

It is a lack of interest in the entire field of the so-called sciences of everyday life, the micro-history. They are still in their infancy despite the approaches of the French *Annales* school – in contrast to the founders of the *Wissenschaft des Judentums*, who pioneered the first works in the field. Even after almost a century, for instance, some of the books by Samuel Krauss as the volumes of the "Archeology of Judaism," as he referred to them, remain pathbreaking and indispensable for scholarship. Further noteworthy are Imanuel Löw's *Flora der Juden*, Lewysohn's *Die Zoologie des Talmuds*, Julius Preuss's *Biblisch-Talmudische Medizin*, and the more recent studies of Saul Lieberman and Daniel Sperber.[72] Recent research includes Mireille Hadas-Lebel's contributions to the Roman religion,[73] in which Lieberman's pivotal and seminal researches in particular are appraised and supplemented via further parallels and sources. Another noteable undertaking is Peter Schäfer's project *The Talmud Yerushalmi and Graeco-Roman Culture*,[74] which resumes the research on the *realia*, thus opening up new vistas for the scholar. Recent developments are the book of Emmanuel Friedheim[75] on 'pagan' polytheist cults, rituals, festivities mentioned in Rabbinic sources, and the important contribution of *The Oxford Handbook of Jewish Daily Life in Roman Palestine*, edited by Catherine Hezser.[76]

The study of the *realia* does not merely have significance in itself but grants historiography precious information that is unobtainable through other

---

[72] Immanuel Löw, *Die Flora der Juden*, 4 vols. (Vienna and Leipzig: Löwit, 1924–34; repr. Hildesheim: Olms, 1967); Ludwig Lewysohn, *Die Zoologie des Talmuds: Eine umfassende Darstellung der rabbinischen Zoologie, unter steter Vergleichung der Forschungen älterer und neuerer Schriftsteller* (Frankfurt: Baer, 1858); Julius Preuss, *Biblisch-talmudische Medizin*. (Berlin Karger, 1911; repr. Wiesbaden: Fourier, 1992), translated by Fred Rosner as *Biblical and Talmudic Medicine* (New York: Sanhedrin, 1978). See further Saul Lieberman, ed. *Tosefta Ki-Fshutah: A Comprehensive Commentary on the Tosefta* [Hebr.], 10 vols. (New York: Jewish Theological Seminary, 1955–88); Daniel Sperber, *Customs of Israel: Sources and History* [Hebr.], 5 vols. (Jerusalem: Mossad Harav Kook, 1990–95).

[73] Mireille Hadas-Lebel, *Le Paganisme à travers les sources rabbiniques des IIe et IIIe siècles: contribution à l'étude du syncrétisme dans l'empire romain* (Berlin and New York: De Gruyter, 1979), 426–441.

[74] Peter Schäfer, ed., *The Talmud Yerushalmi and Graeco-Roman Culture*, vol. 1 (Tübingen: Mohr Siebeck 1998); idem, Catherine Hezser, eds., *The Talmud Yerushalmi and Graeco-Roman Culture*, vol. 2 (Tübingen: Mohr Siebeck, 2000).

[75] Emmanuel Friedheim, *Rabbinism et Paganism en Palestine romaine. Étude historique de Realia talmudiques (Ier–IVème siècles)* (Leiden, Boston: Brill, 2006).

[76] Catherine Hezser, ed., *The Oxford Handbook of Jewish Daily Life in Roman Palestine* (Oxford: Oxford University Press, 2010).

means. One example may be sufficient to illustrate the methodological approach, researching the details of ancient Jewish medicine – from prescriptions to the different healing professions of physicians, apothecaries, barber surgeons, etc., allowing a glimpse at Jewish everyday life. It also permits us to create criteria for assessing the cultural and social levels on which the Jewish minority in Greco-Roman society lived. Through their works, Krauss, Lieberman, Hadas-Lebel, Schäfer, Hezser and Friedheim have contributed to creating a more differentiated image of mutual influences in the cultures of the Greeks, Romans, and Jews. Their detailed studies, however, largely do not offer an analysis of the social importance of the Greco-Roman for the different social layers of Jewry in later antiquity.[77] Yet to my mind, this aspect remains of vital importance for the interest in Roman customs as reflected in the rabbinic literature.

The Jewish reflection of Roman customs and religion does not only point to a theological problem but first and foremost a political and social one, the Jewish authorities had to distance themselves from a culture by means of clear criteria of differentiation. The agents of this culture lived amidst the Jewish minority of the Empire and sought to subjugate this minority politically and culturally. On the other hand, the rabbis could not have simply rejected Roman culture entirely without forfeiting the support of their own people and (which is self-explanatory), provoking the *Roman* authorities in charge. The perhaps largest segment of Jewry that did not belong to the rabbinic elite would not likely have comprehended such a segregation, one that adhered to the presence of tradition without any regard for the costs. However, another possibility was to give a new meaning to customs and mores, presenting them in a new shape amenable to integration into one's own religious identity. This is a topic we will return to below.

In the following discussion of Roman religion as reflected in the Jewish sources, I will limit my interpretation to two subjects: the so-called *darkhe ha-emori*, or "ways of the Amorites," which are mentioned in the rabbinic literature,[78] and the Roman festivals. Another complex which factually belongs with that discussion, the cult of certain deities in *Eretz Yisrael*, is not a topic of focus in the chapter. The decision of separating the two complexes can be explained by the different implications of the topics mentioned. The description of "foreign" customs adds considerably to one's own identity and culture, thus, it

---

77 There are of course many contributions on the social aspects of the rabbinic movement, but very few on Jewish society and culture in relation to and in dependence on Roman society.
78 See also the chapter 6 of this book.

explains the connecting social dynamic of a group.[79] Moreover, honoring a tendency to ignore the festivals of the majority is a political decision with a social component, since it touches on everyday interaction with the foreign element. Quarreling with foreign deities, however, has an ideological dimension moving far beyond the sphere of politics and society. Its treatment would thus exceed the narrow boundaries of this chapter.

3.1 Religious Customs: The Rhetoric of Ethics

3.1.1 "Roman" Sources for the "Rabbinic" Romans

The transmitters of Roman culture in the conquered territories were rarely highly educated representatives who could have left valuable reports on the conditions of life for the peoples governed by Rome. Those who were, such as Pliny the Younger (61–c. 112 CE) in Bithynia, or Tacitus (56–117 CE) in Gaul and Germania, were exceptions. Yet even in respect to their writings, the reader should be cautious, since in reality the ancient reporters rarely adhered to their own ideals of eyewitness accounts as the proof of historical credibility.[80] Pliny's famous uncle, so-called Pliny the Elder, was a literate who did little to be in concrete touch with the environment he describes. Moreover, his concept of *natural science* as in antiquity is "ethically charged,"[81] and even the "Greek sources are criticised by default for being foreign"[82] and therefore also immoral.[83] Thus, we have to view *cum grano salis* the messages on non-Roman or non-Romanised peoples that Roman antiquity has left us.

---

79 On this, see Sacha Stern, *Jewish Identity in Early Rabbinic Writings* (Leiden and New York: Brill, 1994).
80 On Pliny the Elder and Africa se John F. Healy, *Pliny the Elder on Science and Technology* (Oxford: Oxford University Press, 1999), 17 and *passim*. On the Greek sources on Jews, see Bezalel Bar-Kochva, *The Image of the Jews in Greek Literature: The Hellenistic Period* (Berkeley: University of California Press, 2010).
81 See Mary Beagon, *Roman Nature: The Thought of Pliny the Elder* (Oxford: Clarendon, 1992), esp. 102 et seq. and the review by K. Sara Myers in Bryn Mawr Classical Review 04.03.19 from http://bmcr.brynmawr.edu/1993/04.03.19.html (accessed 7 October 2013).
82 Sorcha Carey, *Pliny's Catalogue of Culture. Art and Empire in the Natural History* (Oxford: Oxford University Press, 2003): 25 and Caterina Agostini, "Real, Unreal and Magic in Pliny the Elder's *Naturalis Historia*," in *Proceedings of the Annual Meeting of the Postgraduates in Ancient Literature*, http://ojs.st-andrews.ac.uk/index.php/ampal/article/view/683 (accessed 7 October 2013).
83 *Ibidem*.

However, the same also holds true for the inverted case of the image of Romans transmitted through "barbarian" sources. The reason for that lies in the fact that the living nexus between Roman and non-Roman culture most often was the Roman soldier. He was, in the time of the Caesars, generally not a Roman in origin, at least in the strict sense. The soldier commonly originated from Syria, Germania, Gaul, or Spain. Thus, he was usually a "barbarian" doing military service for the Roman Empire. What he brought with him (besides his equipment) were especially his deities and customs that he imported into the land in which he did his military service. The soldier hoped to become *civis Romanus* with his retirement from the army (if he had not become a Roman citizen before), and to receive a parcel of land or some money.[84] It is unlikely that the soldier had any particular interest in the "other" culture he came in contact with and which *nolens volens* had also influenced him.

In the non-Roman sources – the rabbinic ones in our case – we meet the *stereotype* of the Roman who more or less bellicosely comes into the land to be conquered or which is already a conquered province. Be it soldier or ruler: the stereotype applies to both. Combined and intertwined in these images and characteristics are, in fact, both stereotypical features and realistic ones. Both should be taken into account, since in this way we can learn not only about the historical "reality" but also illuminate the reaction of the *altera pars* to the Graeco-Roman monopoly of power and knowledge.

If, at this point, only the Roman soldier is referred to, this is rooted in the fact that the rabbinic sources do indeed mention meetings with high dignitaries of the Roman administration and rule, even with kings and emperors. However, the historical reliability of these references is very doubtful.[85] In general, these contacts are quite probable. Yet it remains unknown when they actually occurred, how often, and under what circumstances. In any case, the sources do not speak of the details. Their orientation is toward apologetics and edification; often it is exegetic, pointed up by the equalisation of the biblical

---

[84] On the everyday life of Roman soldiers, see Roy W. Davies, "The Daily Life of the Roman Soldier under the Principate," in *Aufstieg und Niedergang der römischen Welt* I.1 (1981): 53–72. For a more general overview, see Benjamin H. Isaac, *The Limits of Empire: The Roman Army in the East* (New York: Oxford University Press, 1990); Ze'ev Safrai, "The Roman Army in the Galilee," in *The Galilee in Late Antiquity*, ed. Lee I. Levine (New York: Jewish Theological Seminary of America, 1992).

[85] However, Moshe Herr defends the credibility of the story. Moshe D. Herr, "The Historical Significance of the Dialogues Between Jewish Sages and Roman Dignitaries," *Scripta hierosolymitana* 22 (1971): 123–150; but see Daniel Krochmalnik, "Der 'Philosoph' in Talmud und Midrasch," in *Terumah* 5 (1996): 137–178; Catherine Hezser, *The Social Structure of the Rabbinic Movement in Roman Palestine* (Tübingen: Mohr Siebeck, 1997), 438 ff.

character of Edom with the world domination of Rome.⁸⁶ Current historical scholarship has to operate in a space strung between text immanence – questioning the motivation of sources – and the necessary transcendence of the source material.

3.1.2 Political and Popular "Religiosity" or Culture: Theatre and the Circenses

The Roman environment is especially reflected in the rabbinic literature through what the rabbis had subsumed under the category "Greco-Roman customs and laws." While there is no question whatsoever about the rabbis' knowledge and unrestrained adaptation of the Greek language and especially their Greek (popular) culture, the sources do not show any significant interest in the Roman tradition. And this is consistent: according to common conviction, Roman culture was inferior to Greek culture.

It can suffice here to mention but a few well-known texts. According to the Midrash Bereshit Rabbah 16:4:

> R. Ḥuna says: Greek rule was superior to this evil (Roman) one in three aspects: in [building of] a temple⁸⁷ [variant: in the form of government⁸⁸], in art⁸⁹ [variant: the book sector⁹⁰], and in language.⁹¹

---

86 "Edom" repeatedly functions as a coded reference to Rome. On the rabbinic sources discussing Rome, see the above-mentioned study by Stemberger, *Die römische Herrschaft*; on Esau-Rome, see Gerson D. Cohen, "Esau as Symbol in Early Medieval Thought," in *Jewish Medieval and Renaissance Studies*, ed. Alexander Altman (Cambridge, Mass.: Harvard University Press, 1967), 19–48; Friedrich Avemarie, "Esaus Hände, Jakobs Stimme: Edom als Sinnbild Roms in der frühen rabbinischen Literatur," in *Die Heiden: Juden, Christen und das Problem des Fremden*, ed. Reinhard Feldmeier and Ulrich Heckel (Tübingen: Mohr Siebeck, 1994), 177–208.
87 נאווסים (MSS London Add. 27169, Munich 97, etc.), from ναός, "Tempel," according to Samuel Krauss, *Griechische und lateinische Lehnwörter im Talmud, Midrasch und Targum*, vol. 2 (Berlin: Calvary, 1899; repr. Hildesheim: Olms, 1964), 355. It might also have derived from ναῦς, "shipping."
88 נימוסין (MSS Paris 149; Oxford 2335 etc.); from νόμος. See *Shemot Rabbah* 15:27. It becomes נימוס מלכות. See Krauss, *Griechische und lateinische Lehnwörter*, vol. 2, 259–360.
89 פנוקטין (MSS London Add. 27169 usw.), griech πινακοθήκη. See Krauss, *Griechische und lateinische Lehnwörter*, vol. 2, 465.
90 פנוקדין (Printed edition, Yalqut) Greek πίναξ, see Krauss, *Griechische und lateinische Lehnwörter*, vol. 2, 466–467.
91 On this text, see Günter Stemberger, *Jews and Christians in the Holy Land. Palestine in the Fourth Century* (Edinburgh: T&T Clark, 2000), 284.

The variants show that there was no common conception regarding what exactly made Greece superior over Rome; only in respect to the Greek language, and thus likely the literature written in Greek, did the texts concur. More meaningful is Shemot Rabbah 42:8, where the language of the Romans is mentioned as the "language of the soldiers." The Palestinian Talmud, Megillah 1:11 (71b) even states that

> There are four languages used in the world. These are: Greek for poetry, Latin[92] for war, Syrian for wailing, and Hebrew for speaking. And, some aver: Assyrian for writing.[93]

The comment here, no doubt polemic, regarding Latin because Latin remained the general language of command in the army. Nearly all military inscriptions, even in Palestine, are in Latin. This understanding is reflected also in a linguistic fact: rabbinic literature has many more Greek loanwords than Latin ones. The few Latin loanwords which Samuel Krauss lists, for instance, had for the most part originated in the language of the administration and the military. However, some of the lemmas that Krauss explains as Greek were likely of Latin origin or used as Latin, e.g. *dux*, *castra*, or *centurio*. It cannot be concluded that the imperial administration and military were the only sectors of Roman life the rabbis came into immediate contact with. What is extant in the sources, however, shows at least that the cultural exchange of philosophical and religious content was not very active and robust. On the other hand, this does not mean that such a cultural transfer did not take place at all, but implies more simply that the rabbis remained silent about it and just discussed the matters directly relevant for Halakhah or Aggadah. And that is the case when it comes to discussion about the theatres and circuses, a world of rabbinic and Roman rhetoric of religion and culture.

Theatres and circuses of late antiquity as well as earlier in imperial times were quite comparable to soccer stadiums and games in the present,[94] a politically privileged place of the imperial and local rulers to satisfy the needs of popular even plebian mass entertainment and diversion. Likened to what some

---

[92] Or also "Byzantine." The Hebrew *Romi* correspondent to ρωμαίοι can mean both "Latin" and "Byzantine."

[93] On the rabbis' knowledge of the Latin language, see Joseph Geiger, "Latin in Roman Palestine," *Cathedra* 74 (1994): 3–35. See also Veltri, *Eine Tora für den König Talmai* (Tübingen: Mohr Siebeck, 1994), 118 et seq.

[94] There is a voluminous literature on the Roman theatre, see for a useful overview Richard C. Beacham, *The Roman Theatre and its Audience* (London: Routledge, 1991); Gerhard Binder, Bernd Effe, eds., *Das antike Theater: Aspekte seiner Geschichte, Rezeption und Aktualität* (Trier: WVT, 1998).

would term "cultural policy" today, the legal and political authorities in late antiquity spent substantial funds on constructing such buildings for amusement and used them as an institution for political self-presentation, a kind of political staging of power and the regime. Attending theatre performances was a parade of political importance for every class, but most especially for the nouveaux riches, or politically important representative groups, all of them mirrored socially by the placement of their seating in the theatre structure, a visible "power geometry" of rank and status. From inscription materials, we have archeological evidence that there were seats set aside for supporters of "green" or "red" parties,[95] but also for Jews and Jewish elders.[96] To attend theatre performances was a consistent step forward in the itinerary of social and political ascent for Jews in the Roman world, a necessary temptation for ruling classes in general anywhere and time.

Even Jewish women seem to have been habitual spectators of theatre performances, a fact confirmed by the redactor of Midrash Rut Rabbah 2:23: "It is not the custom of the daughters of Israel to go to the theatre and the circus of the non-Jews." The sentence bears on women as spectators; however, we may well suspect that they also acted as performers, an element indirectly focused on by the the bishop of Hippo Augustine.[97] In his well-known sermon, the Jews are accused of misusing the Sabbath rest for devoting themselves to all manner of frivolity and voluptuousness. Further on and *ad hominem*, he stresses rhetorically: "It would be much better if the Jews did something useful in their fields than to attend seditious theatre performances; their women would better spin wool in the Shabbat day than dancing indecently the whole day in their (amphitheatre) galleries."[98] Beside the anti-Jewish animus expressed here, a characteristic and constant factor of Augustine preaching,[99] it is noteworthy to

---

[95] As a fanatical supporter of the green party, Caligula should be mentioned here.

[96] Charlotte Roueché, *Aphrodisias in Late Antiquity. The Late Roman and Byzantine Inscriptions Including Texts from the Excavations at Aphrodisias* (London: Society for the Promotion of Roman Studies, 1989), 218–226; see Peter Brown, *Power and Persuasion in Late Antiquity: Towards a Christian Empire* (Madison: University of Wisconsin press, 1992), passim.

[97] See Johannes van Oort, "Jews and Judaism in Augustine's Sermones," in *Ministerium Sermonis. Proceedings of the International Colloquium on St Augustine's Sermones ad Populum*, ed. Gert Partoens, Anthony Dupont & Mathijs Lamberigts (Turnhout-Leuven: Brepols Publishers, 2009): 243–265, here 260–261.

[98] Augustine, *Sermo IX* (*Corpus Christianorum Series Latina*, vol. 41, 110): "uacare enim uolunt ad nugas atque luxurias suas. melius enim faceret iudaeus in agro suo aliquid utile quam in theatro seditiosus exsisteret. et melius feminae eorum die sabbati lanam facerent quam toto die in maenianis suis impudice saltarent." The English translation is mine.

[99] On Augustine's attitudes to the Jews, see Marcel Jacques Dubois, "Jews, Judaism and Israel in the Theology of Saint Augustine. How he Links the Jewish People and the Land of Zion,"

call the attention of the discerning reader to one very intriguing element of this text: Jews are charged not only with attending theatre performances, but also with actively performing (on the stage or in the galleries) in an indecent manner.

As is well-known, the Roman theatres were places of amusement, where nakedness of female performers as well as sexual allusions and open acts of sexual content played an important role. Ovid, an author often accused of shameless use of erotic elements, already was outspoken in denouncing this custom as immoral, even if it was openly funded by the local and imperial hand:

> What if I'd written lewd and obscene mimes,
> that always show the sin of forbidden love,
> in which a smart seducer constantly appears,
> and the skilful wife cons her stupid husband?
> They're seen by nubile girls, wives, husbands,
> sons, indeed most of the Senate attend.
> It's not enough your ears are burned by sinful words:
> your eyes get used to many shameful things:
> and when the lover's newly tricked the husband,
> he's applauded, given a prize, to vast acclaim:
> because it's common, theatre's profitable for poets,
> and the praetor pays for sin at no small price.
> Check the cost of your own games, Augustus,
> you'll scan many pricey items like these.[100]

Some centuries later, the situation still had not changed and the church father Tertullian denounced the decadence of customs by charging Roman cults with immoral attitudes and shameless performances:

Immanuel 22–23 (1989): 162–214; Jeremy Cohen, "'Slay them not'. Augustine and the Jews in Modern Scholarship," *Medieval Encounters* 4 (1998): 78–92; Paula Fredriksen, "Augustine and Israel. 'Interpretatio ad litteram'. Jews, and Judaism in Augustine's Theology of history," *Studia Patristica* 38 (2001): 119–135; Lisa A. Unterseher, "The Mark of Cain and the Jews. Augustine's Theology of Jews," *Augustinian Studies* 33 (2002): 99–121.Paula Fredriksen, *Augustine and the Jews: A Christian Defense of Jews and Judaism* (New York, NY: Doubleday, 2008).

100 Ovid, *Tristia* II: 497 ff.: Quid, si scripsissem mimos obscena iocantes, | qui semper uetiti crimen amoris habent: | in quibus assidue | cultus procedit adulter, | uerbaque dat stulto callida nupta uiro? | Nubilis hos uirgo matronaque uirque puerque | spectat, et ex magna parte senatus adest. | Nec satis incestis temerari uocibus aures; | adsuescunt oculi multa pudenda pati: | cumque fefellit amans aliqua nouitate maritum | plauditur et magno palma fauore datur; | quoque minus prodest, scaena est lucrosa poetae, | tantaque non paruo crimina praetor emit. | Inspice ludorum sumptus, Auguste, tuorum: | empta tibi magno talia multa leges. English translation by A. S. Kline (2003), http://www.poetryintranslation.com/PITBR/Latin/OvidTristia BkTwo.htm (accessed 6 June 2013).

... The very harlots, too, victims of the public lust, are brought upon the stage, their misery increased as being there in the presence of their own sex, from whom alone they are wont to hide themselves: they are paraded publicly before every age and every rank – their abode, their gains, their praises, are set forth, and that even in the hearing of those who should not hear such things. I say nothing about other matters, which it were good to hide away in their own darkness and their own gloomy caves, lest they should stain the light of day. [4] Let the Senate, let all ranks, blush for very shame! Why, even these miserable women, who by their own gestures destroy their modesty, dreading the light of day, and the people's gaze, know something of shame at least once a year.[101]

It is not my aim either to examine the moral value of amusements with regard to mime and pantomime and their social impact on the audience, or to engage in questions relating to gender research and public stage prostitution. Rather, I wish here to focus on a very intriguing aspect of ancient theatre in reference to the power of the amusement and distraction where magic or foreign customs – which are notoriously the specific rabbinic terms for these phenomena[102] – play a significant role. Let us examine a halakhic text on theatre performances which begins with ancient professions that apparently did not necessarily have anything to do with theatre: Jerusalem Talmud, 'Avodah Zarah 1,7 (40a):

> It is taught: He who watches the sorcerers (*naḥashim*) and enchanters (*ḥabbarim*), *mokion, mopion molion, milarin, milaria, sagilarin, sagilaria* – it is prohibited on the count of "sitting in the seat of the scornful."
>
> He who goes up into the theatre – it is prohibited on the count of idolatry, words of R. Me'ir.
>
> And the sages say: "(If one goes up) when they offer sacrifices, it is forbidden on the count of idolatry. But if not, it is only forbidden on the count of "sitting in the seat of the scornful."
>
> He who goes up into the theatre and cries out: If it is for the benefit of the public, it is permitted. But if he conspires (with the non-Jews), it is forbidden.

---

101 Tertullian, *De Spectaculis* XVII,3 ff.: Hoc igitur modo etiam a theatro separamur, quod est priuatum consistorium inpudicitiae, ubi nihil aliud probatur quam quod alibi non probatur. Ita summa gratia eius de spurcitia plurimum concinnata est, quam atellanus *gesticulatur, quam mimus etiam per muliebres repraesentat, sensum sexus et pudoris exterminans*, ut facilius domi quam in scaena erubescant, quam denique pantomimus a pueritia patitur in corpore, ut artifex esse possit. Ipsa etiam prostibula, publicae libidinis hostiae, in scaena proferuntur, plus miserae *in praesentia feminarum*, quibus solis latebant, per que omnis aetatis, omnis dignitatis ora transducuntur; locus, stipes, elogium, etiam quibus opus non est, praedicatur, etiam (taceo de reliquis) ea quae in tenebris et in speluncis suis delitescere decebat, ne diem contaminarent. English translation by S. Thelwall, Tertullian, *The Shows*, in "Early Christian Writings," www.earlychristianwritings.com/text/tertullian03.html (accessed 6 June 2013).
102 See my book, *Magie und Halakha. Ansätze zu einem empirischen Wissenschaftsbegriff im spätantiken und frühmittelalterlichen Judentum* (Tübingen: Mohr, 1997).

> He who sits in the stadium is guilty of bloodshed.
> R. Natan permits (sitting in the stadium) on two counts: first because one cries out and (thereby) saves the lives (of the losers), and (second) because he may give evidence in behalf of the wife (of the loser), so that she may remarry.

This text is a mirror of Jewish life in the Roman province and its cultural and political values. To attend the theatre was among the most frequent entertainments in Roman Palestine and elsewhere in the imperial Roman world. The rabbis as well as their counterpart, the Church authorities, constantly gave their co-religionists an urgent warning to avoid theatre performances, urging them instead to visit the synagogue and attend to the liturgy and weekly sermon. The study of the Torah should accordingly be far preferred to such shameless amusements and dangerous entertainments. In vain, as history was to teach. The council of the African Church in the 5th century lamented a reproachable situation: Christians usually preferred to go to the theatre instead of listening to the Sunday sermon.[103]

However, the meaning of the Yerushalmi text quoted above goes beyond a moral caveat for the masses. In its historical dimension, it reveals a cultural world where amusements and politics played a substantial role. At a deeper layer of the social and historical core and spirit of the text, we are obliged to resolve several exegetical difficulties it raises: the meaning of the Greek or Latin loanwords, the expression "for the public" or according to the parallel Tosefta text ('Avodah Zarah 2:7) "the need of the district," and finally the presence of sorcerers and enchanters (*naḥashim we-ḥabbarim*).

To search for loanwords and explain them is a difficult undertaking, not only negatively because of the unvocalised text, but above all positively because of the multifarious possibilities the consonants offer. That is the case of *mokion, mopion, molion, milarin, milaria, sagilarin, sagilaria* with their textual variants in addition taken from the parallel text of Tosefta 'Avodah Zarah 2:6. I will adopt a quite easy method here, namely to prefer common Greek words and expressions instead of literary and learned parallels. In this I follow the

---

[103] Concilia Africae 345–525 – *Registri ecclesiae Carthaginensis excerpta* (SL 149, 196): De spectacvlis, vt die dominico vel ceteris sanctorvm festivitatibvs minime celebrentvr. Necnon et illud petendum, ut spectacula theatrorum ceterorum que ludorum die dominica uel ceteris religionis christianae diebus celeberrimis amoueantur; maxime quia sanctae paschae octauarum die populi ad circum magis quam ad ecclesiam conueniunt, debere transferri deuotionis eorum dies, si quando occurrerint, nec oportere etiam quemquam christianorum cogi ad haec spectacula, maxime quia in his exercendis, quae contra praecepta dei sunt, nulla persecutionis necessitas a quoquam adhibenda est, sed, uti oportet, homo libera uoluntate subsistat sibi diuinitus concessa.

view that rabbinic Judaism was not primarily interested in learning Greco-Roman (high) culture, but rather only in accepting (and reworking) concepts, traditions and texts deemed necessary for living and daily survival and advantage in an occupied territory. That is the case with the theatre performances.

Mokion: As per Samuel Krauss[104] who follows the reading of the Tosefta, we must read here *Bokiun mukiun* instead of *mokion*, *mopion* of the Jerusalem Talmud. In this case, *Boukkion* would be nothing but *Bucco*, a folklorist comedy, the Atellana, which can be traced back to the City of Atella, near Capua, while *mokion* here represents the third clown of this fable called *Maccus*. This coinage is likewise hazardous, at least highly speculative, and presupposes a detailed rabbinic knowledge of Roman theatre and comedy. There is no proof that Roman soldiers at the *fines imperii* entertained themselves with a form of respectful albeit obscene comedy, to which Cicero contrasts the mime as a clearly deteriorated form of this genre.[105]

In my opinion, *mokion* has nothing to do with a particular form of comedy. A much more common etymology from the word *mōkos*, mockery (see Sirach 36[33]:6) should be favored. Philo of Alexandria uses the corresponding verb, *katamōkaomai* ("to mock at") to describe a theatre performance: "as in a theatre, there was a great noise of people hissing, and groaning, and ridiculing us in an extravagant manner" (*Ad Gaium* 368: *ōs gar men en theátrōi klōsmós syrittóntōn katamōkōménōn*). Another meaning that can also surely be appropriated can be derived from the etymology *mochos*, Latin *moechus*, "adulterer." This lexical import is not far-fetched if we refer to the contents of such comedies predominantly concerned with stories of a sexual matter, usually called in antiquity, at least by Christian authors, "adultery" – as the text quoted above by Tertullian claims.[106] In this context, the Tosefta-term *bukion* can be perfectly

---

104 For the following discussion, see Samuel Krauss, *Griechische und lateinische Lehnwörter*, vol. 1 (Berlin: S. Calvary, 1899; reprint Olms: Hildesheim, 1964), p. 319 ff.; Hans Blaufuss, *Römische Feste und Feiertage nach den Traktaten über fremden Dienst (Aboda zara) in Mischna, Tosefta, Jerusalemer und babylonischem Talmud* (Nürnberg: J. L. Stich, 1909); Mireille Hadas-Lebel, "Le paganisme à travers les sources rabbiniques des IIe et IIIe siècles. Contribution à l'étude du syncrétisme dans l'empire romain," *Aufstieg und Niedergang der römischen Welt* II/19.2 (1979): 397–485; Martin Jacobs, "Theatres and Performances as Reflected in the Talmud Yerushalmi," in *The Talmud Yerushalmi and Graeco-Roman Culture*, ed. Peter Schäfer (Tübingen: Mohr, 1998): 327–347, here p 332–333; Giuseppe Veltri, "Römische Religion an der Peripherie des Reiches: ein Kapitel rabbinischer Rhetorik," *The Talmud Yerushalmi and Graeco-Roman Culture*, ed. Peter Schäfer, Cathrine Hezser, vol. 2 (Tübingen: Mohr 2000): 81–138.
105 *Ad Familiares* IX:16,7: "secundum Oenomaum Accii non, ut olim solebat, Atellanam, sed, ut nunc fit, mimum introduxisti."
106 See also Pat Easterling and Edith Hall, *Greek and Roman Actors: Aspects of an Ancient Profession* (Cambridge: Cambridge University Press, 2002).

understood as *boeiakós,* "of an o(x)en)," probably a negative synonym for "horned," in English colloquially termed "cuckold." Following this interpretation, we would have a perfect account of what Roman performers almost always played out as narrative in their comedies: "The adulterer and the cuckold."

Molion is probably an insult, *mōlys* "week in intellect, dull," as well as *mopion* for *myōpios,* "short-sighted." *Milarin* probably has nothing to do with the celebration of the 1000th anniversary of Rome, a millennium, as Mireille Hadas-Lebel claims, but rather with *myllō, -ein* (literally "to mill"), a word also known in rabbinic literature as a euphemistic expression for having sex,[107] hence *myllas, mylladas* means "prostitutes." The discerning reader will note that all these are expressions and words found in the above-quoted text by Ovid.

More difficult is the word *sagilaria, sagilarin,* interpreted by Samuel Krauss and others as an allusion to the *ludi saeculares,* such games celebrated once every century with theatre performances. I can hardly believe that rabbinic Judaism was halakhically concerned with a holiday occuring once in a century. Here the principle of plausibility should be adopted and preferred over seemingly contextual suitable parallels. I would rather suggest a coinage from "sýnklērōsis," "community" (lat. *consortium*), a common word which clearly refers to Psalm 1:2: *moshav,* translated by the Septuagint with *kathedra* and by Jerome with *conventus.* The reference to Psalm 1 is very important for rabbinic Judaism, because it is the reason for rejecting theatre performances: although going to attend pagan comedies does not go against the law of avoiding idolatry, it is against Psalm 1:2, which condemns the *moshav leṣim.* A similar exegetical tradition can be found in the works of the Church fathers, who connected *cathedra pestium* or *pestilentium* of Psalm 1:2 to going to the theatre. Tertullian in his *De spectaculis* and Ambrose of Milan in his *De officiis* rebuke attending theatre performances for their immoral character (Tertullian: ... *et extra cardines theatri impudicitiae*).[108] Ambrose also reproaches the popularity of such entertainment, where people indulge in wasting their money and inherit-

---

[107] See Bereshit Rabbah 48:17: "The woman (Sarah) (said): As long as the woman can give birth to a child, she menstruates and I, *after I am worn out, will I now have ednah*? *(Ednah)* means period. But *my husband is old* (Genesis 18:12). Rabbi Yehudah said: He grinds but does not produce anything." See also see Job 31:10.

[108] Tertullian, *De Spectaculis* 20: Comparas, homo, reum et iudicem, reum, qui, quia uidetur, reus est, iudicem, qui, quia uidet, iudex est. Numquid ergo et extra limites *circi* furori studemus et extra cardines *theatri* impudicitiae intendimus et insolentiae extra *stadium* et immisericordiae extra *amphitheatrum*, quoniam deus etiam extra cameras et gradus et (apulias) oculos habet?

ance.[109] The argument of wasting one's patrimony could be the intriguing element able to support a scholarly opinion according to which the Yerushalmi text, here commented on, is speaking of elitist groups who were expressly permitted to attend theatre performances in order to "cry out" but not to place a bet. They read *mithashev* of the Jerusalem Talmud as "to place a bet," rejecting the reading of the Tosefta *mithashed* as spurious.[110] To cry out is interpreted following the Halakhah of R. Natan, (see above), according to whom to cry out in the stadium is interpreted as to "save lives" (of Jews in the arena). My first difficulty is how to connect crying out to save lives with placing a bet. In any case, the first part of the Halakhah is concerned with theatre performances and not with horse games, or lions competition against slaves or Jews. To cry out is, on the contrary, to be interpreted in the context of the reaction of the audience to the performances which were always noisy, as attested by Philo of Alexandria, among others. That theatre was a privileged place for sedition was of course not an unproved accusation. The theatre doubtless offered an opportunity for (demagogical) protest because of social discontent, a danger for political authorities who attended such performances.[111] Theatres were a beloved place to organise riots, if we are to give credence to the story of the Apostle Paul in Ephesus in Acts 19.

The rabbis permitted attendance at the theatre, if this can help in representing the Jewish community, as I understand *ṣorekh ha-rabbim* – but not to participate in sedition, a danger for the Jewish communities itself. Jewish personalities who acted as intermediaries between the Jewish community and Roman authorities are allowed to adopt Roman customs if that was deemed to be advantageous to the Jewish community. This element explains why the rabbis begin the Halakhah with the sentence: "He who watches the sorcerer and enchanters," professions who do not usually have anything directly to do with theatrical performances. According to rabbinic Judaism, *nahashim we-habbarim*, technical terms for "divination," were the quintessence of Roman customs

---

109 *De Officiis* 2.2.21, 109 (Clavis Patrum Latinorum 144, 58): Prodigum est popularis fauoris gratia exinanire proprias opes; quod faciunt qui ludis circensibus uel etiam theatralibus et muneribus gladiatoriis uel etiam uenationibus patrimonium dilapidant suum ut uincant superiorum celebritates, cum totum illud sit inane quod agunt, quandoquidem etiam bonorum operum sumptibus immoderatum esse non deceat.

110 In my opinion, even if we read *mitashev*, the difficulty is not resolved, because there is no proof of such use of the verb in the rabbinic literature.

111 Paulinus of Nola, *Epistula* 13,16: Beatus, qui non adisti in tale consilium nec in cathedra pestilentiae, sed in apostoli sede et in ecclesiae coetu id est Christi theatro non seditiosis sed benedicentibus cuneis deo ipso spectatore laudaris, ecclesiae munerarius, non harenae nec inanis gloriae sed aeternae laudis ambitor.

or religion. Therefore, the Halakhah raises the question as to whether to attend theatre performances should be considered '*avodah zarah*, i.e. idolatry.

A parallel text to the halakhic tradition of the Jerusalem Talmud will explain my position: it is transmitted in the Midrash Sifra and bears on the complex of the so-called ways of the Amorites, a list of forbidden customs and beliefs which can be termed magical in definition, a topic I will deal with in Part III. Here I will only mention the main aspect so as to better comprehend the rabbinic attitude.

It is very intriguing to ascertain that in Sifra and in the much longer list of Tosefta, Shabbat 6–7, the first forbidden act to be taken into account has to do with hair styles.

> The following [acts] constitute ways of the Amorite: trimming the front of the hair [according to a Greco-Roman fashion], allowing one's locks to grow long, making a bald-pate (Tosefta, Shabbat 6:1).

In Sifra aḥare, pereq 13 (86a), we find a similar discussion on foreign and forbidden acts, where hair style also plays a role:

> *You shall not walk in their statutes* (Leviticus 18:3). Did the Scripture leave [something] that they did not say? Is it not written: *There shall not be found among you anyone who burns his son or his daughter* (Deuteronomy 18:9) etc., and he *who fascinates* (Deuteronomy 18:11) etc.? What teaching does [the verse] *You shall not walk in their statutes* (Leviticus 18:3), [mean] to convey? [It has been ordered], so that you do not walk in their [religious] customs, in the things ordered to them, as for instance theatre, circuses and amphitheatre.
>
> R. Me'ir says: 'These are the ways of the Amorite, that the Sages taught.' R. Yehudah b. Batira says: '[It has been ordered so] that you do not augur (?), that you grow no sidelock and trim not the front [according to a Greco-Roman fashion].'
>
> Will you say: Those are their statutes, but not ours? It is taught: *You shall do my ordinances and keep my statutes and walk in them. I am the Lord* (Leviticus 18:4). Until now, the evil inclination has occasion (literally hope) to criticize, saying that among them it is more amusing than among us.
>
> It is taught: *Keep them (the statutes and ordinances) and do them; for that will be your wisdom and your understanding* (Deteronomy 4:6).

The focus of the Midrash is the discussion of the suffix -*hem*- of *ḥuqqotehem* and the interpretation of *ḥuqqah* as general "commandment," to be obeyed without any discussion, or as "custom," as the Sifra put it. Their statutes are *nómoi* (*nimusot*), but only for *them* (the Amorites).[112]

---

112 An interesting parallel position can be found in the Greek evaluation of other religions, see Jean Rudhardt, "De l'attitude des Grecs à l'égard des religions étrangères," *Revue de l'Histoire des Religions* 209 (1992): 219–238.

The rabbis are aware of the meaning of the term νόμος used in this context and its implications, as can be seen from the explanation which follows in the above-mentioned quotation of Sifra. Accordingly, there are two kinds of statutes. The first series of ordinances are those of universal validity, directed against acts which are forbidden *per se*, such as robbery, forbidden (sexual) relations, idolatry, cursing the (divine) name, and bloodshed. They are forbidden *per se*, because of their nature, so that if they had not been written in the Torah, they would have had to be added according to logical inference. The second kind of law is specific to the Jewish people and constitutes a constant temptation by the evil inclination, as well as forming a pagan pretext for criticising Jewish customs, for instance the prohibitions against eating pork, wearing clothes of mixed material, the ceremony of ḥaliṣah, the purity norms for lepers and the scapegoat. This second kind of norm is based only on the will of God: "I am God. I ordered (them). You must not argue against them" (*Sifra aḥare, pereq* 13 [86a]).

In addition to the above quoted halakhic debate and the theological discussions on the definition of the others as belonging to another world of reference, we can ascertain here a concern among Jewish authorities to defend Jewish customs. Hence, the unwilling concession that "among them it is more amusing than among us."

If circus and theatre are expressions of the customs of the Romans, i.e. their religious and indeed cultural identity, we can understand why enchanters and sorcerers are deemed to be expressions of this cult, namely because of their function in Roman religion and practices. We read in the Tosefta, Shabbat 7:13:

> Who is an enchanter *menaḥesh* ? One who says:
> My staff has fallen from my hand.'
> My bread has fallen from my mouth.
> Mr. So-and-So has called me from behind me.
> A *raven* has called to me.
> A *dog* has barked at me.
> A *snake* has passed at my right
>   and a *fox* at my left.
> A deer has crossed the road before me.
> Do not begin with me, for it is dawn,
>   it is new moon, it is the end of the Sabbath.

This listing of (especially animal) behaviours interprets them as chiefly bad omens of future events. It is not surprising that a very similar list was recorded by Horace, *Carminum liber* 3,27,1–12:[113]

---

[113] Inpios parrae recinentis omen | Ducat et *praegnans canis* aut ab agro | Rava decurrens *lupa* Lanuvino | Fetaque *volpes*; | Rumpit et *serpens* iter institutum, | Si per obliquum similis

> May the wicked be guided by the omen of a screaming lapwing and a *pregnant dog* or a *red she-wolf* racing down from the Lanuvian fields, or a *fox* that has just brought forth!
> May a *serpent* break the journey they have begun, when, darting like an arrow across the road, it has terrified the ponies! But for whom, I, as a prophetic augur, cherish fear, for him I will rouse the singing *raven* from the east with my entreaties, before the bird that forebodes threatening showers re-seeks the standing pools.[114]

We have no evidence that the rabbis read Latin or any proof of knowledge of Latin in rabbinic sources. The similarities between Horace and the rabbis could nevertheless stem from the Latin Greco-Roman world where they lived. At any rate, both the Latin source and the rabbis agree that peculiar animal behaviours belong to the divinatory science of the Roman religion and beliefs, also practiced in Palestine according to the Tosefta – or at least among Diaspora Jews. For "Do not begin with me, for it is dawn, it is new moon, it is the end of the Sabbath" can be understood only in a Jewish context. For that reason, enchanters and sorcerers, are, according to the rabbis, the quintessence of Roman religion and identity, seen as a public cult performed in theatres and circuses.

According to the above-quoted text from the Jerusalem Talmud, 'Avodah Zarah 1,7, the anonym Halakhah and the sages (ḥakhamim) rejected Rabbi Me'ir's condemnation of theatre performances as idolatrous, accepting only a dismissal of it as waste of time according to Psalm 1:2: "sitting in the seat of scornful." Whoever attends to theatre causes neglect of the Torah.

I suppose that the reader of the Halakhah of the Yerushalmi text cannot be appeased by this statement of a mere distinction between idolatry and Roman customs, idolatry and waste of time. What is the reason for such discussion? To reject considering all the Roman customs and cults as idolatrous would imply that even simple contact with the neighbours as soldiers or workers, merchants or owners of land was also absolutely forbidden, with all the economic and social consequences attendant on the Jewish community under Roman imperial rule. To reduce some of the Roman religious and folkloric activities to customs, prohibited but not idolatrous, made the life of the Jews in the Roman Empire a little more comfortable and rationally more justifiable. On the other hand, to obtain obedience and allegiance must also imply to be prepared to make compromises, especially if the temptation of the Roman way of life was as spatially near as it was popularly attractive.

---

sagittae | Terruit mannos. ego cui timebo, | provido auspex | antquam stantes repetat paludes | imbrium divina avis imminentum, | oscinem *corvum* prece suscitabo | solis ab ortu.
114 Eng. transl. CE Bennett (Loew 33,263).

The rabbi pragmatically accepts some forms of contact with the Romans as a necessary concession which was applied even more in the case of those who were the intermediaries of the Jewish community or who lived in a 'pagan' environment. Especially as a benefit in favor of these categories, the exception regarding attending theatre performances and the adoption of Roman customs was accurately conceived and underpinned by Halakhah. Amusements as well as other social factors belonged to the 'entrance ticket' which every 'barbarian' had to pay. That is why I speak here of the media power of amusements. We should consider a text which exemplifies the political aspect of so-called magic or in the rabbinic terminology, ways of Amorites, namely Jerusalem Talmud,Shabbat 6,1 (7d):

> Three things were allowed to the members of the House of Rabbi: that they look at oneself in the mirror; that they trim one's *qomi*, and they teach Greek to their sons. For they were close to the (Roman) government.

As already quoted in the introduction, to look into one's mirror has nothing to do with hair trimming. It was a mantic practice ascribed to kings and emperors called *specularia*. The author of the *Historia Augusta* tell us that Didius Iulianus

> was mad enough to perform a number of rites with the aid of magicians, such as were calculated either to lessen the hate of the people or to restrain the arms of the soldiers. For the magicians sacrificed certain victims that are foreign to the Roman ritual and chanted unholy songs, *so we are told, before a mirror, into which boys are said to gaze, after bandages have been bound over their eyes and charms muttered over their heads.*[115]

Divination through a mirror is also considered here as a kind of art or science to be attributed to the structure of power. To look into the mirror is the expression of a structure of power strung between magic and politics, directed toward interpreting reality as it is, should be or as is politically convenient. The mirror is thus an instrument of power to act upon reality and world(s) of reference. Divination is also considered here as a kind of art or science to be attributed

---

[115] *Historia Augusta, Didius Iulianus* VII: 9–11: "Nam et quasdam non convenientes Romanis sacris hostias immolaverunt et carmina profana incantaverunt et ea, quae ad speculum dicunt fieri, in quod pueri praeligatis oculis incantato vertice respicere dicuntur, Iulianus fecit. Tuncquem puer vidisse dicitur et adventum Severi et Iuliani decessionem." English translation quoted from *Historia Augusta, Volume I: Hadrian. Aelius. Antoninus Pius. Marcus Aurelius. L. Verus. Avidius Cassius. Commodus. Pertinax. Didius Julianus. Septimius Severus. Pescennius Niger. Clodius Albinus*, Transl. David Magie (Loeb Library, 1921), from http://goo.gl/kW8Qeo, emphasis added). See also Judas Bergmann, "Die Schicksalserforschung der römischen Kaiser in der Agada," *Monatsschrift für Geschichte und Wissenschaft des Judentums* 81 (1937): 478–481.

to the structure of power. This element is also known elsewhere. Among the requirements to be members of the Sanhedrin, we find listed the mastering of magic practices.[116] The reason is perfectly evident: nobody can destroy magic without magic. In this manner, Tiberius learned astrology and mantic practices to counter everyone who tried to challenge his power, as Cassius Dio reports.[117]

Interesting is also the permission of a particular hair style, the *qomi*. It is very difficult to know whether the *qomi* refers to a form of haircut. In any case, either it is a fashionable hairstyle or a hairstyle reserved for some specific groups. We have evidence that a particular haircut was reserved for personalities of "barbarian" origins as well, as Ambrose of Milan wrote.[118] The aversion to this hairstyle in the rabbinic literature is comprehensible, because it was also reserved for slaves and women. According to Philo of Alexandria, this hairstyle was a typical sign of the decadence of Roman customs:

> (50) ... and well-shaped slaves of the most exquisite beauty, ministering, as if they had come not more for the purpose of serving the guests than for delighting the eyes of the spectators by their mere appearance. Of these slaves, some, being still boys, pour out the wine; and others more fully grown pour water, being carefully washed and rubbed down, with their faces anointed and pencilled, and the hair of their heads admirably plaited and curled and wreathed in delicate knots; (51) for they have very long hair, being either completely unshorn, or else having only the hair on their foreheads cut at the end so as to make them of an equal length all round, being accurately sloped away so as to represent a circular line, and being clothed in tunics of the most delicate texture, and of the purest white, reaching in front down to the lower part of the knee, and behind to a little below the calf of the leg, and drawing up each side with a gentle doubling of the fringe at the joinings of the tunics, raising undulations of the garment as it were at the sides, and widening them at the hollow part of the side.[119]

Be that as it may, the particular hairstyle is seen in the Jerusalem Talmud, as a sign of acculturation, set aside only for elitist groups of Jews close to the government and in the position of being a political advantage for the Jewish community.

To conclude on theatres: rabbinic Judaism considers all Roman customs associated with the field of divination to be magic practices. Divination, pro-

---

116 See Babylonian Talmud, Sanhedrin 17b; Talmud Yerushlami, *Sheqalim* 5,1 (48b) and Veltri, *Magie und Halakha*, 52–53.
117 Cassius Dio 57:15; see Marie-Therese Fögen, *Die Enteignung der Wahrsager. Studien zum kaiserlichen Wissensmonopol in der Spätantike* (Frankfurt am Main: Suhrkamp, 1993), 138 and Veltri, *Magie und Halakha*, 52.
118 *De Elia et ieiunio* 13:42 (Patrologia Latina 14:748): "Assistunt pueri coma nitentes, ex gente barvarica ad hos usu electi, per singularum distanciis aetatum vices".
119 *De Vita contemplativa* 50 f.

hibited by the Torah, is allowed to special groups when this can be of political advantage for Judaism and the Jewish community in some way. This confirms the general tendency of the rabbinic academy to reserve the real power of magic to leading classes as *instrumentum regni*, to destroy magic with the power of magic.[120] The rabbinic explanation, namely that only some groups are allowed to follow certain foreign customs prohibited for others, should not obscure the fact that the majority of the people often and without scruples did what the rabbis prohibited. The Halakhah is not a perfect account of everyday life, but rather a mirror of what we can call an attempt to influence moral behaviour.

In addition, the prohibition of theatre performances should not hide the fact that the rabbis likewise did not have a prudish upbringing such as in the Victorian period, or in the age of Puritanism in England and colonial America, when the theatre was in effect outlawed and witchcraft was sensed everywhere. That is especially valid for the Babylonian literature that transmits some fictive or real episode of rabbinic life which can doubtless be compared to mime and pantomime. We read in the Babylon Talmud, Sanhedrin 67b:

> R. Jannai came to an inn. He said to them: Give me a drink of water. And they offered him *shattitha*. Seeing the lips of the woman [who brought him this] moving, he [covertly] spilled a little thereof, which turned to snakes. Then he said: As I have drunk of yours, now do you come and drink of mine. So he gave her to drink, and she was turned into an ass. He then rode upon her into the market. But her friends came and broke the charm [changing her back into a human being], and so he was seen riding upon a woman in public.[121]

We cannot imagine the world evoked by this story of magic. However, all the elements and ingredients of the popular mime and pantomime are present here: a woman, snakes, ass, market, nakedness, conjuration and counter-conjuration. I have a strong impression that we have here a story about sex, magic, and performance at a market, the old place for impromptu theatre, the commedia dell'arte of antiquity, when magic had the power to subjugate all that can influence the world and hence could be countered only by magic. This conclusion may not be particularly edifying, but perhaps for that very reason it lies nonetheless closer to real life, which is a conglomerate of hopes and achievements, amusements and legal tricks.

---

120 On the danger of magic and the need to have recourse to magic against magic, see Babylonan Talmud Pesaḥin 8b, the Responsa of R. Shelomo b. Adret, 1,413, and R. Shelomo ben Yeḥiel Luria, § 3 (bottom): "... to destroy magic by magic" (*le-battel kishshuf be-kishshuf*).
121 *The Babylonian Talmud: Seder Nezikin. Sanhedrin*, Translated into English with Notes, Glossary and Indices by H. Freedman (London: Soncino Press, 1969): 460–461.

3.1.3 The Rhetoric of Ethics

Analysing the Rabbinic attitude to theatre has shown that the rabbis had command over a very clear picture of the Roman religion – at least of the religion as it was reflected in popular transmissions through Roman soldiers and merchants, and in the festivities in the provinces. It is now understandable that the passage of Sifra mentioned above did not refer either to public or private expressions of the Roman religion. The rabbis likely learned the general and the popular conceptions from soldiers and merchants. Comparable notions concerning theatre, circus, and *ludi* are reported from the African province through Tertullian, Augustine, and Jerome, as mentioned above.

Occupation with these subjects as represented in the rabbinic literature is not rooted in a scholarly yet antiquarian interest in the customs of the world's people, but in the fact that these customs were common among the Jewish people. The doctrine of a separation of Israel – as proclaimed in the rabbinic sources – is often emphasised for the reason that the reality was different. Certain "religious" customs were partially allowed explicitly, partially tolerated as long as they were not suspected of being idolatrous. Even the fact that visiting the theatre was allowed if it was necessary to save lives or to witness the death of a husband (as precondition for his widow to remarry) shows a remarkable attitude of the rabbis toward pragmatism. If a custom cannot be eradicated, it is read as useful as far as this is possible. In this we see the actual rabbinic "art of convincing" when facing with the task of reaching the ears of Jews who often oriented their everyday lives toward the gentile environment and its compass of custom and morality. If a certain custom – in the sphere of medicine, for instance – had proven useful it would not be possible to eradicate it, no matter how idolatrous it might appear. Ethical-religious acceptance of an act is rarely proof of a decline in religious conviction, but rather indicates an attempt to bring up to date contents which are difficult to promote.

The rabbinic literature takes a similar stance when it comes to the official religion and cult in respect to festivals. This is a topic associated not only with idolatry but also with the law of the rulers, which needs to be obeyed. A Roman holiday implied abstinence from work through a ban on commerce for the day, but also offered the opportunity to get to know one's "Roman" neighbours. This is the subject of the following sub-chapter.

3.2 Holidays: Religion, Politics, and Social Life

'Avodah Zarah, "Idolatry," is the tractate par excellence that talks about the relationship of Jews to gentiles. One important topic the tractate discusses is

the thorough identification of the mainly Roman festivals on which Jews are not supposed to socialise with non-Jews. This special emphasis on these days is the result of Romans performing practices related to the Roman religion on certain festivals. For this reason, any socialisation of Jews with those Romans would be considered tantamount to accepting idolatry.[122]

3.2.1 On the History of Research

Interest in the rabbinic statements on Greco-Roman festivals began in the early 20th century as a result of the study of *realia*. Two small contributions by Hans Blaufuss deserve mention in this context. They were guided by the conviction that the rabbinic sources were "full of material ... that deserves the attention of archeological circles." This held especially true for the tractate '*Avodah Zarah* in Tosefta, Mishnah and Talmud.[123] Blaufuss proceeded correctly in terms of methodology: he chose as his point of departure Mishnah 'Avodah Zarah 1:3. In order to explain the festivals listed there, he then uses other parallels from the rabbinic scriptures.

Samuel Krauss proceeded differently in his discussion of the *realia*: he offers a list of the respective holidays, but without further attention to the texts mentioning them. Kraus considered the following to be the Greco-Roman holidays the rabbis had listed: the *kalendae, saturnalia*, the γενέσια – the days of birth and death of the Caesars –, the day on which the heathen cuts his hair and beard, the day of landing – κατιτήρια sc. ἱερά –, *sigillaria*, the *saeculares ludi*, the festival of the *Hilaria*, the festival of Jews – which the Romans called ὀργία – and the Greco-Syrian *Mayumas* festivals. Krauss also noted the Persian festivals.

Mireille Hadas-Lebel largely follows Krauss in her listing of pagan festivals and their traces in the rabbinic literature. However, she proceeds more cautiously in her identification of the festivals. The list appears as the following: the festival of *kalendae* for the public festivals, the saturnalia, Kratesis, Geno-

---

122 See, however, Gary G. Porton, "Forbidden Transactions: Prohibited Commerce with Gentiles in Earliest Rabbinism," in *To See Ourselves as Others See Us": Christian, Jews, "Others" in Late Antiquity*, ed. Jacob Neusner et al. (Chico, Calif.: Scholars Press, 1985), 317–335; Porton, *Goyim: Gentiles and Israelites in Mishna-Tosefta* (Atlanta, Ga.: Scholars Press, 1988).
123 Hans Blaufuss, *Römische Feste und Feiertage nach den Traktaten über fremden Dienst (Aboda zara) in Mischna, Tosefta, Jerusalemer und babylonischem Talmud* (Nuremberg: Stich, 1909), 2.

sia, as well as the *ludi*. For the private festivals, she lists cutting of beard and hair, and banquets.[124]

When reading old and recent scholars, one can get the distinct impression that the rabbis had thematically discussed the Roman *feriae* one after another. The rabbis had no interest in discussing the Roman calendar for its own sake. On the contrary, they were interested in discussing certain festivals for their halakhic implications.

In regard to this topic as well, modern scholarship was content with finding (in)congruencies between the rabbinic reflection of the Roman calendar and findings from other sources. The reason why the rabbis had discussed these festivals in mythological and religious terms in their sources had not caught scholarly attention. If the rabbis had *only* been interested in a halakhic discussion, why would they have occupied themselves with the etiology? For the simple reason that the people – and the rabbis – had observed the festivals themselves.

3.2.2 The Calendar

The Roman calendar[125] distinguishes between *feriae publicae*, *feriae gentium* or *familiarum*, and *feriae privatae* or *feriae singularum*. Among the public festivals (*feriae publicae*)[126] were the following:

---

124 Hadas-Lebel, *Le Paganisme à travers les sources rabbiniques*, 426–441.
125 The most important source which presents information on the Roman calendari is the opus magnus by the Neo-Platonic Macrobius Ambrosius Theodosius (5th century CE), *Saturnalia*. It belongs to the genre of symposia literature. Macrobius' symposion is not an original one – neither in respect to the genre (dating back to Plato) nor to its content. It is the work of an "antiquarian" who collected pre-existent material with the purpose of transmitting and discussing it further. Macrobius' *Saturnalia* had been viewed as a kind of encyclopaedia in the Middle Ages. It was often used. On this, see Nino Marione's introduction to *I Saturnali di Macrobio Teodosio*, ed. and trans. Nino Marinone (Turin: Unione tipografico-editrice torinese, 1967), 9–97. Macrobius devotes a rather large part of his symposion to the Roman calendar (*Saturalia*, I,12,2–16,37). On the Roman calendar itself in more general discussions, see Joachim Marquardt et al., *Römische Staatsverwaltung* vol. 3 (Leipzig: Hirzel, 1885), 293; Georg Wissowa, *Religion und Kultus der Römer* (Munich: Beck, 1912); Wissowa, "Feriae," in *Paulys Real-Encyclopädie der classischen Alterthumswissenschaften* VI/2 (1909), col. 2211–2213; Mary Beard et al., *Religion of Rome* 2 vols. (Cambridge and New York: Cambridge University Press, 1998), vol. 1, passim; vol. 2, 60–77.
126 Macrobius, *Saturnalia* I:16,5: "Feriarum autem publicarum genera sunt quattuor. Aut enim stativae sunt aut conceptivae aut imperativae aut nundinae."

- *feriae stativae*, which were set on one specific day of the calendar;[127]
- the *feriae conceptivae*, set on a specific section of the calendar (*in dies certos*), for agricultural duties, for instance, or that were set arbitrarily (*in dies incertos*);[128]
- the *feriae imperativae aut indicate*, which were ordered by officials with an imperium through the magistrates,[129] and;
- *feriae nundinae* – festivals of the villagers at which the (annual) market was conducted.[130]

The private festivals reflected the Roman (sociologic) affiliation which, as is well-known, expressed itself in *praenomen, cognomen*, and *nomen. Feriae gentium* were assigned to the *gens*, a band of several families with common ancestry (e.g. Iulia, Cornelia, Claudia, etc.), and were celebrated through special family customs.[131] However, the *feriae privatae* or *singulorum* were reserved for the individual person. Over the course of time, the differences between *gens* and *familia* declined for the most part in importance – a strict demarcation between the two sociological entities had lost its meaning.[132] Private festivals which concerned the individual were birthdays, the day one escaped lightning, the day of death, and the day of atonement.[133] Regular private festivals of the family – *feriae privatae* – were the *kalendae, nonae*, and the *ides* of each month, the festival of relationship – *Caristia* – on February 22, the *saturnalia*,[134] the birthday of the *pater familias* or one of his friends, and the day of

---

127 See the listing of Varro, *De lingua latina* VI:12 et seq. The definitions of these holidays are found in Macrobius, *Saturnalia*, I:16,6: "Et sunt stativae universi populi communes certis et constitutis diebus ac mensibus et in fastis statis observationibus adnotatae, in quibus praecipue servantur Agonalia Carmentalia Lupercalia."
128 *Ibidem*: "Conceptivae sunt quae quotannis a magistratibus vel a sacerdotibus concipiuntur in dies vel certos vel etiam incertos, ut sunt Latinae Sementivae Paganalia Compitalia."
129 *Ibidem*: "Imperativae sunt quas consules vel praetores quo arbitrio potestatis indicunt."
130 *Ibidem*: "Nundinae sunt paganorum itemque rusticorum, quibus conveniunt negotiis vel mercibus provisuri."
131 *Ibidem*, I:16,7: "Sunt praeterea feriae propriae familiarum, ut familiae Claudiae vel Aemiliae seu Iuliae sive Corneliae, et si quas ferias proprias quaeque familia ex usu domesticae celebritas observat."
132 On this, see Paul Kübler, "Gens," in *Paulys Real-Encyclopädie der classischen Alterthumswissenschaften* VII,1 (1910), col. 1177.
133 Macrobius, *Saturnalia*, I:16,8: "Sunt singulorum, uti natalium fulgurumque susceptiones, item funerum atque expiationum."
134 For this reason, they belonged to the *privatae*. See Marquardt, *Römische Staatsverwaltung*, vol. 3, 127. I have taken this list from there.

death of a family member. The festival consisted of a reverence to the domestic gods.

The rabbinic literature offers a very detailed discussion of the position a festival took in the Roman calendar and thus in Jewish everyday life. The festivals affected Jewish everyday life in so far as the typology of the festivals was concerned, and their halakhic meaning as days of (Roman) rest whose non-observance the Roman literature referred to by the technical term *pollutio* (transgression of law and custom).

3.2.3 The Typology of the Festivals

The Mishnah does not refer to any substantial differentiation between the *feriae publicae, feriae gentium*, and *feriae privatae* in its listing of foreign festivals – which are noted there by the dysphemism איד ("misfortune") or simply as עיד ("festival").[135] It notes:

> The following are the festivals of the pagans: Kalendae, saturnalia, the day of reign (κράτησις), the birthdays of the kings (γενέσια), birthdays and days of death …

The differentiation between public and private festivals is seen for the first time in the Jerusalem Talmud, 'Avodah Zarah 1:2 (39c):

> The birthday and the day of death. Until this sentence, [the Mishnah discussed the festivals] for the public (*le-ṣibbur*); from this point on [it discusses the festivals] for the individual (*le-yaḥid*).

Tosefta, 'Avodah Zarah 1:4 likely presupposes this distinction. In this passage, however, there is also a reference to local and private festivals:

> A city observes the one [festival], [but] another does not.
> One nation observes it, [but] another does not.
> One family observes it, [but] another does not.
> Those who observe it, are forbidden, the others [however] are not.
> The Kalendae:
> Although all observe [the festival], it is only forbidden to those who observe it in a cultic way.
> The saturnalia,
> The day of [the Emperor's] accession to power,
> The day of reign,

---

[135] See, for instance, Babylonian Talmud, 'Avodah Zarah 7b; Jerusalem Talmud, 'Eruvin 5 (22a).

> The birthdays of the kings, the day of each king.
> The king [belongs] to the public as an individual.¹³⁶
> Even his day of marriage and the day he became a commander [belong to the public]
> Rabbi Me'ir says: The day he recovers from sickness is also forbidden.

In the passage of the Tosefta, the king is regarded as a public person in all areas. Thus, not only the dates that are connected to his *curriculum vitae* as ruler are offered as public festivals, but also those that are commonly reserved for the private sphere. This is the meaning of the formula הרי כרבים יחיד / "he belongs to the public as an individual."¹³⁷ Sources have provided proof for the practice of a king assigning the day of his anniversary of his promotion to be a *feria indicta*. This practice became possible by a decision of the Senate in 723 (31 CE) to grant that right to any emperor who became *divus*.

3.2.4 Day of Rest, pollutio, and Permissions of Commerce

There was a need for distinguishing public from private festivals as, according to the Halakhah, commerce was prohibited for three days before the public festival. On the occasion of private festivals, the prohibition was only valid for the day itself, and also only for the person observing the day (Mishnah, 'Avodah Zarah 1:1). There is a reference visible in the Roman legal practice. The legal practice rested on the *feriae publicae*, which could perhaps last for several days. Thus, commerce was hindered as well. Whether or not the Romans had indeed observed their festivals is debatable. The days were listed in the calendar as *nefasti dies*, i.e., on these days it was *"nefas* to pursue bourgeois business."¹³⁸

We find the following explanation in the writings of Marcobius: "fasti sunt, quibus licet fari praetori tria verba solemnia: do dico addico; his contrarii sunt

---

136 This text is difficult to translate. Hadas-Lebel writes, "jour de chaque empereur. Il en est de la collectivité comme des particuliers: cela vaut également pour le jour de son banquet et celui de son entrée en charge" Hadas-Lebel, *Le Paganisme à travers les sources rabbiniques*, 427. See Jacob Neusner, trans., *The Tosefta: Neziqin* (New York: Ktav, 1981), 312: "The day of each and every emperor – lo, it is tantamount to a public festival. As to an individual, even on the day of his banquet or the day on which he was made ruler."
137 Heinrich Lewy's interpretation which sees a caesura between כרבים and יחיד, is less than convincing. He entirely ignores the function of אפילו / "even [more so]/yet" which expands the meaning of the prefix כ even more (!). See Heinrich Lewy, "Philologische Streifzüge in dem Talmud," *Philologus* 52 (1898): 735. See also Blaufuss, *Römische Feiertage*, 1–2, note 5.
138 Werner Eisenhut, "Fasti dies," in *Der Kleine Pauly: Lexikon der Antike in fünf Bänden*, ed. Konrat Ziegler and Walther Sontheimer vol. 2, (München: DTV, 1979), 519.

nefasti."¹³⁹ In English: "*Fasti* are those days on which the praetor is allowed to utter the following three words publicly: I do allow, I do order, I do acknowledge. Otherwise, they are *nefasti*." It is likely a folk etymology which understood *fas* as *fateor* (say). Yet, we may conclude one aspect from this quote: legal practice rested on these days. Macrobius further informs us that every work was forbidden at the festivals.¹⁴⁰ The *flamines* (Roman priests) were even prohibited to *watch* others doing work. Those who transgressed the prohibition were fined and had to sacrifice a pig.¹⁴¹ According to Umbro, who is otherwise unknown, one did not commit *pollution*. In the Jerusalem Talmud, 'Avodah Zarah 39c, it is written:

> Rav said: The festival of *kalendae* is forbidden [for Jews] at all [pagans' houses].
> Rabbi Yoanan said: [For Jews] it is only forbidden at those [pagans' houses] who celebrate [the festival].
> The feast of Saturn is forbidden [for all Jews] at all [pagans' houses] who celebrate this festival.
> The companions asked: Are [in the prohibition to do commerce] the women [of the pagans] who [celebrate the festival] like the [gentiles themselves] who celebrate the festival? Rabbi Abbahu asked: And, [what about the] occupation¹⁴² of Caesarea? Because their majority [consists] of Samaritans, it is the same as with those [gentiles themselves] who celebrate the [festival].
> [How about the] occupation of Duqim? This requires [a further explanation].¹⁴³

While Rav had argued for a total prohibition of contact for the *kalendae* festivals, Rabbi Yoḥanan takes into consideration the *pollutio* committed by the Romans. He thus allows some latitude for the case that gentiles do not celebrate the festival. Then there would be no need for insisting on this prohibition of the Mishnah. Rav's statement does not have to be understood as making the

---

139 Macrobius, *Saturnalia*, I,16,14. On the identification of *nefas* and *fas*, see Georg Schön, "Fasti," in *Paulys Real-Encyclopädie der classischen Alterthumswissenschaften* (= PRE) VI/2 (1909), col. 2015 et seq.
140 Macrobius, *Saturnalia* I:16,9: "Adfirmabant autem sacerdotes pollui ferias si indictis conceptisque opus aliquod fieret."
141 *Ibidem*, I:16,10: „Prater multam vero adfirmabatur eum qui talibus diebus imprudens aliquid egisset porco piaculum dare debere."
142 טקסים, loanword from the Greek τάξ. See Krauss, *Griechische und lateinische Lehnwörter*, vol. 2, 267.
143 דוקים appears only here. See Gottfried Reeg, *Die Ortsnamen Israels nach der rabbinischen Literatur* (Wiesbaden: Reichert, 1989), 203. It most likely is not a place name as Saul Lieberman argues. See Lieberman, "The Martyrs of Caesarea," *Annuaire de l'Institute de Philologie et d'Histoire Orientales et Slaves* 7 (1939–1944): 406. See Reeg, *Die Ortsnamen Israels*, 203, for further bibliographic references.

Halakhah more complicated. Whether the individual Roman had celebrated the *kalendae* festival or not: it is a fact that legal practice rested during that period.

A possible legal argument – which might have resulted from doing commerce – was a risk that the Halakhah had to foresee and eliminate. The Halakhah proceeds in a similar way in regard to the *saturnalia*: Jews were prohibited from having contact with gentiles who celebrated the festival. The fact that the gentiles' wives were mentioned in this context is somewhat problematic. Blaufuss argues on the basis of this text that women did not take part in the celebrations of the festival of Saturn.[144] However, as far as I know from my studies of the Roman religion, I can answer to that argument: there is no other Roman source which would indicate this. As I see it, the sacrifice which was brought to the festival hardly played any role: as we will see later, the *saturnalia* were celebrated in private through the *sacrificium* of a piglet. It is very difficult to prove, indeed highly unlikely, that women were excluded from this *private* cult.

In my view, the "companions" wanted to pose a paradox form of argumentation by offering an implicit *argumentum a maiori*: if it is correct, according to the Halakhah, that in the case of the *kalendae* the prohibition of doing business is lifted because of the Roman *pollutio*, how about the wife of a gentile who celebrates the *saturnalia*? The main question is not so much related to the Roman festivals but rather to the position of the Roman woman in Rome and in the periphery of the Empire.[145] Because it is highly unlikely that a Roman woman could do business without her husband, the risk of the Jewish merchant in the case of *pollutio* would have doubled: a possible legal argument could not be averted, and all rested on the basis of trust. To argue from a halakhic standpoint: if doing business with the pagans, who do not celebrate the festival, was risky, it would be all the more so if done with the women of the pagans who celebrate the festival.

One could point to the fact, as an alternative hypothesis, that the domestic business was entirely in the hands of the wife.[146] Thus, it is reasonable to distinguish between the gentile and his wife. She might of course have finished the domestic business before the festival commenced. No wife, on the other

---

144 Blaufuss, *Römische Feste*, 10.
145 On the position of Roman women in Italy, see Marquard, *Das Privatleben der Römer*, 57–74.
146 See Tertullianus, *Exhortatio Castitatis* 12: "Scio, quibus causationibus coloremus insatiabilem carnis cupiditatem, praetendimus necessitates adminiculorum, *domum administrandum, familiam regendam, claves custodiendas, lanificium dispensandum, victum procurandum.*" My italics. On this subject, see Marquard, *Das Privatleben der Römer*, vol. 1, 58.

hand, was guilty of *pollutio* if she prepared the festival and conducted the usual domestic chores, because *pollutio* was an official term related to cult.[147] Women, however, were excluded from the official cult of the Roman religion: their participation in the cult did indeed constitute a pollution of *religio*.[148] In this case, too, it is argued in terms of Halakhah with the *argumentum a maiori*: if doing business is allowed with the pagan, who does not celebrate the festival, it is *a maiori* allowed to do business with the wives of those pagans who celebrate it, since the wives are not part of the official Roman religion.

It is not surprising that this passage mentions the "occupation" of Caesarea. According to the Jerusalem Talmud, Demai 2:1 (22c), a large number of Samaritans lived there. The attitude of the rabbinic sources was a very polemic one when mentioning the Samaritans.[149] For this reason, the Talmud is not entirely reliable. Our source, however, does not leave room for doubt that the Samaritans were set on a par with the gentiles. This might go back to the involvement of Samaritans in the administration and military, as scholarship assumes.[150]

The importance of defining whether or not the "pagans" worked on certain days also touched on the differentiation between the *feriae stativae*, celebrated on fixed dates, and the *feriae imperativae, indicate,* or *conceptivae*. Such a differentiation only appears in the Tosefta, 'Avodah Zarah 1:1:

> Naum the Meder says: In the [community of] Diaspora, only one day is forbidden before the festivals (לפני אידיהן). This does only hold true for the fixed festivals (אידין הקבועין). On days, which are not fixed (אידין שאין הקבועין), only the very same day is forbidden.

Although doing business is forbidden for three days, this does only concern circumstances which are fixed. A thing which is not fixed is allowed. But a thing which is fixed for purchase of sale is also allowed.

The Tosefta weakens the firm position of Mishnah, 'Avodah Zarah 1:1, which foresees at certain festivals a prohibition on Jews enjoining them from doing business for three days (before and after the actual festival). The Tosefta

---

147 Macrobius, *Saturnalia*, I:16.10: "... opus vel ad deos pertinens sacrorumve causa vel aliquid ad urgentem vitae necessitatem respiciens." On this, see Wissowa, *Religion und Kultus der Römer*, 441.

148 See Titus Livius, 10.23.9–10: "eodem ferme ritu et haec ara quo illa antiquior culta est, ut nulla nisi spectatae pudicitiae matrona et quae uni uiro nupta fuisset ius sacrificandi haberet; uolgata dein religio a ollutis, nec matronis solum sed omnis ordinis feminis, postremo in obliuionem uenit."

149 On this, see Lee I. Levine, *Caesarea under Roman Rule* (Leiden: Brill, 1975), 107–112 [notes 227–230].

150 On this, see Stemberger, *Juden und Christen*, 26.

reduces the days in the Diaspora to no more than two: one before and one after the festival. According to the Tosefta, this is only valid for the *feriae stativae* (באידיהן הקבועים), but not for the non-fixed dates on which only the day of the festival is forbidden for business.

The second paragraph presents the festival from the perspective of commerce. The Mishnah discusses the done deals only, and forbids the market on Roman festivities. The reason was that the market was open on some festivals, and merchandise had possibly included idolatrous "devotional objects" as well. This held especially true for the *kalendae* festival and the *saturnalia* (see below), on which presents were given (the *straenae* and the *sigillaria*, see below). Presents always mean profit from which Jews were supposed to abstain on these occasions if they followed the Mishnah. This, however, is not the opinion as outlined in the Tosefta. The Tosefta presents the case from the perspective of profit: a thing which is fixed for purchase and sale is allowed. It probably refers to the annual market that is always held on these festivities. To prohibit that means to deprive the Jewish merchants of their livelihood. The Jewish merchants were also allowed to sell "devotional objects," such as "idolatrous" statuettes. In the end, we should remember, Jewish producers were allowed to produce "idols" *for* the gentiles.[151]

3.2.5 The Day of Rain: A Judeo-Roman Festival?

According to Devarim Rabbah 7:7, the respective festivals functioned as markers of difference to distinguish Jews from gentiles.[152] It reads:

> It happened once that a gentile asked R. Yoḥanan ben Zakkai.
> He said to him: We have our festivals, and you have yours.
> We have *kalendae, saturnalia*, and [the Day] of Reign,
> And you have *pesaḥ, 'aṣeret*, and *sukkot*.
> What is the day we may celebrate together?
> R. Yoḥanan ben Zakkai answered him: the day it rains.

The order of the festivals/holidays in the list likely corresponded to the importance the redactor assigned to the mentioned festivals of the "goyim" as well

---

151 On this, see Mishnah, 'Avodah Zarah 4:4 and Ephraim E. Urbach, "The Rabbinical Laws of Idolatry in the Second and Third Centuries in the Light of Archaeological and Historical Facts," in *Israel Exploration Journal* 9 (1959): 159 et seq.
152 Saul Lieberman, *Greek in Jewish Palestine* (New York: Jewish Theological Seminary, 1965), 111.

as to those of the Jews. Following the text, Jews and gentiles were not able to celebrate together any other day than the one on which it rains.[153] One may very well grasp the idea that the day it rains is celebrated, especially after a drought. But why would Jews and Romans do that together?

When following the wording of the text, R. Yoanan ben Zakkai seeks the separation of Jews from the Romans: every group has their own holidays. Only after times of distress can the two groups jointly thank (the) god(s). A Jewish celebration on the occasion of rain is proven by Mishnah, Ta'anit 3:9: during an ordered fasting and after the half period of it was already over, it suddenly began to rain.[154] For this, R. Tarfon allowed the people to eat, drink, and celebrate the day. However, there is no reference to the participation of gentiles. Such a participation seems rather absurd if we consider the reasons given which had allegedly caused the drought. Jerusalem Talmud, Ta'anit 66c offers three grave sins in this context: "idolatry, forbidden sexual intercourse (adultery), and the spilling of blood."[155] Thus, sins which the rabbinic literature often associated with the Romans, and which could be witnessed in the theatre or circus were regarded as reasons.

This interpretation can be sustained by Jerusalem Talmud, Ta'anit 1:4 (64b), where a sinner named "Pentekaka" (the name had either derived from πεντήκακα, roughly translatable as "five sins," or from παντοκακός, i.e., roughly translatable as "sinner through and through") is mentioned.[156] Pentekaka called for a prayer for rain. When he was asked for his profession, he answered that he committed five sins each day: he beautified the theatre, he mediated prostitutes, he carried their garments to the bath house, and danced for them by clapping his hands and playing the cymbals.[157] These "sins" would have been enough to disqualify him from praying for rain as God would not listen to him. Yet, as it appears, Pentekaka had demonstrated mercy, at least once, when he used his own money to free a man from prison whose wife had

---

[153] See Midrash Shoḥer Ṭov on Psalms 117: אמר רבי תנחום בר חייא: גדולה ירידת גשמים ממתן תורה, שמתן תורה שמחה לישראל, וירידת הגשמים שמחה לכל העמים ולכל העולם, וגם לבהמה ולחיה ולעופות (thanks to Ronit Nikolsky for the reference).
[154] On rain and the remedies against drought, see Raphael Patai, "The 'Control of Rain' in Ancient Palestine: A Study in Comparative Religion," *Hebrew Union College Annual* 14 (1939): 251–286.
[155] On medicinal remedies, see also Jerusalem Talmud, 'Avodah Zarah 2:2 (40d) and especially *Babylonian Talmud,* Pesachim 25a–b.
[156] See Jacobs, "Theatres and Performances," 342.
[157] On this, see Lieberman, *Greek in Jewish Palestine,* 31–32; see also Martin Jacobs, "Römische Thermenkultur im Spiegel des Talmud Yerushalmi," in *The Talmud Yerushalmi and Graeco-Roman Culture* vol. 1, ed. Peter Schäfer (Tübingen: Mohr Siebeck, 1998), 256.

been forced to prostitution because of his imprisonment. This story actually calls for a thorough analysis, but it may serve solely for our argument: this episode proves, among other things, that the (Roman) business with the theatre and prostitution, like many other customs and institutions, constituted grave sins in the eyes of the rabbis. This does not make it appear very likely that Jews and gentiles (Romans) celebrated a festival together that the rabbis had approved of.

However, that is nothing more than theory. The reality was different as we will discuss. If there had been no festivals/holidays which Jews and Romans had celebrated jointly, we would have no rabbinic sources touching on their meaning for Roman and Jewish life. The rabbinic refusal of any convergence between Jews and gentiles simply proves the necessity of laws regulating reality and keeping the principle. It does not say much about the historical reality.

3.2.6 Kalendae

The first festival the rabbinic literature lists is that of the *kalendae*. In the Roman literature, the term refers to the beginning of a month – rather gloomy days (*tristes kalendae*) as these were also the days for making due payment.[158] When the rabbinic literature mentions the festival of *kalendae*, it is very likely the *kalendae Ianuarii*, the first day of the year which was as much of a religious holiday as a secular holiday, including closed schools. Over the course of time, the word *kalendae* indeed began being applied predominantly to the first day of January, the *kalendae Ianuarii*.[159]

The first day of January was also the common day for officials to assume their offices. This custom dated back to the year 153 BCE, when Consul Q. Fulvius Nobilior had to pay tribute to the war on the Iberian Peninsula, and assumed office on January 1, instead of March 15.[160] The custom had prevailed ever since. It was listed in the rabbinic sources as *dies fastus*, and the *kalendae Ianuarii* gained more importance over time for its religious, political, and social connotations.[161] The first day of the year was the day to pray to God or the

---

[158] Yerushalmi also notes that the *Kalendae Ianuarii* were referred to as the "gloomy kalendae." It also mentions the "black day," which is, however, not related to it as we will discuss below.
[159] Symmachus I:44; X:27; Marquard, *Das Privatleben der Römer*, vol. 1, 94, note 6.
[160] See Werner Eisenhut, "Kalendae Ianuariae," in *Der kleine Pauly* vol. 3, 57–58.
[161] On this, see Georg Schön, "Fasti," in *Paulys Real-Encyclopädie der classischen Alterthumswissenschaften* VI, 2 (1909), col. 2015–2046.

gods, but also to wish well their own relatives and friends.[162] White bulls were sacrificed on that day for the honor of Jupiter. The ceremony was exercised in front of Capitol Hill, the "centre of the state's political potency."[163] The consuls thanked the gods for the protection of the previous year, and afterwards, the first seating of the Senate for this year took place. Typically, the subject of this seating was religious matters.

The celebrations began with a feast on the night before the festival. The day itself was reserved for trading wishes and presents. Pliny is a source of the practise when he emphatically asks:[164] "Why, in fact, upon the first day of the new year, do we accost one another with prayers for good fortune, and, for luck's sake, wish each other a happy new year?"[165] Ovid also mentioned this custom.[166]

The *kalendae*'s importance grew over times, and eventually superseded the *saturnalia* (of which more later). The process of "defeating" the *saturnalia* was largely concluded in the 4th century.[167] The *kalendae* (*Ianuarii*) was not only one of the most important *feriae* of the Roman Empire, but also one of the widest spread.[168] The Christian literature repeatedly mentions the "stubborn clinging" to this festival even in the "Christian era." Aurelius P. Clemens Prudentius (c. 348–405) – who was from today's Spain and likely the greatest Christian author of antiquity – condemned the celebrations of *kalendae*, and also confirmed that they were based on a long tradition.[169]

---

[162] Tacitus mentions the prayer and the praising of the deity in respect to Caesar. See Tacitus, *Annales* IV:70,1: „Sed Caesar solemnia incipientis anni kalendis Ianuariis epistula precatus."
[163] Werner Eisenhut, "Juppiter," in *Der kleine Pauly* vol. 3, 5.
[164] See below, p. 154.
[165] *Naturalis Historia*, XXVIII:5,22: "cur enim primum anni incipientis diem laetis precationibus invicem faustum ominarum?" See also *C. Plinii Secundi Naturalis Historiae Libri XXVIII/C. Plinius Secundus d. Ä. Naturkunde.* Buch XXVIII: Lateinisch–Deutsch, ed. and trans. Roderich König and Gerard Winkler (Munich and Zürich: Artemis, 1988), 25–31.
[166] Ovid, *Fasti* I:175 et seq.:
"At cur laeta tuis dicuntur verba Kalendis,
et damus alternas accipimusque preces?
tum deus (scl. Janus) incumbens baculo, quod dextra gerebat,
„omina principiis" inquit "inesse solent."
[167] Martin P. Nilsson, "Studien zur Vorgeschichte des Weihnachtsfestes," *Archiv für Religionswissenschaft* 19 (1916/19): 52.
[168] The custom of this festival had even reached Bythinia, for instance. See the greetings to Traianus on this occasion in Pliny, *Epistulae*, X:35: "Solemmnia vota pro incolumitate tua, qua publica salus continetur, et suscepimus, domine, pariter et solvimus precati deos, ut velint ea semper solvi semperque signari." See Traianus's reply in Pliny, *Epistulae*, X,36.
[169] *Contra Orationem Symmachi*, I:237–244:
"... Iano etiam celebri de mense litatur
auspiciis epulisque sacris, quas inveterato,

The custom was still followed in the 6th century, which does prove once more just how deeply it was rooted in the society. St. Eligius (588–659) mentions the celebration of *kalendae* among the *paganorum sacrilegas consuetudines* still in existence, in a sermon intended to combat those.[170]

3.2.7 Elements: Wishes and Presents

The Roman well wishes and also the presents for New Year's Day are mentioned in the rabbinic literature. Among the things which were forbidden during the celebrations were the felicitations. It is very likely that the term לשאל שלום in Tosefta, 'Avodah Zarah 1:3 ("asking for the peace, that is well-being, health") has to be understood as a form of well-wishing in this context. The Tosefta reads:

> One is allowed to ask a gentile of his well-being for the peace's sake during his holidays. This is only allowed to the Jewish craftsmen who work in the Jewish house next to the gentile's. It is not allowed in the gentile's home.[171]

---

heu miseri, sub honore agitant, et gaudia ducunt
festa Kalendarum. sic observatio crevit
ex atavis quondam male coepta, deinda secutis
tradita temporibus serisque nepotibus aucta.
traxerunt longam corda inconsulta catenam,
mosque tenebrosus vitiosa in saecula fluxit."

170 He wrote "Nullus in kal. Jan. nefanda aut ridiculosa, vetulas aut cervulos, aut strenas aut bibitiones superfluas exerceat." Quoted in Grimm, *Deutsche Mythologie* vol. 3, 401. Eligious's source likely was Augustinus *De rectitudine catholicae conversationis* (*Patrologia Latina* 40,1172 et seq.). This is not the place to discuss the further development of the *kalendae*. See, however, the decrees of Burchard of Worms (died 1024). Burchards seeks to learn in the "interrogatio": "observasti calendas januarias ritu Paganorum, ut vel aliquid plus facere propter novum annum, quam antea vel post soleres facere, ita dico, ut aut mensam tuam cum lapidibus vel epulis in domo tua praeparares eo tempore, aut per vicos et plateas cantores et choros duceres, aut supra tectum domus tuae sederes ense tuo circumsignatus, ut ibi videres et intelligeres, quid tibi in sequenti anno futurum esset ..." *Sammlung der Dekrete, Köln 1548, 193ᵉ*, quoted in Grimm, *Deutsche Mythologie*, vol. 3, 409. English: Jacob Grimm, *Teutonic Mythology*, transl. by James Steven Stallybrass (London [repr. New York]: Bell & sons [repr. Dover Publications] 1888 [1966]: 755. On the Christian sources for the prohibition of καλάνδια and βρουμάλια, see also Max Grünbaum, "Beiträge zur vergleichenden Mythologie aus der Hagada," *Zeitschrift der deutschen Morgenländischen Gesellschaft* 31 (1877): 277.
171 On this aspect, see Gerald Blidstein, "A Roman Gift of Straena to the Patriarch Judah II," in *Israel Exploration Journal* 22 (1972): 150–152.

The idea behind this is likely the understanding that greeting the gentile in his home is an active participation in the festival or holiday. It is not possible to suspect participation of this sort if in a Jewish home. There the greeting is reduced to what it is, requesting for the well-being of the gentile in the year now beginning.

We know of presents through Jerusalem Talmud, 'Avodah Zarah 1:1 (39b):

> A *ducenarius* [highest ranking provincial procurator, later only mentioned as a title] once sent a disk [δίσκος] to Rabbi Yudan the Prince, full of denarii and as a present for the festival. [The rabbi] took [one denar], and sent the rest [back]. Then he questioned Rabbi Shim'on ben Laqish [about it] who said: Throw the profit [this denar] into the sea of salt.

The Babylonian Talmud, 'Avodah Zarah 6a, tells the story quite differently:

> On his holiday, a *min* once sent an Emperor-Denar to Rabbi Yehudah ha-Nasi. Resh Laqish sat before him. He said to Resh Laqish: What am I supposed to do? If I accept it, he will go on and thank [his deity]. If I do not accept it, he will harbor enmity against me.
> Resh Laqish answered: Take it, and throw it into the well when he is present.
> He said: This will definitely cause enmity against me.
> I meant, with the back of the hand.

Blidstein had convincingly argued that the object of discussion was the so-called *straenae*, the present on occasion of the *kalendae Ianuarii*. Not only does the term באידו (on his, the *min's*, holiday) in the passage of the Babylonian Talmud point to this direction, but also the loanword *discus* in Yerushalmi. It was a Roman custom to give away, as a present, a plaque with the inscription *Annum novum, Annum faustum*.

R. Yehudah is in fact doubly troubled and thus discusses the matter with Resh Laqish in the Babylonian Talmud-version: first, of course, he is worried to offend the gentile if he refuses the present. Second, however, he is worried to accept a gift on the occasion of an idolatrous holiday and thus tacitly accept idolatry.[172] The advice Resh Laqish offers is worthy of a Solomon's: R. Yehudah avoids any transgression through a little deceit, *and* keeps the peace, which is the message of the entire festival.

The present for New Year's Day was an important aspect of the festivities and has survived to this day in some regions. As a side note: when I grew up

---

[172] See this episode in Bereshit Rabbah 78:12: "A woman presented a bowl and a knife to the patriarch. The patriarch only took the knife; the bowl was taken by the Roman: '[he came], he saw it, [and] he liked it and took it." In these three verbs, Lieberman sees a parody of *veni, vidi, vici*. Saul Lieberman, *Texts and Studies* (New York: Ktav, 1974), 143 [note 216]. On this, see also Stemberger, *Die römische Herrschaft*, 117.

in southern Italy, we received presents for New Year's Day, typically coins. In Calabria's dialect, those are *'rina*, a corruption of the Latin *straena*. Anyway, R. Yehuda's story can be interpreted as a confirmation of a practice which likely had found support among the people, and it shows the close evidence according to which a Roman sent a present to a Jew on the occasion of a Roman holiday. The present in our little story is not only important for the emphasis on interpersonal relations, but also for its economic implications. To buy and sell presents is one of the main activities during the annual market on the occasion of the *saturnalia*.

3.2.8 The Rabbinic Explanations of the Origin of the Kalendae

The Jerusalem Talmud provides two explanations of the origin of the *kalendae*. One associates the Roman festival of the new year with the Jewish festival of the new year, Rosh ha-Shanah. The second explanation almost historicises it by linking its introduction to a decree of the Romans.

On the mythical explanation: the Roman festival of *kalendae Ianuarii* did not simply celebrate the beginning of the year, but also the return of the sun. Jerusalem Talmud, 'Avodah Zarah 1:2 (39c) also connects the *kalendae* with the intensifying sunlight. Here creation is a further motif.

> Rav said:
> The festival of *kalendae*[173] was set by the first human. When he saw that the night became longer, he said: Woe is me! Maybe this is the one of whom is written: He will bruise thy head, and thou will bruise his heel [Genesis 3:15]. And he said: The darkness shall envelop me [Psalms 139:11].[174]

---

173 קלנדס, loanword from Latin *calendae*. See Krauss, *Griechische und lateinische Lehnwörter*, 546.
174 The fear of the first man (*Adam ha-Rishon*) of the night is mentioned in another passage of Talmud Yerushalmi, Berachot 8:5 (12b): "*The Fire:* R. Levi said in the name of R. Bezira: The light, which was created on the first day of creation, served for 36 hours, 12 hours before the Shabbat, 12 hours for the night [belonging to] Shabbat, and 12 hours for Shabbat itself; in this light, the first man could see from one corner of the world to the other. Because the light had not ceased to shine, the entire world began to sing hymns of praise, as it is written: *He, whose glory [reaches] the farthest corners of the earth, lets it ring under all the sky* [Job 37:3]. When the end of Shabbat drew near, darkness began to fall; then Adam became frightened and told himself: this is what the scripture mentions when saying: *He will bruise thy head, and thou will bruise his heel* [Genesis 3:15]. Maybe it is coming to bite me, as it is written: *The darkness shall envelop me* [Psalms 139:11]. R. Levi said: On this hour, the Lord, be He blessed, took two stones of gravel and struck one against the other. From this there appeared a flame of light; that is what the scriptures mean when mentioning: *But the night shineth as the day* [Psalms 139:11]. After this, he spoke the benediction: He who creates the lights of fire. Shmu'el said: It is for

When the [first men finally] saw that the days were growing longer again, he said: *qalendas* [which means]: oh my, the day! And this is in accordance with the [scholar] who said that the world was created in [the month of] Tishri; but according to the [scholar] who said the world had been created in Nissan, the [first man had had to] know [that].

Rabbi Yose be-Rabbi Bun said: He who claims that the world had been created on New Year's Day, was Rav. Because in the liturgy for New Year from Rav's school, the [following prayer] has been taught: This day is the beginning of your work, a remembrance of the first day [because it is a law for Israel and a right unto the God of Jacob]. [Accordingly,] it is [to say]: the world had been created on New Year's Day.

The etymology of the term *kalendae* in Hebrew requires some attention: דיא קאלון. Some attempts have been made for identifying this loanword. Typically, it is seen as a contraction of the following elements: the Greek word καλόν – for "oh my!," "how marvellous!" – and the Latin dies/day. As such it is "oh my, the day!," or "what a beautiful day!"[175] This explanation dates back to Mussafia. David Cohen de Lara identifies דיא as διός.[176] Max Grünbaum, on the other hand, is reminded of a popular linguistic form of "day" in connection to ενδιος ευδιος.[177]

However the etymology of the word might be interpreted, we are left with the conclusion that the rabbis used the term *kalendae* in a positive sense, namely for a beautiful day. It was the day on which the light of the sun returns. The two models for explanation, a subject for discussion here, are thus present-

---

this reason that we speak the benediction upon the fire at the end of Shabbat, because it is [the light of fire] which was created at this point. R. Huna [said] in the name of R. Abbahus [who said] in the name of R. Yohanan: At the end of Yom Kippur, too, a benediction is to be said upon [the light of fire], because the light had rested for the whole day [At Yom Kippur, it is forbidden to light a light]." The literary topos of human fear whether or not the sun will ever rise again finds its counterpart in Roman literature, such as Lucretius, V, 975:
"A parvis quod enim consuerant cernere semper / Alterno tenebras et lucem tempore gigni / Non erat ut fieri posset mirarier umquam / Nec diffidere, ne terras aeterna teneret / Nox in perpetuum detracto lumine solis."
    From childhood wont
    Ever to see the dark and day begot
    In times alternate, never might they be
    Wildered by wild misgiving, lest a night
    Eternal should possess the lands, with light
    Of sun withdrawn forever
English translation from *T. Lucreti Cari De rerum natura libri sex*, edited by William E. Leonard and Stanley B. Smith (Madison, Wis: Univ. of Wisconsin Press, 1968).
175 See Blaufuss, *Römische Feiertage*, 7.
176 David Cohen de Lara, עיר דוד *Sive De Convenientia Vocabulorum Rabbinicorum cum Græcis, [et] quibusdam aliis linguis Europæis* (Amsterdam: Ravesteinius, 1648), s. v.
177 Grünbaum, "Beiträge zur vergleichenden Mythologie," 276–277.

ed.[178] According to Rav, the world had been created in the month of Tishri. He concludes the following order: creation of the world, longer night, shorter day; with the winter solstice: longer day, shorter night. Thus, Adam's joy is explained when the days grew longer again after mid-winter. According to the second explanation – namely that Adam set the *kalendae* for the Nissan, the month of spring – the following alternative order appears: creation of the world, longer day, shorter night; with the summer solstice: shorter day and longer night. If the world had been created in the first Jewish month, Nissan, "Adam should have been aware" that the day was growing longer.

The two models of explanation reveal the rabbis' purpose: they wanted to use the meaning of the gentile New Year's Day for the Jewish calendar. However, the *kalendae* was not the festival of light. That symbolism was associated with the *saturnalia*. This misconception is based on the fact that the *kalendae* gained high ground over the *saturnalia*, coming to predominate. With this misconception, we may explain the order of festivals as presented in Mishnah, 'Avodah Zarah 1:2 (first *kalendae*, then *saturnalia*), as well as the dictum of Rav in the Jerusalem Talmud, 'Avodah Zarah 1:2 (39c): "The *kalendae* occur eight days before winter solstice, and the *saturnalia* eight days after [winter] solstice." In fact, it is the other way around *and saturnalia* was celebrated on the occasion of the solstice. Babylonian Talmud, 'Avodah Zarah 6a thus takes a more thorough approach, and also attributes to Adam the invention of the *saturnalia*.[179]

On the polemics against Roman rule: a second explanation for setting the calendar is found in the Jerusalem Talmud, 'Avodah Zarah 1:2 (39c) in the name of Rabbi Yoḥanan:

> R. Yoḥanan did not hold that same opinion [of Rav], but [suggested the following origin of the *kalendae*]: the kingdom of Egypt, and the kingdom of Rome were at war with one another. They said [to each other]: How long are we going to kill one another in battle[180] Come and let us make a rule that whichever kingdom will say to its chief general: Fall on your sword [and kill yourself], and [whose general] will listen to that command – [that kingdom] will seize the power [over both of us] first! The Egyptian [general] did not listen to them. The [general] of Rome was a certain old man with the name of Januarius [Yanubris]. He had twelve sons. [They, i.e., someone] said to him: If you will listen to us [and fall on your sword], we shall make your sons commanders,[181] prefects[182], and generals![183]

---

178 This is based on the traditional explanations as transmitted in the commentaries of the Yerushalmi. On this, see Wewers, *Avoda Zara*, 10, note 57.
179 See Babylonian Talmud, 'Avodah Zarah 8a.
180 פולמוס, Greek loanword: πόλεμος.
181 דוכוסין, Greek loanword from Latin dux, pl. duces.
182 איפרכין, Greek loanword from Ἔπαρχος.
183 איסטליטין, Greek loanword from στρατηλάτης.

> So he listened to them [and fell on his sword]. Thus then did [his sons] cry out for him: קלנדס יינובריס (qalendas Yanubris, Lat. *kalendae Ianuarii*)! From this day on, they mourned for him: the black day.[184]

This explanation is not evidenced elsewhere. Yet, individual elements of this story can be compared to topoi in Greco-Roman literature. Thus the rabbis had a greater knowledge of this literature than it is commonly thought today. Let us look at these topoi.

3.2.8.1 Topos 1: Yanubris and the Calendar

The origin of the *kalendae*, as offered here, is based on a mythical event of Roman history. It apparently reflects the connection of the Roman god Janus with the *kalendae Ianuarii* – together with the historical reminiscence that Rome could prevail over Egypt in questions of the calendar as well. January, the first month of the year since Numa (the second of the Roman kings), does in fact take its name from the war god Janus.[185] Janus was set on a par with Mars as *Janus Quirinus*, and twelve altars were dedicated to him in Rome.[186] They represented the twelve months of the calendar,[187] and were represented by the twelve sons in this passage of the Jerusalem Talmud. The gates of Janus's temple remained open during times of war, which can explain another element in the story, namely the continuous war.

3.2.8.2 Topos 2: A Black Day

The phrase μέλαινα ἡμέρα – "black day," or *dies ater*, in Latin – stands in clear relation to the Roman calendar of festivities as well. The second day of the *kalendae*, the *dies postridiamus*, was seen as *dies ater* in regard to waging war. According to Macrobius, this attribution of a "characterisation of days" dated back to a regulation of the College of Pontiffs (*collegium pontificum*) in 363 BCE[188] At that time, the continuous failures of the Roman army raised ques-

---

[184] מילני אימירא, Greek μέλαινα ημέρα. I have taken the English translation from Peter Schäfer, "Jews and Gentiles in Yerushalmi Avodah Zara," in *The Talmud Yerushalmi and Graeco-Roman Culture*, vol. 3, ed. Peter Schäfer and Catherine Hezser (Tübingen: Mohr Siebeck, 2002), 340.
[185] Macrobius, *Saturnalia* I:13,3: "Ac de duobus priorem Ianuarium nuncupavit primumque anni esse voluit."
[186] Johann B. Keune, "Janus," in *Paulys Real-Encyclopädie der classischen Alterthumswissenschaften* Suppl. III (1918), col. 1181.
[187] Varrus, *Antiquitates*; quoted in Macrobius, *Saturnalia* I:9,16.
[188] Macrobius, *Saturnalia* I:16,22 et seq.

tions about the underlying reasons for such defeats. The *haruspex* Lucius Aquinius concluded that the Romans were defeated repeatedly because they had waged war on days that had immediately followed a holiday. Since then, every day was termed "black day" if it came after *kalendae, nonae*, and *ides*.

3.2.8.3 Topos 3: The Voluntary Death of a King

The topos of the voluntary death of a commander – who thus brings victory to his people – is known through Greek and Roman sources. We might refer to the legend of Κόδρος/Codrus, Athens' last king, and Consul P. Decius Mus who committed suicide in 295 BCE.[189] It is known of Codrus that the forces of Peloponnese had waged war against Athens during his reign. The oracle of Delphi had divined that they would only conquer the city if they did not kill the king, Codrus. Codrus, however, learned of this divination. He dressed as a beggar and left the city. He then met two enemies and began quarreling with them. He killed one, and allowed the other to kill him. When the people of Athens demanded back the corpse of the king, the forces of Peloponnese realised what had happened and immediately ended the siege of the city.[190]

There is a tale that the father and grandfather of Publius Decius Mus had given their lives for Rome. The enemy soldier learned at the Battle of Ausculum against King Pyrrhus of Epirus that Decius sought to follow his brave ancestors, and wished to sacrifice himself for the victory.[191] This news created unrest among them as they all feared that "through his death, they would all be annihilated" (... ἐκφοβούντων ὡς ἐκ του θανεῖν ἐκεῖνον πάντως ἀπολουμένους). Phyrrus attempted to boost his men's morale through the remark that "neither a man who dies can overwhelm the many, nor can charms and magic prevail against weapons and men."[192]

---

189 The only scholar to point to this fact is Israel Lewy. Israel Lewy, "Über die Spuren des griechischen und römischen Alterthums im talmudischen Schriftthum," in *Verhandlungen der 33. Versammlung Deutscher Philologen und Schulmänner* (Leipzig: Teubner, 1878), 83.
190 See the more detailed description in Karl Scherling, "Kodros," in *Paulys Real-Encyclopädie der classischen Alterthumswissenschaften* XI/1 (1921), 984–994; see also Jon Hesk, *Deception and Democracy in Classical Athens* (Cambridge, UK, New York, NY: Cambridge University Press, 2000), 89–102 and passim.
191 According to Dio Cassius X (fragment from Zonaras 8:5): ὁ Δέκιος ἐπιδοῦναι ἑαυτὸν κατὰ τὸν πατέρα καὶ τὸν πάππον.
192 See Dio Cassius, *Dio's Roman History*, trans. Earnest Cary and Herbert B. Foster (Cambridge, Mass.: Harvard University Press, 1914), 351. On this, see Friedrich Münzer, "Decius," in *Paulys Real-Encyclopädie der classischen Alterthumswissenschaften* IV/2 (1901), col. 2285.

The suicide of the king which is interpreted as a victory clearly has a negative connotation: the *kalendae* is a black day on which one is supposed to mourn. Moreover, it was not so much a day of mourning for the Romans themselves – they had achieved the dominance of the then known world – but rather for the other peoples who had lost their autonomy. Thus, it becomes clearer what Rabbi Yudan added to the story in Jerusalem Talmud, 'Avodah Zarah 1:2 (39c): "He said: he who sows peas on this day will not see them thrive." Peas were eaten during the days of mourning; dishes with peas in them were mourning dishes *par excellence*.[193] The Babylonian explanation for that is very vivid, but might be too rationalistic: In the Babylonian Talmud, Baba Batra 16b we read:

> Why peas? (Because) peas do not have a mouth – and the one who mourns has no mouth. Another explanation [is]: Why peas? [Peas] roll, so does the time of mourning.[194]

Thus, for Jews, the festival of *kalendae* is simply a time for mourning which is supposed to "roll" away as soon as possible.

3.2.8.4 The Kalendae: A Detail?

One may wonder why the rabbis had discussed the *kalendae* so thoroughly. There are several reasons for this interest.

1. The most important reason seems to be the contemporary political situation. Despite the fact that the rabbis had continued using the Jewish calendar at least for liturgical reasons, they had to grant the Roman calendar more than only brief attention. Everything was dependent on the Roman calendar: political and military life, as well as commerce with the gentiles. The ignorance of the *kalendae Ianuarii* would have grave consequences for the survival of the Jewish community.

2. It is proof for more than an involuntary acceptance of their own subordination: on the one hand, they present a very positive explanation for the origin of the word "*kalendae*" – as the "beautiful day" of the creation of light; on the other, they provide a quite negative one as the "black day" of Yanubris. The Jewish population had likely adjusted to the loss of political

---

193 Jerusalem Talmud, Berachot 3:1 (6a); Bereshit Rabbah 66:14; Pesikta Rabbati 12:4; *Paulys Real-Encyclopädie der classischen Alterthumswissenschaften* 35:1; *Yalqut toledot* § 110.
194 Other sources in Arthur Marmorstein, "Comparisons between Greek and Jewish Religious Customs and Popular Usages," in *Occident and Orient: Being Studies in Semitic Philology and Literature, Jewish History and Philosophy and Folklore in the Widest Sense – In Honour of Haham Dr. M. Gaster's 80th Birthday*, ed. Bruno Schindler (London: Taylor's Foreign Press, 1936), 419.

autonomy, and probably celebrated this or that festivity with the victors. But not everything went smoothly. We can imagine the existence of two parties among the Jewish intellectuals: one rabbinic party tried to polemically resist in adapting the Jewish tradition to the Roman culture and oppressive government by claiming that the Roman Empire had not had a glorious but rather very dark and sad beginning (suicide). By contrast, the other party put forward pragmatic criteria in order to adopt the Roman calendar. Implicitly and explicitly following this political turning point, they claimed hermeneutically that it was not the Romans who had established the *kalendae Ianuarii* but rather Adam. In plain text, this means that Jews might celebrate the *kalendae* without risking having likewise to adapt to other customs and mores of the Roman rulers. Or, to see it historically, the rabbis had adapted the Roman celebration of the New Year's Day to Jewish practice because it was a way of political acculturalisation.

3.2.9 Saturnalia and Sigillaria

The *saturnalia* were celebrated from December 17 to December 23.[195] Despite the fact that the festival lasted for seven days, the actual period of festivities – on which none engaged in legal practice – was shortened to three days since the time of Emperor Augustus. Emperor Caligula added another day.[196] On December 17, the *saturnalia* began with a *sacrificium publicum* and a public feast – *convivium publicum* – before the temple of Saturn. Both were concluded with the cry "*Io saturnalia.*"[197]

Schools were closed on these three or four days of the holiday, war was postponed, and no death sentence was carried out. There was a private cele-

---

195 See the more detailed discussion in Hendrik S. Versnel, "Saturnus and the Saturnalia," in Versnel, *Inconsistencies in Greek and Roman Religion*, vol 2: *Transition and Reversal in Myth and Ritual* (Leiden et al.: Brill, 1993), 136–227.
196 Macrobius, *Saturnalia* I:10,24. On Caligula's addition, see Suetonius, *Caligula*, 17; Martin P. Nilsson, "Saturnalia," in *Paulys Real-Encyclopädie der classischen Alterthumswissenschaften* II.A,1 (1921), 201 et seq.
197 See Tenentius Varro, 6.23: "Saturnalia dicta ab Saturno, quod eo die feriae eius, ut post diem tertium Opalia Opis." Macrobius, *Saturnalia*, I:10,18: "quo solo die apud aedem Saturni convivio dissoluto Saturnalia clamitabantur." *Historia Augusta*, on Tacitus [M. Claudius Tacitus Augustus, 275–276] IX,5: "addidit ut Aurelianum omnes pictum haberent. divorum templum fieri iussit, in quo essent suis et Parilibus [festival of shephards for the deity Pales, later celebrated as the birthday of Rome itself] et kalendis Ianuariis et votis libamina ponerentur." The *Votorum Nuncupatio* was celebrated on January 3, when wishes for the well-being of the emperor were accepted.

bration at which a piglet was sacrificed. During meals, it was the custom to first serve the slaves who enjoyed a brief respite of liberty during these days. The last day of the *saturnalia* was the *sigillaria* at which little figurines made of clay or dough, the so-called sigillaria, were given out as presents. According to the *Historia Augusta*, Emperor Hadrian used to surprise his friends with presents on the occasion of *saturnalia* and *sigillaria*.[198] The *sigillaria* were followed by several days on which the market was open.[199]

Hebrew and "Roman" "Etymologies"
The rabbinic explanation of the term "*saturnalia*" itself presents some peculiarities. In Babylonian Talmud, ʿAvodah Zarah 8a, the festival is called סטרנורא. According to Max Grünbaum, this is not an error, but intentional and a reference to סטר נורא ("the light which is hidden"). Jerusalem Talmud, ʿAvodah Zarah 39c noted different etymologies which related not so much to the solstice but rather to the political aspect of the festival. The name of the holiday is interpreted as "hidden hatred" – שנאה טמונה. The redactor added, in reference to Gen 27:41 ("And Esau hated Jacob"), "hating, vengeful, resentful one." The Talmud derived these explanations through the exegetic methodology of Notarikon: סטם – "to be hostile to" – becomes סונא, נוטר, נוקם.[200] The political references become more apparent if one reads the message of R. Yiṣḥaq be-Rabbi Leazar which had been transmitted to this context: "In Rome, [the Jews] call this [day] *sanaṭoraya* of Esau." To identify the word *saturnalia* as *sanaṭoraya* presents us with a curiosity: it is the loanword for *senatores*.[201]

The *saturnalia* used to be a predominantly agricultural celebration for the common people, a kind of carnival, when slaves enjoyed freedom for a day (*Saturnalibus tota servis licentia permittitur*), and were able to speak their minds to their masters without risking punishment.[202] The *senatores* mentioned had little to do with it. During the time of the Caesars, there was a custom to replace the Emperor with a "carnival prince," the *Saturnalicius prin-*

---

[198] David Magie, ed. and trans., *Scriptores historiae Augustae* vol. 1 (Cambridge, Mass.: Harvard University Press, 1921), 52: "saturnalicia et sigillaricia frequenter amicis inopinantibus misit et ipse ab his libenter accepit et alia invicem dedit. ad deprehendendas obsonatorum fraudes cum plurimis sigmatibus pasceret, fercula de aliis mensis etiam ultimis sibi iussit adponi. omnes reges muneribus suis vicit."
[199] Macrobius, *Saturnalia* I:10,24: "sed Sigillariorum adiecta celebritas in septem dies discursum publicum et laetitiam religionis extendit."
[200] On this, see Wewers, *Avoda Zara*, 12, note 74.
[201] See also Bereshit Rabbah 67:8.
[202] Macrobius, *Saturnalia*, I:10; Horace, *Satirae* II,7. On this, see André, *Griechische Feste*, 136.

ceps, for the duration of this time of "carnival."²⁰³ This "carnival prince" was later expelled by the *refugium*.²⁰⁴ The rabbinic literature does not mention this at first glance.

A more thorough analysis, however, reveals what might have been the "senatores," or better, the "senatoria." It likely was a reference to the *senatoria* (*dignitas*), the dignity of the senator's office – exactly what the *saturnalia* did not wish to express. The celebration was an opportunity for the people to release tension, and during which the ridiculous and the non-dignified became the dignified. It was a kind of controllable and ritualised rebellion of those who were impotent at other times. The saying *not semper Saturnalia erant*, the *saturnalia* are not celebrated at all times, was a reminder not to forget the reality during the celebration.²⁰⁵ If the rabbis had in mind the *dignitas senatoria* when speaking of the *sanaṭoraya of Edom*, their references are not meant ironically, but sarcastically. The *saturnalia* represent the ridicule of Roman might and dignity; they thus become the impersonation of *romana insanitas*.

Babylonian Tradition

Other elements are present in the representations of the Babylonian Talmud. A festival has to be celebrated on the 1ˢᵗ of the month of Ṭevet according to Mishnah, Ta'anit 4. According to Babylonian Talmud, 'Avodah Zarah 8a, the mythical *Adam ha-Rishon* had celebrated *tequfat ṭevet* for eight days, after he had fasted for eight days at the beginning of *tequfat tammuz*.²⁰⁶ This is the mythologisation of the beginning of winter and summer.²⁰⁷ The sacralisation of the seasons was presented in two other parallel traditions: the four-day lamentation of Israel's girls for the sacrifice of Jephthah's daughter (Judges 11:40) at the beginning of *Ṭevet*; and the cyclic transformation of water to blood (according to Exodus 7:14, see Midrash, Leqaḥ Ṭov on shemot 8:10).²⁰⁸ There is

---

203 Publius Papinius Statius, *Silvae* 1.6.82
"tollunt innumeras ad astra voces
Saturnalia principis sonantes,
et dulci dominum favore clamant:
hoc solum vetuit licere Caesar."
204 André, *Griechische Feste*, 136.
205 Seneca, *Apocolocyntosis* 12.2–3: "ex his unus, cum uidisset capita conferentes et fortunas suas deplorantes causidicos, accedit et ait: 'dicebam uobis: non semper Saturnalia erunt." See also Versnel, "Saturnus and the Saturnalia," 163.
206 See also Babylonian Talmud, Shabbat 129a and Mark Geller, review of *Astral Magic in Babylonia*, by Erica Reiner, *Orientalische Literaturzeitung* 93 (1998): 456–457.
207 See, however, Meir Friedmann, *Onkelos und Akylas* (Vienna: Lippe, 1896), 20–21.
208 On this, see Avigdor/Victor, Aptowitzer, "Issur shetiyat mayim be-sha'at ha-tequfa," *Ha-Zofeh me-Erez Hagar* 2 (1912): 122–126; Louis Ginzberg, *The Legends of the Jews*, vol. 6 (Philadelphia: Jewish Publication Society of America, 1969), 203–204, note 109.

little reason to think that these traditions reflect the Roman *saturnalia* other than that they were celebrated at the beginning of the month of Ṭevet. Over the course of time, they then became a mythical-magical lamentation in the Jewish Aggada – and it was reinterpreted as fasting in a kind of "demonisation of foreign holidays."[209]

The Banquet

Both *kalendae* and *saturnalia* were the occasions for a banquet, as we have noted above. Eating habits, and thus banquets, are the most profound reflections of the acceptance or rejection of foreign customs. This was true in antiquity as it is true today. They are a part of everyday life, but also an expression of the *feriae*, that is, special times at which work had to rest. They are a reflection of society and a gauge for its tolerance, economic success, morale, political customs or decadence. The meal was also a social moment, an event during which there was a socialisation of closed societies. The pressure and the responsibility to accept or decline an invitation were considerable. The Jerusalem Talmud reflects this fact when recommending the following as a norm, in 'Avodah Zarah 1:3 (39c):

> The [Jewish] inhabitants of Gader[210] asked R. Ammi: Is one allowed to [attend] the banquet of the gentiles? He argued it was possible to allow them that [for the sentence] "for the sake of peace."
> R. Ba told him: Yet R. Ḥiyya taught: The day of a banquet with the gentiles is forbidden. R. Ammi said [to this]: If it had not been for R. Ba, we would have allowed their idolatry. The sublime one may be blessed, however, that he has kept us from doing so.[211]

The inhabitants of Gader, who lived at the border of Eretz Yisrael,[212] asked whether they were allowed to attend the banquets of the gentiles with whom they apparently were in social contact. The reply was clear: the permission to do so would be tantamount to a permit for idolatry. Of course, it is impossible to learn from this Halakha whether the people had indeed followed the direct-

---

209 The reference is made in the article by Matitjahu Mieses. Unfortunately, he did not discuss the *saturnalia*, and basically concentrated on the Shabbat. See Matitjahu Mieses, "Die Dämonisierung fremder Feiertage: Die Umkehrung heidnischer Dekadenendtage durch die Hebräer," *Jahrbuch für jüdische Volkskunde* 26/27 (1925): 292–306.
210 On the form, see Reeg, *Die Ortsnamen Israels*, 167–168.
211 See also Jerusalem Talmud, Demai 4,6 (24a/71–74). Wewer's translated (into German), "that he kept away [the gentiles]." What is meant is not the gentiles but their idolatrous practises ('*avodah zarah*).
212 See Tosefta, 'Eruvin 6:13; Jerusalem Talmud, 'Eruvin 5:1 (22d) and Babylonian Talmud, 'Eruvin 22ab.

ive of R. Ba. It is more likely that R. Ammi's reply was closer to actual lived reality. There is some evidence available for this, as we know that Jewish banquets had been significantly influenced by the Greco-Roman model. But we cannot delve into the matter any further here.[213]

3.2.10 Κράτησις

The Mishnah[214] mentions a festival called קרטסים.[215] It is typically rendered as κράτησις. Modern scholarship offers two explanations for this holiday. The first relies on several papyri from the 1st century CE and dated as τῆς Καίσαρος κρατήσεως. This was likely the date when Emperor Augustus entered Alexandria on August 1st, 30 BCE[216] The second explanation refers to a usage of the 3rd century, according to which κράτησις is an emperor's accession to the throne. If we follow this, the festivals referred to would be the *dies imperii*, or *natalis imperii*, which was celebrated on April 16.

Blaufuss and Krauss follow this second interpretation. According to them, Tosefta confirms it in 'Avodah Zarah 1:4. There a sentence appears in a list *before* קרטסים. יום שאחז בו את המלכות "the day of empowering, qratesim." The suffix of plural may indicate the "empowering(s)" of several emperors. Although it is a historical fact that every emperor celebrated his own accession to the throne, it is difficult to see κράτησις being rooted in this. It is not substantiated beyond doubt that the term קרטסים and the phrase יום שאחז בו את המלכות were used synonymously in the passage of Tosefta. Under no circumstances is it wise to read the second sentence as an explanation of the loanword, since it stands *before* the first. Rather, it is probable that Tosefta referred to *both* festivals: the *natalis imperii* on April 16, and the *dies imperatoris*.

---

213 On this, see Siegfried Stein, "The Influence of Symposia Literature on the Literary Form of the Pesa Haggadah," *Journal of Jewish Studies* 7 (1957) 13–44; Liliane Vana, "Les relations sociales entre juifs et païens à l'époque de la Mishna: la question du banquet privé," *Revue des Sciences Religieuses* 71 (1997): 147–170.
214 See Adolf Schulten, "Dies imperii," in *Paulys Real-Encyclopädie der classischen Alterthumswissenschaften* I/9 (1903), 477–478.
215 The form of this loanword has been debated for quite a while: whether there is a ם or a ס at the end. See the *status questionis* in Hadas-Lebel, *Le Paganisme à travers les sources rabbiniques*, 431.
216 *Berliner griechische Urkunden* (Berlin 1985), 175; mentioned in Hadas-Lebel, *Le Paganisme à travers les sources rabbiniques*, 431; Dio Cassius LI:19,6; Lieberman, *Greek in Jewish Palestine*, 10. See also the references and sources there.

Jerusalem Talmud, 'Avodah Zarah 39c offers the following perspective of interpretation in this context:

> This is the day on which Rome received the rule.
> Have you not learned it before?
> Rabi be-Rabbi Bun said: The empowering has happened twice.[217]

The Gemara refers to the festival of *kalendae* where there is also mention of a celebration on the occasion a Roman ascended to power. Babylonian Talmud, 'Avodah Zarah 8b identifies this ascension with the one during the days of Cleopatra, and under the Greeks:

> Rome has been empowered twice: once in the days of [Egyptian] Queen Cleopatra [VII. Philopator, 69–30 BCE], and once in the days of the Greeks. Then, that is to say, Rav Dimi came [to Babylon], and said: There were 32 battles the Romans had waged against the Greeks and could not conquer them until they had allied with Israel.[218]

The empowering under the Greeks that this text mentions, when Romans and Jews became allies, likely refers to the Maccabean era, as Stemberger, for instance, argues. However, the second empowering remains unclear. Yerushalmi's Gemara mentions the *kalendae*, and thus the story of Yanubris. As we have discussed before, it is a legend with a mythological-magical dimension, and it assigned the victory over Egypt to the death of the king. In this context, however, it is important to also note a special ritual which was connected to both saturnalia and *kalendae*: a person, typically a criminal, was named "king" and executed at the end of the celebrations. We might also identify this ritual in the story concerning Jesus being crowned king as told in the New Testament.[219] In this case, however, it is again an ironic-sarcastic reference to the villainous might of Rome.

It is rather probable that the Talmud refers to the date τῆς Καίσαρος κρατήσεως, that is, when Augustus entered Alexandria. The temporal description "under Cleopatra" in this context is thus the representation for the annexation of Egypt after the Battle of Actium. Victory in that battle marked the "empowering" of Rome over the eastern half of the empire.[220]

---

217 See also Babylonian Talmud, 'Avodah Zarah 8b and Stemberger, *Die römische Herrschaft*, 61.
218 With my translation, I follow the German one in Stemberger, *Römische Herrschaft*, 61.
219 On this, see Stefan Weinstock, "Saturnalien und Neujahrsfest in den Märtyreracten," in *Mullus. Festschrift Theodor Klauser*, ed. Alfred Hermann and Alfred Stuiber (Münster in Westfalen: Aschendorff, 1964), 391–400.
220 See Stemberger, *Römische Herrschaft*, 63.

3.2.11 Feriae Imperatoris

The memorial days for Julius Caesar and Augustus were made *feriae publicae* and thus entered the calendar of holidays through a decision by the senate (*feriae ex s[enatus] c[onsulto] quod eo die* etc.). As a consequence, the old calendar, which had not been altered for some time prior to this, was again changed in respect to festivals/holidays.[221] The same occurred later for emperors who became *divi*.[222] It is not surprising that the rabbis note two days of the emperor in their listing of holidays. In the province, the soldiers in particular celebrated the emperor's birthdays, those of the emperor's relatives, and the days when the Caesars ascended to the throne – the patriotic holidays. This fact is evidenced by a military calendar from Dura Europos for the years 223–227.[223] Tosefta presupposes this when writing: "The γενέσια, the day of each king. The king [belongs] to the public as an individual. Even his day of marriage and the day he became a commander [belong to the public]."

3.2.12 Birthday and Day of Death

The list of the Mishnah and the parallel traditions mention at this place the גנוסיא, which is usually rendered as γενέσια. In classical Greek, the term was τα γενέθλια – the day of birth. Γενέσια corresponded to the Latin *natalis* (*dies*). The passage in the Mishnah has some difficulties: following יום גנוסיא של מלכים, it continues as "the day of birth and the day of death." The sentence probably has to be understood as a specification: the *genesia* of the king is the celebration of his birthday and his day of death. In classical Greek, τα γενέθλια or γενέσια refer to the birthday of a deceased person – Herodot had emphasised that this was a Greek custom.[224] If one was to consider that the celebration of the emperor's day of death was also the celebration of his ascension to the world of *divi*, it is likely that the *genesia* had kept this meaning in Roman culture. The Roman calendar had incorporated the birthday of Caesar only after his death.[225]

---

221 Dio Cassius XLVIII,18,5; Wissowa, *Religion und Kultus der Römer*, 343 et seq.
222 Wissowa, *Religion und Kultus der Römer*, 365–381.
223 On this, see Robert O. Fink, Allan Hoey, and Walther F. Snyder, "The Feriale Duranum," *Yale Classical Studies* 7 (1940): 1–222; Beard and North, Price, *Religions of Rome*, vol. 2, 71–74.
224 Herodot, *Historiae* 4:26,7: παῖς δὲ πατρὶ τοῦτο ποιέει, κατά περ Ἕλληνες τὰ γενέσια.
225 Dio Cassius 47:18.

Texts of the 1st century predominantly mention γενέσια in the meaning of a birthday celebration for a person who is alive. We also know this from the New Testament, Mark 6:21, where it reads: ὅτε Ἡρῴδης τοῖς γενεσίοις αὐτοῦ δεῖπνον ἐποίησεν τοῖς μεγιστᾶσιν αὐτοῦ καὶ τοῖς χιλιάρχοις καὶ τοῖς πρώτοις τῆς Γαλιλαίας ("On his birthday Herod gave a banquet for his high officials and military commanders and the leading men of Galilee"). The people celebrated the birthday of ruling emperors, as the inscriptions of Pergamon report, as well as their day of accession, as Babylonian Talmud, ʿAvodah Zarah 10a discusses in detail.[226] The literary sources, too, prove this custom. It was not only customary in Rome itself, but also in Egypt. In the 2nd century BCE, Poseidon mentions the birthday celebrations of Cleopatra; Philo of Alexandria mentions those of Pharao, etc.[227] The military calendar of Dura Europos, for instance, shows in particular the birthdays (of *divi* and *divae*), "empowering" and accession (Antony on February 4, Marcus Aurelius on March 13, Alexander Augustus on March 14, etc.), and *dies imperii* (April 21).

3.2.13 Apotheosis

Like the Mishnah, the Jerusalem Talmud also lists the day of death of an emperor as a public holiday. It reads:

> But, as it is written, thou shalt die in peace; and with the burnings of thy fathers ... so shall they make a burning for thee [Jeremy 34:5].

The Mishnah is to [be understood] in this way: When, in the case of death, there is fumigation and a burning, it is idolatry; and where there is no fumigation and burning, it is not idolatry.

The rabbis did not so much treat the day of death of the king as a description of a Roman holiday representing the apotheosis of the emperor. It was rather an exegetic problem. Tosefta, Shabbat 7:18 transmits the following tradition:

> They ignite a fire in honor [or: on the occasion] of kings' deaths.
> This is not the way of the Amorites.
> As it is said thou shalt die in peace; and with the burnings of thy fathers ... so shall they make a burning for thee [Jeremy 34:5].

---

226 On this, see Beard, North, and Price, *Religions of Rome*, vol. 2, 255.
227 Fragment 150.10 apud Diodorus 34/35,14; see also Diodorus Siculus, *Bibliotheca historica*, 34/35,14.1.12. Philo, *Joseph* 97:3.

As they ignite a fire in honor of kings, as they do in the case of *nesi'im*, but not in the case of a private person.
What is burnt? His bed and the objects of his use.
Ma'ase: When Rabban Gamli'el the Elder died, Onqelos the Proselyt ignited [in his honor] a fire worth more than seventy mane.²²⁸

This is a Midrash to I Samuel 32:12 and Jeremy 34:5. The rabbis seek to justify the biblical custom and to bring it up to date. I Samuel 31:12 clearly mentions the cremation of the king. The Targum to this passage adds: "they ignited a fire in their honor [literally, "for them"], as one would ignite a fire for kings." According to the rabbis, it was a salute. Other sources – Jerusalem Talmud, Sanhedrin 2:8 (20c) and Tosefta, Sanhedrin 4:2 – specify this even further: they burn the horse, the arm chair, the crown and the scepter, all objects he used. The problem was that cremation was seen as the "way of the Amorites."²²⁹ Babylonian Talmud, Sanhedrin 52b presents this tradition in another context:

> [*Mishna*] The procedure of decapitation consists of beheading him [the punished one] with a sword – the way the government typically proceeds. R. Yehudah says: This is a disgrace for him. [Rather] should his head be placed on a block and cut off with an axe. He was answered: There is no death more disgraceful than this.
>
> *Gemara*. It is taught. R. Yehudah told them, the Ḥakhamim: I know that there is no death more disgraceful than this [i.e., through an axe]. But, what am I supposed to do if Torah clearly states: *Ye shall not walk in their statutes* [Leviticus 18:3]?
>
> And the Rabbanan? Because [the execution by] the sword is already rooted in the biblical teachings, we have not adopted anything from them [the government].
>
> If you do not want to adopt [this conclusion, how do you explain] the teachings that one is allowed to burn in honor of kings and this is not seen as a way of the Amorites? How can we burn [if] it is written: *Ye shall not walk in their statutes* [Leviticus 18:3]? Burning is rooted in the biblical teaching, as it is written *thou shalt die in peace; and with the burnings of thy fathers ... so shall they make a burning for thee*. Thus, we have not adopted that [custom] from them [the Amorites].
>
> Neither have we adopted this [way of execution] from them, because [decapitating] by the sword is already rooted in the biblical teachings.

Decapitation by sword becomes a problem because the rabbis are reminded of the Roman practice. According to the tradition of the Mishnah, however, R. Yehudah perceived this form of execution as a disgrace. He would have preferred the execution by axe over execution by the sword. When following the Gemara, R. Yehudah questions the beheading by sword because it violates the

---

228 One *mane* was worth 100 denars in the first two centuries CE. See Daniel Sperber, *Roman Palestine, 200–400*, vol. 1: *Money and Prices* (Ramat-Gan: Bar-Ilan University, 1974), 35 et seq.
229 On this custom, see also Erwin Rohde, *Psyche: Seelencult und Unsterblichkeitsglaube der Griechen*, vol. 1 (Tübingen and Leipzig: Mohr, 1903), 24 et seq.

biblical principle of rejecting foreign customs. For the justification of an already updated custom – the fire as a *salute* to the king, rather than his cremation – the rabbis recur to the biblical teachings. Even a fire *saluting* the dead might be of gentile heritage and thus violates the principle from Leviticus 18:3.

While the passage of Tosefta is concerned with reserving for the Jewish princes – the *nesi'im*, – the same or similar rights as the "gentile" kings have, the Babylonian Talmud only discusses an exegetic question: Whether or not decapitation by sword and cremation can be identified with Roman, Amorite or foreign customs. In both cases, cremation is mentioned as a practice for the kings.

There is no doubt, of course, that it was a special day when the emperor died – not because his body was cremated. Typically, the day of death was also the day when the emperor became *divus*.[230] The cremation of his body – or a wax copy of it, as in the case of Pertinax in 193 CE – was a ceremony through which the emperor became immortal. This element, and not the fire itself, had likely caught the attention of the rabbis. It was, of course, an idolatrous act beyond any doubt to participate in the apotheosis of the emperor. The custom of cremation, however, was acceptable, since it was a way of honoring a king or ruler.

3.3 Conclusion

The rabbinic transmissions of Roman culture and religiosity are a precise representation of what the dominating power – Rome – believed in and celebrated at the periphery of the empire. It was also a representation of their military and religious practices. According to the sources we have at hand, the interest was limited to a discussion of elements which were concerned with ethics or Halakhah.

Yet, one may read between the lines and learn aspects of the social acceptance of the Roman way of life which the majority of Jews had probably adopted. When differentiating between the majority of the population and the minority of the rabbinic elite, I do not only rely on the rabbinic sources for the conclusions outlined at this point. Archeological findings have proven the existence of foreign cults in Palestine. The findings have by and large been evaluated. The question remains if these cults are only remnants of the Roman *colonia*, or whether they were indeed practiced among the Jewish population. The pene-

---

230 Beard, North, and Price, *Religions of Rome*, vol. 1, 206–210.

tration of Greco-Roman cults and views of the world into everyday life do not have to be limited to the astrological aspects of synagogue decoration. It affected every segment of life. Common customs, the ways of the Amorites, the world of science, medicine and astrology, the Roman holidays, theatre, bath culture, etc.: these are all part of this complex of transfer and influence.

If the rabbis had dedicated a large part of their teachings to idolatry, the practices of the strangers and their "sciences," this suggests that they were not solely seeking to combat the *hypothetical* threat of a "gentile" intrusion into the Jewish community. It shows that the intertwining of the foreign and one's own had progressed, and that foreign elements had already been absorbed into Jewish practice. There is a clear agenda when attempting to transfer the meaning of certain Roman holidays, such as *kalendae* and *saturnalia*, onto their own holidays: for instance, to create a mythological background for the Jewish New Year which was comparable to the Roman one. This tendency of Christianity to absorb and legitimate Greco-Roman holidays, such as Christmas and the like, is also visible in the rabbinic sources. However, the difference is that the rabbis had reinterpreted their calendar but had not adopted it.

It is justified to speak of a special rhetoric of the rabbinic ethics and community politics in this context. Rhetoric is not simply the art of speech and discourse in this sense. It is the (forensic) power of persuasion the rabbis had to display in order to present something new in an old wrapping, and to update the old. The new reality is reflected not only in the existence of foreign, Greco-Roman cults, but also in the contact with merchants, soldiers, administrators, and the rulers. This daily contact had created social ties for which the rabbis had to devise new categories. The strict refusal to enter the gentile's home for fear of idolatry led to social, economic, and political consequences that neither the individual nor the Jewish community wished to be burdened with. Attending a banquet on the occasion of holidays or weddings, etc. was not easy to avoid. In all likelihood, celebrating *kalendae* and *saturnalia* together, Jews and Romans, was more common than modern scholarship acknowledges. If R. Ammi allows socializing with the idolaters at a banquet "for the sake of peace," and R. Ba forbids it, it does not mean that the common Halakhah follows R. Ba. It means that there were two forms of the religious law. The instructions of the rabbinic tradition are not only a historical mirror of this period, even if it is *sui generis*, but also a "canonic" document for the generations to come. It was the clear intention of the Talmud's redactors to give the Talmud not only meaning for the contemporary generation but also for future ones. The rabbinic literature thus also had a normative function which the final redactors sought to emphasise by rendering the Halakhah anonymous, as well as by introducing a certain halakhic terminology like "another interpretation," or "some say," etc.

The rabbis present a practical-pragmatic attitude to "foreign" elements which have no connection with the Torah. This does not only hold true for astrology and medicine – the sciences of antiquity – but also for customs and holidays at the periphery of the Roman Empire. The rabbis allowed attending the theatre and the circus in order to witness the death of the victims, albeit for positive reasons. It shows the rabbinic willingness to accept the social, political, and religious dimension of contact with the strangers on the condition that it was achievable by means of a reinterpretation of one's own tradition.

The rabbis' thorough treatment of Roman holidays is evidence for the practice in the province. The reason the typical Roman holidays like *parilia*, *burmalia*, etc. have not been discussed here is simply based on one fact: Roman soldiers did not celebrate them in the periphery, like the province of *Iudaea*. However, *kalendae*, *saturnalia*, *sigillaria*, the birthday of Rome itself, and the *dies imperatoris* were part of the common military calendar. I have put special emphasis on the *kalendae Ianuarii* because it gradually superseded the *saturnalia*. The rabbis, as well as the church fathers, attempted to emphasise the importance of light for the holiday, so as simply to stress the Jewish or Christian liturgy at the same time. Through these means, the Roman holiday was updated to comply with Jewish or Christian needs. The rabbis do not proceed any differently in respect to the cult concerning the emperor at the celebration of *dies imperatoris*. The meaning of this celebration for the Jewish community is stressed, for instance, by the fact that the Tosefta qualifies as a celebration for the public, *le-ṣibbur*, if it is connected to the king (birthday, wedding, etc.). The subtle or not-so-subtle criticism of the power of Rome – the *romana insanitas* – could not obscure or elude a sovereign fact: namely דִּינָא דְּמַלְכוּתָא דִּינָא – the law of the country (or king) is binding.

Part III: **Performing the Craft of Science & Magic**

4 The Science(s) and "Greek Wisdom"

According to the mainstream of modern research in the sciences of late antiquity,[231] rabbinic Judaism is not considered a fertile field for pursuing anything of theoretical interest or concerning scientific development. It is regarded at best as a conglomeration of popular, magical and religious practices and beliefs.[232] Scholars of the history of sciences tend to avoid dealing with these "dark" Middle Ages. They claim to find their appropriate object in the Golden Age of the Jewish "mediation" of science, that is, in the period from the Arabic conquest until the expulsion from Spain. At that time, medicine as well as mathematics and astronomy penetrated the organic life of the Jewish educated classes, and Judaism became the vector of *adab*, the Arabic *paideia* which made possible the translation, adaptation, and interpretation of the Greek sciences. They were thus mediated and transmitted anew to the European cultures.[233]

This is nothing but a very simplified and naïve conception – not only of historical development as such, but also of the history of science. Rabbinic Judaism already contains the cultural premises which enabled the so-called

---

[231] This chapter is based on some ideas taken from my *Habilitationsschrift* which was published as *Magie und Halakha: Ansätze zu einem empirischen Wissenschaftsbegriff im spätantiken und frühmittelalterlichen Judentum* (Tübingen: Mohr Siebeck, 1997). This essay was inspired by Jacob Neusner's thesis on Rabbinic Judaism in *The Making of the Mind of Judaism: The Formative Age* (Atlanta, Ga.: Scholars Press, 1987); see also Neusner, "Why No Science in Judaism?," *Shofar* 6 (1988): 45–71. Reprint in J. Neusner, *Neusner on Judaism* (Ashgate Contemporary Thinkers on Religion. Collected Works), Aldershot: Ashgate, 2005, vol. III 307-338.
[232] This tendency is confirmed by the lack of secondary literature on the theoretical aspect of science in rabbinic Judaism. The following works largely exhaust the material: Saul Lieberman, "The Natural Science of the Rabbis," in *Hellenism in Jewish Palestine: Studies in the Literary Transmission, Beliefs and Manners of Palestine in the I Century BCE–IV Century CE*, ed. Lieberman (New York: The Jewish Theological Seminary, 1962), 181–193; Gerd A. Wewers, "Die Wissenschaft von Natur im rabbinischen Judentum," *Kairos* 14 (1972): 1–21; Abraham Wasserstein, "Astronomy and Geometry as Propaedeutic Studies in Rabbinic Literature [Hebrew]," *Tarbiz* 43 (1973): 53–57. The only author I am aware of who deals with the topic even in its theoretical aspect is Menachem Fisch, *To Know Wisdom: Science, Rationality and Torah-Study* [Hebrew] (Jerusalem: The Van Leer Jerusalem Institute/Hakibbutz Hameuchad, 1994).
[233] See, for instance, in Arturo Castiglioni, "The Contribution of the Jews to Medicine," in *The Jews: Their History, Culture, and Religion*, ed. Louis Finkelstein, vol. 2 (New York: Harper & Row 1960), 1358–1359. Castiglioni writes, "For many centuries the Jews were concentrated in the Mediterranean countries. Here their medicine had its most important development. A remarkable period of this development is connected with the Arab conquest of the Mediterranean countries. The Jews were the great intermediaries of the Mediterranean ..." *Ibidem*, 1350. On the *adab* see Anwar G. Chejne, *Muslim Spain: Its History and Culture* (Minneapolis: University of Minnesota Press, 1974), 196–218; notes on 447–450.

Middle Ages to absorb "foreign" knowledge: not to ignore or reject it outright because of mere religious misgivings or even bans. The underlying premise of the ideological framework of modern attitudes to ancient Judaism is the theoretical, purely Hegelian view, according to which the mutual influence of cultural units can exist only as a process of intellectual interaction.

The first consequence of this approach is the perennial question of how to understand the rabbinic attitude to Greek wisdom (ḥokhma yewwanit).[234] It is, by the way, claimed to be the matrix of the ancient sciences.[235] Modern scholarship is torn between whether the study of Greek philosophy and science was common among the rabbis, or if there was any contact between Jews and Greeks at all. Thus, scholars of rabbinic Judaism are either keen detectives who carefully seek every trace, however minute, of influence, or severe judges who declare almost every alleged Greek reference to be inadequate by explaining everything on the basis of immanent rabbinic concepts and beliefs.

A second, complementary and related consequence is the concentration of modern scholarship on researching the mutual exchange between the Jewish and Greco-Roman cultures from the point of view of intellectual history. Mere traces of philosophical, theological, hermeneutical and religious ideas have been treated in detail as main areas of influence, whereas everyday life, folklore, science and empirical knowledge have rarely been the focus of scholarly attention.[236] This is all the more surprising as rabbinic Judaism had not transmitted tractates on philosophy or theology the way contemporary neo-Platonic teachers had. The principal activity of rabbinic Judaism was, as is well-known, the exegetical combination of the literary and traditional past (the written Torah) with the demands of the present by means of exegetical methods, that is, via the hermeneutics of the oral Torah.

---

234 On learning "foreign" sciences, see Dov Rafal, *Shevaʻ ha-ḥokhmot: Ha-wikuaḥ ʻal limmude ḥol be-sifrut ha-ḥinnukh ha-yahadut ʻad ha-haskala* (Jerusalem: Misrad ha-ḥinnukh we-ha-tarbut, 1989).
235 See, however, André Pichot, *Die Geburt der Wissenschaft: Von den Babyloniern zu den frühen Griechen*, review by Jan Assmann, *Frankfurter Allgemeine Zeitung* Nr. 258 (November 6, 1995), 17.
236 The term empirical "science" as a characteristic of rabbinic medicine has been supported by many scholars. The adjective "empirical" is often understood, however, to have a negative connotation as opposed to "scientifically proved." Castiglioni, for instance, writes that "Biblical-talmudic literature permits us to trace the evolution of medical thought among the Jews from fundamental magical beliefs and conceptions common to all primitive peoples to an empirical and religious medicine." Castiglioni, "The Contribution of the Jews to Medicine," 1358–1359. On the contribution of the Aristotelian school to the development of empirical knowledge, see Fritz Jürss, "Bemerkungen zum naturwissenschaftlichen Denken in der Spätantike," *Klio* 43–45 (1965): 385.

The thesis of this section is that although the rabbis had some difficulties about accepting purely theoretical Greek conceptions, the ancient empirical sciences constituted the main area where they tacitly or consciously accepted gentile customs and findings, or even their *Weltanschauung*. This attitude was rooted in their pragmatic approach to judging non-"Jewish" sciences. It is this pragmatism which proves to be a key for the understanding of the "medieval" acceptance or refusal of "theoretical" and empirical sciences.

4.1 Greek Wisdom and Everyday Sciences

Since publication of the *magna charta* of the *Wissenschaft des Judentums* published in 1818 – Leopold Zunz's *Etwas über die rabbinische Litteratur* – the rabbinic attitude to Greek culture has been an often discussed question.[237] At least two generations of scholars have tried to shed light on the relationship between Judaism and its Greek environment (and vice versa, of course).[238] The theoretical premises and the scholarly results of researching this material are well-known: some scholars deny any influence of Greek culture on Judaism while others emphasise it. Prudence is the guideline of a third category of scholars who avoid speaking of *the* influence or of *the* encounter between Hellenism and Jewish culture but rather of two different cultural and social units with some points of contact.[239]

---

237 Leopold Zunz, "Etwas über die rabbinische Litteratur [1821]," in *Zunz Gesammelte Schriften*, vol. 1 (Berlin: Louis Gerschel Verlagsbuchhandlung, 1875): 3–31. An abridged English translation is available with Paul Mendes-Flohr and Jehuda Reinharz, eds., *The Jew in the Modern World: A Documentary History* (New York: Oxford University Press, 1995), 221–230. The main effort of the new *Wissenschaft des Judentums* was the promotion of an awareness that the Jewish Talmudic culture contributed to European cultural development. Moreover, the analysis of Talmudic literature aimed at proving its antiquity. For instance, Zacharias Frankel's studies on the Septuagint intended above all to date Talmudic imformation. See Frankel's *Vorstudien zu der Septuaginta* (Leipzig: Vogel, 1841), viii.
238 To my knowledge, Israel Lévi made the first comprehensive contribution to this issue. See his "Über die Spuren des griechischen und römischen Alterthums im talmudischen Schriftthum," in *Verhandlungen der Versammlung Deutscher Philologen und Schulmänner* (Leipzig: Teubner, 1878), 77–88
239 On these three tendencies, see Yiṣḥaq Baer, "The Historical Foundations of the Halakha [Hebrew]," *Zion* 17 (1952): 1–55; Baer, "On the Problem of Eschatological Doctrine During the Period of the Second Temple [Hebrew]," *Zion* 23–24 (1958–1959): 3–34, 141–165; Lieberman, *Hellenism in Jewish Palestine*; Lieberman, "How Much Greek in Jewish Palestine," in *Biblical and Other Studies*, ed. Alexander Altmann (Cambridge, Mass.: Harvard University Press, 1963), 123–141; Lieberman, Lieberman, *Greek in Jewish Palestine* (New York: Jewish Theological Seminary, 1965); Lieberman, *Texts and Studies* (New York: Ktav 1974). On the Homeric and Rabbinic

The Jewish attitude to Greek culture and language was, in my opinion, a positive one: Greek was even supposed to be the language that was spoken from the beginning of the world up to the time of the Tower of Babel (see Jerusalem Talmud, Megillah 1:11 [71b]). It might be assumed with some certainty that the ban on Greek culture, as ordered in rabbinic Judaism, concerned only special circumstances and certain periods at most, while its relationship to Greek was generally an interaction that is comparable to those of other peoples and cultures.[240]

The Mediterranean peoples, and most of the Central/Southern Asian peoples as far as Bactrian India, were fascinated by Greek literature, philosophy, and its way of life. Yet, not every group was brought into cultural and political subjugation to such a degree that its people and especially the higher classes replaced/adjusted their own traditions entirely. The resistance to Hellenism grew in Judaism, for instance, into a military confrontation when the Maccabeans and their followers refused to be assimilated by denying the local deity and customs. Their response to the assimilation process was the "high praises of God in their mouths, and the two-edged sword in their hand" (Psalms 149:6).

Without going into details regarding a very difficult question, it might be accepted as based on thorough studies that the cultural response to the infiltration of Greek ideas was not always one of openly aggressive or subversive resistance.[241] It was a creative reaction to the new cultural demands and impuls-

---

exegesis, see E. E. Hallewy, "The Writers of the 'Aggada and the Greek Grammarians [Hebrew]," *Tarbiz* 29 (1959): 47–55; Halleway, "Biblical Midrash and Homeric Exegesis [Hebrew]," *Tarbiz* 31 (1961): 157–169, 264–80. For a general view see Henry A. Fischel, *Essays in Graeco-Roman and Related Talmudic Literature* (New York: Ktav, 1977); Nicholas de Lange, "Sem et Japhet: Les Juifs et la langue grecque," *Pardès* 12 (1990): 90–107; de Lange, "Judaeo-Greek Studies: Achievements and Prospects," *Bulletin of Judaeo-Greek Studies* 17 (1995): 27–34.

240 See Mishnah *Soṭa* 9:14 and parallels with a reference to the war of Titus (or Quietus?). On the alleged ban of Greek wisdom, see Lieberman, *Hellenism in Jewish Palestine*, 100–114; E. E. Hallewy, "Concerning the Ban of Greek Wisdom [Hebrew]," *Tarbiz* 41 (1971): 269–274.

241 See, however, Louis H. Feldman who writes: "The question, then, is not how thoroughly Jews and Judaism in the Land of Israel were hellenised, but how strongly they resisted Hellenisation. In other words, what was the power of Judaism that enabled it to remain strong despite the challenge of Hellenism and later of Christianity and even to counterattack through conversion of non-Jews to Judaism?" Louis H. Feldman, *Jew and Gentile in the Ancient World: Attitudes and Interactions from Alexander to Justinian* (Princeton: Princeton University Press, 1993), 44. Rightly, Martha Himmelfarb in her review of Feldman's book notes: "In this short passage one can discern both the shadow of the Middle Ages and the shadow of the present. If it is not 'lachrymose' in its conception, it has certainly erected barricades between the Jews and the rest of the world." Martha Himmelfarb, review of *Jew and Gentile in the Ancient World: Attitudes and Interactions from Alexander to Justinian* by Louis H. Feldman, *Judaism* 43 (1994): 328–334.

es rather than a "stubborn" rejection of Hellenistic ideas. Without doubt, some βάρβαροι/barbarians – as the Greeks referred to "uncivilised," foreign peoples – attempted to resist the pervasive Greek influence on their culture. The danger of being entirely assimilated, however, spurred the barbarians into productive thinking and apologetic reworking of their traditions by stressing their illustrious origins and ancient nature of their cultures.[242] Thus, the Hermetic tradition claimed that the Greeks had derived (or better, "stolen") most of their own wisdom from the Egyptians, while in Judaism, Greek wisdom was widely believed to be based on the Mosaic Law.

It is therefore apparent why Judaism of the centuries before and after the beginnings of the Common Era apologetically claimed that the Greek philosophy and culture had "stolen" their wisdom. According to them, Plato, for instance, was guilty of plagiarism. Aristobulos, a philosopher of the Greek Diaspora, states that "There is no doubt that Plato followed our legislation."[243] In another fragment, taken from his lost work, he maintains:

> In my opinion, Pythagoras, Socrates, and Plato who tried to answer these questions as good as possible, did follow in his [Moses] footsteps. They maintained that they heard a divine voice gazing at the shape of the universe, created and permanently supported by God.[244]

It is questionable whether the doctrine of the Graeco-Roman "theft" of the Jewish ancient wisdom, as claimed by Jewish sources, refers to the entire body of philosophy, literature, and science, or rather to the barbarian origin of certain ideas and findings. Aristobulos, Aristeas, Artapanus, Philo, and Josephus referred to a Jewish superiority only when speaking of certain findings and concepts. It is possible that they were aware of the pervasive power of Greek literature and *weltanschauung*, and that they were aware of their superiority over the Greeks in other sectors of the sciences. The idea of an ontological character of the possession of wisdom developed only after the advent of Christianity.

---

[242] An important result of this positive reaction was the translation of the Torah into Greek. It was used not only in the Greek Diaspora but also in *Eretz Yisrael*. For the rabbinic attitudes to the so-called *Septuaginta*, see Veltri, *Eine Tora für den König Talmai* (Tübingen: Mohr Siebeck, 1994); and *Libraries, Translations, and 'Canonic' Texts. The Septuagint, Aquila, and Ben Sira in Jewish and Christian Tradition* (Leiden, Boston: Brill, 2006).
[243] See also Clemens Alex., *Stromata*, 5:14–97,7, in *Apocalypsis Henochi graece: Fragmenta pseudepigraphorum quae supersunt graeca una cum historicorum et auctorum judaeorum hellenistarum fragmentis* [PVTG 3], ed. Albert-Marie Denis and Matthew Black (Leiden: Brill, 1970), 228.
[244] *Apud* Eusebius, *Praeparatio Evangelica* 13:12,2, in Denis, *Fragmenta pseudepigraphorum*, 222–223.

Christian writers stressed that *all* wisdom belonged to them as the *verus Israel*.[245]

The difficulty in understanding the relationship between Hellenism and Judaism is mainly a problem of hermeneutics. Modern philosophy and linguistics since the semiotics of de Saussure at least, have taught us that the standpoint is the determinative factor in perceiving and judging "reality" and text. If we take as our starting point rabbinic Judaism, or alternatively Roman literature, we have two very different images of their mutual interconnections. The reason is that the thing/object/subject which one wishes to compare is almost always the measure of the one it is being compared to. From the Graeco-Roman point of view, one wonders why Jewish literature contains no reception of Plato, Aristotle, Hippocrates, Galen, Cicero, or others.[246]

In explaining the absence of a reception of Greek philosophy and scientific thought, modern scholars have projected a typical 19th-century ideological and religious simplification: the non-acceptance of philosophy in rabbinic Judaism is to be attributed to the centrality and exclusiveness of the preoccupation with the Torah. Judaism is the religion and culture of a people of rabbis who are concentrated on the study of the law as a mythical entity. Greek philosophy, however, is allegedly concerned with the sphere of the logos, the reign of rationality.[247] From the rabbinic point of view, it is surprising that Graeco-Roman, and also Christian authors, were ignorant when it came to the nature of Judaism itself. While knowledge of the written Torah, even in its Greek form, is scarcely attested in "pagan" sources, the oral Torah is even more unknown, with the exception of Christian polemical and admittedly distorted references. One wonders whether the mutual ignorance was only a problem rooted in the difficulty of translation, or whether Jewish culture did not interest Romans at all.[248]

---

245 On the whole question, see G. Veltri, "Dalla tesi giudeo-ellenistica del 'plagio' dei Greci al concetto rabbinico del verus Israel: Disputa sull'appartenenza della *sofia*," *Revista Catalana de Teologia* 17 (1992): 85–104.

246 Very notable exceptions are the references to Homer and the *epikursim*. These possibly designated an obscure group of heretics as well as a popular image of the Epicurean.

247 Castiglioni writes: "We may pass ... only a general judgment on the practice of medicine and believe that the Jewish physicians of those days accepted the diagnostic rules and therapeutic means prescribed by Greek medicine, but did not care too much for the clinical doctrines or the theoretical scientific explanations that were the characteristic elements of Greek science. Jewish physicians acknowledged the facts, but were cautious and skeptical in adopting doctrines which appeared to them heterodox from the point of view of their strong religious faith, whose central belief was expressed by the words of Divine revelation, 'I am the Lord, that healeth thee' (Ex. 15:26)." Castiglioni, "The Contribution of the Jews to Medicine," 1359.

248 See Arnaldo Momigliano, *Alien Wisdom: The Limits of Hellenization* (Cambridge: Cambridge University Press, 1975), 91 et seq. On the knowledge of the biblical text among non-

In my opinion, the alleged relationship rests on a mistaken supposition. To begin with a perhaps categorical statement, I would like to stress that rabbinic Judaism, and Hellenism in its Graeco-Roman shape, are two sociological and historical units of a different magnitude. We cannot compare Judaism and Hellenism with reference to their mutual influence for two important reasons. First, the rapport of influence is chronological, which presupposes a language or unique system of reference. In other words, it is a dangerous task to compare ideas if the respective texts are not written in the same or related languages. The creation *ex nihilo*, the uniqueness of God, the divine providence – the might of the word – are Jewish as well as "pagan" ideas and concepts. Second, students of comparative religions and cultures should ask which form of Judaism they wish to compare with which form of Hellenism. The concept "Hellenistic culture" is neither a homogenous phenomenon nor a unique historical event. There is not *one* single Hellenistic theology, not *one* Hellenistic philosophy, not *one* Hellenistic culture. Monotheism, dualism, and polytheism were, in different periods and in various areas, simultaniously an expression of the "Hellenistic mind." The adjective Hellenistic can refer to Greek "influences" as far away as Bactrian India and Egypt in the Graeco-Roman period (thus, former conquests of Alexander the Great). It can also be extended to Britain, Gaul and Germany. If we compare some sayings from Mishnah Avot with philosophical conceptions of the Stoa or with neo-Platonic ideas, we have to solve the question of how the Stoic and neo-Platonic conceptions reached the Jewish teachers. The mere quoting of Pythagoras, Plotin, Seneca, together with the Sayings of the Fathers is, in my opinion, methodologically dubious.

The situation changes, of course, if we turn to the empirical and natural sciences: botany, zoology, medicine, agronomy, etc. It is astonishing how similar Graeco-Roman knowledge and methods were to those of Jewish teachers. Immanuel Löw's *Flora der Juden*, Ludwig Lewysohn's *Die Zoologie des Talmuds*, Julius Preuss's *Biblisch-talmudische Medizin*, as well as other works, among them the material collected by Saul Lieberman and Daniel Sperber, clearly demonstrate in many details how close the rabbinic teachers were to their Graeco-Roman colleagues.[249] The list of *realia* doubtless can be extended

---

Jews, see Giancarlo Rinaldi, *Biblia Gentium: Primo contributo per un indice delle citazioni, dei riferimenti e delle allusioni alla Bibbia negli autori pagani, greci e latini, di età imperiale* (Rome: Libreria Sacre Scritture, 1989); David Rokeaḥ, "The Jewish Bible and the New Testament in the Pagan World [Hebrew]," *Tarbiz* 40 (1991): 451–464.

249 See Immanuel Löw, *Die Flora der Juden*, 4 vols. (Vienna and Leipzig: Löwit, 1924–34; repr. Hildesheim: Olms, 1967); Löw, *Aramäische Pflanzennamen* (Leipzig: Engelmann, 1881; repr. Hildesheim: Olms, 1973); Löw, *Fauna und Mineralien der Juden*, ed. Alexander Scheiber (Hildesheim: Olms, 1969); Ludwig Lewysohn, *Die Zoologie des Talmuds: Eine umfassende Darstellung*

to the bathing culture, the plays, and so on, revealing a spectrum of "influences" or, as I prefer to denote it, the *humus* in which rabbinic Judaism developed.[250]

Also in this academical branch – where the methodological correctness of quoting parallels and similar *realia* cannot be seriously contested – we have to wonder whether the similarity of procedures is the result of a tacit reception of common sciences. This procedure might methodologically be called "eclectic pragmatic activity." Or is it rather a process of conscious acceptance of scientific findings? Only on the basis of the second possible explanation, namely the conscious process, can we seriously identify the rabbinic attitudes to theoretical and practical science as a universal system of useful knowledge. The mere gathering of data and *realia* is certainly not proof of influence or relationship. The implications of this statement remain a *terra incognita* down to the present.

4.2 Empirical Science: Medicine

The history of the ancient and modern sciences is neither linear nor consequent. The optimistic approach of the 19th century, which tried to interpret classical Greek attitudes to the sciences as being rationally and scientifically proven, is no longer credible. Of course, modern scholars attempt to view and trace the history as a linear development, for every handbook has to present material carefully ordered in a logical way to facilitate learning. History, how-

---

der rabbinischen Zoologie, unter steter Vergleichung der Forschungen älterer und neuerer Schriftsteller (Frankfurt: Baer, 1858); Julius Preuss, *Biblisch-talmudische Medizin* (Berlin: Karger, 1911; repr. Wiesbaden: Fourier, 1992); Joseph Bergel, *Studien über die naturwissenschaftlichen Kenntnisse der Talmudisten,* (Leipzig: Friedrich, 1880). Saul Lieberman, ed. *Tosefta Ki-Fshutah: A Comprehensive Commentary on the Tosefta* [Hebr.], 10 vols. (New York: Jewish Theological Seminary, 1955–88); Daniel Sperber, *Customs of Israel: Sources and History* [Hebr.], 5 vols. (Jerusalem: Mossad Harav Kook, 1990–95); Sperber, "Studies in Loan Words and their Textual Variant," *Te'uda* 7 (1991): 149–153; Sperber, *Material Culture in Eretz-Israel during the Talmudic Period* [Hebrew] (Ramat Gan: Bar-Ilan University Press, 1994); Sperber, *Magic and Folklore in Rabbinic Literature* (Ramat Gan: Bar-Ilan University Press, 1994).

250 The Hellenistic influence on constructions and building as well as on social behaviour and custom – for instance, *symposia, ludi* – is not a proof of rabbinical acceptance of the theoretical system therein. It is rather a reference to their practical-pragmatical attitude. We have indeed neither evidence that the rabbis attributed any theoretical value, for example, to the mosaics of the synagogue building of Naaran, Beth Alpha, Tiberias and Husifa. Nor do we have any tractate, text or at least a tradition about the cultural implications of bathing or the symposia.

ever, is known to be anything but an Aristotelian and scholastic exercise of logical deduction and induction. There hardly is indeed any proof, and no solid evidence, as to whether the Babylonian and the Egyptian healing methods provided the seed of the theories of Hippocrates and Galen.[251] The main difference between the Babylonian and Egyptian sciences and the Greek sciences is the speculative reflection on human health. We have numerous lists of medical recipes, human parts, *materia medica ac magica*, plant names, and symptoms in Akkadian as well as in Egyptian texts. However, they offer no theory of how the human being and body work and function, or, in fact, what constituted health and disease.

Moreover, the modern conception of science and the ancient approach to the *sciences* differ profoundly. Modern natural scientists, such as botanists or zoologists, aim at finding rules and theories which can explain conclusively one or many phenomena. If an outdated rule fails to explain a new phenomenon, scientists change it in order to explain the old and new phenomena. Neither the old Babylonian nor the late Jewish sciences followed this modern scientific praxis. A recipe, a medicine, a plant could be used as a *possible* cure.[252] Palestinian as well as Babylonian sources contain numerous discussions about a medicine, a preparation or a medical-magical procedure. The discussions are not only based on the traditional exegetic premise of rabbinic hermeneutics to discuss everything at length, but also on the nature of the empirical sciences. Pliny's encyclopaedic work, Columella's dissertation on agriculture, Dioscurides' *Materia medica* as well as at Marcellus Empiricus, *De Medicamentis*, follow the same or at least a similar method for presenting medical-magical findings and beliefs.

It is a truism that science is chiefly the interaction of both the observation of phenomena and their evaluation with the aid of theories. Surely, modern scholars do not adhere acritically to Edgar Zilsel's thesis that the beginnings of modern science are the experiments of the plebian classes of artists, engineers, and surgeons whose empirical findings were not re-evaluated, even theoretically, before Roger Bacon, Galileo Galilei and William Gilbert since the Renaissance period.[253] One cannot deny that empirical experimentation is useful

---

251 See, however, Dietlinde Goltz, *Studien zur altorientalischen und griechischen Heilkunde: Therapie – Arzneibereitung – Rezeptstruktur* (Wiesbaden: Steiner, 1974).
252 But see the discussion on amulets – the "proved one" (*mumḥe*) – in Mishnah, Shabbat 6:2; Babylonian Talmud, Shabbat 53b; Tosefta, Shabbat 4(5):10 und Jerusalem Talmud, Shabbat 6:2 (8b).
253 Edgar Zilsel, "The Sociological Roots of Science," *American Journal of Sociology* 57 (1942): 245–279.

for confirming and contrasting theories. This could be the reason why rabbinic authorities insisted on empirical and pragmatic criteria in judging customs, medical procedures and medicines as such.

With reference to this very important attitude, some texts and traditions, which were transmitted in early rabbinic tractates, are fully intelligible: we know the halakhic examination of foreign customs which were called the "Ways of the Amorite."[254] According to biblical sources, the Amorites are among the former inhabitants of Canaan whose "abominable" practices the Israelites were not allowed to adopt.[255] In rabbinic discussions, the "ways of the Amorite" became a Halakhic category which included most kinds of forbidden foreign customs.

The whole list of the "customs of the Amorite" is a conglomeration of different magical genres, superstitions, and medical-magical recipes, which can be compared to Graeco-Roman magic literature, as for instance the *Papyri Graecae Magicae*, but also with the works mentioned by Pliny and Columella. The customs which were forbidden or allowed by the rabbis under this label "ways of the Amorite" encompass all aspects of everyday life and point up the broad variety of procedures and beliefs taken into consideration by the rabbis. The contextualisation of the customs of the Amorite attests to two characteristics of the category: it is synonymous with "foreign customs," and at the same time it is an anti-category calling attention to what deserves to be considered "healing" versus "quackery" or even dangerous cures.

The method the rabbis used to examine the validity of customs or medical recipes, is an empirical one: "whatever is used to bring about healing does not belong to the ways of the Amorite."[256] This principle has to be emphasised for its scientific and modern value. With little reason to believe otherwise, the statement proves that rabbinic authorities accepted certain "foreign" customs for healing purposes and did not forbid them altogether. We do not know whether "Jewish skill in effecting cures" attracted non-Jews to Judaism, as Louis H. Feldman claims.[257] On the contrary, the above-mentioned Halakhah might only show that rabbinic Judaism was open to "pagan" influences as long as they brought about effective cures. Therefore, according to the Palestinian Talmud, even a pagan physician was allowed to treat a Jew (Jerusalem Talmud, 'Avodah Zarah 2:1 [40c]).

---

254 See chapter 3.2 in this volume.
255 For the references see below, p. 132–158.
256 Jerusalem Talmud, Shabbat 6:10 (27d: דרכי האמרי 'משו בו אין מרפא שהוא כל). For further details see below, p. 135 ff.
257 Feldman, *Jew and Gentile*, 381.

A similar principle in accepting foreign knowledge also appears in Pliny's work, especially in connection with magic.²⁵⁸ Moreover, there are some similarities between the rabbinic attitudes to empirical sciences and those of the Greek school of the Empiricists (ἐμπειρικὴ ἀγωγή) who opposed the dogmatic school of medicine and based their science on the therapeutic art and pharmacology. Very interesting and similar to "rabbinic" practice are their three principles: πεῖρα ("experience"), ἱστορία ("the use of foreign observations"), and τοῦ ὁμοίου μετάβασις ("analogical method").²⁵⁹ With reference to these similarities, I assume it is not surprising to learn that one Marcellus Empiricus transmitted a remedy which he attributed to Rabban Gamli'el. Moreover, the principle *similia similibus*, which is a typical empirical principle, can also be found in rabbinic literature, even with the same application which we find in Marcellus Empiricus. We read in Tosefta, Shabbat 7:21: "If a bone got stuck in one's throat, one may put on his head a bone of that sort." We can quote Pliny, who relates to this custom as "commenta magorum":

> Should a fish bone stick in the throat, they say it comes out if the feet are plunged into cold water; if however it is another kind of bone, bits of bone from the same pot should be applied to the head; if it is a piece of bread that sticks, pieces from the same loaf must be placed in either ear.²⁶⁰

Of course, a similar method can also be found in Marcellus Empiricus.²⁶¹ I do not believe that the rabbis had contacts with the Empirical School. Neither did

---

258 See chapter 7.1 in this volume, pp. 154–157.
259 See Marquis Berrey, "Early Empiricism, Therapeutic Motivation, and the Asymmetrical Dispute Between the Hellenistic Medical Sects," *Apeiron* 47 (2013): 141–171.
260 Pliny's Latin: "Si quid e pisce haeserit faucibus, cadere in aquam demissis frigidam pedibus; si vero ex aliis ossibus haeserit faucibus, inpositis capite ex eodem vase ossiculis. Si panis haereat, ex eodem in utramque aurem addito pane." Plinius, *Naturalis Historia* XXVIII:12,49. See the English translation in Pliny the Elder: *Natural History* vols. vi–viii [Loeb Classical Library, 418], trans. William H. S. Jones (Cambridge, Mass.: Harvard University Press, 1945). The same use is to be found in the *Testament of Solomon* 18:34–40 according to *Pap. gr. Vindobonensis* 330. There is written: "I am the Lord, my name is Rex Alleborith. If a person eats birds and gulps a bone down and [thereafter] he gets ill, if he takes a bone of the same kind and coughs, I will go away from mine kibōrion [?] ..." See the text with its German translation in Karl Preisendanz, "Ein Wiener Papyrusfragment zum Testamentum Salomonis," *Eos* 48 (1956): 161–167. The Babylonian Talmud adds a conjuration for the same purpose: If one has a bone in the throat, he should bring one of the same sort, place it on his head, and say thusly: one by one, go down, swallow, swallow, go down, one by one. This is not considered a way of the Amorite. For a fish bone he should say thus: Thou art stuck in like a pin. Thou art locked up as in a cuirass, go down, go down.
261 Marcellus also recommended a conjuration. See Marcellus, *De Medicamentis* VIII:172; XV:108 ("os Gorgonis basio") and *Physica Plinii Sangallensis*, no. 11 ("Lafana piscatoris, exi et

they read Marcellus' work. The similarities between the rabbis, Pliny, Marcellus and the Empirical School could nevertheless originate from the concepts of the Latin Graeco-Roman world in which they lived, i.e., through cultural contacts.

The empirical principle of examining first and then accepting new sciences and findings contributed to the development in Judaism of an Halakhic tradition which permitted the use of any medicine, tool, herb, plant, custom, etc., as long as it was unrelated to idolatrous customs. The rabbis allowed the use of all amulets except those which had traces of idolatry. Yet, in the judgement of special cases, the rabbinic practice stressed that the principle of healing is much more important than the danger of idolatry. The empirical principle thus realised its greatest significance: religious beliefs are dependent on health-related necessities. What the principle of *Piquaḥ-Nefesh*[262] permitted in certain life-threatening situations, is thus valid in every situation.[263]

Concluding this part on the empirical value of rabbinic Judaism, I have to emphasise once more that the cultural settings in which the Jewish attitude to science developed were not the academic institutions and the philosophical schools of their age, but merely the challenges of everyday life. Their preoccupation with the Torah was not the determining factor in accepting foreign knowledge; rather, salient were the actual demands of the day: whatever is considered to be useful for healing should be accepted. In this respect, the Amoraic and Tannaitic teachers were innovative, because the written Torah is against medicine: accordingly, the only physician can be God alone.

4.3 Theoretical Science: Astrology

The concept of theoretical science is an epistemology where knowledge is gained and established without experimenting on the basis of principles or axiomata. Euclidean geometry, for instance, presupposes that only one line can cross two points, and that two parallel lines meet each other in *infinitum*. Whoever does not accept these principles has to turn to the so-called non-Euclidean geometries. A theoretical science is apodictically correct, because it is based on postulates which *per definitionem* do not need to be demonstrated.

---

fac quae te iussit Iuppiter"). See *Incantanta magica Graeca Latina*, collegit disposuit edidit Richardus Heim (Leipzig: Teubner, 1892), 490.

262 See Babylonian Talmud, Ketubbot 5a, 15b, 19a; Yoma 84a etc. On the principle see Hirsch Jacobs Zimmels, *Magicians, Theologians, and Doctors: Studies in Folk Medicine and Folklore as Reflected in the Rabbinical Responsa* (London: E. Goldston, 1952), 9 f.

263 Zimmels, *Magician, Theologians, and Doctors*, 9, et seq.

The spectrum of possibilities from empirical, practical to abstract, theoretical sciences offers a second pattern of interpretative reality. This second pattern combines abstract theory with empirical observation. This correlative pathway, which is recognised by other sciences, for instance astronomy or physics, is the empirical observation of phenomena which are noted with the senses. Such observations enable us to predict other similar phenomena. The postulate consists of the premise that the laws observed by perceiving a phenomenon, such as the influence of the moon or some events on earth, are also valid for other phenomena. If an apple falls when it loses its support, it is reasonable to believe that this happens with all bodies having a mass (as Newton put it). The explanation why this happens is not of an empirical nature but rather is theoretical.

This second method of science is the basis of the success of astrology, known in the ancient world by different names all of which had something to do with heavenly bodies, observation, or calculation (ἀστρολογία, ἀστρομαντεία, ἀστροσκοπία, γενεθλιακή, μαθηματική, ὡρονομική, ὡροσκοπική, *astrologia, mathematice, mathesis, scientia sideralis*). The names are also related to their supposed inventors: the Chaldeans (Χαλδαϊκή, *ars Chaldaeorum*). Despite the controversy, already present in antiquity regarding the origins of astrology, we can assume with some certainty that its origins were Babylonian. Diodorus of Sicily, who tracked down the main points of astrological theory, depicted the Chaldaeans of Babylon (... περὶ τῶν ἐν Βαβυλῶνι Χαλδαίων) as being similar to the priests of Egypt. Dioderos wrote, "For being assigned to the service of the gods they spend their entire life in study; their greatest renown being in the field of astrology."[264]

At the end of the 4th century BCE, astrology became known in the Mediterranean world. The first testimony is Theophrastus's: Περὶ σημείων.[265] The wide diffusion of astrology was based on the the Alexandrian conquest, which allowed diviners and astrologers to fan out to all corners of the empire.

Diodoros of Sicily tells us about the principles of Chaldean philosophy, thereby suggesting a reason for the dissemination of astrology throughout the Mediterranean world.[266]

---

264 Greek: πρὸς γὰρ τῇ θεραπείᾳ τῶν θεῶν τεταγμένοι πάντα τὸν τοῦ ζῆν χρόνον φιλοσοφοῦσι, μεγίστην δόξαν ἔχοντες ἐν ἀστρολογίᾳ. Diodorus, II, 29,1–3. See *Diodorus Siculus*, ed. and trans. Charles H. Oldfather (Cambridge, Mass., and London: Harvard University Press, 1946), 445.
265 According to Riess *PRE* II,2 (1896): 1811.
266 Diodoros II, 30:1 ff. Eng. tr. Charles H. Oldfather (Cambridge MA, London: Harvard University Press, 1946), p. 445.

Now, as the Chaldaeans say, the world is by its nature eternal; it neither had a first beginning nor will it at a later time suffer destruction; furthermore, both the disposition and the orderly arrangement of the universe have come about by virtue of divine providence; and to-day whatever takes place in the heavens is in every instance brought to pass, not at haphazard nor by virtue of any spontaneous action, but by some fixed and firmly determined divine decision.

And since they have observed the stars over a long period of time and have noted both the movement and the influence of each of them with greater precision than any other men, they foretell to mankind many things that will take place in the future.

Diodoros tells us that the scientific activity of the Chaldeans was based on their observation of the stars over a long period of time; i.e., they first empirically registered the positions of the heavenly bodies and then calculated mathematically the movements of the planets and the stars. Their first aim was doubtless to calculate the calendar so as to predict when a new month would begin, or when an intercalary month was needed. With their proven experience in calendar calculation, they extended their authority by claiming to be able to determine also the influence of the heavenly bodies on human beings, which is what astrology claims. The success of astrology is nothing but the success of astronomy which is, in fact, but a by-product of astrology.

The scientific value of astrology is confirmed by a Palestinian story, also transmitted in the context of the "Ways of the Amorite" in Jerusalem Talmud, Shabbat 6:10:[267]

> Two disciples of R. Hanina were going out to cut wood. They saw an astrologer (איסטרולוגוס). [He said:] "These two will go out but not come back."

---

[267] It is not my intention to deal extensively with the complex topic of astrology, neither do I intend to provide a complete list of references. On astrology in Rabbinic Judaism, see, for example, Salomon Funk, *Bibel und Babel* (Wien and Leipzig: Orion 1913), 241–250; Isidor Scheftelowitz, *Die Altpersische Religion und das Judentum. Unterschiede, Übereinstimmungen und gegenseitige Beeinflussungen* (Gießen: Töpelmann, 1920), 224–227; David Feuchtwang, "Der Tierkreis in der Tradition und im Synagogenritus," *Monatsschrift für Geschichte und Wissenschaft des Judentums* 59 (1915): 241–267; Ludwig Wächter, "Rabbinischer Vorsehungs- und Schicksalsglaube" (PhD diss., University of Jena, 1958); Wächter, "Astrologie und Schicksalsglaube im rabbinischen Judentum," *Kairos* 11 (1969): 181–200; Günter Stemberger, "Die Bedeutung des Tierkreises auf Mosaikfußböden spätantiker Synagogen," in *Studien zum rabbinischen Judentum*, ed. Stemberger (Stuttgart: Verlag Katholisches Bibelwerk, 1990), 177–228; Gideon Foerster, "The Zodiac in Ancient Synagogues and its Place in Jewish Thought and Literature," *Eretz Israel* 19 (1987): 225–234; Lester J. Ness, "Astrology in Judasim in Late Antiquity," *Archaeology in the Biblical World* 2 (1992): 44–54. On Jewish astrological literature, see the very extensive work of Reimund Leicht, *Astrologumena Judaica: Untersuchungen zur Geschichte der astrologischen Literatur der Juden* (Tübingen: Mohr Siebeck, 2006).

When they went out, an old man met them and said to them: "Acquire merit by helping me, for I have gone three days without tasting any food." They had with them a single circle of figs, which they divided and half of which they gave to him. He ate it and prayed for them. He said to them: "May you live out this day, just as you have helped me to live out this day." They went forth whole and came back whole.

There were people in that place who had heard the (prediction of the astrologer). They said to him [to the astrologer]. "Now did you not say to us that these two would go out and not come back." He (the astrologer) said: "I am a liar, for my astrological science has fooled me."

Even so (אפילו כן), they went and investigated and found (in the bundles they were bearing) a snake cut in half, one part in the knapsack of one of them, one part in that of the other. They said to the disciples: "Now what sort of thing did you do today?" They repeated the story. He said: "Now what can I do, when the God of the Jews is appeased by a half-circle of figs!"[268]

From the literary point of view, the story is similar to other Graeco-Roman and Christian stories about miracles occuring through piety. The new aspect in our literary piece is the acceptance of the occupation of the astrologer as a scientific one which is governed by universal laws from which we cannot escape. The astrologer said: my science is a liar. But the successive research reveals that he was right. Only the intervention of the "God of the Jews" in the natural scheme of things brought forth an exception to the rule. Accordingly, astrology is not fraudulent deceit, but science. The divine intervention, i.e., the intervention of the God of the Jews, is not accepted as a rule but as an exception. This is the underlying philosophical reason for the theoretical rejection/acceptance of astrology by the rabbis.

The belief in the power of the celestial bodies is a constant which we can find throughout the antiquity and the Middle Ages. There are, of course, also some critical statements and refutations of astrology.[269] The rabbinic teachers did not attempt to found a new, theoretical science that denied the validity of astrology in a scientific way. They understood the intervention of God for the benefit of pious Jews as an exception.

---

268 The text used the third person singular: ההוא גברא שקר דאיסתרולוגיא גיגיה שקרין. The translation of the Jerusalem Talmud text is a radical adaptation from the American text by Jacob Neusner, *The Talmud of the Land of Israel: A Preliminary Translation and Explanation*, vol. 11: Shabbat (Chicago and London: University of Chicago Press 1991).

269 See the defence of astrology in Claudius Ptolemaeus, *Tetrabiblos*, ed. and trans. Frank E. Robbins (Cambridge, Mass. and London: Harvard University Press, 1948). The school led by Carneades, attacked the validity of astrology in particular. The Stoic school, however, defended astrology.

4.4 Conclusion

Medicine and astrology are the only two sciences of empirical and theoretical "scientific" value to Palestinian rabbinic Judaism. They were acceptable, despite the fact that the written Torah issued an anathema against physicians and astrologers for acting against divine unity and providence. This hints at a solution to the question: how did foreign ideas influence Judaism? The usefulness of medicine and the scientific solidity of astrology were generally accepted in late antiquity. That does not mean, of course, that there were no discussions regarding the validity of medical practices or the reliability of astrologers.

Medicine and astrology are also discussed in the Jerusalem Talmud in the context of foreign knowledge: in the so-called *darkhe ha-emori*. According to the rabbinic way of thinking, foreign knowledge could not be rejected outright as idolatrous or harmful, even though a contrary opinion had been expressed in the Torah. This signifies a new aspect of rabbinic Judaism, which surely cannot be underestimated: the attitude toward science as a complementary aspect of their preoccupation with the Torah. New and old sciences are accepted or repudiated solely on the basis of their practical-pragmatic, "scientific" dynamics. They were not accepted or spurned because the Torah specifically supported or condemned them. The Babylonian Talmud summarises this aspect in the well-known dictum we find in Babylonian Talmud, Megillah 16a:

> Whoever, even among the people of the world, says words of science/wisdom, has to be considered a wise man (כל האומר דברי חכמה אפי' באומות העולם נקרא חכם).

5 On Magic: Past and Present Research

A substantial number of studies already exist on topics related to magic, superstition, healing, and sciences in Graeco-Roman Palestine and its vicinity, especially as far as the political and cultural environment of rabbinic Judaism is concerned. It is impossible to provide a comprehensive account of the various aspects of practical and theoretical magic in ancient Judaism here. This chapter will therefore restrict itself to offering an outline of the major research questions and scholarship on magic and science, assisting the reader in his or her future study of these topics.

5.1 Magic in Past and Present Scholarship

Modern studies on the magical tradition in Judaism go back to the German *Wissenschaft des Judentums*/Science of Judaism in the nineteenth century. Initially, only sporadic studies were conducted on the subject, but eventually scholarly interest in these issues increased, and a new discipline was created which investigated the extent and nature of Jewish magic and healing in antiquity and the Middle Ages. Interest in magic developed especially out of the incipient folklore studies of the early nineteenth century, and was based on a re-evaluation of the phenomenon of Jewish mysticism. After almost two centuries of scholarship and research, we can now distinguish between the following trends in the literary, cultural and anthropological study of magic:
1. the polemic-apologetic approach of the last century
2. studies based on new discoveries in the archaeological and philological realms
3. folklore and folk life studies
4. the impact of the study of Jewish mysticism on magic, and finally
5. the Halakhic-theological approach.

5.1.1 The Polemic-Apologetic Approach

The study of rabbinic texts on magic, superstition and healing was not the primary interest of the scholarly advocates of the *Wissenschaft des Judentums*. Quite the contrary, they avoided broaching the subject, largely because they had an enlightened vision of Judaism as a rational religion. They feared that by focusing on magic, the entire Jewish tradition risked being viewed as an extension of the medieval mystical movement of Kabbalah. Nevertheless, from the second half of the nineteenth century onward, the intentional ignoring of the topic evolved quite naturally into an expression of 1. a rationalist polemic against the "obscurantist" earlier centuries, when Judaism was affected by magical beliefs, and 2. an anti-apology for the Jewish adoption of "foreign customs," non-Jewish magical traditions and superstitious practices, mostly encompassing Kabbalah and Jewish mysticism.

A second reason for the interest in magic and superstition that needs to be considered was the typical tendency of the new philological "science" of Judaism to collect and "encyclopaedise" every piece of literature and tradition, whether Jewish in origin or by adoption. In the "manifesto" of the *Wissenschaft des Judentums* composed by the "father" of the new "science," Leopold Zunz, the presence of magic traditions in rabbinic literature is denied, or at least their significance belittled.[270] In his monumental work on liturgy (*Die gottesdienstlichen Vorträge der Juden, historisch entwickelt*, 1832) no mention is made of the huge number of magical traditions scattered throughout liturgical texts, for example, in *siddurim, maḥzorim* (prayer books) and their corresponding fragments.

Yet by no means were discussions on the value of magic and superstition a terra completely incognita. In 1807, Johann Andreas Lebrecht Richter (1772–1844) had already published some thoughts and reflections on the value of magic in religion.[271] These were published in *Sulamith*, the first German-language periodical for Jewish and non-Jewish readers alike.[272]

The first modern treatise on Jewish magic was written by Gideon Brecher (1850), a physician in Prossnitz (today's Prostějon in Moravia, Czech Republic).[273] In the treatise, Brecher pointed out in 1850 that he considered magic an

---

[270] Leopold Zunz, *Etwas über die rabbinische Litteratur. Nebst Nachrichten über ein altes bis jetzt ungedrucktes hebräisches Werk* (Berlin: Maurer'schen Buchhandlung, 1818); reprint *Gesammelte Schriften*, ed. Zunz' Stiftung (Berlin, 1875–1876; Hildesheim, New York: Olms, 1976), p. 14: "Die unheilige rabbinische Litteratur hat keine hierobotanica, hierozoica, physicas und medicas sacras aufzuweisen, obgleich es billig gewesen wäre, nicht stets vom Aberglauben zu schreien, ohne seine Gegnerin, die Physik, angehört zu haben. Ihr zur Seite geht die *Medicin*, gestützt auf die Kenntnisse der Natur, des Menschen (d. h. Psych- nebst Anthropo- und Physiologie) und die geschickte Anwendung dieser Kenntnisse."

[271] "Fragmente einiger Betrachtungen: Über den Aberglauben in der Religion," *Sulamith* 1 (1807): 82–86.

[272] On the journal, see Werner Grossert, "'Sulamith,' die Friedliebende aus Dessau (1806–1848): Die erste jüdische Zeitschrift in deutscher Sprache und deutscher Schrift," in *Jüdische Bildung und Kultur in Sachsen-Anhalt von der Aufklärung bis zum Nationalsozialismus*, eds. Giuseppe Veltri and Christian Wiese (Berlin: Metropol, 2009), pp. 133–146.

[273] See Gideon Brecher, *Das Transcendentale: Magie und magische Heilarten im Talmud* (Vienna: Klopf and Eurich, 1850).

incidental phenomenon in Judaism, adopted from the non-Jewish environment in the biblical and rabbinic periods. A similar approach was adopted by Rabbi David Heymann Joël (1883), who collected rabbinic legal and narrative sources on the topic. His book was aimed at proving that biblical and tannaitic sources (rabbinic sources of the first two centuries CE) were free of magical beliefs and practices. It was an erroneous view also shared by Israel Finkelscherer in his brief book on Maimonides.[274] In addition to these publications, some detailed studies on particular aspects of rabbinic folklore appeared at that time. Amongst others, the works of the following should be mentioned: Max Grünbaum (1877) and Israel Lévi (1878), who pointed to parallels to Jewish magic in the Graeco-Roman world.[275]

The scholars who wrote these early studies of ancient Jewish magic and superstition were primarily concerned with upholding a rationalist image of Judaism in the post-Enlightenment period, rather than with actually analysing ancient rabbinic discourse. Nevertheless, their work is important in mapping out magic in ancient Jewish literature and tradition – an indispensable foundation stone in the modern scientific study of the topic. And this is also the case with the great bibliographer Moritz Steinschneider. Steinschneider concerned himself with magic in several publications. Already in 1848, he had published the magic folkloric book *Alpha Beta de-ben Sira*.[276] In 1863, he devoted himself to the genre of oneirology[277] and, twenty years later, to the genre of divination.[278] Another example of his immense curiosity manifested itself in his concern with the meaning of numbers. In two articles, he investigated the symbolic meaning and values of the numbers 70, 71, 72 and 73 in both Islam and

---

[274] See David H. Joël, *Aberglaube und die Stellung des Judenthums zu demselben*, 2 vols. (Breslau: Jungfer, 1883); Israel Finkelscherer, *Moses Maimunis Stellung zum Aberglauben und zur Mystik* (Breslau: Schottländer, 1894).
[275] See Max Grünbaum, "Beiträge zur vergleichenden Mythologie aus der Hagada," *Zeitschrift der deutschen Morgenländischen Gesellschaft* 31 (1877): 183–359; Israel Lévi, "Über die Spuren des griechischen und römischen Alterthums im talmudischen Schriftthum," in *Verhandlungen der Versammlung Deutscher Philologen und Schulmänner* (Leipzig: Teubner, 1878), 77–88.
[276] *Alfa Beta de-Ben Sira: rishonah u-sheniyah, 'im ha-perush ha-yashan ha-kolel meshalim u-ma'asiyot u-midrashot*. *Alphabetum Syracidis* (Berlin: Typis Friedlaender, 1848); new critical edition by Eli Yassif, *The Tales of Ben Sira in the Middle Ages. A Critical Text and Literary Studies* (Jerusalem: Magnes, 1984), see also Dagmar Börner-Klein, *Das Alphabet des Ben Sira* (Wiesbaden: Marixverlag, 2007).
[277] "Das Traumbuch Daniels und die oneirokritische Litteratur des Mittelalters," *Serapeum* 24 (1863): 193–201, 209–216.
[278] "Losbücher," *Hebräische Bibliographie* 6 (1863): 120 ff.

Judaism.²⁷⁹ These publications are also of great philological, cultural, and historical interest, being mostly encyclopaedic accounts of traditions and texts.

His "theoretical" concern with magic is episodic, with (to my knowledge) only one notable exception, namely his lecture before the Association of Young Merchants (*Verein Junger Kaufleute*) in Berlin in 1900.²⁸⁰ This text of Steinschneider's is little known, because it was printed as part of an obscure series, contrary to Steinschneider's declared policy of publishing only in highbrow journals – a marketing ploy that revealed a "mercantile spirit" ["*merkantiler Geist*"], as Ludwig Geiger called it.²⁸¹ Yet, his concern with magic belonged to the pedagogical resources of his enlightenment program, a preoccupation fully evident in his lecture. According to Steinschneider's worldview, magic literature belongs neither to the beautiful nor to the true and good.²⁸² It therefore has no place in the Olympus of the intellectual canon. He then states that magic belongs to the notorious, yet unreflected things that cannot be explained – a task which scholarship will set itself in future generations, he adds hopefully.²⁸³

5.1.2 Archaeological and Philological Research

At the end of the nineteenth century, the publication of philological commentaries on Aramaic texts from Babylonia, and the interest in Greek magical papyri opened up a new era of research, offering a deeper insight into the world of magic from Babylonia to the Mediterranean coast. For the study of Jewish magic, the discovery of Greek and Aramaic parallels constituted a decisive step forward in research, which culminated with the handbook of Jewish magic

---

279 "Die kanonische Zahl der muhammedanischen Secten und die Symbolik der Zahl 70–73, aus jüdischen und muhammedanisch-arabischen Quellen nachgewiesen," *Zeitschrift der deutschen Morgenländischen Gesellschaft* 4 (1850): 145–170; 57 (1903): 474–507.
280 See note 1. Associations of Young Merchants were very popular in 19th- and 20th-century Germany. See the entry in *Meyers Großes Konversations-Lexikon*, vol. 10 (Leipzig: Bibliographisches Institut, 1907), p. 772; online at http://www.zeno.org/Meyers-1905/A/Kaufm%C3%A4nnische+Vereine (last accessed December 2, 2008).
281 In *Berliner Tagesblatt* no. 160, quoted by W. Ahrens, "Zum Charakterbilde Moritz Steinschneiders," *Ost und West* 16:8 (1916): 349–352.
282 On the concept, see Steinschneider's *Allgemeine Einleitung in die jüdische Literatur des Mittelalters. Vorlesungen* (Jerusalem: Bamberger & Wahrmann, 1938 [1859–1897]), p. 12.
283 For further details on Steinschneider's concepts of magic, see my study *Language of Dissent & Conformity. The Imaginative Grammar of Jewish Intellectuals in the Nineteenth and Twentieth Centuries* (Boston: Academic Studies Press, 2013), 179–191.

created by Lajos/Ludwig Blau (1898).²⁸⁴ This short work has remained a classic work of Jewish ethnological studies down to today. The Babylonian Aramaic incantation bowls – first published by Thomas Ellis in 1853²⁸⁵ – initiated a new epoch of philological research. Nearly half a century later, in 1913, James A. Montgomery presented a collection of the Aramaic incantation texts.²⁸⁶ Indeed, since the early 1900s, research on the magic bowls has continued almost without interruption. Important here are Edwin Yamauchi's publication of Mandaic texts,²⁸⁷ Victor P. Hamilton's work on Syriac incantation bowls (1971), and Charles D. Isbell's study on Aramaic texts (1975).²⁸⁸ In the last twenty years, the interest in Aramaic texts has been revived by the publication of new archaeological discoveries²⁸⁹ that shed fresh light on the Aramaic literary production of both Palestinian and Babylonian Judaism in late antiquity.

Another very important branch of scholarship is the publication of new literary texts, fragments, papyri, and other documents relating to Graeco-Roman magic.²⁹⁰ It would go beyond the scope of this chapter to list only a fraction of the huge scholarly output in this area. It should suffice to mention the well-known collection of Karl Preisendanz (1928).²⁹¹ New texts have in recent times been published by Merkelbach and Totti (1990–1992) and by Daniel and Maltomini (1990–92). Hans-Dieter Betz (1992) published an English translation.²⁹² Furthermore, the very important studies on the *defixiones* (curse tab-

---

284 See Ludwig Blau, *Das altjüdische Zauberwesen* (Strassburg: Trübner, 1898).
285 Austen H. Layard, *Discoveries among the Ruins of Nineveh and Babylon* (New York: Harper, 1853), 434–445.
286 James A. Montgomery, *Aramaic Incantation Texts from Nippur* (Philadelphia: University Museum, 1913).
287 See Edwin Yamauchi, *Mandaic Incantation Texts* (New Haven: American Oriental Society, 1967). See also William S. McCullough, *Jewish and Mandean Incantation Bowls in the Royal Ontario Museum* (Toronto: University of Toronto Press, 1967).
288 Victor P. Hamilton, "Syriac Incantation Bowls" (PhD diss., Brandeis University, 1971); Charles D. Isbell, *Corpus of the Aramaic Incantation Bowls* (Missoula: Society of Biblical Literature and Scholar Press, 1975).
289 See Joseph Naveh and Shaul Shaked, *Aramaic Incantations of Late Antiquity* (Jerusalem: Magnes, 1985); Naveh and Shaked, *Magic Spells and Formulae: Aramaic Incantations of Late Antiquity* (Jerusalem: Magnes, 1993); Shaked, ed. *Officina Magica: Essays on the Practice of Magic in Antiquity* (Leiden: Brill, 2005).
290 See a bibliography until 1994 in William M. Brashear, "The Greek Magical Papyri: An Introduction and Survey; Annotated Bibliography (1928–94)," in *Aufstieg und Niedergang der Römischen Welt* II, vol. 18.5 (1995): 3381–3684.
291 See Karl Preisendanz, *Papyri Graecae Magicae: Die griechischen Zauberpapyri*, 3 vols. (Stuttgart. Teubner, 1928; repr. 1973–1974).
292 See Reinhold Merkelbach and Maria Totti, *Abrasax: Ausgewählte Papyri religiösen und magischen Inhalts*, 3. vols. (Opladen: Westdeutscher Verlag, 1990–92); Robert Walter Daniel

lets), amulets, gems, and other magic devices by August Audollent (1904), John G. Gager (1999) and Roy Kotansky (ed. 1994–99) deserve mention.[293]

When analysing Jewish magic and superstition in Roman Palestine, the comparison with Graeco-Roman texts and traditions is of course obligatory. Yet, students of Jewish magic should be very careful when comparing Jewish and Graeco-Roman magical texts. The newly developed scholarly interest in Jewish and Greek magic reintroduces the old question of the relationship between Greek magical papyri and amulets, and biblical and post-biblical Jewish tradition. As Morton Smith has emphasised, the very difficulty in determining what is Jewish in Greek papyri and amulets lies in the notorious problem of defining Judaism in the first centuries CE[294] Since magic was an eclectic phenomenon, it is almost impossible to distinguish between Jewish and Greek elements in magic (for instance, with regard to angelology and *nomina barbara*, "unheard of words," "foreign words," or "mysterious words"). A naïve and hastily claimed interest in purported "parallels" is best avoided when investigating the origin and context of certain themes and motifs. The main question is whether it is correct to assume that one particular motif in a Greek amulet or papyrus (e.g., Solomonic power over demons) qualifies the text as "Jewish."

The definition of what constituted Jewish identity in antiquity is also important for the choice of the relevant texts for comparative studies.[295] The literary creativity of Judaism in the earliest centuries CE was mainly conducted orally, and only in a relatively late period was it put down in writing. For that reason, students of ancient religion and folklore should not merely focus on biblical and post-biblical Greek Jewish literature but also take the later rabbinic literature into account.

---

and Franco Maltomini, ed., *Supplementum Magicum* (Opladen: Westdeutscher Verlag, 1990–92); Hans Dieter Betz, ed. *The Greek Magical Papyri in Translation: Including the Demotic Spells* (Chicago: University of Chicago Press, 1992).

293 See Auguste Audollent, *Defixionum tabellae quotquot innotuerunt tam in Graecis Orientes quam in totius Occidentis partibus praeter Atticas in corpore inscriptionum Atticarum editas* (Paris: Fontemoing, 1904); John G. Gager, *Curse Tablets and Binding Spells from the Ancient World* (New York: Oxford University Press, 1999); Roy Kotansky, ed. *Greek Magical Amulets: The Inscribed Gold, Silver, Copper, and Bronze Lamellae*, 2. vols. (Opladen: Westdeutscher Verlag, 1994–99).

294 Morton Smith, "The Jewish Elements in the Magical Papyri," *Society of Biblical Literature Seminar Papers* 25 (1986): 455. See also Daniel Sperber, "Some Rabbinic Themes in Magical Papyri," *Journal for the Study of Judaism* 16 (1985): 93–103.

295 See Gideon Bohak, *Ancient Jewish Magic: A History* (Cambridge, UK, and New York: Cambridge University Press, 2008).

5.1.3 Folklore and Folk Life Studies

Motivated by the general interest in anthropology and ethnography at the beginning of the twentieth century, scholars began to focus their research on Jewish folklore. A famous forerunner in this field was the Romanian Rabbi Moses Gaster, *Hakham* (chief rabbi) of the Spanish and Portuguese congregation in London, who was a member of the executive councils of various societies of folklore studies. He published widely on Jewish magical texts, superstitions, and amulets.[296] Although the quality of his philological work is often not of a high calibre and his theories are sometimes questionable, Gaster distinguished himself as a polymath with a substantial interest in folklore and ancient and medieval literature. The Ashkenazic (German Jewish) Rabbi Max Grünwald can also be considered amongst the scholarly progenitors of Jewish folklore studies. He edited a journal and year book, was one of the principal founders of the Hamburg Jewish Museum, and published a huge number of essays mostly based on his collection of texts, manuscripts, and amulets.[297] Equally indispensable for the study of ancient Jewish folklore is the monograph by Joshua Trachtenberg (1939), based almost entirely on Ashkenazic tradition.[298] His book has been republished several times and still constitutes the most often consulted and quoted handbook on Jewish magic in the Middle Ages. Trachtenberg's monograph should be read together with Hirsch J. Zimmels's contribution on the work of the magician, it represents the first attempt to describe Jewish magic on the basis of the medieval rabbinic Responsa literature.[299]

Modern approaches to magic and folklore have been developed by many scholars in Israel, Europe, and the US. A survey of the state of research can be found in Veltri (1997) and most recently in Harari (2006; see also Bohak, *Ancient Jewish Magic*), who is concerned with the definition of magic, the occult, demons, divinations and astrology in rabbinic literature.

5.1.4 Mysticism, Kabbalah, and Jewish Magic

A peculiar chapter in the history of scholarship on magic is the investigation of the relationship between Jewish magic and mysticism (Kabbalah). In the

---

[296] See Moses Gaster, *Studies and Texts in Folklore, Magic, Medieval Romance, Hebrew Apocrypha and Samaritan Archaeology*, 3 vols. (London: Maggs, 1925–28).
[297] See Max Grunwald, "Folklore and Myself," [Hebr.] *Edoth* 2 (1944–45): 1–22.
[298] Joshua Trachtenberg, *Jewish Magic and Superstition: A Study in Folk Religion* (New York: Behrman's Jewish Book House, 1939; repr. Philadelphia: University of Pennsylvania Press, 2004).
[299] Hirsch J. Zimmels, *Magicians, Theologians, and Doctors: Studies in Folk Medicine and Folklore as Reflected in the Rabbinical Responsa* (London: E. Goldstone, 1952).

nineteenth and early twentieth century, the prevailing attitude to Jewish mysticism was extremely negative, since mysticism was deemed a product of irrational and irreligious thought, comparable to superstition. Until recently, scholars who studied early Jewish mystical texts (Hekhalot literature) distinguished between what they considered "high mysticism" and elements which are regarded as a product of magical beliefs.[300] The famous bibliographer Moritz Steinschneider and the historian Heinrich Graetz avoided dealing with the subject altogether, except for some negative comments belittling its significance.[301]

Only with the work of Gershom Scholem did Jewish mysticism become a *bona fide* field of scholarly inquiry, developing into an academic discipline. Scholem's interest in Jewish mysticism was profoundly influenced by the romantic and idealistic intellectual milieu of his German cultural environment. His inclination for the mystical and the mysterious, the fragmentary and the imperfect, in which he believed to have recognised the essential motive of (Jewish) existence, is reminiscent of the cosmological and linguistic ideas of Neoplatonist and Hermetic provenance (e.g., the conception of mystical language).[302] Exploring the development of the concept of micro-and macrocosm, and the rise of mystical and magical trends that culminated in early Jewish mysticism and Kabbalah, Scholem's interest extended to every imaginable genre of Jewish esoteric literature.[303] By being traced back to Hermeticism and Neoplatonism, the mystical and magical elements in Judaism that were rejected by such rationalists as Maimonides regained their philosophical respectability.

Although Scholem published physiognomic texts and conjuration formulae, he was not interested in the practical, pragmatic use and misuse of divine power, names, conjurations, recipes, etc.[304] Rather, his concern was with the theurgic interpretation as the core of Jewish mysticism and magic. Despite modern criticism of Scholem, it is undeniable that the study of Jewish mysticism, magic, and superstition owe much to his sustained scholarship, which helped create a new sub-discipline that is still a powerful magnet for a new generation of students and scholars today.

---

[300] Peter Schäfer, "Merkavah Mysticism and Magic," in *Gerschom Scholem's Major Trends in Jewish Mysticism*, edited by Peter Schäfer and J. Dan (Tübingen: Mohr-Siebeck, 1993), 73.
[301] Giuseppe Veltri, *Magie und Halakha* (Tübingen: Mohr-Siebeck, 1997), 12–13.
[302] On this aspect, see Gerschom Scholem,"Der Name Gottes und die Sprachtheorie der Kabbala," *Neue Rundschau* 83 (1972): 470–495.
[303] Veltri, *Magie und Halakha*, 12–16.
[304] See Gerschom Scholem, *Major Trends in Jewish Mysticism* (Jerusalem: Schocken, 1941); Scholem, *Jewish Gnosticism, Merkabah Mysticism and Talmudic Tradition* (New York: Jewish Theological Seminary, 1965); Veltri, *Magie und Halakha*.

A further decisive impulse to the study of magic and superstition (demonology, chiromancy, physiognomic, astrology, etc.) was given in the last decade of the twentieth century by new research on mysticism and magic, and the publication of magical texts and fragments from the Cairo Genizah. This new research was initiated and carried out by Peter Schäfer and Shaul Shaked, Joseph Naveh, and Lawrence Schiffman and Michael Swartz.[305] The newly published texts raised fresh questions about the relationship between magic and liturgy, mysticism, rabbinic Judaism and the Graeco-Roman environment, and the significance of magic in Palestinian Judaism. Ancient and medieval texts have been newly discovered and edited, initiating new studies and debates, such as the *Sword of Moses,*[306] *Havdalah de Rabbi Aqiva, Sefer Ha-Malbush, Sefer ha-Yashar,*[307] *'Inyan Soṭa,*[308] *Sefer Ha-Razim.*[309]

5.1.5 The Halakhic-Theological Approach

A Halakhic-theological debate on the value of magic can already be found in rabbinic texts, as outlined below. The modern (largely Orthodox) discussion of Jewish magic was deeply influenced by the view that Jewish mysticism was a culture of the common people (*'am ha-areṣ*), a conclusion based on the sociological approach.[310] As far back as the 1960s, Saul Lieberman suggested that magic belonged to the culture of the so-called masses.[311] Accordingly, it was assumed that ancient rabbis looked at the phenomenon with a sense of resig-

---

305 Peter Schäfer and Shaul Shaked, ed. *Magische Texte aus der Kairoer Geniza*, 3 vols. (Tübingen: Mohr-Siebeck, 1994–99); Joseph Naveh and Shaked, *Magic Spells and Formulae: Aramaic Incantations of Late Antiquity* (Jerusalem: The Hebrew University Magnes Press, 1993); Lawrence H. Schiffman and Michael D. Swartz, ed. *Hebrew and Aramaic Incantation Texts from the Cairo Geniza* (Sheffield: JSOT, 1992).
306 Yuval Harari, ed. *The Sword of Moses: A Critical Edition and Study* [Hebr.] (Jerusalem: Academon Press, 1997).
307 Irina Wandrey, *Das Buch des Gewandes und Das Buch des Aufrechten* (Tübingen: Mohr-Siebeck, 2004).
308 Veltri, "Inyan Sota: Halakhische Voraussetzungen für einen magischen Akt nach einer theoretischen Abhandlung aus der Kairoer Geniza," *Frankfurter Judaistische Beiträge* 20 (1993): 23–48.
309 See Bill Rebiger and Peter Schäfer, et al. *Sefer ha-Razim I und II: Das Buch des Geheimnisse I und II* (Tübingen: Mohr-Siebeck, 2008–09); Veltri, *Magie und Halakha*, 262–264.
310 On Hekhalot literature, David J. Halperin, *The Merkabah in Rabbinic Literature* (New Haven: American Oriental Society, 1980).
311 Saul Lieberman, *Greek in Jewish Palestine* (New York: Jewish Theological Seminary, 1965), 91–114.

nation, being unable to stamp out superstitious practices and beliefs which originated in a Graeco-Roman environment. Even Orthodox scholars conceded that rabbis may have adopted some magic practices. But they stressed that the elite strata of society were enlightened. A slightly different view was adopted in Reform Jewish circles, as Louis Jacobs claims: In his view, rabbinic Judaism applied the category of *ḥuqqot ha-goy*/laws of the Gentiles to magic.[312] Magic is seen as an adoption of Graeco-Roman customs which gradually penetrated Judaism.

This ideologically inspired approach does not take into consideration the fact that we possess evidence only of the rabbinic perspective on magic. The world beyond rabbinic literature cannot be conceived as a simple struggle between the common people and the elite. We lack literary evidence of ancient Jewish popular culture, which rabbis present from the viewpoint of the intellectual elite.

5.2 Magic and Methods in Studying Magic

The primary issue in studying magic concerns the meaning of the term. This aspect involves the scholar in the complex and much-discussed problem of religion's relationship to science, and the question of whether it is appropriate to use the label "magic" for certain ancient phenomena. The term "magic" has been burdened with ideological connotations since the Enlightenment, not to mention its religious and legal implications since the dawn of the written tradition. Yet, there is no semantic substitute for describing this phenomenon, and for distinguishing it from religion and science. Therefore, one should continue to use the term because of its practical and heuristic value.

Evans-Pritchard states:

> To try to understand magic as an idea in itself, what is the essence of it, as it were, is a hopeless task. It becomes more intelligible when it is viewed not only in relation to empirical activities but also in relation to other beliefs, as part of a system of thought.[313]

I suggest that we put the question differently, because I do not think that one can speak of magic as (part of) a "system of thought." The term "system" implies the organisation of ideas – a typical philosophical objectification. When

---

[312] Louis Jacobs, *A Tree of Life: Diversity, Flexibility and Creativity in Jewish Law* (Oxford: The Littman Library and Oxford University Press, 1984).
[313] Edward P. Evans-Pritchard, *Theories of Primitive Religion* (Oxford: Clarendon Press, 1965), 111.

speaking of magic, it is preferable to see its semantic and historical environment as the "holistic world," the world in which human beings live and operate. Yet Evans-Pritchard is correct in stressing that magic is understandable only in relation to many different aspects of human life.

The category of magic itself is an empty concept for defining a historical and existential relationship between subjects and their respective environments. The magician as practitioner illustrates how his or her (real or illusive) power can only be understood in terms of a relationship. Like an actor, the magician cannot exist or act without an audience. In almost every historical period the magician was the most consulted, but also the most despised member of his or her community, because he claimed and was attributed a special power over things, people, and coming events. He or she was supposed to be an especially skilled master, able to control not only supernatural forces and energies required for healing and the prediction of the future, but also for injuring or even killing people. To understand the power of the magician in ancient society, it is necessary to stress that a magician's authority was based on true or illusionary success in doing things that others could not do. From this point of view, it is clear why ancient scholarship was so eager to determine the nature of magic and to identify the real, authentic magician. If magic is to be defined as a hermeneutic effort to interpret and change reality, the achievements of ancient scholarship in understanding the power of its hermeneutics (by critique, avoidance, or acceptance) were considerable.

The implications of this understanding of magic for its relationship to rabbinic Judaism are obvious. Rabbis were a scholarly elite, for whom the hermeneutical method was virtually the only key to gaining knowledge and, consequently, to defending rabbinic power against undesirable competitors, such as magicians, physicians, and astrologers. It was not fear of the power of magic that compelled rabbis to analyse, oppose, or accept magic, but rather the magician's claim to be able to change reality, contrary to common experience and the "natural" rules governing human existence.

In the ancient and early medieval period, rabbis were confronted with many hermeneutic, scientific, philosophical, and theological questions which originated from the debate about magic and its efficiency: were magicians' and physicians' successes merely due to illusions and tricks, or to the genuine application of supernatural or unknown natural powers? If the magician really utilised supernatural powers, how was his handling of such energy possible and theoretically justifiable? As a direct consequence of monotheistic beliefs, a theological dilemma arose: if magic comes from the one and only God – and it must come from him – might it be used against his will? Or is God's power independent of his will? The assumption of the existence of a second, perhaps evil, but supreme and autonomous, power in heaven would undermine every monotheistic concept.[314]

In rabbinic discussions of magic and magicians, two very important aspects of rabbis' mentality are revealed:
1. the readiness to accept sources of knowledge other than the biblical text and the oral tradition, since rabbis absorbed the achievements and practices of medicine and astrology.
2. the perseverance in criticising magic by trying to unveil the innumerable tricks and strategies of the magician.

Rabbis' pragmatic attitudes to the *scientiae et artes* were almost always coupled with a belief in the magic and theurgic power of the word, substantially a Neoplatonic and Hermetic idea.

The tendency to stress (or to overemphasise?) the above mentioned intellectual aspects of rabbinic Judaism is indirectly based on the tacit premise that rabbis represented the literati of Judaism in late antiquity, an enlightened class aware of their own authority in developing Halakhah and conscious of the practical difficulties in uprooting popular customs and "foreign" ideas. Rabbis obviously maintained contacts with their Gentile neighbours, whose "idolatrous" practices they rejected, and whose philosophical ideas they accepted only in part, as many modern scholars claim.[315] The biblical and rabbinic emphasis on monotheism,[316] as well as an idealistic nineteenth-century vision of history, led modern scholars to the questionable distinction between the rabbinic elite and the "others," that is, the common people.

There were some noteworthy differences in legal competence between the Roman rulers and the rabbis. The Roman emperors tried to suppress the occult sciences, such as magic practices and astrology, because they allegedly attempted to undermine the imperial claim to be the sole authority and interpreter of history.[317] By incriminating these "alternative" sciences, the emperors tried to stem the erosion of their political power. Rabbis also tried to impose their will upon others, but they could do so only by means of argumentation,

---

[314] Alan F. Segal, *Two Powers in Heaven: Early Rabbinic Reports about Christianity and Gnosticism* (Leiden: Brill, 1977).
[315] Ephraim E. Urbach, *The Sages: Their Concepts and Beliefs* (Cambridge, Mass. and London: Harvard University Press, 1975). 97 et seq.; Lieberman, *Greek in Jewish Palestine*, 91 et seq.
[316] See Peter Hayman, "Monotheism – A Misused Word in Jewish Studies?," *Journal of Jewish Studies* 42 (1991): 1–15.
[317] See Marie-Theres Fögen, *Die Enteignung der Wahrsager. Studien zum kaiserlichen Wissensmonopol in der Spätantike* (Frankfurt am Main: Suhrkamp, 1993).

by persuading their followers and the common people. Rabbis had no power to impose capital punishment upon those who practiced magic.

To describe rabbinic attitudes toward magic and science in terms of an enlightened minority's confrontation with the "pleasures and fears" of the common people, as Saul Lieberman did,[318] must be considered inappropriate – if not outright dangerous. The mutual flow of ideas between rabbis and their environment can be encountered in the confrontation with, and tacit acceptance of, widespread patterns of behaviour, as I try to explain below.

---

[318] Lieberman, *Greek in Jewish Palestine*, 91–114.

6 "Ways of the Amorite" and Hellenism in Jewish Palestine

How much and how deeply did Greek culture (or, more precisely, the Hellenistic version of Greek culture) permeate rabbinic Judaism is an often discussed question.[319] Most modern scholars have concentrated mainly on researching the mutual exchange between these two cultures from the point of view of intellectual history. Mere traces of philosophical, theological, hermeneutical, and religious ideas have been treated in detail as prime areas of influence, whereas everyday life, folklore, science and empirical knowledge have rarely been in the focus of scholarly attention.[320]

This tendency in researching rabbinic Judaism is indirectly based on the tacitly accepted premise that the rabbis represented the intelligentsia of Judaism in late antiquity. They are considered an enlightened class aware of their own authority in developing the Halakhah, and were conscious of the practical difficulties in uprooting popular customs and "foreign" ideas. The rabbis, of course, were in contact with their Greco-Roman neighbours, whose (idolatrous) interpretation of history and *weltanschauung*, however, they largely rejected. And, whose (philosophical) ideas they accepted only within limits, or so many modern scholars claim.[321] The biblical and rabbinic accentuation of monotheism as well as a typically idealistic 19th century vision of history caused

---

319 See chapter 3 in this volume.
320 Scholars who added to the work of the scholars' of the 19th century "*Wissenschaft des Judentums*" are Samuel Krauss, Immanuel Löw, etc. There are some noteworthy approaches that have appeared more recently. See, for instance, Danniel Sperber, *Customs of Israel: Sources and History* [Hebr.], 5 vols. (Jerusalem: Mossad Harav Kook, 1990–95). Concerning science, David Ruderman commented: "I was unable to find any extended discussion of the possible connections between magical and 'scientific' activity in ancient Judaism – as one might find, for example, in Greek, Roman, or medieval culture – other than the mere mention of the links between magic and medicine." David B. Ruderman, ed. *Jewish Thought and Scientific Discovery in Early Modern Europe* (New Haven, Conn: Yale University Press, 1995), 382. See also Philip S. Alexander, "Bavli Berakhot 55a–57b: The Talmudic Dreambook on Context," *Journal of Jewish Studies* 45 (1995): 245, note 30: "A history of early Jewish science is a meaningful project which is yet to be written."
321 Scholars who maintain that Judaism of late antiquity shared beliefs about magic and superstitions with their Greco-Roman environment emphasise, on the other hand, the eclectic nature of the "common people," while the rabbis played the role of the enlightened teachers. See Ephraim E. Urbach, *The Sages: Their Concepts and Beliefs* (Cambridge, Mass. and London: Harvard University Press, 1975), 97 et seq., and Saul Lieberman, *Greek in Jewish Palestine* (New York: Jewish Theological Seminary, 1965), 91 et seq.

modern scholars to sociologically refer to a two-class system: the rabbinic elite and the "others," the common people.[322]

There is little factuality in this interpretation of the social circumstances in which the rabbinic phenomenon grew and asserted itself. Rabbanism was in fact a movement to which different social strata belonged.[323] Ignoring the various facets of the rabbinic movement's social dimension elevates the rabbis to the status of a leading class which more or less was a political caste – like the Romans in ancient Israel. As already stated above, between the Roman ruler and the rabbi there were noteworthy differences in respect to legal competence. The Roman emperors attempted to suppress the "other" sciences, such as magic practices and astrology, because these allegedly sought to undermine the imperial claim of sole authority.[324] The rabbinic "class" – whether or not we should insist on that term at all – tried of course to impose its will and its interpretation of history on the people. The medium of reaching this goal could be nothing other than *argumentatio*: the dialectic conviction of followers and of the "common" people in the truth of their belief. In this context it should not be forgotten that rabbinic Judaism had no power of physical or legal coercion, such as passing capital punishment sentences in accordance with Halakhah for crimes as such "magic."[325]

Rabbinic Literature is a product of the teachings in the schools and academies. There, beliefs and customs of the "common" as well as the "authoritative" classes were discussed with a reference to the Bible, tradition, and the exigences of everyday life. To describe the rabbinic attitudes toward magic and science in terms of an enlightened minority's actions in dealing with the "pleasures and fears" of the common people, as Lieberman maintains, is inappropriate, to say the least. We have to understand that the mutual flow of ideas between Judaism and its environment lay not in academic discussions,

---

[322] See, however, Peter Hayman, "Monotheism – A Misused word in Jewish Studies?," *Journal of Jewish Studies* 42 (1991): 1–15.

[323] On this topic, see Catherine Heszer, "Social Fragmentation, Plurality of Opinion, and Nonobservance of Halakha: Rabbis and Community in Late Roman Palestine," *Jewish Studies Quarterly* 1 (1993–1994): 234–251.

[324] For a further ongoing discussion of this topic, see Marie-Theres Fögen, *Die Enteignung der Wahrsager. Studien zum kaiserlichen Wissensmonopol in der Spätantike* (Frankfurt am Main: Suhrkamp, 1993).

[325] This is a *vexata quaestio*. On Origen's problematic claim in *Epistula ad Africanum* 20, according to which there were in some *secret* trials Rabbinic Judaism that ended with capital sentences, see Martin Jacobs, *Die Institution des jüdischen Patriarchen: Eine quellen- und traditionskritische Studie zur Geschichte der Juden in der Spätantike* (Tübingen: Mohr Siebeck, 1995), 248–251.

although rabbinic Judaism used to present fictive encounters with high dignitaries and anonymous philosophers about Jewish and "pagan" convictions and ideas. This flow was in the confrontation with and tacit acceptance of widespread patterns or models. There is indeed no proof that the rabbis actually read Plato, Aristotle, Cicero, or Pliny. On the other hand, we have more than scattered evidence that some ideas, such as the eternity of matter, the demiourgos, the nature of man as androgyn, etc., were influenced by the Greeks and Romans; as were customs (like the bath culture, theatres), and language (loanwords, for example). This cultural exchange between Judaism and Greek culture grew out of the daily contacts of Jews with other ordinary, common people, a sort of popular "fusion," as I shall attempt to show in this section. Essentially, we have to understand cultural contacts especially through their "bottom-up" dimension.

The sector that can be conceived as a sensitive barometer of the impressive interchange between Judaism and its environment is magic and folklore. Both constitute a large field where eclecticism was the rule, one adopted, borrowed, and copied from others as one pleased.[326] This phenomenon developed not only in the "lower classes," but doubtless had pervaded the entire society. Some widespread customs and beliefs were, in fact, common to every social group, sect, and religion. The rabbinic legislation about the adoption of foreign usages and "superstitions" was not aimed at limiting assimilation by forbidding or tolerating foreign customs. It was rather aimed at showing the Halakhic path of judging the exploitability of old and new customs, findings, usages and "scientific" achievements of the Jewish and pagan world.[327]

In explaining my interpretation of rabbinic Halakhah on magic and science, I would like to employ a semantic-phenomenological method, based on the evidence of the sources. For rabbinic literature uses a category which groups all forbidden customs and practices, the so-called "ways of the Amorite." It was a category related to the empirical knowledge acquired according to the Talmudic principle: "whatever is used to bring about healing does not belong to the ways of the Amorite" (see below). This category can be compared to those which Pliny refers to as the *magicae vanitates* in describing and criticising the "foreign" customs of the *magi*.

---

[326] A very impressive example of eclectic borrowing of traditions is the "conjuration of the womb." See later in this chapter.
[327] On similar results in other sectors of Rabbinic life see Martin Jacobs, "Römische Thermenkultur im Spiegel des Talmud Yerushalmi," in *The Talmud Yerushalmi and Graeco-Roman Culture* vol. 1, ed. Peter Schäfer (Tübingen: Mohr Siebeck, 1998).

The emphasis of this chapter will therefore be threefold. First of all, I will point out the background of some customs and beliefs of the "Amorite" and their similarity to Greco-Roman practices. In a further step I will attempt to identify the Halakhic principles which led the rabbis to forbid or to permit a custom. Finally, I will compare Pliny's attitudes on magic and experimental science to those of the rabbis.

6.1 The *darkhe ha-emori*

The descriptive expression "ways of the Amorite" (*darkhe ha-emori*) appears in the Mishnah and the related Gemarot. It was used there in the context of the enumeration of things permitted or forbidden on Shabbat (Mishnah, Shabbat 6:10), in the Tosefta in chapters 6 and 7, apparently in the same context, and in the Midrash Sifra as a commentary to Leviticus 18:3.[328] According to biblical sources, the Amorites belonged to the former inhabitants of Canaan (Genesis 10:16 and Exodus 8:17), whose "abominable" practices the Israelites were not allowed to adopt (Deuteronomy 20:17 f. and Ezekiel 21:29 et seq.). As early as in the biblical literature, the "Amorite" is merely a term used *pars pro toto* to roughly identify the former peoples inhabiting Canaan (see also Tosefta, Shabbat 7:25, and Mekhilta de-R. Yishmaʻel pisqa 18).

The "ways of the Amorite" became a Halakhic category in rabbinic discussions in which most kinds of forbidden foreign customs were included.[329] Their

---

[328] On the references of Talmudic data concerning the *darkhe ha-emori*, as well as a more extensive and detailed coverage of the topic see G. Veltri, *Magie und Halakha. Ansätze zu einem empirischen Wissenschaftsbegriff im spätantiken und frühmittelalterlichen Judentum* (Tübingen: Mohr Siebeck, 1997), 93–220.

[329] See Heinrich Lewy, "Morgenländischer Aberglaube in der römischen Kaiserzeit," *Zeitschrift des Vereins für Volkskunde* 3 (1893): 23–43; 130–143; 238; Ludwig Blau, *Das altjüdische Zauberwesen* (Strassburg: Trübner, 1898); Isidor Scheftelowitz, *Alt-Palästinensischer Bauernglaube in religionsvergleichender Beleuchtung* (Hannover: Lafaire, 1925); Yitzhak Avishur, "Darkhe ha-emori. Ha-reqaʻ ha-kenaʻani-bavli we-ha-mivne ha-sifruti," in *Studies in the Bible and the Hebrew Language offered to Meir Wallenstein on the Occasion of his Seventy-Fifth Birthday*, ed. Chaim Rabin, et al., (Jerusalem: Jewish Society for Bible Research in Israel and the Tarbut Society, 1979), 17–47; Saul Lieberman, ed. *Tosefta Ki-Fshutah: A Comprehensive Commentary on the Tosefta* [Hebr.] vol. 3 (New York: Jewish Theological Seminary, 1962); Mireille Hadas-Lebel, *Le Paganisme à travers les sources rabbiniques des IIe et IIIe siècles: contribution à l'étude du syncrétisme dans l'empire romain* (Berlin and New York: De Gruyter, 1979); Daniel Sperber, *Minhagei Yisra'el: Meqorot we-telodot*, 2 vol. (Jerusalem: Mossad harav Kook, 1990–1991), 33–34; Veltri, "Defining Forbidden Foreign Customs: Some Remarks on the Rabbinic Halakha of Magic to the "Chapters of the Amorite,'" in *Proceedings of the Eleventh World Con-*

importance is shown by the fact that the rabbis taught a complete lesson on them. It is documented in both the Babylonian Talmud and the Halakhic Midrash Sifra that a special "chapter" was part of rabbinic teaching and was concerned with the "ways of the Amorite." In the Sifra and in the Tosefta, the first forbidden acts to be taken into account deal with hair styles (Tosefta, Shabbat 6:1):

> The following [acts] constitute ways of the Amorite: trimming the front of the hair [according to a Greco-Roman fashion], allowing one's locks to grow long, shaving a bald-pate for [or to ward off] the Medusa.[330]

In the text of Sifra aḥare, pereq 13 (86a/22–30) we find a similar discussion on foreign and thus forbidden acts as discussed above:[331] The redactor(s) of the Sifra introduce(s) the Halakhah of the Amorite through dealing with the question of how a Jew should act with his (pagan) neighbour. Some of the customs are referred to as *ḥuqqat ha-goy* (Leviticus 20:23), as "pagan law." They are thus forbidden by definition because of their idolatrous connotations.This interpretation also appears in the Babylonian commentary (Gemara) to the Mishnah, 'Avodah Zarah 1:3 (see the Babylonian Talmud, 'Avodah Zarah 11a–11b). There, the redactor denies that the procedure of burning the body of the king after his death, on a funeral pyre, could be considered as pagan law.[332] In this case, the redactor identifies *darkhe ha-emori* with *ḥuqqat ha-goy*, the pagan law which is not to be followed according to Leviticus 18:3: "you shall not walk in their statutes."

---

gress of Jewish Studies. Div. C, Vol. 1: Rabbinic and Talmudic Literature (Jerusalem: World Union of Jewish Studies, 1994), 25–32.
330 The English translation of The Tosefta was taken, with some changes, from Jacob Neusner, trans., *The Tosefta: Neziqin* (New York: Ktav, 1981). This translation, however, is not the common one. The following readings of the text are of importance: first edition: HMGBH LGWDGDIN; manuscript Vienna: HMGBH LGWGDWN, Yalqḥare § 587: HMGBIH LGWRGRWN. Jastrow 1886/1903: 218 translates: "he who shaves his head (makes a bald-pate) for good luck [a superstitious practice]." There is, however, no reference for this superstitious practice. Lieberman reads HMGBḤ LGWDGDIN/LGWRGRIN / "Who barks for luck or for seed.". Lieberman, ed. *Tosefta Ki-Fshutah*, 81–82. It seems more likely that this practice also has something to do with "hair," as the use of L-GBḤ suggests. In Leviticus 13:42–43, this verb refers to shaping a bald-pate on the forehead. GWRGRWN can be interpreted as a Greek loanword from *Gorgoneion*: the "head of the Medusa" with its horrible hair, which is the most reproduced apotropaic figure of antiquity. It is also used as an *apotropaicum* against the evil eye. Shaving one's bald-pate for the Medusa can be consequently interpreted as an apotropaic measure against the evil eye.
331 See above, p. 58–59.
332 See also above, ibidem.

To the best of my knowledge, only these two rabbinic sources (the Midrash Sifra and the Babylonian Gemara) classify the ways of the Amorite in the category "pagan law." They interpret this tradition as a Jewish attempt of self-definition in response to the gentile world.[333] It is noteworthy that the interpretation of the "ways of the Amorite" as pagan laws appears only in the relatively early Halakhic Midrash, the Sifra, and also in the relatively late Babylonian Talmud. This is, however, not too surprising. The redactor of the Midrash Sifra attempted to base this rabbinic-tannaitic Mishnah on the Bible.[334] In the attempt to clarify what was meant by "their statutes" (Leviticus 18:3), the redactor refers to Leviticus 19:27, which attributes certain haircutting styles to "pagan" neighbours. For the Babylonian Talmud, the question is of a different nature. It seeks to harmonise the biblical custom of "burning" (in honor of) the king – in I Samuel 32:12 and Jeremy 34:5 – with the Mishnaic ban on "burning on the occasion of the king's death." Although this custom is condemned as "pagan," it is allowed on the basis of the biblical usage. The designation "pagan law" accordingly is only an exegetical notion to classify a custom which *apparently* contradicts the oral law, but which was actually grounded on a biblical precedent.

The Mishnah mentions the "ways of the Amorite" in the context of the laws of the Shabbat and the problem of "healing" (*refu'ah*): "whatever is used to bring about healing does not belong to the ways of the Amorite," as the Palestinian Talmud puts it. The "ways of the Amorite" are thus the *other* sciences and the *other* customs which, after empirical examination, are either allowed because they were useful or rejected because they were idolatrous or had tendencies of "superstition."

The entire list of the "customs of the Amorite" is a conglomeration of different magical genres, superstitions, and medical-magical recipes. It can be compared to the Greco-Roman magic literature, such as the *Papyri Graecae Magicae* or the numerous "magical" manuscripts of the Middle Ages. The "ways of the Amorite," or the customs forbidden or allowed by the rabbis under this label encompass all aspects of everyday life. They show the variety of procedures and beliefs the rabbis took into consideration.

It is no longer surprising that a comparison of most of the "ways of the Amorite" with Greek and Latin customs, as mentioned in sources of the imperi-

---

[333] This interpretation of the *darkhe ha-emori* is supported by Louis Jacobs. Louis Jacobs, *A Tree of Life: Diversity, Flexibility and Creativity in Jewish Law* (Oxford: The Littman Library and Oxford University Press, 1984), 94 et seq.

[334] There is a very detailed discussion as to whether the Midrash Sifra or the Mishnah is the original stratum of rabbinic literature. See, for instance, Ronen Reichmann, *Mishna und Sifra: Ein literarkritischer Vergleich paralleler Überlieferungen* (Tübingen: Mohr Siebeck, 1998).

al period, reveals how closely attuned the rabbinic mind was to Greco-Roman scholarship in classifying magic, folklore and science. To illustrate this and what is meant by the influence of Hellenistic culture on Hebraism, let me present some examples of allowed and forbidden customs.

Mishnah, Shabbat 6:10

> [On Sabbath] it is allowed to go out with a locust's egg, with a fox's tooth with a nail [from the gallows] of an impaled convict, for medical purposes: That is the teaching of R. Yose. R. Me' ir says: it is forbidden even on weekdays for they are ways of the Amorite.

Both the Palestinian and the Babylonian Talmud identify the objects enumerated here as medicinal amulets which presumably were in circulation in the Talmudic period:[335]

Palestinian Talmud, Shabbat 6:10 (8c)

> It is allowed to go out with a locust's egg: it is good for [her] ear; with a fox's tooth: it is good for her tooth; with a nail of an impaled convict: it is good against a spider's bite.

Babylonian Talmud, Shabbat 67a

> It is allowed to go out with a locust's egg: for they use [it] for the foetus; with a fox's tooth: for they use the tooth of a living [fox] for sleep; [the tooth] of a dead [fox] to stay awake; with a nail of an impaled convict: they use it for *zirpa* [inflammation].

It is a widespread and traditional belief that amulets are good for certain illnesses.[336] Several theoretical principles are implicitly employed: The use of a tooth against toothache comes from the magic-medical principle according to which *similia similibus* / "like cures like."[337] Pliny notes in his *Naturalis Historia* XXVIII:78, 257 that "the tooth of a wolf tied on as an amulet keeps away childish terrors and ailments due to teething."[338] According to Pliny, the magi were accustomed to make use of the teeth of hyaenas: "They [the magi] add

---

[335] On the medicinal purposes of amulets, see Julius Preuss, *Biblisch-talmudische Medizin* (Berlin: Karger, 1911; repr. Wiesbaden: Fourier, 1992), 167–171; Hirsch J. Zimmels, *Magicians, Theologians, and Doctors: Studies in Folk Medicine and Folklore as Reflected in the Rabbinical Responsa* (London: E. Goldstone, 1952), 136.
[336] See, for instance, Dioscurides, *De Materia Medica*, II, § 126 on the efficacy of the root of the plantain ("plantago major") as an amulet against glandular swelling.
[337] See Zimmels, *Magicians, Theologians, and Doctors*, 115.
[338] Latin: "Dens lupi adalligatus infantium pavores prohibet dentiendique morbos."

that a hyaena's tooth relieves toothache by the touch of the corresponding tooth, or by using it as an amulet."[339]

The application of a nail from the cross, or pieces from the gallows of an executed convict also has a parallel in Pliny as a magical custom:

> These also wrap up in wool and tie around the neck of quartan patients a piece of a nail taken from a cross, or else a cord taken from a crucifixion, and after the patient's neck has been freed they hide it in a hole where the sunlight cannot reach.[340]

Pliny accepts the idea that medicinal amulets are good for healing. His doubts about their customs originate in the further explications of the magi and contents of their practices (see for instance Pliny, *Naturalis Historia*, XXVI:9,18–20 and below). From an analysis of rabbinic literature, it can be inferred that the rabbis also believed in the power of amulets.[341] However, some principles limit their use: An amulet, a *qame'ah*, was only permitted when it had been tested (*mumḥeh, probatum*).[342]

The rabbis allowed the use of all amulets except for those which had traces of idolatry. Yet, when ruling special cases, the rabbinic practice stresses the principle of healing as being more important than the danger of idolatry. According to the Babylonian Talmud, 'Avodah Zarah 55a, using even idolatrous remedies is permitted in order that the patients do not lose their trust in God. In the Middle Ages, the principle of healing develops to the point of not only permitting the use of gentile names, the so-called *nomina Barbara*, but even the use of the name "Jesus" because of its therapeutic value (see below).

Tosefta, Shabbat 6:2

> If a piece of bread fell from his hand, whoever says: Give it back to me,
> so that my blessing may not be lost … This is a custom of the Amorite.

---

339 *Naturalis Historia* XXVIII:27,95: "dentes eius dentium doloribus tactu prodesse vel alligatos ordine." This an all other English translations are taken from: Pliny the Elder, *Natural History* vols. vi–viii [*Loeb Classical Library, 418*], trans. William H. S. Jones (Cambridge, Mass.: Harvard University Press, 1945).
340 Pliny, *Naturalis Historia*, XXVIII:11,46: "Iidem in quartanis fragmentum clavi a cruce involutum lana collo subnectunt aut spartum e cruce, liberatoque condunt caverna, quam sol non attingat." On these customs, see Lewy, "Morgenländischer Aberglaube in der römischen Kaiserzeit," 141.
341 Preuss, *Biblisch-talmudische Medizin*, 167.
342 For further references to the magical-medical therapy and to the indication of the "very approved ones," see Zimmels, *Magicians, Theologians, and Doctors*, 112.

Some customs and beliefs concerning dropping bread from the table and leaving crumbs on the table, have been transmitted from antiquity. Pliny, for example, considers the following "superstitions" to be deeply rooted in *conscientia* (the Roman mind):

> Food also that fell from the hand used to be put back at least during courses, and it was forbidden to blow off, for tidiness, any dirt; auguries have been recorded from the words, or thoughts of the diner who dropped food, a very dreadful omen being if the chief priest (*pontifex*) should do so at a formal dinner. In any case, putting it back on the table and burning it before the household deity (*Lares*) counts as expiation.[343]

Pythagoras, however, asked his disciples not to pick up fallen crumbs. He did that either to accustom them to eating moderately, or – the more superstitious explanation – because they should not tamper with a person's life. Even for Aristophanes, crumbs belonged to the heroes. In his *Heroes*, he says: "Nor taste ye of what falls beneath the board."[344]

A very interesting rational and magical explanation of the custom of picking up crumbs is transmitted by Abbaye in the Babylonian Talmud (Ḥullin 105b). The purpose of picking up fallen crumbs is to be tidy or, rather, to avert poverty:

> Abbaye said: At first I believed that the reason why one [usually] picks up [fallen] crumbs was merely tidiness. My master said to me that it might lead to poverty.[345]
>
> The angel of poverty was following a man [in order to catch him at fault], but he could not [catch him] because he was careful about [fallen] crumbs. One day he was eating some bread [outdoors] and [then] some crumbs fell among the *yavleh*.[346] [The angel of poverty] said: "Now, he will surely fall into my hands!" [Because he would not be able to pick up every fallen crumb from the grass.]

---

343 *Naturalis Historia*, XXVIII:5,27: "Cibus etiam e manu prolapsus, reddebatur, utique per mensas, vetanbantque munditiarum causa deflare; et sunt condita auguria, quid loquenti cogitantive id acciderit, inter exsecratissima, si pontifici accidat dicis causa epulanti. in mensa utique id reponi adolerique ad Larem piatio est."
344 Diogenes Laertius, VIII, 8, 34. "He bade his disciples not to pick up fallen crumbs, either in order to accustom them not to eat immoderately, or because connected with a person's death; nay, even, according to Aristophanes, crumbs belong to the heroes." The translation is taken from Diogenes Laertius, *Lives of Eminent Philosophers* vol. 2, trans. Robert D. Hicks (Cambridge: Mass.: Harvard University Press, 1972=1925), 349– 351.
345 See Babylonian Talmud, Pesaḥim 111b: "[to leave] crumbs lie in the house leads to poverty."
346 It is a kind of grass. For this translation, see Markus Jastrow, *A Dictionary of the Targumim, the Talmud Babli and Yerushalmi, and the Midrashic Literature* (London: Luzac, 1903), 561.

> After he had eaten, he took a spade and dug up the *yavleh* and threw it into a river.[347] [Then] he heard [the angel of poverty] saying: Alas, he has driven me out of his house!

Tosefta, Shabbat 6:9

> He who says: Do not clasp your hands behind your back, so that you should obstruct the work for us.

The text seems to describe a custom which was very popular in antiquity. Pliny writes:

> To sit in the presence of pregnant women, or when medicine is being given to patients, with the fingers interlaced comb-wise, is to be guilty of sorcery (*veneficium est*), a discovery made, it is said, when Alcmena was giving birth to Hercules.
> The sorcery is worse (*peius*) if the hands are clasped round one knee or both, and also to cross the knees first in one way and then in the other. For this reason our ancestors forbade such postures at councils of war and officials, on the ground that they were an obstacle to the transaction of all business.[348]

To untie and to bind are technical terms both in judicial and magical terminology. The basic principle of the procedure is that legal and magical authorities have the power to obstruct someone's action. The concept occurs in the Aramaic translation (Targum) of Deuteronomy 24:6: "Nobody is allowed to bind the brides because this is sorcery."

Tosefta, Shabbat 6:11

> He who pours out water onto the street and says: HD' – This is a custom of the Amorite. If he did so [to warn] people who are on the street, or passing by this is permitted.

To pour water onto the street was common in times without sewerage. In their daily housecleaning, housewives were accustomed to throw what they wished to dispose of into the street. See for instance the Palestinian Talmud, Moʻed Qatan 3: [81d]. Politeness, however, dictated the necessity to warn passersby.[349]

---

347 Demons are afraid of water. See Ignaz Goldziher, "Wasser als Dämonen abwehrendes Mittel," *Archiv für Religionswissenschaft* 13 (1910): 20–46; Scheftelowitz, *Alt-Palästinensischer Bauernglaube,* 72 et seq.
348 Pliny, *Naturalis Historia,* XXVIII:7,59: "Adsidere gravidis, vel cum remedia alicui adhibeantur, digitis pectinatim inter se inplexis veneficium est, idque conpertum tradunt Alcmena Herculem pariente; peius, si circa unum ambove genua; item poplites alternis genibus imponi. ideo haec in consiliis ducum potestatiumve fieri vetuere maiores velut omnem actum inpedientia."
349 See Lewy, "Morgenländischer Aberglaube in der römischen Kaiserzeit," 36.

However, both crying out and pouring water onto the floor or out the door, could be interpreted as magical procedures performed to avert bad luck. Pliny refers to the custom of pouring water in his examination of superstitions at the dinner table: "If during a banquet fires have been mentioned we avert the omen by pouring water under the table."[350]

Petronius speaks about the custom of pouring wine under the table if a cock should crow at an inopportune moment:

> Just as he [Trimalchio] was speaking a cock crew. The noise upset Trimalchio, and he had wine poured under the table, and even the lamp sprinkled with pure wine. Further, he changed a ring onto his right hand, and said: 'That trumpeter did not give his signal without a reason. Either there must be a fire, or some one close by is just going to give up the ghost. Lord, save us.'[351]

Tosefta, Shabbat 6:17

> She who sets hens to brood and says:
> I will let only a virgin set them [to brood].
> I will set them only naked.
> I will set them only with the left hand.
> I will set them only with both hands.
> These [procedures and utterances] are [among] the ways of the Amorite.

Customs and beliefs about setting hens to brood are widespread in an agricultural society and reflect fear of events which depend upon fortune and chance. A naked woman as well as nakedness per se were reputed to be a good remedy for some illnesses. Columella, a popular writer of the 1st century, recommends using the presence of a menstruating virgin as the *ultima ratio* against the plague.[352] According to Pliny, naked menstruating women are an antidote against vermin.[353] He notes also the following "medical" procedures:

---

350 Pliny, *Naturalis Historia*, XXVIII:5,26: "Incendia inter epulas nominata aquis sub mensam profusis abominamur."
351 Petronius, *Satyricon*, 74: "Haec dicente eo gallus gallinaceus cantavit. Qua voce confusus Trimalchio vinum sub mensa iussit effundi lucernamque etiam mero spargi. Immo anulum traiecit in dexteram manum et 'non sine causa' inquit 'hic bucinus signum dedit; nam aut incendium oportet fiat, aut aliquis in vicinia animam abiecit'." See *Petronius*, trans. William H. D. Rouse, (New York: Putnam's Sons, 1913), 170–171.
352 Columella, *De re rustica*, X:357–361: "At si nulla valet medicina repellere pestem, Dardaniae veniant artes, n u d a t a q u e p l a n t a s F e m i n a, quae, iustis tum demum operata iuvencae Legibus, obscaeno manat pudibunda cruore, Sed resoluta sinus, resoluto maesta capillo, Ter circum areolas et sepem ducitur horti."
353 Pliny, *Naturalis historia*, XXVIII:23,78: "quocumque autem alio menstruo si n u d a t a e segetem ambiant, urucas et vermiculos scarabaeosque ac noxia alia decidere."

Superficial abscess is cured by panaceas in honey, plantain with salt, cinquefoil, root of persolata administered as for scrofula; also by *damasonium* and by *verbascum,* pounded with its roots, sprinkled with wine, wrapped round with its root, and heated, thus prepared, on embers, so that it may be applied hot. Those with experience have assured us that it makes all the difference if, while the patient is fasting, the poultice is laid upon him by a maiden, herself fasting and naked, who must touch him with the back of her hand and say: 'Apollo tells us that a plague cannot grow more fiery in a patient if a naked maiden quench the fire.'"[354]

There are many superstitions concerning the (good or bad) "action" of the left hand.[355] The herb *eruca* has to be gathered with the left hand (Pliny, *Naturalis Historia*, XX,49,126: "tria folia silvestris erucae sinistra manu decerpta"). The same procedure has to be followed in gathering iris.[356] Care has to be taken in this procedure when mentioning the name of the patient (Pliny, *Naturalis Historia* XXI:83,143: "praecipitur ut sinistra manu ad hos eruatur colligentesque dicant cuius hominis vitiisque causa eximant"). In *Naturalis Historia* XXI:104,176, Pliny repeats the same formula for the *parthenium* but instead of writing the usual *praecipitur*/"one advises," he attributes the use to the magi ("magi contra tertianas sinistra manu evelli eam iubent dicique cuius causa vellatur nec respicere").[357]

Tosefta, Shabbat 6:19

> She who sets out a brood of chicken in a sieve or puts pieces of iron among a brood of chicken: These [procedures are among the] ways of the Amorite. But if she did so because of thunder or because of lightning: This is permitted.

The same procedure appears both in Pliny's and Columella's descriptions. Against thunder, Pliny suggests putting iron nails under straw:

> If it thunders while the hen is sitting, the eggs die, and if she hears the cry of a hawk they go bad. A remedy against thunder is an iron nail placed under the straw in which the eggs lie, or some earth from the plough.[358]

---

354 Pliny, *Naturalis Historia,* XXVI:60,93: "... experti adfirmavere plurimum referre, si virgo inponant nuda ieiuna ieiuno et manu supina tangens dicat: 'Negat Apollo pestem posse crescere, cui nuda virgo restinguat'; atque ita retrorsa manu ter dicat totiensque despuant ambo."
355 Saul Lieberman, "How Much Greek in Jewish Palestine," in *Biblical and Other Studies,* ed. Alexander Altmann (Cambridge, Mass.: Harvard University Press, 1963) 90, note 75.
356 On gathering herbs and using them as a conjuration for a magical procedure, see Thomas Köves-Zulauf, *Reden und Schweigen: Römische Religion bei Plinius Maior* (Munich: Fink, 1972), 162–163.
357 See also Pliny, *Naturalis Historia* XXII:24,50: "folium eius sinistra decerpi iubent magi, et cuius causa sumatur dici tertianisque febribus adalligari."
358 Pliny, *Naturalis Historia* X:75,152: "Si incubitu tonuit, ova pereunt, et accipitris audita voce vitiantur; remedium contra tonitrus c l a v u s f e r r e u s sub stramine ovorum positus aut terra ex aratro."

Columella recommends fasting underneath heads of garlic with iron nails:

> Very many people also lay a little grass under the litter in the nest-boxes and small branches of bay and also fasten underneath heads of garlic with iron nails, all of which things are regarded as preservatives against thunder by which the eggs are spoilt and the half-formed chickens killed before they can reach complete perfection in all their parts."[359]

Tosefta, Shabbat 7:5

> He who says: "Healing!" This is a custom of the Amorite.
> R. El'azar b. R. Ṣadoq says: They do not say "Healing" because that is a waste of time for the study of Torah. The members of the household of R. Gamli'el would not say "healing" because of the ways of the Amorite.

The custom of wishing health to sneezers is a well-documented procedure still in use today (Italian, "salute," French, "à vos souhaits," German, "Gesundheit," or English "bless you"). Two elements of this magical procedure should be distinguished: wishing health to sneezers, and the meaning of sneezing itself.[360] The Tosefta and the Babylonian Talmud in this context speak *only* of the former.

The Tosefta refers to a discussion in the rabbinic academies in which the reason for the prohibition of this widespread custom was not formulated unanimously. The Tosefta statement, i.e., the first quotation without a tradent, follows the opinion of the household of R. Gamli'el, while R. El'azar b. R. Ṣadoq attributes to the prohibition of the wish not to a danger of "magic," but only to a very practical value. He said "healing" for the sneezers necessarily interrupts the lecture of the teacher, thus causing a waste of time during the study of the Torah.

---

359 "Plurimi etiam infra cubilium stramenta graminis aliquid et ramulos lauri, nec minus alii capita cum clavis ferreis subiciunt: quae cuncta remedio creduntur esse adversus tonitrua, quibus vitiantur ova, pullique semifornes interimuntur antequam toti partibus suis consummentur;" Columella, *De re rustica* VIII:5,12. The English translation is taken from Columella, *On Agriculture*, vol. 2, trans. E. S. Forster and Edward H. Heffner (Cambridge, Mass.: Harvard University Press, 1941–1955), 349.
360 Peter Van der Horst, for example, discusses only the second aspect of the topic. This is, however, not the main point of the "way of the Amorite." See Peter van der Horst, "Two Notes on Hellenistic Lore in Early Rabbinic Literature," *Jewish Studies Quarterly* 1 (1993–1994): 255–262; Veltri, "Zur Überlieferung medizinisch-magischer Traditionen: Das màtra-Motiv in den Papyri Magicae und der Kairoer Geniza," *Henoch* 18 (1996): 157–175; Nicholas de Lange "Jewish Traditions in Greek Amulets," *Bulletin of Judaeo-Greek Studies* 18 (1996): 37–39.

Concerning the practice of wishing health to sneezers in the context of customs which are deeply-rooted in the Roman *conscientia*, Pliny observes:

> Why do we say: 'Good health' to those who sneeze? This custom, according to report, even Tiberius Caesar, admittedly the most gloomy of men, insisted on even in a carriage, and some think it more effective to add to the salutation the name of the sneezer.[361]

Tosefta, Shabbat 7:21

> If a bone got stuck in one's throat: One may put on his head a bone of that sort.

The "medical" and magical principle used here is the well-known *similia similibus*. We can again quote Pliny, who relates this custom to a "*commenta magorum*":

> Should a fish bone stick in the throat, they say it comes out if the feet are plunged into cold water; if however it is another kind of bone, bits of bone from the same pot should be applied to the head; if it is a piece of bread that sticks, pieces from the same loaf must be placed in either ear.[362]

The same use is found in the *Testament of Solomon* 18:34–40 according to *Pap. Gr. Vindobonensis* 330:

> I am the Lord, my name is Rex Alleborith.
> If a person eats birds and gulps a bone down and [thereafter] he gets ill,
> if he takes a bone of the same kind and coughs,
> I will go away from mine kib-orion(?) ...[363]

The Babylonian Talmud, Shabbat 67a, adds a conjuration for the same purpose:

> If one has a bone in his throat, he may bring of that kind, place it on his head, and say thus:
> one by one
> go down

---

[361] Pliny, *Naturalis Historia* XXVIII:5,23: "Cur sternumentis salutamus? quod etiam Tiberium Caesarem, tristissimum, ut constat, hominum, in vehiculo exegisse tradunt. et aliqui nomine quoque consalutare religiosius putant."

[362] Pliny, *Naturalis Historia* XXVIII:12,49: "Si quid e pisce haeserit faucibus, cadere in aquam demissis frigidam pedibus; si vero ex aliis ossibus haeserit faucibus, inpositis capite ex eodem vase ossiculis. Si panis haereat, ex eodem in utramque aurem addito pane."

[363] See the text with its German translation in Karl Preisendanz, "Ein Wiener Papyrusfragment zum Testamentum Salomonis," *Eos* 48 (1956): 161–167.

> swallow, swallow
> go down
> one by one.
> This is not considered as ways of the Amorite.
> For a fish bone he should say thus:
> Thou art stuck in like a pin
> Thou art locked up like a cuirass
> go down
> go down.

A conjuration is also recommended by Marcellus, *De Medicamentis* VIII:172; XV:108 – "os Gorgonis basio" –, and by the *Physica Plinii Sangallensis*, no. 11: "Lafana piscatoris, exi et fac quae te iussit Iuppiter."[364]

Tosefta, Shabbat 7:23

> One may whisper [a conjuration] over an eye, a serpent, a scorpion. But one may not whisper over words of demons.
> R. Yose says: Even on an ordinary day one may not whisper [using] words of demons.

Maimonides (*Hilkot 'Avodah Zarah* 11:11–12) tries to rationally justify the rabbinic acceptance of whispering. The rabbinic Halakhah would allow it to prevent the patient from losing his mind.[365] Of course, as Maimonides maintains, the rabbis were aware of the inefficacy of whispering for curing mental sickness. It would simply not lead to healing.

Despite the interpretation of Maimonides, however, we have evidence that the rabbis did believe in the power and efficacy of whispering as a remedy. To whisper on a wound is not forbidden according to Mishnah, Sanhedrin 10:1 – except if one utters at the same time Exodus 15:26: "I will put none of the diseases upon you which I put on the Egyptians; for I am the Lord, your physician." In other words, only the (mis)use is forbidden, one would properly say the improper *shimmush*, of the Bible in connection with whispering on a wound. Prohibiting the "use" of the biblical text is perhaps due to the fear of abuse by bibliomancy.

The Greco-Roman neighbours of the Jews also believed in the magical property of the word. The history of medicine shows that whispering as a remedy was well-known, for instance, to Galen:

---

364 See *Incantanta magica Graeca Latina*, collegit disposuit edidit Richardus Heim (Leipzig: Teubner, 1892), 490.
365 See Preuss, *Biblisch-talmudische Medizin*, 166; Lieberman, ed. *Tosefta Ki-Fshutah*, 103.

Some think that conjurations are fairytale inventions [maintained by] old wives. This was also my opinion in the past. On the basis of the evidence of my own eyes, I have gradually been convinced that they have power. I examined their usefulness relating to scorpion bites and to the case of a bone which stuck in someone's throat and was coughed up by means of conjuring. The conjurations performed their own aim.[366]

However, one must add that the question was controversial as to the effectiveness of whispering and conjuring. Pliny noted the power of whispering as a medical remedy:

There is indeed nobody who does not fear to be spell-bound by imprecations. A similar feeling makes everybody break the shells of eggs or snails immediately after eating them, or else pierce them with the spoon they have used. And so Theocritus among the Greeks, Catullus and quite recently Vergil among ourselves, have represented love charms in their poems.

Many believe that by charms pottery can be crushed, *and not a few even serpents*; that these themselves can break the spell, this being the only kind of intelligence they possess; and by the charms of the Marsi they are gathered together even when asleep at night. It is not easy to say whether our faith is more violently shaken by the foreign, unpronounceable words, or by the unexpected Latin ones, which our mind forces us to consider absurd, being always on the look-out for something big, something adequate to move a god, or rather to impose its will on his divinity.[367]

6.2 Halakhic Attitudes to Magic and Science

The entire material – procedures, conjurations, divinations, etc. – which was taken into account by the rabbis as *darkhe ha-emori*, is nothing but a small part of the practices and beliefs that were common in Talmudic times. It does, however, reflect various aspects of everyday life in the first centuries CE, especially in the sectors of agriculture and household obligations. This world is

---

366 Alexander von Tralles, *Original-Text und Übersetzung nebst einer einleitenden Abhandlung: Ein Beitrag zur Geschichte der Medicin*, vol. 2, ed. and trans. Theodor Puschmann (Amsterdam: Hakkert, 1878), 475.
367 Pliny, *Naturalis Historia* XXVIII:4,19–20: "defigi quidem diris deprecationibus nemo non metuit. hoc pertinet ovorum quae exorbuerit quisque calices coclearumque protinus frangi aut isdem coclearibus perforari. hinc Theocriti apud Graecos, Catulli apud nos proximeque Vergilii incantamentorum amatoria imitatio. multi figlinarum opera rumpi credunt tali modo, *non pauci etiam serpentes*; ipsas recanere et hunc unum illis esse intellectum contrahique Marsorum cantu etiam in nocturna quiete. etiam parietes incendiorum deprecationibus conscribuntur. neque est facile dictu externa verba atque ineffabilia abrogent fidem validius an Latina inopinata et quae inridicula videri cogit animus semper aliquid immensum exspectans ac dignum deo movendo, immo vero quod numini imperet." My emphasis.

also depicted by gentile (pagan and Christian) writers of the period, such as Pliny and Columella, and by documents such as the so-called "Magical Papyri." If the rabbis felt able or obligated to legislate on these customs, these were common practices in that period or earlier, either among Jews and/or their neighbours. Books or reference manuals on many usages, occasions, and necessities were in circulation. But it is possible that the rabbinic authorities aimed at dealing with practices which affected the "subliminal" behaviour or *conscientia*, as Pliny the Elder called it: the unreflective behaviour of mankind with reference to matters which are not in the domain of an empirical investigation. This could be the reason why rabbinical authorities insisted on empirical and pragmatic criteria in judging certain customs: whatever has a practical value can be used, provided it does not belong to the category of idolatrous practices.

The main problem in dealing with the "customs of the Amorite" is that the rabbis tend to offer no reasons why they allow or forbid a custom or procedure. A very typical example is Tosefta, Shabbat 6:4, which reads:

> He who stops up a window with thorns,
> He who ties [a piece of] iron to the leg of the bed of a woman in childbirth,
> he who sets a table before her,
> These [procedures are among] the ways of the Amorite.
> But he who stops up a window with a blanket or with tufts,
> they who set before her a bowl of water,
> and they who tie up a chicken for her
> so that it look after her.
> These do not belong to the "ways of the Amorite."

There is no reason to suppose that the rabbis allowed the customs which were introduced by *aval* ("but") because of rational considerations, as Lewy and Scheftelowitz claim. The latter base their interpretation on the custom of tying a chicken for the woman in childbed, "to keep company."[368] If we take into consideration the apotropaic function of the hen, namely to avert evil, the custom has to be interpreted as "magical," not rational.

A pragmatic mentality led the rabbis to look for clear-cut criteria in order to judge customs and widespread beliefs. They clearly wanted to reassess some procedures/customs which were deeply rooted in everyday life. Some of the principles which helped them to reinterpret the "past," that is, discussing common conventions and habits, are the following:

---

368 Quoted in Jacob Neusner, *The Tosefta: Moed* (New York: Ktav, 1981), 20.

6.2.1 Good Manners

Tosefta, Shabbat 6:8

> He who pours out water onto the street and says: HD'
> This is a custom of the Amorite.
> If he did so [in order to warn] people who are on the street or passing by this is permitted.

Tosefta, Shabbat 7:12

> He who says:
> Do not come between us so that our love does not fail.
> This is a custom of the Amorite [i.e. superstition].
> But if this was said in order to pay respect, it is permitted.

Both shouting while pouring water in order to keep out demons, as mentioned above, and the conjuration against being separated by chance here have been reinterpreted as being good manners: to warn someone on the street and to pay respect to a loved one.

6.2.2 Common Sense

Tosefta, Shabbat 6:8

> He who says:
> Do not sit on the plough
> in order that you do not make the work hard for us.
> Do not sit on the plough
> in order that it should not be broken
> These are ways of the Amorite.
> But if he said this so that it really should not break, this is permitted.

Sitting on a plough may be interpreted as an act or procedure of "binding" the tool to render it unusable. In that case, the warning "do not sit" would not have a well-founded explanation. However, if there is a real danger that the plough could be broken because of the excess weight, the warning is based on observable experience.

Tosefta, Shabbat 6:10

> He who strikes a fire against the wall and says: HD'
> This is a way of the Amorite.
> But if [he did so] because of sparks, this is permitted.

This probably refers to putting out, literally, "sealing," a fire. This was done perhaps before retiring to bed. The rabbis seem to distinguish between the "normal" procedure which may be performed by striking the burning log against a wall, and a "magic" variant. However, it is not quite clear whether the rabbis consider uttering the word HD' a part of both.

6.2.3 Established and Deep-Rooted Convictions

Tosefta, Shabbat 6:12

> He who throws a piece of iron into a cemetery and says HD'
> This is a way of the Amorite.
> But if he did so because of witchcraft, this is permitted.

Tosefta, Shabbat 6:13

> He who puts a staff of wood or iron under his head,
> This is a custom of the Amorite.
> But if he did so in order to keep them, this is permitted.

The rabbis' permission was based on the popular and widespread magical belief in the power of iron on the one hand, and in the power of sorcery and witchcraft on the other. Rabbinic as well as pagan and Christian authorities were convinced that sorcery indeed had power *per se*. It was therefore allowed to protect oneself against these influences, even through magic. It was also not forbidden to keep pieces of iron for the same purpose. All magical activity as such was forbidden, however, and if carried out, punishable by death.

6.2.4 Empirical Observation

Tosefta, Shabbat 6:14

> She who shouts at an oven [for] not to let the bread fall,
> She who puts splinters into the handle of a pot that it should not boil over,
> These are ways of the Amorite.
> But she may put splinters of mulberry or shards of glass into the pot, so that it will boil more quickly.
> [However], the Ḥakhamim said that she should not do so with those made out of glass, because of the danger to life.

Pliny makes a clear case, in *Naturalis Historia* XXIII:64,127, that certain kinds of twigs were usually put into the pot so that it could boil more quickly. The rabbis allowed this custom, but rejected the use of glass because of the danger to life. This is a typical example of their empirical-pragmatic mentality. They did not allow shouting at an oven, perhaps because of the "magical" thinking this evoked, and putting splinters into the handle, maybe because of their use as amulets.

The examples I have presented show the attitude of rabbinic Judaism toward magic, superstitions, and science. Evident in all examples is a practical and pragmatic tendency which should not be overlooked. Yet it should also be emphasised that the introduction of the principle of "intention" into discussions of the "ways of the Amorite" illustrates the difficulty in finding clear-cut criteria to define a procedure or belief. Everywhere else it is emphasised that in order to make a proper decision according to the relevant Halakhah, it is necessary (especially in criminal justice) to ascertain the facts and the nature of the case, for example, through witnesses. The intention behind an act, however, cannot be ascertained and intention plays little or no role in determining the permissibility of an act, unless it was plainly obvious. The fact that the non-stated intention here is seen as the critical factor suggests that the rabbis were trying to reinterpret certain worrying practices. These were practices that in fact were forbidden but continued to exist. The rabbis used "intention" as a loophole through which to make the forbidden permissible.

Another principle of rabbinic Halakhah concerning the "ways of the Amorite" has to be emphasised for its "scientific" and modern value: the Palestinian Talmud, Shabbat 6:10 (8c/37–39) reads: "whatever is used to bring about healing does not belong to the ways of the Amorite." This points to the fact that rabbinic authorities did accept certain "foreign" customs for healing purposes and did not forbid them, although they were foreign. We do not know whether "Jewish skill in effecting cures" attracted non-Jews to Judaism, as Louis Feldman claims.[369] We can only infer from the above-mentioned Halakhah that rabbinic Judaism was open to "pagan" influences as long as they were believed to be effective. Therefore, according to the Palestinian Talmud ('Avodah Zarah 2:1 [40c]), even a pagan physician was allowed to treat a Jew.

6.3 Pliny and the "Foreign" Customs of the Magi

The rabbis' attitude to *darkhe ha-emori* is paralleled in many ways by Pliny's attitude to magic. The attitudes are both sympathetic and critical. Pliny allows

---

[369] Louis H. Feldman, *Jew and Gentile in the Ancient World: Attitudes and Interactions from Alexander to Justinian* (Princeton: Princeton University Press, 1993), 381.

an impressive picture of how scholars and scientists of antiquity and late antiquity approach the sectors of life which escape an empirical explanation in a phenomenological way. Above all, it is the power of the word which fascinates and repulses Pliny.[370] Pliny writes that

> Of the remedies derived from man, the first raises a most important question, and one never settled: have words and formulated incantations any effect? If they have, it would be right and proper to give the credit to mankind. As individuals, however, all our wisest men reject belief in them, although as a body the public at all times believed in them unconsciously.[371]

Pliny cannot deny that some customs and beliefs are rooted in the consciousness of humankind, we might say in the collective unconscious mind. For this reason he writes, "I should like to reinforce this part of my argument by adding [some beliefs from] the consciousness of the individual".[372] These beliefs are nothing but "superstitious practices," as we usually call them. Among them were the following: To wish one another luck on New Year's Day; to express belief in evil; to declare that a dead person's memory is not being attacked while mentioning the deceased; to believe in the power of odd numbers; to wish "good health" to someone who sneezes, etc. According to Pliny, these are commonly accepted customs. They form the *conscientia,* the common feeling of people. Pliny respects the *conscientia* and therefore does not transmit some *formulae* because of the feelings they may evoke:

> We certainly still have formulas to charm away hail, various diseases, and burns, some actually tested by experience, but I am very shy of quoting them, because of the widely different feeling they arouse. Wherefore everyone must form his own opinion about them as he pleases.[373]

---

370 See Alfred Ernout, "La magie chez Pline l'Ancien," in *Hommages à Jean Bayet,* ed. Marcel Renard and Robert Schilling (Brussels-Berchem: Latomus Revue d'Études Latines, 1964); Köves-Zulauf, *Reden und Schweigen;* Änne Bäumer, "Die Macht des Wortes in Religion und Magie, Plinius *Naturalis Historia* 28: 4–29," *Hermes* 112 (1984): 84–99.
371 Pliny, *Naturalis Historia,* XXVIII:3,10: "Ex homine remediorum primum maximae quaestionis et semper incertae est, polleantne aliquid verba et incantamenta carminum. quod si verum est, homini acceptum fieri oporteret conveniat, sed viritim sapientissimi cuiusque repuit fides, in universum vero omnibus horis credit vita nec sentit."
372 *Ibidem,* 5:22: "Libet hanc partem singulorum quoque conscientia coarguere."
373 *Ibidem,* 5:29: "Carmina quidem extant contra grandines contraque morborum genera contraque ambusta, quaedam etiam experta, sed prodendo obstat ingens verecundia in tanta animorum varietate. Qua propter de his ut cuique libitum fuerit opinetur."

Pliny's liberal attitude in letting everyone decide "as he pleases" does not extend to the inventions of the magi, which he calls *magicae vanitates* ("deceits"). He notes:

> Above all Asclepiades was helped by magician deceits, which prevailed to such a degree that they were strong enough to destroy confidence in all herbal remedies. It was believed that by the plant aethiopis rivers and pools are dried up; that by the touch of onothuris all things shut are opened; that if achaemenis is thrown on the ranks of an enemy the lines turn their backs in panic; that latace was want to be given by the Persian king to his envoys, so that wherever they went they might enjoy an abundant supply of everything, with much similar nonsense ...
>
> It would certainly be wonderful that the credulity of our forefathers, though it arose from most sound beginnings, reached the height it did, if in any matters man's wit knew moderation, and I were not about to show, in the appropriate place, that this very system of medicine invented by Asclepiades has surpassed even magician nonsense. It is without exception the nature of the human mind that what begins with necessities is finally carried to excess.[374]

Pliny refuses the *magicae vanitates* not because they are "magic," but only because they are *vanitates*, i.e., an exaggerated claim in the efficacy of plants in non-medical (or empirical) sectors. He does not shy away from using foreign (and strange) healing methods, if they are comprehensible. At the beginning of Book XXVIII of his *Naturalis Historia*, which deals with the remedies taken from animals, he adds:

> Surely I must, and I shall devote all my care to the task, although I realised the risk of causing disgust, since it is my fixed determination to have less regard for popularity than for benefiting human life. Furthermore, my investigations will include foreign things and even outlandish customs (*externa quoque et barbaros etiam ritus indagabimus*).

Even in the mind of Pliny the Elder, the usefulness of a cure is the criterion for its "scientific" value. Foreign and "barbarian" procedures, too, can be of proven medical value. This is not the case of the pseudo-medical knowledge of the *Magi*, a sociological category which in Pliny's terminology corresponds to the rabbis' Amorites. Their inventions are only "deceits" (*vanitates*) because these cannot be proven empirically. The same opinion is revealed in a law issued by Emperor Constantine on May 23, 318 CE.[375] Constantine makes punishable the

---

374 Pliny, *Naturalis Historia* XXVI:9,18–20.
375 *Codex Theodosianus* 9.16.3, a.321/4 (318 Seek): "Idem A. et Caes. ad Bassum P(raefectum) V(rbi). Eorum est scientia punienda et severissimis merito legibus vindicanda, qui magicis adcinti artibus aut contra hominum moliti salutem aut pudicos ad libidinem deflexisse animos detegentur. Nullis vero criminationibus inplicanda sund remedia humanis quaesita corporibus aut in agrestibus locis, ne maturis vindemiis metuerentur imbres aut ruentis grandinis lapidatione quaterentur, innocenter adhibita suffragia, quibus non cuiusque salus aut existimatio

science (*scientia*) of those who support the magical arts (*magicis adcinti artibus*), and who act against human health (*contra hominum moliti salutem*) or morals (*pudicos deflexisse animos*). Constantine does accept without reservation, however, the remedies for healing (*remedia humanis quaesita corporibus*). In the same manner, he had no objection to agricultural devotions for rain or to prayers for a good harvest, etc., because they are not harmful.[376] Pliny, Constantine, and the Rabbis all agree in the main feature of their legal and scientific ideals: whatever cannot be verified (and/or is harmful) is called magic and superstition. It therefore should be avoided. These practices do not aid mankind's salvation or moral life. By contrast, non-magical practices help to heal and to sustain people's lives and should consequently be accepted from whoever has invented or (improved) them.

After the analytical discussion, I wish to pose a more theoretical question: how can we compare the attitudes of Pliny and the rabbis toward magic and the empirical sciences? Although they were similar, they obviously did not stem from the same socio-cultural environment, same religious or philosophical ideas. In fact, Pliny belonged to the Roman establishment, the elite of Latin scholarship. The Jews, on the other hand, were among the minority subject peoples under Roman imperial rule scattered from Orient to Occident.

To understand the similarities, we do not necessarily have to speak of mutual influences. There is, as a matter of fact, no evidence that the rabbis ever read the *Naturalis Historia*. Nor can we prove that Pliny had informants among the rabbis. I dare say he had none. The best explanations of the common approaches are certain tendencies in the first centuries CE until Byzantine Emperor Justinian's rule (527–565), when the medical schools and academies were gradually losing their influence, and the records of encyclopaedists like Pliny, as well as Dioscurides, were sought to be kept for posterity.

Neither Pliny nor the rabbis were experimenters in scientific matters; their purpose was to examine, judge and record past and present experiences, which perhaps could prove helpful for everyday life. It is likely that both the rabbis

---

laederetur, sed quorum proficerent actus, ne divina munera et labores hominum sternerentur. Dat. x Kal. Iun. Aquil(eiae) Crispo et Constantino Caess. Conss." Marie-Theres Fögen, *Die Enteignung der Wahrsager: Studien zum kaiserlichen Wissensmonopol in der Spätantike* (Frankfurt am Main: Suhrkamp, 1993), 323. See also the comment there.

376 This should not be compared to the more modern idea of a "black" and a "white" magic, as Fögen suggests. as the *scientia* to be avoided and punished is that science deemed harmful to salvation or moral life. Therefore, a love charm, which in modern terminology would be considered white magic, is forbidden. The sciences to be followed are, of course, medicine, and "religious" agricultural devotions, because they are not directed against the salvation or the dignity of people. Fögen, *Die Enteignung der Wahrsager*, 42.

and Pliny learned their (relatively pseudo-)medical recipes, prescriptions and pharmaceutical knowledge almost exclusively from books and informants.[377] They had not been students of particular schools of medicine, but tried to base their knowledge on the (intellectual) experience of reality. The intellectual element of rabbinic Judaism would seem at times to be the main feature of its exegesis of traditions and texts. The area of thought common to both Pliny and the rabbis was, in conclusion, only the pragmatic attitude toward reality and the method of recording past experience.

We should not overlook a further question concerning the use of the label *darkhe ha-emori* as a rhetoric category. The terms "ways of the Amorite," as well as Pliny's "magic deceits," surely belong to a rhetoric dimension: They attribute certain customs to "foreign," fictitious elements or peoples. They are used to explain, even distinguish, the "common" practices and modes of behaviour as categories. The rhetoric of separation was nothing but the use of a category of social identity to forbid something that was, for whatever reason, deemed unacceptable. We might ask as to why the rabbis transmitted both forbidden and allowed customs, and did not alternatively censor them. They did so, perhaps, because they could not suppress them all. On the other hand, both the rabbis and Pliny aimed to provide records of events, procedures, and medical knowledge which were categorised as either helpful or dangerous. It was up to their readers or commentators to accept or reject their findings.

The principle of empirical evidence, as expressly noted by both Pliny and the rabbis, is surely a "modern" aspect, however it should not be exaggerated. "Magic" or "science" in late antiquity were not only terms to encompass scientific phenomena and religious practices, they had legal consequences as well. The supporters of magic were to be prosecuted and severely punished. In rabbinic Halakhah and Roman law the penalty for *effective*, that is, proven magical procedures was death. In other words, magic was considered both a real and potential danger to public and private life. That is why one could defy "magic" with the help of one's own magic.

The empirical principle of first examining and then accepting new sciences and findings – *remedia quaesita corporibus* – was also an achievement of Roman law. Yet it was a brief achievement largely confined to the rule of Constantine the Great. In Judaism, it formed a Halakhic tradition which flourished most particularly in the Middle Ages, when Greek medicine once more addressed the question of the legitimacy of "foreign" customs through the mediation of Arabs.

---

[377] On Pliny's method in his *Naturalis Historia*, see Geoffrey E. R. Lloyd, *Magic, Reason and Experience: Studies in the Origin and Development of Greek Science* (Cambridge: Cambridge University Press, 1979), 137 et seq., 148 et seq. The ancient sources show evidence of a very small number of Jewish doctors who were trained in medical schools.

The examples of lore, magic, and custom which we have discussed show the similarities of the Jewish and Roman minds. It is hard to say whether Jews borrowed such customs from the Romans or *vice versa*. The term *darkhe ha-emori* may even be a metathesis of *darkhei ha-romi* which would mean "ways of the Roman."[378] The main point to be emphasised, in conclusion, is that the Jews and Greeks, Pliny in particular, show parallels in their attitudes toward magic and sciences more than in their *realia*. Widespread customs and beliefs were tested for their usability or harm. In judging magic and science(s), rabbis and Pliny reflect a pragmatic mentality, and the intent to accept or avoid what could be helpful or dangerous for everyday life.

Another aspect: Asclepiades, the physician, was supported by magic deceits which prevailed to such a degree that they were strong enough to destroy confidence in all herbal remedies. It was believed that the plant *aethiopis* dried up rivers and pools; that by the touch of *onothuris* all things shut were opened; that if *achaemenis* is thrown on the ranks of an enemy, the lines turn their backs in panic; that *latace* was once given to his envoys by the Persian king so that wherever they went they might enjoy an abundant supply of everything. The list of this and much similar nonsense is long.

It certainly would be wonderful if the credulity of our forefathers, although it arose from quite sound beginnings, had not reached the height it did through the elevation of superstition and magic. It is a curious fact, that the very system of medicine invented by Asclepiades, the epitome of Greek medicine and thus science, surpassed even magician nonsense. It is without exception the nature of the human mind that what begins by necessity is finally carried to excess.[379] Pliny shows an ambivalent attitude toward magic where it suits him.

In concluding this part on the empirical value of rabbinic Judaism, I wish once more to emphasise that the cultural settings where the Jewish attitude to science developed were not in the academic institutions and the philosophical schools of their age, but amid the challenges of everyday life. Their preoccupation with the Torah was not the determining factor for accepting or condemning foreign knowledge, but the actual demands of their day: whatever is to be considered healing should not be avoided. In this respect, the Amoraic and Tannaitic teachers were innovative. Let us not forget, the written Torah is strongly against medicine: The only physician is God.

---

378 See Judah Goldin, "The Magic of Magic and Superstition," in *Aspects of Religious Propaganda in Judaism and Early Christianity*, ed. Elisabeth Schüssler Fiorenza (Notre Dame, Ind.: University of Notre Dame Press, 1976), 117.
379 Pliny, *Naturalis Historia* XXVI:9,18–20.

Appendix: A Comparison between Pliny and Tosefta Shabbat

The main source for our knowledge of Roman religious customs is Pliny the Elder's *Naturalis Historia*.[380] Pliny is especially close to the rabbinic concepts of magical deeds when he speaks of the Roman *conscientia*. This is a commonly accepted Roman custom that is not necessarily related to reason or *religio*. When Pliny discusses summoning – whose power he doubts, but against which he is unable to argue sufficiently – Pliny lists the following customs which also show surprising similarities to the rabbinic "ways of the Amorite."[381] For clarification, I have added the corresponding rabbinic opinion in small caps.

> I would appeal, too, for confirmation on this subject [conscientia], to the intimate experience of each individual.
> Why, in fact, upon the first day of the new year, do we accost one another with prayers for good fortune, and, for luck's sake, wish each other a happy new year?
> Why, too, upon the occasion of public lustrations, do we select persons with lucky names, to lead the victims?
> Why, to counteract fascinations, do we Romans observe a peculiar form of adoration, in invoking the Nemesis of the Greeks; whose statue, for this reason, has been placed in the Capitol at Rome, although the goddess herself possesses no Latin name?
> Why, when we make mention of the dead, do we protest that we have no wish to impeach their good name?
> Why is it that we entertain the belief that for every purpose odd numbers are the most effectual; – a thing that is particularly observed with reference to the critical days in fevers?
>> [TOSEFTA, SHABBAT 6:18: "THE WOMAN WHO THROWS EGGS AND HERBS AGAINST A WALL AND SQUEEZES THEM OUT [AGAINST HERSELF], AND COUNTS SEVEN AND ONE. THESE [ACTIONS/UTTERANCES] ARE THE WAYS OF THE AMORITES.]
>
> Why is it that, when gathering the earliest fruit, apples, on pears, as the case may be, we make a point of saying "This fruit is old, may other fruit be sent us that is new?"
>> [TOSEFTA, SHABBAT 7:6: "HE WHO SAYS: MORE, AND THERE WILL BE LEFT [EVEN MORE]! THIS [WISH] IS THE WAY OF THE AMORITES. R. YEHUDAH SAYS: HE WILL HAVE NOTHING IN HIS HOUSE [LEFT], AND [THUS] THERE WILL BE [NOTHING LEFT]."]
>
> Why is it that we salute a person when he sneezes, an observance which Tiberius Cæsar, they say, the most unsociable of men, as we all know, used to exact, when riding in his chariot even? Some there are, too, who think it a point religiously to be observed to mention the name as well of the person whom they salute ...

---

380 See Giuseppe Veltri, "The Rabbis and Pliny the Elder: Jewish and Greco-Roman Attitudes to Magic and Empirical Knowledge," *Poetics Today* 19 (1998): 63–89; "The 'Other' Physicians: The 'Amorites' of the Rabbis and the Magi of Pliny," *Koroth* 13 (1998–1999): 37–54.
381 On the entire passage, see Thomas Köves-Zulauf, *Reden und Schweigen: Römische Religion bei Plinius Maior* (Munich: Fink, 1972); Änne Bäumer, "Die Macht des Wortes in Religion und Magie, Plinius *Naturalis Historia* 28: 4–29," *Hermes* 112 (1984): 84–89.

[TOSEFTA, SHABBAT 7:5: "HE WHO SAYS: BLESS YOU! THIS [WISH] IS THE WAY OF THE AMORITES. R. EL'AZAR B. R. SADOQ SAYS: ONE DOES NOT SAY "BLESS YOU" BECAUSE THIS MEANS LOSING TIME FOR THE STUY OF THE TORAH. THE HOUSE OF RABBAN GAMLI'EL DOES NOT SAY "BLESS YOU" AS THIS IS THE WAY OF THE AMORITES."]

To salute summer lightning with clapping of the hands, is the universal practice with all nations.

[TOSEFTA, SHABBAT 6:2A: "HE WHO CLAPS [WITH HIS HANDS] ON THE SHOULDERS, OR THROW'S ONE'S HANDS UP, OR DANCES BEFORE THE FIRE: THESE [ACTIONS] ARE THE WAYS OF THE AMORITES."]

If, when eating, we happen to make mention of a fire that has happened, we avert the inauspicious omen by pouring water beneath the table ...

It has been remarked, too, that there is never a dead silence on a sudden among the guests at table, except when there is an even number present; when this happens, too, it is a sign that the good name and repute of every individual present is in peril.

In former times, when food fell from the hand of a guest, it was the custom to return it by placing it on the table, and it was forbidden to blow upon it, for the purpose of cleansing it. Auguries, too, have been derived from the words or thoughts of a person at the moment such an accident befalls him ...

[TOSEFTA, SHABBAT 6:2B: "IF SOMEBODY DROPS A PIECE OF BREAD [FROM HIS HANDS] : THE ONE WHO SAYS: HAND IT BACK SO MY BLESSING MAY NOT BE LOST ... THIS [ACTION] IS THE WAY OF THE AMORITES."]

There are in existence, also, certain charms against hail-storms, diseases of various kinds, and burns, some of which have been proved, by actual experience, to be effectual; but so great is the diversity of opinion upon them, that I am precluded by a feeling of extreme diffidence from entering into further particulars, and must therefore leave each to form his own conclusions as he may feel inclined.[382]

As seen, many superstitious beliefs Pliny mentions in this excerpt have their correspondence in the Tosefta, and are typically referred to as the "ways of the Amorites." This congruence equally is, it would seem no accident. Rather, it points to the fact that the term "Amorite" could very well mean "Roman." The actions and customs mentioned appear *de facto* as common customs in Pliny's description and also that of the rabbis. By identifying them as "foreign," the rabbis express very plainly their disapproval of observing them. The rabbis proceeded with the customs in such a way that they tacitly accepted them *if* they were compatible with pragmatic-empirical knowledge or religion. Otherwise they outlawed them.

It is easy to see that the rabbis as well as Pliny referred to customs which were very deeply rooted in the everyday lives of the people, and for which there were no real reasons. However, these were also customs that would not

---

[382] The English text is taken from: Pliny the Elder, *The Natural History*, trans. John Bostock, vol. XXVIII,5, *Perseus Digital Library of Tufts University*, www.perseus.tufts.edu/hopper/text?doc=Plin.+Nat.+toc (accessed January 12, 2013).

cease to be followed. They simply belonged to the *conscientia* (of Romans, Jews, and any other people under Roman influence). The question of these actions' legitimacy was often raised. According to the answer to this question, the respective custom was either allowed or prohibited.

It was not only the rabbis who had sought to fence themselves off from pagan customs. There are similar examples in the church history of the late antiquity. One such example is the Christian author Eligius (588–659), who devised a list of *paganae consuetudines* / "pagan customs."[383]

English Translation	Latin Original
I especially wish to announce and conjure: do not follow any idolatrous and pagan customs …	Ante omnia autem illud denuntio atque contestor, ut nulla Paganorum sacrilegas consuetudines observetis …
At the same time, you are not supposed to pay attention to divination, or (divination through sneezing,[384]	Similiter et auguria vel sternutationes nolite observare
Or some singing birds at the side of the path one has begun to travel.[385]	Nec in itinere positi aliquas aviculas cantantes attendatis …
No Christian is supposed to pay attention to the time of day at which he leaves the house or returns to it,[386]	Nullus Christianus observet, qua die domum exeat, vel qua die revertatur
As God had created all days. Nobody is supposed to pay attention to the [time of] day and moon when beginning a work.	Quia omnes dies deus fecit; nullus ad inchoandum opus diem vel lunam attendat;
On the first day of January, nobody is supposed to do the *nefanda*, the ridiculous, the ugly, the *cervulos*, or the *iottocos*.	nullus in kal. Jan. nefanda aut ridiculosa, vetulas aut cervulos aut jotticos faciat,
Nobody is supposed to put up a table [simply] because of the night;[387]	neque mensa super nocte componat

---

[383] See the parallels to the ways of the Amorites as quoted above. I have taken excerpts of the Latin text, including these parallels to rabbinic texts, from Jakob Grimm, "Aberglaube," in *Deutsche Mythologie* vol. 3 (Göttingen: Dieterische Buchhandlung 1854; repr. Berlin: Ullstein 1981]). As far as I know, this text is rarely discussed in scholarship.
[384] See Tosefta, Shabbat, 7:5: "This [wish] is the way of the Amorites."
[385] See Tosefta, Shabbat 6:5: "Caw: He who tells it: Caw! [If] a raven caws: He who tells it: Return! These [actions] are the ways of the Amorites."
[386] See Tosefta, Shabbat 7:14: "Who is a *me'onen*? R. Ishma'el says: He who moves something before the eye. R. Aqiva says: They are those who offer times, like those who say: This present day is right for going out. This present day is right for doing purchase. On this day, the sun will hide behind the clouds. Tomorrow, there will be rain."
[387] See Tosefta, Shabbat 6:3 (work); Tosefta Shabbat 7:13: "He who sets the table before her. This [action] is the way of the Amorites."

English Translation	Latin Original
nor is he supposed to exercise the omen or the unnecessary drinking.[388]	Neque strenas aut bibitiones superfluas exerceat
On the occasion of the festivities of St. John or any other festivity honoring the holy solstice, nobody is supposed to do saltations [?], dances,[389] *caraulas* [?], or sing devilish songs.	Nullus in festivitate S. Joannis vel quibuslibet sanctorum solemnitatibus solstitia aut vallationes vel saltationes Aut caraulas aut cantica diabolica exerceat.[390]

This passage is not important for the stunningly similar motives of the customs in question. Its importance lies far more in the list's composition and consistency. Eligius and the rabbis condemn everything that was remotely connected to idolatry, perceived to be so, or simply deemed morally unfit. For Eligious, these customs were *consuetudines paganorum*, for the rabbis *darkhe ha-emori*. Both reflect Greco-Roman customs which had penetrated Judaism and Christianity. The Greco-Roman heritage could not be eradicated entirely, despite all those prohibitions. It thus had to be interpreted anew, like the *saturnalia*, which continue their existence in Christian Christmas and Jewish Hanukkah.

The rabbis reserved other customs for themselves that were unique to the Roman elite, or associated with it. This is an outcome of the political position of Judaism after the loss of political autonomy.

---

388 See Tosefta, Shabbat 7:7: "He who says: Drink and leave a rest. This [utterance] is the way of the Amorites. Drink and leave a rest. This [utterance] is not the way of the Amorites." *bShab* 67b/12–14: "Drinking and leaving a rest, I will drink and leave a rest. This is [forbidden] because of the ways of the Amorites."

389 See Tosefta, Shabbat 6:2a: "He who slaps on the shoulder with his hands, or who claps his hands, or dances before a flame. These [actions] are the ways of the Amorites."

390 The Latin text continues: "Nullus cristianus ad fana, vel ad petras, vel ad fontes, vel ad arbores ad cellos vel per triviam luminaria faciat. Nullus sibi proponat fatum vel fortuna aut genesin quod vulgo nascentia dicitur ut dicat 'qualem nascentia attulit taliter erit.' Nullus se inebriet, nullus in convivio suo cogat alium plus bibere quam oportet. Nullus vel in qualibet minima causa diaboli sequatur adinventiones, nullus sicut dictum est observet egrediens aut ingrediens domum, quid si occurat, vel si aliqua vox reclamantis fiat, aut qualis avis cantus garriat [see above] vel quid etiam portantem videat, *quia qui haec observat ex parte paganus dignoscitur*."

7 The Magician/Magush in Rabbinic Judaism

The challenge is a very old one to define magic, science and arts, to limit the sphere of influence, and to legislate on the consequences of the handling of their *subjecta agentia*, their professional qualifications. The question of how to understand magic and medicine, for instance, was of vital importance because of its legal implications. That is the reason why the preparation and the use of *farmaka*/potions was already punishable as a capital offence in a law code dating back to 479 BCE.[391] Hippocrates, the famous father of the Greek medical school, advised physicians and midwives not only to refrain from believing in demons and evil forces, but indeed to be *adeisidaímones*/non-superstitious.[392] Plato dealt with the consequence of injuring or killing by poisoning in chapter 11 of his *Laws* (933d–e):[393]

> He who employs poison to do any injury, not fatal, to a man himself, or to his servants, or any injury, whether fatal or not, to his cattle or his bees, if he be a physician, and be convicted of poisoning, shall be punished with death; or if he be a private person, the court shall determine what he is to pay or suffer. But he who seems to be the sort of man who injures others by magic knots, or enchantments, or incantations, or any of the like practices, if he be a prophet or diviner, let him die; and if, not being a prophet, he be convicted of witchcraft, as in the previous case, let the court fix what he ought to pay or suffer.[394]

The decisive criterion in this legal discussion is not the deed as such (causing an injury, fatal or not), but the degree of professional competence of the practitioner.[395] A physician must be aware of the danger of poisoning; a prophet or diviner has to be concerned with the effects of his handling. Consequently, it is the professional qualification of the subject that distinguishes the physician from the private person. It is the physician who is aware of the effects of his

---

[391] Wilhelm Dittenberger, ed., *Sylloge Inscriptionum Graecorum* vol. 1, (Leipzig: Hirzelium, 1915), no. 37; see also the introduction in John G. Gager, *Curse Tablets and Binding Spells from the Ancient World* (New York: Oxford University Press, 1999).
[392] See Ludwig Edelstein, "Greek Medicine in Its Relationship to Religion and Magic," in *Ancient Medicine: Selected Papers of Ludwig Edelstein*, ed. Owsei Temkin, C. Lilian Temkin (Baltimore: The Johns Hopkins University Press, 1967), 220 et seq.
[393] W. D. Amundsen, "The Liability of the Physician in Classical Greek Legal Theory and Practice," *Journal of the History of Medicine and Allied Sciences* 32 (1977) 172–203.
[394] Plato, *Laws: Book XI*, trans. Benjamin Jowett. It is widely accessible online.
[395] See also the parallel discussion on prophecy in my contribution "The False Prophet and the Magician," in *Scritti in onore di Horacio Simian-Yofre S. J.*, ed. Elzbieta M. Obara, Giovani Paolo D. Succu (Rome: GBP, 2013): 343–357.

ministrations. The consciousness of being magus or doctor, prophet or diviner, connected with the proof thereof, is the main element of rabbinic discussion on the subjecta agentia.[396]

Ancient Judaism dealt with magic at length. In the rabbinic academies of the 1st century CE, a very intensive discussion took place about the identification of forbidden customs, professions and beliefs (see above). The starting point of this Halakhic debate was the biblical text, following the usual and traditional way of teaching and learning. This premise of rabbinic Judaism is also the first methodical difficulty for modern research. For it is not easy to ascertain where the boundaries were set between exegesis and historical actualisation; between empirical facts and legal precedents (ma'ase); between what was purely derivative hermeneutics from the Bible text and what was taken from experience. Rabbinic Halakhah oscillates between Bible and history, rhetoric and experience. What we gain from the rabbinic texts perhaps has nothing to do with the real conditions of that period, but it cannot simply be assumed that it was only an academic exercise. Applying methodological doubt to rabbinic literature is the only way to accept its statements as historical facts.

A second additional aspect should be taken into consideration and borne in mind when we deal with magic for its legal value. Because the rabbis no longer held executive power, the verdicts of their courts, if any, were potentially ineffective. In Greco-Roman and rabbinic legislation, magic was chiefly dealt with in criminal law and its punishment comparable to that of premeditated murder. We might wonder – and have every reason for doing so – how the rabbis could have reconciled their impotence to execute a sentence with the "artificial" halo of legal freedom which they communicate while ignoring the real situation.[397]

7.1 Magus & Physician

In dealing with the rabbinic concept of magicians, we face a terminological difficulty.[398] The Babylonian Talmud's final redaction(s) occurred no earlier

---

[396] This criterion plays an important role. See, for example, the discussion on the official Meturgeman in the Babylonian Talmud, Qiddushin 49a, and Veltri, *Eine Tora für den König* (Tübingen: Mohr Siehbeck, 1994), 210 et seq.

[397] This is a *vexata quaestio*. On Origen's claim who affirmed that in the rabbinic period some *secret* trials ending with capital sentences took place, *Epistula ad Africanum*, 20, see Martin Jacobs, *Die Institution des jüdischen Patriarchen: Eine quellen- und traditionskritische Studie zur Geschichte der Juden in der Spätantike* (Tübingen: Mohr Siebeck, 1995), 248–251.

[398] I rely, not rarely almost literally, on notes concerning the Magi in rabbinic and Roman sources as I have discussed them in my following works: *Magie und Halakha*; Veltri, "The

than the 5th century CE It is the only rabbinic source which identifies the *Magi* as a class of Persian priests, and knows them by their factual name: *magushta,* or *magusha*. The Babylonian teachers were aware of their functions. According to Babylonian Talmud, Soṭa 22a, a Tanna is similar to a *magush* because both of them mnemonically repeat what they do not really understand (*raten magusha we-la' yada' ma'y amar tane tanna we-la' yada' ma'y amar*).[399] The Babylonian teachers were also aware of their chief activity: Babylonian Talmud, Shabbat 75a identifies Magus with astrologer in a Halakhic discussion to establish whether a Magus's activity should be considered "sorcery" or "blasphemy."

Palestinian sources, which are older than the Babylonian Talmud, ignore the term *magush*. This is all the more surprising inasmuch as this term and its meaning were known throughout the Mediterranean world. In fact, the *magush* was no longer just merely a Persian priest, but in the ancient mind represented the concept of a non-Greco-Roman foreign body of knowledge which could be harmful and useful at the same time. The Magi were considered *malefici* (literally "producers of evil things"), and the *vulgus*/common people were afraid of them because of their knowledge of poisons and sorcery.[400] On the other hand, the Magi were considered guardians of an arcane science. The Neo-Platonic

---

Rabbis and Pliny the Elder: Jewish and Greco-Roman Attitudes to Magic and Empirical Knowledge," *Poetics Today* 19 (1998) 63–89; Veltri, "On the Influence of 'Greek Wisdom': Rabbinic Attitudes to Theoretical and Empirical Sciences," *Jewish Studies Quarterly* 5 (1998): 300–317; Veltri, "The 'Other' Physicians: the 'Amorites' of the Rabbis and the Magi of Pliny," *Koroth* 13 (1998–1999): 37–54.

399 Jonas Greenfield suggested that *raten magusha*, as used in this text, is nothing but the description of a typical mnemonic technique used in Sassanian schools. See Jonas Greenfield, "raten magusha," in *Joshua Finkel Festschrift: In Honor of Joshua Finkel*, ed. Sidney Benjamin Hoenig and Leon D. Stitskin (New York: Yeshiva University Press, 1974), 63–69.

400 See Apuleius, *Apologia* 26–27; Lucius Apuleius, *La magia*, ed. and trans. Claudio Moreschini (Milan: Biblioteca Universale Rizzoli, 1990), 19 et seq.; Fritz Graf, *La magie dans l'antiquité Gréco-Romaine: Idéologie et pratique* (Paris: Les belles lettres 1994), 57–61. On the Magi as evil doers with poison, see *Codex Theodosianus* IX,16,6, a. 358: "si quis magus vel magicis contaminibus adsuetus, qui maleficus vulgi con suetudine nuncupatur, aut haruspex aut hariolus aut certe augur vel etiam mathematicus aut narrandis somniis occultans artem aliquam divinandi"; *Codex Theodosianum*, IX,16,4: "Chaldaei ac magi ac ceteri, quos maleficos ob facinorum magnitudinem vulgus appellat." On the Magi themselves, see Arthur Darby Nock, "Greeks and Magi," in *Essays on Religion and the Ancient World*, vol. 2, ed. Zeph Stewart (Oxford: Clarendon Press, 1940), 516–526; Elias J. Bickerman, "Darius I, Pseudo-Smerdis, and the Magi," in *Religions and Politics in the Hellenistic and Roman Periods*, ed. Bickerman (Como: Edizioni New Press 1978), 617–641; Marie-Theres Fögen, *Die Enteignung der Wahrsager: Studien zum kaiserlichen Wissensmonopol in der Spätantike* (Frankfurt am Main: Suhrkamp, 1993); Albert de Jong, *Traditions of the Magi: Zoroastrianism in Greek and Latin Literature* (Leiden: Brill 1997).

Numenios of Apamea (2nd century CE) observes the similarity of the idea in the thinking of Plato, Pythagoras, and the Brahmans, Jews, the Magi and the Egyptians.[401] Sextus Empiricus (c. 160–210 CE) reports of the "Persians and those of them who were considered expert in wisdom, i.e., the Magi."[402] The Suda, the famous Byzantine encyclopedia of the Mediterranean world, considers them to be "Magi: Persian philosophers and pious men."[403]

As the Babylonian Talmud shows, the best known characteristic of the Magi was their expertise in astrology. Cicero (who dedicated a whole treatise to divination) presented them as *augures*/diviners.[404] They were known for their skills in predicting the future. Thus, the Magi were considered very dangerous by Roman Imperial authorities. This consideration led to their expulsion from Rome or even execution.[405]

Our main source on the Magi is Pliny the Elder's *Natural History*, chapter XXX, as mentioned above.[406] There, he inquires into the origin of the *magicae vanitates*/magical deceits. Apparently, Pliny deals with the "fraudulent lies" of the Magi because their deceitful art had held "complete sway throughout the world for many ages."[407] Pliny ascribes the success of the Magi to the combination and interaction of three factors as one single feature:[408]

- The origins of magic in medicine which sustains and makes their promise of health credible;[409]

---

401 Numenios, *De Bono, apud* Eusebius, *Praeparatio Evangelica*, IX,7,1. See Menahem Stern, *Greek and Latin Authors* vol. 2: From Tacitus to Simplicius (Jerusalem: Magnes, 1980), no. 364a–b [211–212].
402 Ancient Greek: "Persai kai malista autân hoi sophian askein dokountes, hoi Magoi." Sextus Empiricus, *Pyrrh. Hypotyposes* III, 205.
403 Ancient Greek: "magoi: para Persais hoi philosophoi kai philotheoi." See, however, the Suda's pejorative definition of magos 25 (III,307): "magos ekaloun toys pseudeis phantasias peritithentas heautois. apo toutou de kai tous pharmakoys magous elegon." See Ada Adler, ed. *Suidae Lexicon* (Munich: Saur, 2001). Several editions exist of the Suda.
404 In Cicero's original Latin: "In Persis augurantur et divinant magi, qui congregatur in fano commentandi causa et inter se conloquendi." Cicero, *De Divinatione* 1:23,46.
405 On the expulsion from Rome in the years 16 and 17 CE, see Frederick H. Cramer, "Expulsion of Astrologers from Ancient Rome," *Classica et mediaevalia* 12 (1951): 9–50; Fögen, *Enteignung*, 106–108; Veltri, *Magie und Halakha*, 52.
406 See above, p. 113.
407 Latin: "vel eo ipso quod fraudulentissima artium plurimum in toto terrarum orbe plurimisque saeculis valuit."
408 Latin: "auctoritatem ei maximam fuisse nemo miretur, quandoquidem sola artium tres alias imperiosissimas humanae mentis complexa in unam se redegit." *Naturalis Historia* XXX:1,1.
409 Latin: "natam primum e medicina nemo dubitavit ac specie salutari inrepsisse velut altiorem sanctioremque medicinam." *Naturalis Historia*, XXX:1,2:

- magic is added, moreover, to the power of religion, "about which even today the human race is quite in the dark," and,
- to the power of astrology, "because there is nobody who is not eager to learn his destiny, or who does not believe that the truest account of it is that gained by watching the skies."[410]

The collaboration of these three powers in magic impressed and influenced a substantial segment of humankind. Yet, Pliny stressed in his history of magic that the Magi were foreign people whose magic permeated all the Mediterranean regions, and as far beyond as Britain. Pliny, however, also considered magical healing as such a deceit.[411]

The question whether a specific ethnic group is meant by the term "magus" is not an easy one.[412] Perhaps the "Magus/Magi" as used in Pliny's work refers to a body of literature which was "capable of challenging or infecting traditional learning or tempting a more intellectual audience."[413] As already stated above,[414] Pliny rejects the *vanitates* of the *magi* because of the exaggerated claims for the efficacy of plants in non-medical (or non-empirical) sectors were taken to be. The Magus does not shy away from using foreign (and strange) healing methods. Even in the mind of Pliny the Elder, the usefulness of a cure is the criterion for its "scientific" value. Foreign and "barbarian" procedures can also be of a medical value. The inventions of the "magi," on the other hand, are only *vanitates* because these cannot be reproduced empirically.

If Pliny rejected the procedures of the Magi, why did he transmit them? The first argument he offers is that he wants to contrast them in this way.[415] He discusses these "fraudulent lies" because he seeks to warn people about

---

[410] Latin: "... ita blandissimis desideratissimisque promissis addidisse vires religionis, ad quas maxime etiamnunc caligat humanum genus, atque, ut hoc quoque successerit, miscuisse artes mathematicas, nullo non avido futura de sese sciendi atque ea e coelo verissime peti credente." *Naturalis Historia* XXX:1,2.

[411] See Pliny's celebration of Roman "enlightenment" in *Naturalis Historia*, XXX:4,13: "nec satis aestimari potest quantum Romanis debeatur, qui sustulere monstra, in quibus hominem occidere religiosissimum erat, mandi vero etiam saluberrimum." On Pliny the Elder's attitude to medicine, see Geoffrey E. R. Lloyd, *Magic, Reason and Experience: Studies in the Origin and Development of Greek Science* (Cambridge: Cambridge University Press, 1979), 135–149.

[412] On this aspect, see Mary Beagon, *Roman Nature: The Thought of Pliny the Elder* (Oxford: Clarendon, 1992), especially 102 et seq.

[413] Beagon, *Roman Nature*, 105. Such an identification fits in very well with the depiction of the "Amorite" in rabbinic literature. See Veltri, *Magie und Halakha*, 184–220.

[414] See above, p. 150.

[415] Latin: "inritas fieri Magorum artes, generis vanissimi, ut aestimare licet." *Naturalis Historia* XXVIII:23,85.

them. This idea is, however, only half the truth. Pliny transmits a number of magical procedures attributed to the Magi without factually doubting them. The reason for his acceptance of magical customs and recipes is a pragmatic one: he seeks to offer an alternative where official medicine fails.[416]

A similar pragmatic, empirical approach can be observed in rabbinic literature with regard to the Amorites. Rabbinic authorities use an expression that placed all forbidden customs and practices in a nutshell: the so-called "ways of the Amorite." It is a category that is related to empirical knowledge. Like the Magus, the Amorite is not an entirely negative subject: he is a charmer, a diviner, and a quack, although also a pious man.[417] Nevertheless, such an ambivalent image is also evidence of the diffuse nature of xenophobia/-philia in the ancient world. According to Roman sources, the Magi were foreigners who were no longer in their own land. According to Porphyry (233–301/5), they were, moreover, *hoi peri to theion sophoi*/lovers of God.[418]

The conviction is widespread in Judaism that the Amorite as well as the Magus was a diviner. The compiler of the *Chronicles of Jerahmeel* 67, a medieval compilation from different sources, gives some details about the "idolatrous" tendencies of these people.[419] They are supposed to have seven golden images, the "holy Nymphs", which were decorated with gems. These idols informed the Amorites at specific intervals of the deeds they were about to perform.[420] The complex of the *darkhe ha-emori* also transmits customs and beliefs that are common to the Roman diviners.

---

[416] Alfred Ernout quotes Pliny's Latin phrase: "In quartanis medicina clinice propemodum nihil pollet. Qamobrem plura eorum (scil. magorum) remedia ponemus primumque ea quae adalligari iubent." See Alfred Ernout, "La magie chez Pline l'Ancien," in *Hommages à Jean Bayet*, ed. Marcel Renard and Robert Schilling (Brussels-Berchem: Latomus Revue d'Études Latines, 1964), 193. See also Columella, *De re rustica*, 10,357–361: "At si nulla valet medicina repellere pestem, Dardaniae veniant artes, nudataque plantas Femina quae, iustis tum demum operata iuvencae Legibus, obscaeno manat pudibunda cruore, ..."

[417] According to Rabban Gamli'el (Tosefta, *Shabbat* 7:25), "there is no people as patient as the Amorite. They believed in God and emigrated to Africa. And God gave them a land as beautiful as they had had."

[418] Porphyrios, *De Abstinentia* IV:16.

[419] *The Chronicles of Jerahmeel*, trans. Moses Gaster [revised by Haim Schwarzbaum] (New York: Ktav 1971), 165 et seq. On the problems which are inherent to the *Chronicles*, see G. Veltri, "Die Entstehung der LXX in der jüdisch-mittelalterlichen Historiographie," *Laurentianum* 33 (1992): 105–110.

[420] On the Amorites, their idols, and the stones, see Leopold Cohn, "An Apocryphal Work Ascribed to Philo of Alexandria," *Jewish Quarterly Review* 10 (1898): 294–298. On the wars between the Amorites and the sons of Jacob, see the bibliographic review in Gaster/Schwarzbaum, *Chronicles*, 48–49.

That the Amorite is a pseudo-physician does not need to be stressed. The context of the *darkhe ha-emori* in contrast with the *refu'a* (the principle of "healing") is the best evidence for this. We read this in the above quoted text of Mishnah *Shabbat* 6:10, to which I refer here. The Amorite practices have to be contrasted with true healing since "whatever is used to bring about healing does not belong [to those forbidden practices considered to belong] to the ways of the Amorite." This expression is in my opinion, the key to understanding the reception of medical procedure, science, and arts, as above mentioned.[421] On the other hand, it is a reference to rabbinic acceptance of foreign knowledge on the basis of an empirical, pragmatic principle: if something works, it must be true.

The rabbis do not question the reason *why* something has an effect – that would be an Aristotelian enquiry which follows the principle of "the *effectus* leads to the *causa*" – but rather *whether* there has been any true effect at all. It was a pragmatic and empirical approach shared, for example, by Pliny. The Aristotelian interpretation of reality was, according to the satirist Lucian of Samosata (120–c. 180 CE), concerned with the *logical or natural cause* of reality. In the case of a conjuration, Lucian states that he might believe in the power of the word, *provided* his opponents could show him evidence of the *natural* reason for the superiority of the power of the word over the fever or a swelling. If experience does not have a *natural* explanation, the opinion of his opponents is only the yarn of old women.[422]

Let us summarise the opposite positions: Lukianos belongs to a theoretical rationalist school. The school taught that only those facts are real and true which can be explained. Where a natural explanation is lacking, facts are untrue and unreal. The rabbis follow an empirical-natural conception with a tautological logic: if something has an effect, for whatever reason, it is factual. If something – recipes, conjurations, herbs, or certain kinds of metal – does not have an effect, it is not necessarily not-factual or ineffective. It may well have an effect in the future or in other circumstances. Factuality is thus circumstantial.

7.2 Magician and Illusionist

A very similar, empirical tendency is to be found in the rabbinic discussion on the difference between the magician and the illusionist. Mishnah, Sanhedrin 7:4, for instance defines

---

[421] On this aspect, above, p. 99–114 (Greek Wisdom).
[422] Lukianos, *Philopseudes* 9.

> The sorcerer: He that performs some act is culpable, and not he that [only] deceives the eyes.
>
> Rabbi Aqiva in the name of Rabbi Yehoshuaʽ says: If two were gathering cucumbers, one gatherer may not be culpable and the other may be culpable. He that [indeed] performed the act is culpable, but he that [only] deceived the eyes is not culpable.

Although both of them do the same thing (they gather cucumbers), only the first one must be stoned, since he is considered a sorcerer. The illusionist does not deserve to be punished.

To identify a magician, only one empirical criterion is offered: the magician manipulates something (*mekhashef, ʽose maʽase*), the non-magician only blinds his or her eyes (*huʼ oḥez et ʽenayim*). Consequently, magic is a negative concept. It has originated from the difference between the medium that only does tricks, and the magician who indeed alters something.

Such a pragmatic solution for distinguishing true from false magic calls to mind the biblical judgement concerning prophecy, as outlined in Deut. 18:22: "When a prophet speaks in the name of the Lord, if the word does not come to pass or come true (ולא-יהיה הדבר ולא יבא), that is a word which the Lord has not spoken."

The similarity between prophecy and magic is not surprising. According to an ancient, perhaps stoic conception of divination, reflected, for instance, by the view of Philo of Alexandria: true magic is *optikē epistēmē* / the "visional science/knowledge." It belongs to the Magi who manifests divine knowledge in the pure form (*hierofantoyn-tai te kai hierofantoysi*). In contrast to false magic (*magikē sofisteia*), visional science refers to the nature of the gods, and so reveals its divine nature.[423]

But let us return to the conception of the rabbis. What does the magician do, and through which medium does he operate? In Tannaitic Judaism, there is no definition of magic as an action as such; the stories or acts are very detailed in the Palestinian and the Babylonian Gemara that serve to illustrate and comment on this Halakhah. Yet the examples do not offer an explanation as to the nature of magic, exactly what it is.

However, one source which understands magic as a medium to do something is Babylonian Talmud, Sanhedrin 67b (see also Shemot Rabbah 9:11). It is a Midrash discussing the meaning of two very difficult words in Exodus 7:11 and 7:22:

> R. Abbaye bar Nagri said [in the name of] R. Ḥiyya bar Abba: בלטיהם [Exodus 7:22] refers to the effect by demons; בלהטיהם [Ex 7:11] refers to the effect by sorcery. For it has been

---

[423] Veltri, *Magie und Halakha*, 60–62.

written: *The glow of the sword, which swings around itself* [Genesis 3:24]. R. Abbaye said: He who cares for the vessel he uses, operates through demons; he who does not care, operates through magic.

Both בלטיהם and בלהטיהם refer to the Egyptian magicians in the Torah. For the rabbinic exegesis, as a rule, a difference in spell is also a difference in meaning. Rabbi Abbaye does not equate magic with the work of demons. Magic and demons are the tools of the magician. The sentence "He who cares for the vessel he uses" refers to the magic practices which are carried out by means of bowls or amulets in order to capture demons. The demons are thus brought under the dominion of the magician. Magic is a power in itself. However, in Shemot Rabbah 9:11 we find a similar tradition which ends with the sentence: "For the operation of the magician happens through the angels of destruction."[424] Here there are no theories about the nature of magic – only that it worked either through the demons or its own agency.

We also have a clear statement about the nature of magic in Babylonian Talmud, Sanhedrin 67a: כישוף/sorcery "lessens the power of the divine agencies."[425] This statement is preceded by the quotation from Deuteronomy 4:35: "There is nobody except for him." The text clearly suggests that there is no power except the divine power. If the sorcerer operates, he must operate through his power. This is the reason why the magician lessens the power of God. In this theological view, the power of God can act without his explicit will.

That the name of God can act independently of his will is a typical magical conviction. It can be found in pagan, Jewish and Christian texts. We find in Luke 9:49–50 that Jesus' name was used as a valuable and powerful word (*nomen barbarum*, or *vox magica*) to drive out evil spirits through exorcism. By imposing a prohibition against conjuring the name of Jesus, the disciples obviously wanted to reserve this right for themselves. But Jesus disagreed with their protective zeal and allowed this use, "for he that is not against you is for you." If the magician uses the name of Jesus as a powerful word, he essentially believed in his theurgic power.[426] On the other hand, when justifying this use,

---

424 For the identification of magic with demonology in Augustin, see Jean-Claude Schmitt, "Les 'superstitions,'" in *Histoire de la France religieuse*, Vol. 1: *Des dieux de la Gaule à la papauté d'Avignon (des origines au XIV*^{e} *siècle)*, ed. Jacques Le Goff et al. (Paris: Seuil, 1988); Robert A. Markus, "Augustine on Magic: A Neglected Semiotic Theory," *Revue des études augustiennes* 40 (1994): 375–388.
425 See also Simcha Fishbane, "'Most Women Engage in Sorcery': An Analysis of Sorceresses in the Babylonian Talmud," *Jewish History* 7 (1993): 28.
426 On the magical power of Jesus' name, see Morton Smith, *Jesus the Magician* (Cambridge: Harper & Row 1978, reprint 1981), 114–115; David E. Aune, "Magic in Early Christianity," in

Jesus accepts that the practice was independent and separate from his own authority.[427] The efficiency of conjuration is thus autonomous and free from any (legal) authority.

The Jerusalem Talmud reports that by conjuring the name of Yeshu ben Pandera, R. Yehoshua ben Levi was healed.[428] A similar concept occurs in the medieval *Responsa* literature. The use of gentile names such as Jesus is permitted for their therapeutic value. Rabbi Menaḥem of Speyer (1340–1410) remarked that "The sounds produce the healing, not the words."[429] In pointing out the difference between the sound and the word (or contents), the statement of R. Menaḥem refers indirectly to the Hermetic and neo-Platonic philosophy, according to which only the sound of a word is endowed with great power.[430] The halakhic principle on which the rabbi based his statement is however without doubt the already above quoted talmudic Halakhah: "What heals does not belong to the ways of the Amorite."[431]

The discussion regarding a "permitted use" of the Jewish divine name, the *tetragramma*, can be traced to the rabbinic period. Then the Halakhic impor-

---

Aufstieg und Niedergang der Römischen Welt, vol. 2.23/2, ed. Wolfgang Haase (Berlin and New York: De Gruyter 1980), 1545–1549.

427 We can find the adjuration: "the name which cannot be said" in magical texts. See *Defixionum tabellae*, No. 271/16 (Provincia Byzacena); Ludwig Blau relates this expression to the name as unpronounceable. Ludwig Blau, *Das altjüdische Zauberwesen* (Strassburg: Trübner, 1898), 124. See also the similar expression *ho to onoma oude theoi dyna(n)tai phtheg(ng)esthai*, in Karl Preisendanz, *Papyri Graecae Magicae: Die griechischen Zauberpapyri* vol. 2 (Stuttgart. Teubner, 1928; repr. 1973–1974), 125.

428 Jerusalem Talmud, 'Avodah Zarah 2:2 (40b). See also Jerusalem Talmud, Shabbat 14:4 (14d) and Qohelet Rabba 10:5; Tosefta, Ḥullin 1:22 and 2:22, et seq. See also Larry O. Hogan, *Healing in the Second Temple Period* (Fribourg and Göttingen: Vandenhoeck & Ruprecht, 1992), 253. For a different interpretation, see Johann Maier, *Jesus von Nazareth in der talmudischen Überlieferung* (Darmstadt: Wissenschaftliche Buchgesellschaft, 1978), 193–198; Hogan, *Healing in the Second Temple Period*, 253.

429 Gloss from a *Mordecai* MS, quoted in Joshua Trachtenberg, *Jewish Magic and Superstition: A Study in Folk Religion*, (New York: Behrman's Jewish Book, 1939; reprint New York: Atheneum, 1970), 200, note 15; Zimmels, *Magicians, Theologians, and Doctors*, 141.

430 See, for instance, *Corpus Hermeticum*, 16:2: "Turned into our own native tongue, the sermon (logos) keepeth clear the meaning of the words (logoi) [at any rate]. For that its very quality of sound, the [very] power of the Egyptian names, have in themselves the bringing into act of what is said" "The Corpus Hermeticum and Hermetic Tradition," *The Gnostic Society Library*, http://gnosis.org/library/hermet.htm (accessed 17 February 2013); see G. Veltri, "Übersetzbarkeit und Magie der 'heiligen' Sprache: Sprachphilosophien und Übersetzungstheorien," in *Tradition und Translation: Zum Problem der interkulturellen Übersetzbarkeit religiöser Phänomene: Festschrift für Carsten Colpe zum 65. Geburtstag*, ed. Christoph Elsas and Carsten Colpe (Berlin and New York: De Gruyter, 1994), 306–307.

431 Jerusalem Talmud, Shabbat 6:10 (27d).

tance of God's name was emphasised in reference to the books which were to be concealed in the Genizah or saved from fire. We read in Midrash, Sifre Ba-Midbar 16:

> Do we not find here the use [of the hermeneutic rule] of the *qal va- ḥomer*? Regarding the reconciliation of a man and his wife, if God says: The book which was written in holiness is to be erased by water, [*a maiori*], the books of the Minim should be taken out of the world because they cause hostility, hatred, jealousy and war.
> R. Yishma'el [says]: *Sifre Minim:* What about them? The name of God has to be cut out and the rest must be burn.
> R. Aqiva says: They are to be completely burnt because they have not been written in holiness.[432]

The state of the name was altered entirely because it was not written according to the biblical and rabbinic laws of purity. There is no doubt that the redactor of *Sifre* brought the Halakhah from Numberi 5 up to a contemporary standard. He did so by referring to the similarity of the act of writing curses by the priest on the parchment/book and the rabbinic laws about writing a Torah book which "pollutes the hands." This "modernisation" would be incomprehensible if we did not bear in mind that writing on parchment was also considered the precondition for the theurgic value of a written text. Only *tefillin* or *mezuzot*, written according to the Halakhah, have the power of protection (Mishnah, Megillah 1:8).[433] It is not the characters of the tetragramma, or other divine names, that possess theurgic power. But characters written according to the Halakhah of purity do have this power. Only if we follow this interpretation can we understand the argumentum *a maiori*:

1. *praemissa*: A book which was written in holiness is to be erased by water (meaning, it can be reused);
2. *conclusio*: the books of the Minim, where the divine name was also written, must be removed from the world (meaning, they must be burnt entirely);
3. *argumentum*: all the more so because they were not written in holiness.

Here then is also proof of the anti-theurgic tendency in rabbinic Judaism. Consequently, the naked characters of the tetragramma have no inherent power.

---

[432] On this Halakhah and parallels, see Johann Maier, *Jüdische Auseinandersetzung mit dem Christentum in der Antike* (Darmstadt: Wissenschaftliche Buchgesellschaft: 1982), 26–33.
[433] Deuteronomy 6:4–9 and 11:13–21 were commonly written on the parchment for a *mezuza*. In Qumran 8Q (DJD III), a *mezuza* was found with a longer text (Deuteronomy 10:12–11:21). According to the Babylonian Talmud, Menaḥot 32b, the improper fixing of a *mezuza* might be the source of bad luck. Rashi adds that the house would still be protected against demons.

Let us conclude the rabbinic evaluation of magic: Tannaitic literature does not offer a definition of magic. Even the power of the divine name is not effective unless it is written by Jewish writers and in a spirit of holiness. Amoraic literature, and almost all of Babylonian literature, seek the power of magic in a theological manner: There is no one besides God; therefore there is no power and energy besides His. Thus, if magic has a power in itself, it must have originated in God. For that reason, magic always works without constraints of religion (or for that matter, constraints of race).

7.3 Medieval Developments

The tendency of the Babylonian Talmud to attribute every effect to the divine name finds a natural continuation in medieval Judaism. The Cairo Genizah contains some documents which interpret the rabbinic distinction between "illusory tricks" and "true magic" as being two different forms of magic. According to T.-S. Misc. 9.57, fol. 1a/1 ff., the mere illusion (*aḥizat 'enayim*) consists of the formula: "That is the great and powerful name," and from the biblical verses Isaiah 29:10, Psalms 69:24, Psalms 58:9, and Isaiah 29:11, "to blind the eyes so that the public does not discover the tricks of the magician!" In these examples, the divine power, which is the magic energy in rabbinic texts, also becomes the work of illusory magic.

In other texts from the Genizah, the two forms of magic are identified by the *shem be-tum'ah we-shem-be-tohara*/name of God in the state of purity and impurity. The Genizah material offers us a new interpretation of these very difficult termini. Some fragments from the Taylor Schechter Collection in Cambridge and the Etan Adler Collection of the Jewish Theological Seminary in America criticise the use of the expression *shem be-tum'ah we-shem-be-tohara*. In T.-S. K 1.37, fol. 1a, it is unfortunately very fragmentary text:

> Those, who say: 'name of the purity and name of the impurity' and 'illusion' and 'magic,' know the name but not their principle and their execution.
> Know and understand, that they are first mistaken in respect to their name because they say 'name of the purity and name of the impurity.'
> Heaven forbid, that there would be "the name of impurity"!
> The (right) name is 'name in purity and name in impurity'.

The Karaite Abū Yūsuf Ya'qub al-Qirqisāni (c. 1160–1199) mentions that the Rabbanites used the 'name of purity and name of impurity' to perform theurgy. The author of the Genizah text is opposed to this expression, and therefore to its use. According to him, there could not be a "name of impurity," because it would be a *contradictio in terminis*. There is only good magic which is performed by means of the divine name in the state of purity. The use of the name in the state of impurity is bad magic, and therefore has to be condemned.

But how are we to understand the expression "name in impurity"? To my knowledge, Arthur Marmorstein was the first scholar who recognised the importance of the Cairo Genizah for understanding everyday life in Judaism from late antiquity until the early medieval period. In 1925, he published a very interesting fragment which he considered important for the history of sects in Judaism. We refer to the *'Inyan Soṭa* ("dealing with the woman suspected of adultery").[434] It was republished in *Magische Texte aus der Kairoer Geniza*.[435] *'Inyan Soṭa* is a medieval (perhaps Ashkenazic) modernised version of the *parashat soṭa* of Numeri 5:11–31. Numeri 5:11–31 deals with the case of a woman who is suspected of adultery. Her husband, jealous of his wife, has to bring her to the priest. The priest puts holy water in an earthen vessel. He then takes some of the dust from the floor of the tabernacle and puts it into the water. Thereafter, the priest requires that the wife swear an oath that she has not committed adultery. Afterwards, the priest writes the weighty curses of perjury down in a book and washes them off into the water of bitterness, requiring the woman to drink it. "If she has defiled herself and has acted unfaithfully against her husband, the water that brings the curse shall enter into her and cause bitter pain, and her belly shall swell."

The novelty of the medieval version of the Cairo Genizah should not be seen in the magic connotation of this procedure. However, it does present itself in the speculation about the power which causes the belly of the woman to swell if she is indeed guilty of adultery. The power is the energy of God's name

---

[434] Arthur Marmorstein, "Beiträge zur Religionsgeschichte und Volkskunde," *Jahrbuch der jüdischen Volkskunde* 25 (1924–1925): 377–383. As far as I know, only Gerschom Scholem and Moshe Idel mention this text, in the context of the topic of the Golem. See Scholem, *Zur Kabbala und ihrer Symbolik*, (Zürich: Rhein-Verlag 1960), 285et seq., note 63; Moshe Idel, *Golem: Jewish Magical und Mystical Traditions on the Artificial Anthropoid*, (Albany, N.Y.: State University of New York Press, 1990), 63 and related notes.

[435] Peter Schäfer and Shaul Shaked, *Magische Texte aus der Kairoer Geniza III* (Tübingen: Mohr, 2000), 17–45; See Veltri, "Inyan Sota: Halakhische Voraussetzungen für einen magischen Akt nach einer theoretischen Abhandlung aus der Kairoer Geniza," *Frankfurter Judaistische Beiträge* 20 (1993): 23–48; Peter Schäfer, "Jewish Liturgy and Magic," in *Festschrift für Martin Hengel* vol. 1: Judentum, ed. Schäfer (Tübingen: Mohr Siebeck, 1996), 541–557. See also Schäfer, "Magic and Religion in Ancient Judaism," in *Envisioning Magic: A Princeton Seminar and Symposium*, ed. Peter Schäfer and Hans G. Kippenberg (Leiden, New York and Cologne: Brill, 1997), 32 et seq. The text is transmitted in the fragment JTSL ENA 3635, fol. 17a–d and partly in the Cambridge Collection (Box K 1), (ENA 3635, 17a/1–17b/4 = T.-S. K 1.56, fol. 1a/3–19). There are almost no significant variants.

in an impure state.[436] To speak in the categories of modern physics: the divine name causes an explosion if its positive energy meets a negatively charged particle.

According to these texts, the name of God has to be confronted with a power that depends on the halakhic position of those people who perform the action in their own pure or impure state. Only if they perform something in impurity do they cause destruction and not the desired effect of catharsis. These texts from the Genizah do not contain traces either of rabbinic rationalism in judging magic or of the theological implication concerning the divine power that is unrelated to His will. Clearly, the authors of these texts did not doubt that the nature of God is torn between His power and His will. Or, to express it paradoxically: God has no power over his own power.

The concept of the name in impurity must possibly be interpreted as an attempt to resolve the question of the origin of evil. Evil is not supposed to be within God, but nevertheless originates from God in an unnatural state. Yet His power is divided into two states which do not depend on His will. This is a philosophical premise which permitted medieval Judaism to follow the neo-Platonic and Hermetic speculations on the power of the name(s), and the word as an autonomous force which can be used for (good or evil) magic. The idea does indeed imply an uncritical yet very fertile reception of "pagan" philosophy.

---

436 On the parashat sota and its historical changes, see Louis M. Epstein, *Sex Laws and Customs in Judaism* (New York: Ktav, 1948), 116–134.

8 "Watermarks" in the MS *Munich, Hebr. 95*

At the end of the Massekhet Berakhot which is transmitted in the Manuscript Munich Hebr. 95 after the Seder Moʻed, the scribe copied out some magical formulae which deal above all with the topic of water and the creation of living beings.[437] In his catalogue, Moritz Steinschneider did not pay any attention to this last text, but described the manuscript in toto as "the possibly *most valuable* Hebrew codex in Munich."[438] This is not surprising when we take into account the very negative opinion of magic held by the great bibliographer[439] and also shared by other contemporaries, such as Heinrich Graetz and David Heymann Joël.[440] The description of the manuscript by Moritz Altschüler,[441] which is notoriously inaccurate, adds no relevant information. The more precise introduction to the facsimile by Hermann L. Strack mentions only that on fol. 157b there is no text (of the Gemara).[442] In the description of the manuscript and its text in his edition of Mishnah Zeraʻim, Nissin Sacks does not refer to the content of this page, although he does evaluate the colophon at the bottom.[443]

The editors of the Babylonian Talmud adopted an attitude of reserve towards the most complete manuscript of the Babylonian Gemara. This attitude is understandable only for Strack, since he published the reproduction of Munich 95 with the explicit intention to avert anti-Semitic prejudice against the Talmud. However, there is no excuse for the other scholars because the writer of the Gemara, Shelomo ben Shimshon, is, without any doubt, also the writer (and more likely than not author) of the magical recipes. When we consider that there are several empty pages in the manuscript and that only this page

---

437 See fol. 157b in Hermann L. Strack, ed. *Talmud Babylonicum codicis Hebraici Monacensis 95: Der Babylonische Talmud nach der Münchener Handschrift Cod. Hebr. 95* [Faksimile] (Leiden: A. W. Sijthoff's Uitgevers Maatschappij 1912), 306.
438 German: "vielleicht de(n) *wertvollste(n)* hebr. Cod. in München." The emphasis is Steinschneider's. Moritz Steinschneider, *Die hebräischen Handschriften der K. Hof- und Staatsbibliothek in München* (Munich: Palm'sche Hofbuchhandlung, 1895), 60.
439 See Steinschneider's unequivocal position in his popular published lecture *Der Aberglaube* (Berlin: Verlagsanstalt und Druckerei A.-G. [vormals J. F. Richter], 1900).
440 On the history of the evaluation of magic in the *"Wissenschaft des Judentums,"* see the introduction to G. Veltri, *Magie und Halakha. Ansätze zu einem empirischen Wissenschaftsbegriff im spätantiken und frühmittelalterlichen Judentum* (Tübingen: Mohr, 1997), 1–18.
441 See Moritz Altschüler, ed. *Cod. Hebr. Monac. 95. Die Pfersee-Handschrift,* Vol. 1 (Leipzig and Vienna: Lumen 1908).
442 Strack, *Talmud Babylonicum* [Faksimile], iii.
443 Nissin Sacks, ed. *Mishna Zeraim* [Hebrew], vol. 1 (Jerusalem: Institute of the Complete Israeli Talmud 1972), 69–70.

was filled with this particular magical material, we have to conclude that the writer must have had a very good reason to do so. In view of the content of the recipes, we may suppose that Shimshon added these texts because he thought they were exceptionally important either for preserving the manuscript or for himself. That is what I attempt to demonstrate below.

8.1 Notes on the Manuscript

The text is transmitted at the end of the Massekhet Berakhot (in this manuscript this is also at the end of the Seder Mo'ed: וסליקא מסכת ברכות ואשור) כוליה סדר מועד). It consists of:
1. one column, graphically at the left side of the concluding lines of the text of the Gemara (13 lines),
2. one continuous text of 3 lines after the Gemara, ending with
3. two columns (on the left 12 lines, on the right 9 lines).

The right column consists of divine names, framed by little boxes, mainly permutations of the Tetragramma and other divine names and attributes. At the margin of this column, there are two glosses (in the second and fifth line).

The writer uses common abbreviations, characterised by a double dot on the designed letters (something like a ṣere): פ"ז for פעמים 'ז (line 1), 'מ'א'פ'ב'פ (line 5 and 9) משביע אני פלוני בן פלוני; also the common abbreviation מ'א'ע for משביע אני עליך (line 23) is used. Numbers are also abbreviated: see for example 'ז (line 1); ל"ו (line 27); מ"ב and כ"ב (line 26).

As usual for magical texts in general and amulets in particular, biblical verses are also presented in abridged form.[444] The peculiarity of this text is that the writer or his *Vorlage* gives both the full text and also the abridged form: see line 17 (full text) and line 18 (abridged form); but see line 21 (abridged form) and line 22 (full text). Moreover, in the full text, the abridged characters of the abbreviation are particularly stressed by little dots.

8.2 A Page, or Fragments of a Handbook?

The writer copied the text from a *Vorlage*, probably a handbook containing different magical recipes. There are some hints to confirm this working hypothesis.

---

[444] For a list of abridged biblical verses, see Theodore Schrire, *Hebrew Magic Amulets: Their Decipherment and Interpretation* (New York: Behrman House 1982); Eli Davis and David A.

1. Line 3 is, or could be, incomplete: במשך is vocalised as a *nomen barbarum*, but may also be an indirect indication of the continuation of the practice: "After so and so one has to say "so and so" while you ..." (or "during").
2. The chain of tradition (lines 15–16) is clearly abridged and very peculiar. To my knowledge, it is also unique in that it runs from Michael to Yehudah and "the sons of Hasmonai."
3. Lines 19/20: The sentence בזה הצורך ובזה הדחק ויתענה, written as an introduction to ויאמר belongs, perhaps, to the precedent *segulla*. At any rate, it makes no sense if it is really an introduction to the instruction: "say."
4. The word *Seleq* in line 21 indicates that the *segulla* ends at the lines 21, or, perhaps better, that the verse from Gen. 1:9 was inserted from another context.

Text

1a

לרוח סערה סים יאמר ז"פ וַזֻ֨ג	1
יֵיֵל אחיַ מֶשָׁה רֶוֶם	2
אחר זָמֵע זַעַן בְּמִשָׁךְ:	3
לעבור כל מיני מים בלא גשר	4
ובלא ספינה יאמר מ'א'פ'ב'פ'	5
עליך דֶּ וכל כחך דַּרְבִּיאֵל	6
לְאֲכֵרֶךְ דְצִיַהֵן עֲפָנָא צ'ט':	7
ולהעמיד כל נהר ים ומצולה	8
ולשבר גלים יאמר מאפ'ב'פ'	9
עליך דַּוּ טכך דַּרְנִיאֵל	10
ויש אומרים דַרְנִיאֵל לְאֵינְרֶךְ	11
דַחְפִיאֵל לְאֵיפְחֵד	12
צְעֵיפִיֶץ מְמַמְלְנָאַ:	13
כתוב על חרש חדש בטהרה שמות טלו והשלך במים ויבשו ותעבר ביבשה וכשתקח החרס יחזרו לאחתנם ואם תשימהו על המת יחיה וכש	14
תסירנו ישוב לעפרו.. ואם תכתבנו על ציץ או טס זהב ותשונו בזרועך תושע כל סוס רודף אחריך יפול וכל חרב וכל חץ לא חזהקוך מיכאל	15
מסרו ליהודה ויהדה לבני חשמונאי.. ואם תרמה לפעול מהם קח צץ קטן ויזה עליו מן טל של כשירים מן נטף שחלת וחלבנה ותשאנו	16
להקות מים ויאמר אלהים י'ק'ו ה'מ'ים מ'ת'ח'ת ה'שמים' אל מקום	17
אחד ותראה היבשה ויהי כן: יְקָהֶם מַתֶת הֵם משביעכם	18
אני פב'פ' שתראוני כחכם בזה זצורך	19
ובזה הדחק ויתענה ויאמר משביעכם אני שתברַאו לי	20

Frenkel, *The Hebrew Amulet. Biblical-Medical-General* [Hebrew], Jerusalem: The Institute for Jewish Studies 1995), 171–209.

21 ... בַּר בַּר אֶל אֱלֵי אֲהוָה יְקָהַם מַתָּת הַם. סליק
22 ב׳ר׳אשית ב׳ר׳א א׳ל׳הים א׳ת ה׳שמים ו׳את ה׳ארץ
23 בַּר בָּךְ אֶל אֱלֵי אֲהוָה מ׳א׳ע׳ שמות הקדושים שתבראו לי
24 את הבריאה הזאת והנה היא שם הבריאו:
25 להעלות המים במורדן ישביע אַסָיו בשם יי״ו אלהי ישראל
26 ובשם המפורש ממ״ב ומכ״ב שיעלו המים למקום שירדו:
27 לסער הים עַלְבְּבִיאֵל ל״ו פעמים ויאמר קודם י״ג פעמים יי״ו רועי לא
28 אחסר

1b

1 | הִיהָא | הִי | הָא | אוֹ | אוֹ | אוֹ | אוֹת | אוֹ | אַה | אֲהֶיֶה |
2 | חִי | אָה | יהוה | אָהָא | [??] | (אֵל) | אֱלֹהִים | צָח | הוּ |
3 | חַי | אַדִּיר | צְבִי | צְבָאוֹת | אַדִּירִים | אָיוֹם | ונורא |
4 | יָהּ | וְהוּ | אָרוֹ | בְיָה | בְהוּ | צַח | חַץ | וַץ | פַּץ | יְהִיוּ |
5 | וַת | זֶבֶק (יש אמ׳ זהך) | רַלְיָה | אֲהֶיֶה | צְבָא | הָיָה | שְׁמוֹ | שַׁדַּי | שׁוֹךְ |
6 | עַד | צִיָּה | אִישׁ | מלחמה | לְעוֹלָם | צְבִי | אַגָּא | נוֹרָא | יָהּ |
7 | שׁוֹכֵן | שׁחקים | וְהָ | יהוה | וְיהִיוּ | יְהָא | וַהֹוהּ | וְהָ | יָהּ |
8 | זָרָה | יְזְמִין | אמון | אמון | סל | סל | סל | סל | סל | סל | סַל | וְהָ | וְהָ |
9 | וְהָ וַהֲ וְהֹ וַהֲ וַהֲ | וְהָ וְהָ וֶהֲ וְהֹ וְהֹ וְהָ וְהָ |

Translation

1a

1 For (against) a storm wind on the sea:[445]
2 one has to say seven times[446]
  WZG | YYL
  'HY MŠH RWM
3 after that [say]
  ZM' Z'N BMǨ
4 To cross every kind of water

---

445 ויעמר רוח סערה ותרומם גליו ויאמר, see Psalms 107:25: לרוח סערה בים. See Babylonian Talmud Berachot 24b; Semahot 1:4. This text belongs to the "enumeration" example: "four אמר רב: ארבע צריכין להודות – יורדי הים, הולכי מדברות, ומי שהיה should praise the Lord": הולה ונתרפא, ומי שהיה חבוש בבית האסורים, ויצא. יורדי הים, מנלין-דכתיב יורדי הים בניות אמר רב יהודה וגו׳.
On the storm wind, see Joshua Trachtenberg, *Jewish Magic and Superstition* (New York: Atheneum 1939), 34. See also Jerusalem Talmud, Ḥagiga 1:1 (87a) (on the top): God created a wind storm as an amulet; *Ḥarba de-Moshe* in *Synopse zur Hekhalot-Literatur*, ed. Peter Schäfer, (Tübingen: Mohr 1981), § 619: ואם היית בים וקם סער עליך עצוד נכח הגלים, ואצור חרב והם נותשים. וכת׳ בטס או בחרס או בעץ ותיה לפני הספינה ולא תטבע.
446 The number "seven" is supposed to help against sorcery, see Babylonian Talmud, Shabbat 66b; see also Shabbat 65b.

5	without a bridge | and without a ship
	one has to say: I, N. N., conjure
6	you D(W)[447] and all your power
7	DRKY'L | L'YKRD
	DṢYHW 'PN' ṢṬ
8	To let stay every river, sea and the depths[448]
9	and to break waves one has to say:
10	I, N. N., conjure
	| you DW and all your power
	DRNY'L
11	some say DRNY'L
	L'YNRD
12	DḤPY'L L'YPḤD
13	Ṣ'YPYṢ MMMLN'
14	Write on a new vessel in purity these names
	and cast (it) into the water
	and in this manner it will be dried and you can go ashore.
	If you take the vessel away
	it again obtains its normal condition.[449]
	If you put it on a dead person,
	he/she will live.
15	If you take it away
	he will return to dust.
	If you write them on a gold plate or foil
	and wear it on your arm
	you will be in security.
	Every horse, which runs after you, will fall down.
	Neither sword nor arrow will hurt you.
16	Michael transmitted (it) to Yehudah and Yehudah to the sons of Hasmonai.
	If you would like to use (it)
	take a small wood
	and sprinkle on this ritually permitted *dew of (sweet spices) stacte, onycha, and galbanum* (cp. Ex. 30:34) and wear it.
17	To gather water [say]:
	And God said: Let the waters under the heavens be gathered together into one place,

---

447 If this text was written in Ashkenazi, it is possible to read the nomen as German "du" ("you"). Another possible interpretation is "Deu(s)."
448 Irina Wandrey, "Das 'Buch des Gewandes' und das 'Buch des Aufrechten': Zwei hebräische magische Texte aus dem Mittelalter" (PhD diss., Free University Berlin, 1997), 200 et seq.; see now Irina Wandrey, *Das Buch des Gewandes und Das Buch des Aufrechten* (Tübingen: Mohr-Siebeck, 2004).
449 חזר לאיתנם, halakhic terms, see Babylonian Talmud, Niddah 48b.

18 *and let the dry land appear." And it was so* (Gen. 1:9).[450]
    YQHM MTḤ HM
    I conjure you,
19 I, N. N., that you show me your power.
    In this time of need
20 and in the case of emergency.
    And he shall fast
    and has to say:
    I conjure you that you create for me:
21 *In the beginning God* my God *created the heavens and the earth*
    (Gen. 1:1).
    And let the water be gathered under the heavens (Gen. 1:9).
    Seleq.
22 *In the beginning God* my God *created the heavens and the earth*
    (Gen.1:1)
23 *In the beginning God* my God *created the heavens and the earth*
    (Gen. 1:1).
    I conjure you, holy names, that you create for me
24 this creation. And this creation is there.
25 To let the waters rise, when they come down:
    One has to say conjure
    'SYW with the name YYW the God Israel, and
26 with the *shem ha-meforash* of forty-two and twenty-two (letters),
    that the waters rise to the place where they come down.
27 For Against a sea-storm: (say) thirty-six times 'LBB'L.
    First you should say thirteen times *My God is my shepherd, I will
    not perish* (Psalms 23:1)

    1b

1   'HYH HY H'
    'W 'W 'W
    'WT 'W
    'H 'HYH
2   HY 'H
    YHWH 'H' [??] ('L)
    'LHYM ṢḤ HW
3   ḤY 'DYR ṢBY
    ṢB' WT 'DYRYM
    'YWM WNWR'
4   YH WHW 'RW
    BYH BH
    ṢḤ ḤṢ WṢ PṢ
    YHYẆ

---

450 The Revised Standard Version, 2nd ed., Nashville 1952, was used for the English translations from the Bible; several slight modifications were made.

5	WT ZBQ
	(some say ZBK)
	RLYH 'HYH ṢB'
	HYH ŠMW ŠDY ŠWKN
6	'D ṢYH
	'YŠ MLḤMH
	L'WLM
	ṢBY 'G' NWR' YH
7	ŠWKN ŠḤQYM WH YHWH WYHYW
	YH' WHWH WH YH
8	ZRH YZMYN 'MWN 'MWN
	SL SL SL
	SL SL SL
	WH WH
9	WH WH
	WH WH WH WH
	WH WH WH WH
	WH WH WH

8.3 Water, Waters, Creation, and other Mirabilia

The recipes of Shelomo ben Shimshon are concentrated on a precise topic: the water(s). It is useful to examine this very curious collection. The *segullot* are structured following the typical *Lamed* formula, which serves as the structural keyword:

1a/1–3: "For (against) a storm wind on the sea" (לרוח סערה בים);

1a/4–6: "To cross every kind of water without a bridge and without a ship" (לעבור כל מיני מים בלא גשר ובלא ספניה);

1a/8–15: "To let stay every river, sea and the depths and to break waves" (להעמיד כל נהר ים ומצולה ולשבר גלים);

1a/15–16: Intermezzo with the '*Im tirṣe*-formula and a chain of tradition (אם תרצה לפעול מהם);

1a/17–24: "To gather water" (להקות מים);

1a/25–27: "To let the waters rise, when they come down" (לעלות המים במורדן);

1a/27: "For/against a sea storm" (לסער הים).

Although one might think that there could not be much speculation about the nature of recipes taken from a handbook, surprisingly enough, our text ends with a recipe text (*segulla*) that is the exact opposite of the first one (a kind of rhetorical *inclusio*). The first *segulla* is concerned with the question of how to *master* a storm on the sea, while the last one deals with the opposite situation, namely how to *provoke* a sea storm. To pacify a sea storm was of course a necessity of life and death at a time when navigation on seas and rivers was not safe at all. The reason why one would like to provoke a sea storm, is enigmatic, especially in light of the verse used for this purpose, which is taken from Psalm 23:1: This speaks of "God as Shepherd." The author intends perhaps to provoke a storm against his enemy on the assumption that God will rescue himself from this danger: In fact, the psalmist goes further: "He leads me beside still water, he restores my soul" (על מי מנוחות ינהלני).[451]

The formula to "let stay every river, sea and depths and to break the waves" is of course an imitation of the Exodus story where Moses divided the waves. To understand this *segulla*, it is necessary to refer to Psalms 107:23–30:[452]

> Some went down to the sea in ships,
> doing business on the great waters,
> they saw the deeds of the LORD,
> his wondrous works in the deep.
> For he commanded, and raised the stormy wind,
> which lifted up the waves of the sea.
> they mounted up to heaven, they went down to the depths;
> their courage melted away in their evil plight;
> ... he made the storm be still,
> and the waves of the sea were hushed.
> Then they were glad because they had quiet,
> and he brought them to their desired haven.

The procedure according to which names are to be written on a new vessel in purity and cast it into water is also attested. According to *Mekhilta de-Rabbi Yishmaʿel beshallaḥ petiḥta*,[453] Moses wrote the holy name on a golden plaque and cast it into the Nile to find the bones of Joseph[454] (לוח זהב וחקק בה שם המפורש וזרק לתוכו). In a text from the Cairo Genizah, a very similar procedure is described (T.-S. AS 142.13, fol. 1a/7–11: "Take a clay shard from the sea (חרס מן הים) and write on it: *And an angel of the LORD arose* (Exodus 14:19.) etc.

---

451 The psalm is used in the Shimmushe Tehillim for oneiromantic purposes, see MS Oxford Michael 9, fol. 183b/19; MS New York JTSL 1878, fol. 81a/7; MS London Wellcome Institute Hebr. 34, fol. 7a/15; all of them in Bill Rebiger, "Der magische Gebrauch der Psalmen im Judentum. Sefer Shimmush Tehillim" (M.A. thesis, Free University Berlin, 1998).
452 In *Shimmushe Tehillim*, the psalm is used against fever. See Rebiger, "Der magische Gebrauch."
453 See Arthur Marmorstein, "Beiträge zur Religionsgeschichte und Volkskunde," *Jahrbuch für jüdische Volkskunde* 1 (1923): 281–287.
454 See also *Oṣar Midrashim* 356.

And he came between the camps of Egypt (Exodus 14:20) etc. *And Moses stretched out his hand* (Exodus 10:22) etc. You holy names, bring to me with your great strength a fish which weighs so and so many pounds. Amen. Amen. Sela."[455]

The property of the golden plaque with the divine name put on a dead person is also known as a kind of "mantic procedure." We read in Targum Pseudo-Yonatan on Gen. 31:19 and Pirqe de Rabbi Eli'ezer 36 that it was a pagan custom to put a golden plaque with the holy name under the tongue of a slaughtered first-born. The mantic procedure was to obtain responses to questions.[456] In our *segulla*, the aim of the procedure is to make a dead person come alive. Taking it away will cause the person to return to dust. This procedure is nothing but the actualisation of Babylonian Talmud, Sanedrin 65b:

> Rava created a man and sent him to R. Zera. He (R. Zera) spoke to him but he did not answer. Thereupon he said to him. You are coming from the fellows – return to your dust.

The use of Genesis 1:1 to create a creature is embedded in the *segulla* "to collect water." It is itself based on Genesis 1:9: "Let the water under the heavens be gathered together into one place, and let the dry land appear." This is not an exegetical failure, because it is precisely in this verse that the heavens, dry land and water are named together, the elements from which a "golem" is formed. Genesis 1:1 supplies through its author the holy names needed to create the creature. "And this creation is there."[457]

---

455 The text was published by Peter Schäfer and Shaul Shaked, *Magische Texte aus der Kairoer Geniza III* (Tübingen: Mohr, 2000).
456 Johann Maier, "Magisch-theurgische Überlieferungen im mittelalterlichen Judentum: Beobachtungen zu 'Terafim' und 'Golem'," in *Die Juden in ihrer mittelalterlichen Umwelt: Protokolle einer Ring-Vorlesung gehalten im Sommersemester 1989 an der Universität Wien*, ed. Helmut Birkhan (Bern: Lang, 1992), 263 et seq. For other parallel traditions, see Veltri, *Magie und Halakha*, 74–75.
457 On the Golem in Jewish magic and mysticism, there has recently been a very fertile scholarly discussion. The following (alphabetically arranged) articles and books can be recommended: Moshe Idel, "The Golem in Jewish Magic and Mysticism," in *Golem!: Danger, Deliverance and Art*, ed. Emil D. Bilsky (New York: State University of New York Press, 1988), 15–35; Idel, *Golem: Jewish Magical and Mystical Traditions on the Artificial Anthropoid* (Albany, NY: SUNY, 1990); Bilsky, *Golem* [Hebrew] (Jerusalem: Schocken, 1996); Gerold Necker, "Warnung vor der Schöpfermacht: Die Reflexion der Golem-Tradition in der Vorrede des Pseudo-Sa adya-Kommentars zum *Sefer Yeṣira*," *FJB* 21 (1994): 31–67; Peter Schäfer, "The Magic of Golem: The Early Development of the Golem Legend," *JSJ* 46 (1995): 249–261; Maria Incarnación Varela Moreno, "La Leyenda del 'golem': origenes y modernas derivaciones," *Miscelanea de estudios Árabes y Hebraicos* 44 (1995): 61–79; Gerd A. Wewers, "Die Wissenschaft von der Natur im rabbinischen Judentum," *Kairos* 14 (1972): 1–21.

8.4 A Veritable "Watermark"

The custom of using both free pages and filling free spaces of tractates with magical materials is neither new nor surprising. It also occurs in medieval Latin sources, as D'Alverny has already observed: "Il arrive aussi que des scribes perverses tracent des formules, des recettes ou des invocations dans les espaces blancs d'une marge ou de la fin d'un cahiers."[458] By using the adjective "perverse," perhaps to be translated as "outrageous," for a widespread scribal procedure, the author reveals her attitude to magic: in her opinion, it should be considered scandalous and dangerous material. That was, of course, not the opinion of ancient and medieval writers and their clients, who evidently did not protest against this custom. The same procedure can also be found, for example, in Hebrew and Aramaic documents from the Cairo Genizah. In T.-S. AS 143.340, fol. 1a–2b, Mishnah Yoma 5:3–4 and several *segullot* are transmitted together.[459] In some cases, the writer of the manuscript also has to be considered the writer (and perhaps author) of the magical text, and as is the case with the MS Munich, partly written by Shlomo b. Shimshon.

The reason for this usage can be attributed to the scarcity of parchment or of paper. But it must be remembered that magical and non-magical sectors of life in late antiquity and the Middle Ages were not separated from each other. A "handbook" was first of all a collection of materials, used for the multifarious aspects of life. At the beginning or end of a book or a tractate, a magical or imprecatory text could be used as a magical defence against a possible misuse of the text; as, for instance, the writer of T.-S. 12.41 put it:

> [the Sefer Tora] should not be sold or redeemed. Whoever sells it, steals it, or takes it out in order to sell or steal it, shall be under the ban of the God of Hosts ...[460]

However, the text of Munich 95 is peculiar. If we take a look at the contents of the examined *segullot* transmitted in the MS Munich 95, we note with astonishment that they involve two special topics, a few recipes which have something to do with water and the creation of living beings in connection with the primordial water. It is, of course, known that the Babylonian Gemara was the first

---

[458] See Marie-Thérèse D'Alverny, "Survivance de la magie antique," in *Antike und Orient im Mittelalter*: Vorträge der Kölner Mediaevistentagungen, 1956–1959, ed. Paul Wilpert (Berlin: De Gruyter, 1962), 157.
[459] The text was published in Schäfer and Shaked, *Magische Texte*.
[460] Text and translation in Joseph Naveh and Shaul Shaked, *Magic Spells and Formulae: Aramaic Incantations of Late Antiquity* (Jerusalem: The Hebrew University Magnes Press, 1993), 212–214.

source of material to provide traces of the idea of creating a living being[461] in connection with the so-called *hilkhot yeṣira*. Because this was the main Shabbat activity of Rabbi Ḥanina and R. Oshʻaya according to Babylonian Talmud Sanhedrin 67b. Yet the insertion of the creation of a living being into the water recipes, and especially the reference to Genesis 1:9 (dry land and the primordial water), are somewhere awkward.

The fomulae transmitted by the Babylonian Gemara in the Munich Manuscript Hebr. 95 are very interesting, not only because they are in the Gemara of this manuscript of the Babylonian Talmud, but (and in my opinion, above all) because they bind together some traditions about the Golem. The structure of the small handbook directs the reader to the topic of water being the main element which Jews have to deal with. Water is not there for purification, but as a hostile element to be contended with, or as a powerful tool to be utilised. The Golem traditions are embedded in this context and refer implicitly to other traditional materials such as the *Sefer ha-Malbush* and the *Sefer ha-Yashar*, where water, the golden plaque and the appearance of beings play an important role.

The most peculiar aspect is the mentioning of the creation of living things in connection with Genesis 1:9: "And let the water be gathered under the heavens." Of course, it is possible that the writer copied out some recipes, but he did not care for the meaning of the texts. On the other hand, it may be that this text was influenced by the traditions of the *Ḥaside Ashkenaz*, which stressed in particular the role of running water in cultic and revelatory practices. According to *Sefer ha-Malbush*, running waters are a very essential element to provoke the apparition of a living being.[462]

But what was the real necessity for copying some water-*segullot* on a page of this valuable manuscript of the Babylonian Talmud? I suppose that it was to preserve it from the not uncommon floods in northern European countries. If we look at the year of transcription of the manuscript, 1342 in Paris, we can find a historical reason for the writer's preoccupation with water(s). From Paris to the Baltic Sea, the period between 1340 and 1380 was marked by a "little ice age," with repeated floods and deluges. In August 1342, Germany, for instance, was afflicted by a disastrous flood, the worst in the entire century. These circumstances explain the preoccupation of the writer with copying several water-*segullot* and powerful names as an *apotropaicum*, namely to avert the danger of water from the manuscript and, I daresay, he ended up leaving us a veritable example of a "watermark" in historical context.

---

461 On a different view, see Veltri, *Magie und Halakha*, 40–42.
462 On the *Sefer ha-Malbush* and its traditions, see Irina Wandrey, "Das 'Buch des Gewandes.'"

9 The Meal of the Spirits, the Three *Parcae* and Lilith

Becoming familiar with magical concepts and delving into the subject is a fascinating undertaking. The scholars, initially with few suspicions, find themselves enchanted by the texts that they seek to explain, texts whose secrets the scholar believes to be penetrable by means of analysis and critique. Yet, the deeper scholars and readers venture into the dark forests of magic, often drawn into them involuntarily like Hansel and Gretel, the more the scholar's awe and wonder are infused by the sensation of helplessness. Scholars have to face a chaotic spectrum of uncertainties. They are often overwhelmed by a complex net of works which had been created by authors and practitioners who could be called "artists" of magic. The scholar can only escape these uncertainties and this complexity by identifying the internal structure of spectrum, and breaking complexity into its smallest elements. The elements may then function as signposts for unfolding the underlying motifs of a tradition or a text. Then only are scholars able to step out onto the path leading through the dark forests of magic. And, more importantly, venturing down this path, they may find their way out again.

Martin Heidegger defines *a-letheia* "philologically" as the nature of truth in speaking of the un-concealed-ness of the manifestation of Being. This applies even more to magical concepts. The nature of magic lies, philologically, in the process which leads from the hidden to the undisclosed, and vice versa. Neither origin nor aim is magic. The trajectory of how the tradition of elements from one culture moves into another is central, even though its contents are rarely understood or of interest. This idea suggests that the magicians are uninterested in being occupied with theory. They are concerned with the effects of a text and the practice. They deal with magical formulae which stipulate cures *hic et nunc*, here and now. It is not only the content of magic that is uncovered but in the main the energy that magic sets free when meeting the right conditions. However, even a practice that brings about success does not necessarily mean a stringent causality. Success merely extends the spectrum of possibilities.

Magic is an empirical science par excellence, which is most evident in its affinity to medicine. Both sciences apply to human beings in their respective fields and times. Both sciences claim the empirical totality of their achievements. In this claim, we find the same paradox found in the subjects of the humanities – of which magic is, in fact, a part. In other words: the knowledge of medicine and magic is empirically bound by the parameters of their respective times. Yet their claims are empirically absolute, beyond any temporal framework.

Empirical totality simply refers to the magician's understanding that something might be of absolute importance for one particular individual, but cannot be defined or is not appreciated by another. Contrary to certain speculations, the essence of every magical concept lies within man himself – in his very own *humus*. It is not *super-stitio* that inspires the worldview and value system, but it inspires what is perceived anthropologically as the "I" or ego. Everything else serves human beings, just the way colours and imagination serve a painter. As they are equipped with this understanding, magicians study the provable and the proven, the possible and the impossible. They study what *they* might use as *materia magica*. The magicians are not bound to any religion. They are neither monotheists nor polytheists. They are pragmatists.

We are not always able to identify the structure and the interwoven texts of magic spheres. We are often unable to separate the tangle of their substructures from the at times innumerable threads of tradition they are infused with. The reason for that is quite simple: we lack an overview of all the necessary threads, but not because the magical techniques used by the ancient practitioners are so concealed. It is not the case that magic has a structured nature, as we often believed, marked by esotericism and exotericism. We lack the overview because of our ignorance of how magical traditions are transmitted.

We rarely have at our disposal detailed texts which might explain the origins and developments of certain practices and beliefs. Even in the few known examples where we do, such as those of the Roman writer Apuleius (c. 125–c. 180), the Neo-Platonist Iamblichus (c. 245–c. 325), or the Church Father Origen (c. 184–c. 254),[463] it is always advisable to ask whether their explanations indeed fit the facts at hand or whether they represent "clumsy" attempts at doing so. As a rule, we only know of isolated traditions and customs which are duly classified generically in handbooks, anthologies, and *excerpta*. At times, they are treated as deviations in legal texts (law codices), or described and prosecuted in case files, notably in the files of the Inquisition, as capital crimes.

---

463 On Apuleius, see Adam Abt, *Die Apologie des Apuleius von Madaura. Beiträge zur Erläuterung der Schrift* De magia (Gießen: Töpelmann, 1908); Raffaella Garosi, "Indagini sulla formazione del concetto di magia nella cultura romana," in *Magia: Studi di storia delle religioni in memoria di Raffaella Garosi*, ed. Paolo Xella (Rome: Bulzoni, 1976), 13–93; Fritz Graf, *La magie dans l'antiquité gréco-romaine* (Paris: Les belles lettres, 1994); Veltri, *Magie und Halakha* (Tübingen: Mohr, 1997), 53 et seq. On Origen, see Hans D. Betz, "The Formation of Authoritative Tradition in the Greek Magical Papyri," in *Jewish and Christian Self-Definition*, vol. 3: Self-Definition in the Greco-Roman World, ed. Ben F. Meyer and Ed Parish Sander (Philadelphia: Fortress Press, 1982), 162. See also Naomi Janowitz, "Theories of Divine Names in Origen and Pseudo-Dionysus," *History of Religions* 30 (1991), 359–371.

We also hardly need to emphasise that legal texts, such as the *Shulḥan 'Arukh*, or the confessional books of Early Modern Period, are an inexhaustible source of folkloric and mythical beliefs. The first category comprises behavioural codices which tried to regulate every aspect of life; including private and intimate spheres. The second consists of a series of questions for the believer about whether or not he or she had been guilty of performing certain practices which were usually of a sexual nature or deemed "superstitious." The indirect goal of this inquiry was (and how could it be otherwise?) to educate people about the things they were supposed to avoid. It should not be forgotten that the most effective propagators of so-called superstitious practices were the very churches which, in their zealous campaigns against superstition, eventually advertised them.

As a generic category, the confessional books are easier to characterise than the eagerly sought-after case files of the Inquisition, which still attract the special attention of historians of the *nouvelle école*. Admittedly, the files of the Inquisition are among the best sources for folk beliefs. They are, nevertheless, only usable as sources if taken *cum grano salis*. The explanation for that is easy to follow: the Inquisitors used torture and the threat thereof on the suspected magicians and witches. In order to avoid the physical and psychological stress of the interrogations, suspects often caved in and admitted everything they were accused of.[464] The Inquisition files thus should be accused of psychological plagiarism, where seeming "facts" simply reflected the accuser's imagination rather than the defendant's reality.

Unlike the Inquisitors, however, the father confessors were hardly interested in luring or torturing people, especially women, into confessions about crimes they had not committed. When discussing both inquisitorial material as well as canonical texts, the scholar thus must be cautious. These sources provide only a distorted image of what individuals may have believed, either personally or according to their social context.

The works on magic in the area of Greco-Roman Palestine are numerous and cover a spectrum of topics: magic, superstitions, healing, and sciences in the political and cultural environment of rabbinic Judaism. Thus, it is not my aim to give an exhaustive account of the detailed aspects concerning a world of practical and pragmatic systems of life, beliefs, and behaviour. I wish rather to offer only some outline and guideposts for future inquiries into the subject by exploring an array of considerations on magic and science.

The leitmotif in the present chapter is the magical coping with female feelings of anxiety, in particular during the perinatal period or shortly thereafter.

---

464 See below chapter 10 Evidence and Plausibility, pp. 203–213.

We will also discuss the function of magic for dealing with problems arising from fertility and infertility. According to popular belief, certain forces are at work here which must be influenced, tamed or appeased in a magical manner:
1. the womb as an autonomous addressee,
2. the anxieties of the early postnatal phase, when the danger of an infant's sudden death is most acute, and, above all,
3. the general feeling of anxiety arising from trying to cope with everyday problems.

9.1 A Decree by Burkhard, Bishop of Worms: The Table Set for the Three *Parcae*

In the decrees issued by Bishop Burkhard of Worms (d. 1024), written between 1007 and 1014 but not published as a collection until 1548 in Cologne (198^d), we find the following questions. These were supposed to enlighten the confessants and to overcome the *ignorantia crassa ac supina*:

> Have you done what some women used to do in earlier times? Namely to set a table in your house, having placed on the table your food and drink with three knives, in order that or in case they come: the three sisters whom the ancient following and the ancient stupidity called the *Parcae*, [who] can fortify themselves there? Have you taken away from the divine religion [*pietas*] its power and its name and given them over to the devil? As a believer, I mean to ask whether the three who you say are the three sisters can be of assistance to you either today or in the future?[465]

Burkhard, or rather the source assigned to him, presents us with the mosaic picture that I tried to depict above. The small pieces which make up the motifs

---

[465] Burkhard's decree in the original Latin: "Fecisti quod quaedam mulieres in quibusdam temporibus anni facere solent, ut in domo tua mensam praepareres et tuos cibos et potum cum tribus cultellis supra mensam poneres, ut si venissent tres illae sorores, quas antiqua posteritas et antiqua stultitia Parcas nominavit, ibi reficerentur. et tulisti divinae pietati potestatem suam et nomen suum, et diabolo tradidisti, ita dico, ut crederes illas quas tu dicis esse sorores tibi posse aut hic aut in futuro prodesse." Quoted from Jakob Grimm, *Deutsche Mythologie* vol. 3 (Göttingen: Dieterische Buchhandlung 1854 [reprint Berlin: Ullstein 1981]), 409. See Hermann Usener, *Dreiheit: Ein Versuch mythologischer Zahlenlehre* (Bonn; Georgi, 1903; repr. Hildesheim 1966), 12; Maximilian Ihm, "Der Mütter- oder Matronenkultus und seine Denkmäler" (Ph.D. diss., University of Bonn, 1887), 66 et seq., 98 et seq.; Maximilian Siebourg, "De Sulevis Campestribus fatis" (Ph.D. diss., University of Bonn, 1886); Carolus Friederichs, *Matronarvm monvmenta congessit congesta digessit* (Bonn: Georgus, 1886). On Burkhard and his sources, see Wilhelm G. Solden, Heinrich Heppe and Max Bauer, *Geschichte der Hexenprozesse* (Munich: Müller, 1911).

of the questions simply cannot be cut out of the whole image. The three sisters are evidently the *Parcae* (the Fates) who originally were goddesses of birth, and since their days as Greek Μοῖραι, were also considered to be deities of fortune. According to the Roman scholar Marcus Terentius Varro (116 BCE–27 BCE), the sisters' names are Nona, Decuma and Morta.[466] The names seem to have some connection with stillbirths. The sisters' function is to decide one's fate and to protect the infants during birth.[467]

The three *Parcae* have a positive image in non-Christian texts, and they are associated with the parturient, birth and the infant. By contrast, the Christian tradition demonised the Parcae altogether as demons of the afterlife. The *Ars Laureeshamensis, Expositio in Donatum maiorem III, De Tropis*, (sec. ix, page 234) defines the sisters as: "Parcae are the three sisters Allecto, Tesiphone and Megera; they live in hell and are called Parcae as an antonym, because they spare no one."[468] The mix-up with the three Furies is clear, for the (Greek) names of the *Parcae* were Clotho, Lachesis and Atropos.[469] The reference to the antonym is an indirect quotation from Latin folk etymology, as shown for instance in the work of Maurus Servius Honoratus (4th century CE).[470]

Despite resistance from the church authorities, Burkhard's decree proves that the belief in the *Parcae* continued to thrive. It should be noted, however, that mythological characters tend to fuse with others in the popular imagination. Thus, people then were hardly interested in clearly distinguishing the *Parcae* from other *dramatis personae*. The features of the three *Parcae*, as clear-

---

466 Source 3:16, 10.
467 See Konrad Ziegler and Walther Sontheimer, ed. *Der Kleine Pauly: Lexikon der Antike in fünf Bänden* vol. 4 (München: DTV, 1979), col. 509.
468 Latin: "PARCAE dicuntur tres sorores. Allecto Tesiphone et Megera, quae apud inferos sunt et dicuntur Parcae per contrarium, eo QVOD NEMINI PARCANT, habent enim secundum fabulas serpentes pro crinibus flagella que ignita tenentes in manibus intonant ore et flagellant animas hominum peccatorum; dum ergo nulli parcant, per contrarium Parcae uocantur."
469 Latin: "Huic quoque etiam tres Furias deseruire dicunt; quarum prima Allecto secunda Tisiphone, tertia Megera; Allecto enim Grece inpausabilis dicitur; Tisiphone autem quasi tuton phone, id est istarum vox; Megera autem quasi megale eris, id est magna contentio." Fulgentius Mythographus, *Mitologiarum libri tres* 1,7, 20. See, for instance, 171.1.3. He wrote, "Cum Althaea Thestii filia una nocte concubuerunt Oeneus et Mars, ex quibus cum esset natus Meleager, subito in regia apparuerunt Parcae Clotho Lachesis Atropos." Also online http://latin.packhum.org/loc/1263/1/77#77 (accessed 4 November 2013). English translation *Myths of Hyginus*, transl. and ed. Mary Grant (Lawrence: University of Kansas Press, 1960).
470 See, *Maurus Servius Honoratus*, Aeneis *1.22* 1.22.8: "Volvere Parcas aut a filo traxit 'volvere' aut a libro; una enim loquitur, altera scribit, alia fila deducit. et dictae sunt parcae kata antiphrasin, quod nulli parcant, sicut lucus a non lucendo, bellum a nulla re bella. nomina parcarum Clotho Lachesis Atropos.

ly defined in Roman mythology, were continuously subject to alteration and development. In the mediaeval *Romanusbüchlein*, which deals with medical-magical themes, we find the *Parcae* mentioned in a womb incantation[471]:

English Translation	German
In front of the womb:	Vor die [Ge-]Bärmutter:
Three women are sitting in the sand,	Es sitzen drei Weiber im Sand,
they have human (horse, livestock)	sie haben des Menschen (Roß, Vieh)
entrails in their hands.	Gedärm in der Hand.
The first moves them,	die erste regts,
the second shoots them,	die zweite schießt,
the third lays them out again.	die dritte legts wieder zurecht.

In magical texts and the literature dealing with it, the *Parcae* typically appear as the "three sisters," "three virgins," or "three sows," as in several *Adynata-Historiolae*. They supposedly help against lower abdominal pains.[472]

Back to Burkhard's text: What exactly do the sisters offer, given the fact, that their hoped-for assistance appears to be of importance? Burkhard does not provide an immediate answer. Therefore, we should break down the text into its elements in order to understand the image. Three elements are relevant: the prepared or set table, the three knives (*mensam praeparares et tuos cibos et potum cum tribus cultellis supra mensam poneres*) and the transmission of the divine name to the devil (*tulisti divinae pietati potestatem suam et nomen suum, et diabolo tradidisti*). I will discuss each of them separately.

9.2 The Prepared Table

Servius, the commentator on Virgil (on Aeneis, 10:76), reports about the custom of making a bed for Pilumnus and Pitumnus at the birth of a child, that

---

[471] Quoted in Ricardus Heim, *Incantamenta Magica Graeca Latina* (Leipzig: Teubner, 1892), 497. On *Romanusbüchlein*, see Adolf Spamer, *Romanusbüchlein: Historisch-philologischer Kommentar zu einem deutschen Zauberbuch* (Berlin: Akademie Verlag, 1958).

[472] See Marcellus (ca 400 CE), *De Medicamentis* XXI:3: "Adid (scl. corcum) aliud carmen: 'corce, corcedo stagne, pastores te invenerunt, sine manibus collegerunt, sine foco coxerunt, sine dentibus comederunt. Tres virgines in medio mari mensam marmoream positam habebant; duae torquebant, una retorquebat. Quomodo hoc numquam factum est, sic numquam sciat illa Gaia Seia corci dolorem.'" Also, Marcellus, *De Medicamentis*, XXVIII,74: "Ad rosum tam hominum quam iumentorum praecantatio sic: pollice sinistro et duobus minimis digitis ventrem confricans dices: 'Stabat arbor in medio mare et ibi pendebat situla plena intestinorum humanorum, tres virgines circumibant, duae alligabant, una resolvebat.' Hoc ter dices et ter pari modo terra contacta exspues." On the *Adynata* and the *Historiolae* see Alf Önnerfors,

is, to prepare a meal for these deities.[473] They were thought to be protective spirits for the neonate. Such a custom is also known to Rabbi Yeruḥam ben Meshullam (1290–1350), who dismisses the custom as idolatrous. He stated

> Why are people in certain lands used to preparing a table and placing food [literally: dishes] on it during the night before the day a child is to be circumcised? They said that they do it for the luck of the child born.[474]

The Rabbi's source text likely was the Tosefta, Shabbat 6:4a: "Whosoever prepares the table in front of her (the parturient); this (act) is an Amorite custom." The Amorites were looked upon as the archetypal strangers and thus classified as "magical" (see above). Setting a table did not necessarily mean that the spirits (the *Parcae* or Plimunus and Pitumnus) would eat the food. Admittedly, it is documented that according to the Babylonian Talmud, the spirits could also eat and drink (Hagiga 16a); however, a set table is only the sign of preparedness on the part of the practitioners of this custom. The spirits themselves consume nothing.

On this point, I would like to call your attention to an Aramaic inscription on silver platelets (two amulets) discovered in Agabeyli (Turkey) and published by André Dupont-Sommer in 1950/51.[475] The text caused a lively interest among scholars which is documented by later studies. The later studies carefully re-examined its contents from the 1960s onward, as did Gershom Scholem, Baruch A. Levine, and Joseph Naveh/Shaul Shaked.[476] The import of the

---

ed., *Antike Zaubersprüche* [Greek/Latin and German] (Stuttgart: Reclam, 1991), 21–24. See also Burkhard's decree and Heim, *Incantamenta*, 496.

473 Latin: "Pilumnum et Pitumnum infantium deos esse ait eisque pro puerpera lectum in atrio sterni, dum exploretur an vitalis sit qui natus est." See also "Proinde nobilibus pueris editis in atrio domus Iunoni lectus, Herculi mensa ponebatur." Servius on Vergilius *Eclogae*, 4,62 (according to the Scholion):

474 See Jehuda Bergmann, "Zur Geschichte religiöser Bräuche," *Monatsschrift für die Geschichte und Wissenschaft des Judentums* 71 (1927), 169; Saul Lieberman, *Tosefta Ki-Fshutah: A Comprehensive Commentary on the Tosefta* [Hebr.], vol. 3 (New York: Jewish Theological Seminary of America, 1962), 84, note 37. See, however, *Bet Yosef on Yore De'a* § 179. Eligius (588–659) wrote: "nullus in kal. Jan. nefanda ut ridiculosa, vetulas aut cervulos, aut jotticos (ulerioticos) faciat, neque mensas super noctem componat, neque strenas aut bibitionis superfluas exerceat." Quoted in Grimm, *Mythologie*, vol. 3, 401.

475 André Dupont-Sommer, "Deux lamelles d'argent à inscription hébréo-araméenne trouvées à Agabeyli (Turquie)," *Jahrbuch für Kleinasiatische Forschung* 1 (1950/51), 201–217.

476 Gerschom Scholem, *Jewish Gnosticism, Merkabah Mysticism, and Talmudic Tradition*, New York: Jewish Theological Seminary, 1965), 84–93; Baruch E. Levine, "The Language of the Magical Bowls," in *A History of the Jews in Babylonia*, ed. Jacob Neusner, vol. 5: *Later Sasanian Times* (Leiden: Brill, 1970), 360–361; Joseph Naveh and Shaul Shaked, *Amulets and Magic*

text depends on the epigraphic reading, which in turn should shed light on the question as to whether the amulet was produced for a "womb" (Dupont-Sommer), in the name of "Metatron" (Scholem), or simply for "Demetrius" (Naveh/Shaked). As Scholem and subsequently Levine have emphasised, the entire text can only be understood if the three *dramatis personae* included in the text are understood as well. The text reads as follows:

> These three: the first (of them) is hungry, but doesn't eat; the other is thirsty, but doesn't drink; the (third) is sleepy, but doesn't sleep. I say to the hungry (person): Why are you hungry and do not eat? (I say) to the thirsty (person): Why are you thirsty and do not drink? (I say) to the sleepy (person): Why are you sleepy and do not sleep?[477]

In 1941, Cyrus H. Gordon published a report on a magic bowl whose inscription speaks of spirits standing before the door (literally "on the roof"). The spirits are asked to enter: "Come inside! Here is meat to eat and wine to drink."[478]

It seems reasonable to suppose that this *historiola* is to be understood here as *Adynata*, namely instructions in a story impossible to carry out that are predominantly supposed to keep an illness at bay. In other words, they make it impossible, analogous to the impossibility of the situation described, and as such are reminiscent of the Tantalus formula. The latter is naturally linked to the myth of Tantalus, whose wish to have a life like that of the gods is fulfilled by Zeus. But Zeus suspends a large rock over Tantalus' head, threatening to crush him, and "tantalises" him with fruit and water, but never allows him to satisfy his hunger and thirst, thus depriving him of any pleasure in life. The myth is the very embodiment of the frustrated wish for a godlike existence.[479] It also gave rise to magical ideas which, at times exorcistic, at times ironic or hospitable, nevertheless attest to the great variety and fantasy of the magical acts. A Greek amulet published by Campbell Bonner reads: διψᾷς Τάνταλε, αἷμα πίε. Bonner renders the inscription as: "You, Tantalus, are a thirsty (snake), drink the blood!"[480] διψᾷς (dipsaō, literally "thirst after") refers to a snake whose bite, according to ancient belief, caused thirst. Moreover, the creature is illustrated on this amulet together with a womb motif. Bonner ar-

---

Bowls: Aramaic Incantation of Late Antiquity (Jerusalem/Leiden: Magnes, 1985), 68–77. See also David Sperber, "On a Meaning of the Word hlm," *Revue des Études Juives* 125 (1966): 385–389.
477 Naveh-Shaked, *Amulets*, 70 – 71.
478 See Cyrus H. Gordon, "Aramaic Incantation Bowls," *Orientalia* NS 10 (1941): 342–343.
479 See *Der kleine Pauly*, vol. 5, 512–513.
480 Campbell Bonner, *Studies in Magical Amulets Chiefly Graeco-Egyptian* (Ann Arbor et al.: University of Michigan Press, 1950), 88–89. See a picture of the amulet at "Magical Gem: Ares, Tantalos-historiola (A) womb, voces (B)," *The Campbell Bonner Magical Gems Database*, http://www2.szepmuveszeti.hu/talismans/cbd/754?collection=4 (accessed 21 February 2013).

gues that the amulet itself is supposed to protect against menorrhagia. I assume that this also illustrates an impossible situation: just as the thirsty Tantalus is not allowed to drink, the womb of the amulet wearer is not supposed to bleed or "drink blood."

Another confirmation for the idea that the womb might be held responsible for this is a verse from Transylvania:

English Translation	German
Midwife, womb,	Wehmutter, Beermutter
You want to lick blood,	Du willst Blut lecken,
Push away the heart,	das Herz abstoßen
Stretch the joints	die Glieder strecken!
Stretch the skin!	die Haut strecken
You should not do it,	Darfst es nicht tun
You must rest.	Du must ruhn
In the name of God!	Im Namen Gottes![481]

In this example, the womb or uterus is personalised as having its own will, as in many texts of the ancient, mediaeval and early modern world. It is described as a conscious entity within the body which may cause pains or even asphyxia (*globus hystericus*).[482] The Greek physician Aretaeus of Cappadocia (1st century CE) describes the uterus as such:

> The uterus is completely like an animal, for it moves within the flanks here and there, upwards to the cartilage of the rib cage, sideways to the right to the liver and the spleen, also downwards until just on top of the genitals; in short, it wanders within the whole body here and there, is therefore like an animal and is one, too.[483]

---

[481] Rudolf Kriss, *Das Gebärmuttermotiv: Ein Beitrag zur Volkskunde nebst einer Einleitung über Arten und Bedeutung der deutschen Opfergebräuche der Gegenwart* (Augsburg: Filser, 1929), 31.

[482] Alfons A. Barb, "Diva Matrix: A Faked Gnostic Intaglio in the Possession of P. P. Rubens and the Iconology of a Symbol," *Journal of the Warburg and Courtauld Institutes* 16 (1953): 214, note 23. See also Heinrich von Staden, "*Apud nos foediora verba*: Celsus' Reluctant Construction of the Female Body," in *Le latin medical: La constitution d'un langage scientifique Réalités et langage de la médicine dans le monde romaine*, ed. Guy Sabbah (Saint-Étienne: Publication de l'Université de Saint-Étienne 1991), 294 et seq.

[483] Aretaues, *De causis et signis acutorum morborum*, 2,11.1–3. See further Bonner, *Studies in Magical Amulets*, 9; Kriss, *Das Gebärmuttermotiv*, 35. See also the discussion there on the meaning of this quotation in the history and story of the conception of the womb as an animal. See also G. Veltri, "Zur Überlieferung medizinisch-magischer Traditionen: Das màtra-Motiv in den Papyri Magicae und der Kairoer Geniza," *Henoch* 18 (1996): 157–175; "Jewish Traditions in Greek Amulets," *Bulletin of Judaeo-Greek Studies* 18 (1996): 37–39; Jeffrey Spier, "Medieval Byzantine Magical Amulets and their Tradition," *Journal of the Warburg and Courtauld Institutes* 56 (1993): 25–62 (6 plates), esp. 42 et seq.

We find a comparable idea with Galen.[484] From this, the concept of "hysteria" was developed. The connection between the womb motif and the three figures or *Parcae* is not the outgrowth of a scholar's excited but capricious imagination. It is present in the word-for-word rendering of a German-Jewish conjuration in Old High German published by Moritz Güdemann in 1875. This contribution, unfortunately, soon sank into oblivion. The text is in Hebrew letters and very difficult to decipher. The following is Güdemann's (German) transcription, additions are mine:

1. bermuter legdich
2. bist as alt als ich
3. bringst du mich zu der erde
4. du must mit mir begraben werden
5. ein buch heist d'bible.
6. bermutter leg dich nidre.
7. Du solt dich legen nider an dîn rechte stat
8. das gbot dir di heiligen goltes kraft
9. vermut un hege mut.
10. Un lege mut un das fige [?Feige, Engl. Fig].
11. un wilia tara das vare under mîn sol.
12. Darunder kanichs wol verduldne.
13. Da vlust under ein bodemloser sê
14. da gat in ein gratloser visch den solt essen.
15. Un solt menschlichs gar vergessen.
16. Aschaschanda an sanda (?) drie mêr mindu.
17. Die haten zhanda mîn gederme.
18. D'ein schlehts.
19. D'ander rêhts.
20. d'drite insteht rukts
21. wilius. E wilius (?) wiliatar alie (?) bracha
22. das wilia tar [Engl. "tear," Ger. zerreißen] entzwei
23. das sol mir sîn zbus vir di bermutter
24. das so war in goltes namen amen.[485]

Some remarks are needed for this text. The first part (1–8) is the well-known conjuration of the womb which is also contained in a manuscript published by Max Grünwald in 1907:

---

484 See, however, Soranus *Gynaekologie*, 4,36,4; Bonner, *Studies in Magical Amulets*, 91.
485 Moritz Güdemann, "Vermischungen von Jüdischen und Heidnischem aus neuer und alter Zeit," *Monatsschrift für die Geschichte und Wissenschaft des Judentums* 24 (1875): 271.

Bärmutter leg dich auf deiner rechten stat
das gebiert dir bei Gotts kraft
un' bei seiner heiligen engel macht
brengstu mich zu der erden
du musstu mit mir begraben werden.
So gebiet ich dir bei neun dorot [Geschlechtern] un' bei
neun sefer torot [Torarolle] un bei drei malakhim [Engel] Gottes,
die im Himmel sein,
damit soll der allmächtige Gott mein Helfer sein.[486]

The verses 13–14 mention a fish which the womb has to eat: *Da vlust under ein bodemloser sê da gat in ein gratloser visch den solt essen. Un solt menschlichs gar vergessen.* Güdemann identifies the fish as a penis.[487] Nothing like it: the fish is a reference to the word "delphus," a synonym for "womb" and is at the same time an allusion to dolphin (German: *Delphin*). In Italian, the reference is clearer. It reads: *"nuota come pesce,"* or in English: "[I]t (the womb) swims like a fish."[488] The second part of the text (v. 16 ff.) deals with the three Parcae on the sea, a motif mentioned above. A writer of the text has added (f. 89v) a detailed, more explicit version of this *historiola* in the margins (f. 89v): די אינא בראט דן ודם די אנדרא בושט דן שדן די דריטא הטא אינן אינגיל.[489] In modern German, the verse would read: *die eine bereitet den Faden, die andere büßt den Schaden, die dritte hat einen Engel*; in English "the [first] one prepares the thread; the other one expiates the damage, the third one has an angel."

Let us return to the set table: the dishes are prepared for the three spirits (or *Parcae*), so that they may refresh themselves and enter into the service of the practitioner(s). However, they are not expected or supposed to eat anything. What is the purpose of the three knives/swords and the handing over of the divine name? In the realm of magic, there barely is room for spontaneity or chance. Therefore, each element has a purpose. *Cultellus* means both "small knife" as well as "sword." The *cultelli* and the handing over of the divine name are the elements which qualify the action of the three *Parcae* or spirits: both elements unmistakably refer to the Sideros-Lilith complex.

---

486 Max Grünwald, "Kleine Beiträge zur jüdischen Volkskunde: Aus Hausapotheke und Hexenküche II," *Monatsschrift der jüdischen Volkskunde* NF 3 (1907): 134. The additions are Grünwald's. See also MS 232 of the *Gesellschaft für jüdische Volkskunde*, recipe 24 (Bärmutter), which Grünwald quotes in the same journal.
487 See Güdemann's commen in "Vermischungen von Jüdischen und Heidnischem," 272.
488 See Spier, "Byzantine Amulets," 49, note 141.
489 Güdemann, "Vermischungen von Jüdischen und Heidnischem," 272.

9.3 Sideros (Iron), Lilith, and the Name of God

The three *cultelli*, whether knives or swords, are neither mere table ornaments nor parts of the table setting. In the Middle Ages, a man's knife was an essential tool for defense, for the meal, etc., and was carried at all times. Thus, the mere reference to *cultelli* does not provide an indication of their function. In this context, a sword could have two functions. First, the presence of the sword hints at the continence of man and woman. In the Babylonian Talmud (Sanhedrin, 19b), it is said of Palatiel that he abstained from all contact with his wife by placing a sword between himself and her. Moses achieved the same effect when he married the widowed Queen of Ethiopia by not touching her, at least according to the mediaeval *Chronicle of Moses*.[490]

Second, iron is known to be a repellent against demons. Thus, the Tosefta text, cited above, records: "[Among the practices of the Amorites is the following:] the man who binds a [piece of] iron to the feet of a woman in childbed." Iron allegedly protected against demons who want to suck out the blood of children.[491] Iron supposedly protected the children against the Babylonian demon *Lamashtu*, the Jewish *Sideros* and *Lilith*, the Greek *Gellos*, and the Roman *Lamiae*. They all were female demons, or vampires.[492] According to *Sefer 'Alilot Devarim*, the custom of placing a piece of iron, a sword, into the puerperal had persisted in German regions well into the modern period.[493]

---

490 See *Bet ha-Midrash* II,6 (Chronicle of Moses). On this story see Moses Gaster, "Beiträge zur vergleichenden Sagen- und Märchenkunde," *Monatsschrift für die Geschichte und Wissenschaft des Judentums* 29 (1880): 127.
491 On the use of iron, see Blau, *Zauberwesen*, 159–160; Ignaz Goldziher, "Eisen als Schutz gegen Dämonen," *Archiv für Religionswissenschaft* 10 (1907): 41–46; Immanuel Löw, "Das Eisen," *Monatsschrift für die Geschichte und Wissenschaft des Judentums* 81 (1937): 50–52; Arthur Marmorstein, "Eine angeblich korrupte Borajta," *Monatsschrift für die Geschichte und Wissenschaft des Judentums* 72 (1928): 392, note 1; Samuel Krauss, "Die religionsgeschichtlich erklärte Barajta," *Monatsschrift für die Geschichte und Wissenschaft des Judentums* 72 (1928): 479; Naveh and Shaked, *Amulets*, 121, note 23.
492 Moses Gaster, "Beiträge zur vergleichende Sagen- und Märchenkunde. X. Lilith und die drei Ängel," *Monatsschrift für die Geschichte und Wissenschaft des Judentums* 29 (1880): 553–565; Gaster, "Two Thousand Years of a Charm against the Child-Stealing Witch," *Folk-Lore* 11 (1900): 129–161; Gershom Scholem, "New Chapters in the Story of Ashmedai and Lilith [Hebrew]," *Tarbiz* 19 (1948): 166, note 25; Wilhelm Ahrens, *Hebräische Amulette mit magischen Zahlenquadraten* (Berlin: Lamm, 1916); Wilhelm Bacher, "Lilith, Königin von Smargad ," *Monatsschrift für die Geschichte und Wissenschaft des Judentums* 19 (1870): 187–189; Joseph Dan, "Samael, Lillith and the Concept of Evil in the Early Kabbalah," *AJS Review* 5 (1980): 17–40. Nitzah Abarbanel, *Éavah we-Lilit* (Bene-Brak: Bar-Ilan University Press, 1994); Vera Zingsem, *Lilith: Adams erste Frau* (Tübingen: Klöpfer & Meyer, 1999).
493 *Oṣar Neḥmad* 4 (1863): 189 and 204.

Every scholar in the field of magic and medicine knows in general that in antiquity, at least in the empirical school, the principle of *similia similibus* (like cures like) was applied. For example, only something red like blood could supposedly heal a red wound in the eye. Thus, it may not come as a surprise to learn that *Sideros* is a term also used for the piece of iron, or the sword, supposedly fending off bad spirits. *Sideros* is nothing other than the Greek word for iron. Thus, we find the following in a text edited by Christa Müller:

1. And Smmomit bore twelve children [sons] and the treacherous Sideros killed them all. And
2. she arose and fled from him, and she went to a mountain whose name is unique in the world; and she practiced
3. sorcery with copper and iron. And there came Saunios [and] Saunios. They knocked and told her "Open to us!" And she told
4. them: "I will not open [the door] to you." And they told her: "[There] is the place through which we will pass and enter." And she arose and opened [the door] to them; and Sideros entered with them
5. and killed her son, and strangled him to death; and she arose and screamed because of him: "O Saunios [and] Saunios! What did they do to him?" And they arose and
6. pursued him at the Pelagos, the great sea, and attempted to kill him and to strangle him to death. And he told them: "Let me be, and I
7. besiege you in the name of the one who measures the water in his palm [Isaia 40:12] that I will – at every place which reminds one of the names of Saunios ([and] Saunios – neither
8. kill nor strangle, nor do harm to any child [sons] Hormizdux[t] bat Maro[y] and Nipra[y] bar Maroy have or will have." Bound is Lilith, bound is Mebakalta,
9. bound is Sheda, bound is Dew, bound is Danḥish, bound is Dini, bound is Zakya, bound is Patikar.[494]

Joseph Naveh and Shaul Shaked report on an earlier parallel yet fragmentary text dealing with an amulet in the Israel Museum in Jerusalem. In the same book they give the text; they also published the inscriptions on two magic bowls in the Jewish National and University Library in Jerusalem, and in the Metropolitan Museum in New York, which also contain the same story. This tale therefore belongs to a complex of texts which enjoyed an astonishingly widespread popularity from medieval to modern times, from Sephardic to Slavic lands. Three figures, or four, as in the example, are received by a woman, albeit with suspicion, in her own house (is hospitality the motive here?). Evil Sideros sneaks in with them and kills her child. The three or four figures pursue the evil one and wrest from it a promise that the demon will not kill the children of those parents who mention, remember, speak about or write down

---

[494] Christa Müller-Kessler, *Die Zauberschalentexte in der Hilprecht-Sammlung, Jena, und weitere Nippur-Texte anderer Sammlungen* (Wiesbaden: Harrassowitz, 2005), 22–23. My translation of the text.

the names of the three figures. This is a *historiola* which forms the basis of the production of amulets for births. Note that the *nomina barbara* of these angels, or demons or saints are nothing but the transcription or permutations of God's name ("Saunios" in the translated text, but also Sanoy, Sansanoy, Samangelof). In Greek SNWY, SNSYNUI, SMNGLUF (or SMNGR) can correspond to the following SEMNOS SEMNOS SEMNAI GRAFAI. Semnos is synonymous with agios and means "sacred, noble, majestic, exalted."

In this context, one could quote a text from the *Papyri Graecae Magicae* (*PGM*) IV, 665 et seq., where the goddesses of fate (the seven τύχαι) are presented as "noble and gracious virgins". The *PGM* also knows the expression *semna onomata* as a reference to the sacred names of Selene, the Goddess of the Tartaros.[495] The divine name, which also plays a role in the custom Burkhard described, is the defensive power of the amulet against Sideros or the evil spirit which might kill the child. It is likely that the set table refers to an amulet on which God's name is written. The link between the three *Parcae* and the divine name is seen when the divine name is handed over to the devil, a practice which Burkhard reprimands. If we consider that the woman followed this magical procedure, protecting her child before the child was baptised or circumcised, then the criticism might be understood. Christian and Jewish authorities likely understood it as idolatry par excellence, since it represents the exploitation of the divine name even before the child formally becomes a Christian or a Jew.

It is interesting to note that in a later magic bowl inscription we find the role of the pursuer played by Elijah instead of the three spirits or angels.[496] The three are mentioned as *nomina* only at the outset of the text: "SNWY, SNSYNUI, SMNGLUF, Adam, YHWH, Qadmon, Eva, in the name of the Lord God of Israel etc."[497] Elijah's empty chair (*Kisse shel Eliyyahu*) is a fixed feature of the circumcision rite and symbolises the presence of the prophet. As the Midrash *Tanḥuma, Ṣaw* 14 records that the letter *yod* from God's name is marked on the boy's penis instead of on the foreskin during the ceremony, it is a clear reminder of the *sphragis*, the seal of baptism.[498] In his *Massa'e Yisrael*, David Gordon

---

[495] *Papiri Graece Magicae* V,2345.
[496] See James A. Montgomery, *Aramaic Incantation texts from Nippur*, Philadelphia: University Museum 1913.
[497] See Ida Fröhlich, "Two Apotropaic Texts from the Jewish Museum of Budapest," in *Proceedings of the Colloquim on Popular Customs and the Monotheistic Religions in the Middle East and North Africa*, ed. Alexander Fodor and Avihai Shivtiel (Budapest: Eötvös Loránd University Chair for Arabic Studies, 1994), 295–303. The article is based on Psalm 21 and with reference to Elijah and Lilith.
[498] On this tradition and its mystical and kabbalistic perspective, see Elliot R. Wolfson, "Circumcision and the Divine Name: A Study in the Transmission of Esoteric Doctrine," *The Jewish Quarterly Review* 73 (1987): 77–112.

mentions the North African Jewish custom of preparing a feast on every evening of the first week after the birth of a boy. The first meal is called the "meal of the prophet Elijah."[499]

In the above-mentioned text from the *Sippure Ben Sira*, Lilith promises not to drink the child's blood or eat the bone marrow or flesh *if* the woman mentions Lilith's name (or wears an amulet with her name). Among the various forms which Lilith assumes in the Oriental, Jewish, and Christian traditions, there is also the form of the devourer of children. The Midrash *Be-Midbar Rabbah* 16:25 expressly speaks of her as the murderer of children: "Like Lilith, who, if she finds no other children, beats her own children to death." It is difficult to analyse the name Lilith in philological and historical-traditional terms. It seems to be similar to the Babylonian demon *Labartu* or *Lamashtu* with reference to its characteristic feature of killing children. It is true that she is mentioned in the Talmud, but it is her sexual curiosity and appetite and her demon status which are especially emphasised there. Apart from the Midrash *Be-Midbar*, the first source which outspokenly deals with the myth of Lilith as Adam's first wife, and child murderer, is the medieval tractate *Alphabetum Siracidis*.

Several special features of this text should be mentioned: the three angels are referred to as "Angels of Medicine" (*maleakim shel refu'a*). This would be incompehensible if we were to see the three angels as less than the transcription of God's name: according to the bible, only God is the Doctor-Healer. The angel of medicine is Rafa'el, literally "God's healing." The second new feature of *Alphabetum Siracidis* is the introduction of Lilith as Adam's first wife. She leaves him after an argument over a sexual position. The angels pursue her to the middle of the sea, and demand her return. She refuses, and tells them: "I've been created to cause sickness to children. If it is a male child, I have power over him for 8 days, if a female one, for 20 days." She is urged again to come back. Her reply: "Whenever I see your names or pictures on an amulet, I shall have no power over the children." The eight days in which she has power over male infants evidently are those preceding a circumcision. Only iron and mentioning the divine name – two elements which play important roles at a circumcision – effectively protect the child from her.

Lilith, the child-devouring notoriety, has a parallel in Latin literature, the *Lamiae*, vampire-like female beasts. The Christian bishop Isidorus Hispalensis (c. 560–636) described the creatures as: "*Lamias quas fabulae tradunt infantes corripere ac laniar solitas, a laniando specialiter dictas.*"[500] In his commentary in *Isaiam*, the church father Jerome (c. 347–420) considers Lamia, the mother

---

499 On Elijah, see Bergmann, "Zur Geschichte religiöser Bräuche," 168–170.
500 Isidorus Hispalensis, *Etymologiarum sive originum libri XX* (CPL 1186,8), ch. 11, para. 102.

of the Lamiae, to be Lilith.⁵⁰¹ *Lamia* is the translation found in the *Vulgata* for the Hebrew *tannin* in the Book of Lamentations. It is a term which is usually understood and translated today as "dragon" or "mythical snake." The medieval theologian Paschasius Radbertus (c. 790–869) not only adopted the string of identification (*Lamia* – *tannin* – Lilith) but claimed further that Lilith was in fact one of the *Parcae*.⁵⁰² And so the itinerary has reached its full circle. Not only in the Babylonian, Greek, and Jewish traditions but also in Christian tradition, the three figures (called Parcae, etc.) do not offer protection for the child but instead constitute a danger. They pose a threat to the child which can only be averted through certain practices. In the end, a magical paradox prevails in the following three considerations which lead to only one conclusion: it seems that the hunter and the game identify with each other! The stipulations are these:

1. only the three figures who bring in Sideros can effectively work against him;
2. only Lilith's name can keep her away from the infants, and
3. only if someone helps the Parcae will they help him or her.

9.4 Concluding Thoughts

Burkhard's decree served in this chapter as the tool to find our trail, somewhat like Hansel and Gretel's trail of white pebbles. The decree evokes a net of relationships, a spectrum of possibilities that can and must be subdivided into various interpretative patterns. Nevertheless, the interpretative possibilities in this article are not presented in full but aim at providing food for thought. My starting point was the observation that the *Parcae* are connected to birth and birth-related complications. The evidence for this can be seen in the set table, in the citation of God's name and iron. It should be recalled these had the very same function in Roman mythology as well.

---

501 Jerome wrote: "ceterum qui tropologiam sequuntur, expulso populo iudaeorum sub bestiarum et portentorum nominibus, idololatras et uariis superstitionibus seruientes in hierusalem habitaturos esse confirmant; et hos esse onocrotalos et hericios, ibin et coruum, dracones et struthiones et onocentauros, et daemonia et pilosos et lamiam (quae hebraice dicitur lilith; et a solo symmacho translata est lamia, quam quidam hebraeorum erinun, id est furiam, suspicantur)." Hieronymus, *Commentarii in Isaiam* 10:34,8 (SL 73–73A).
502 Radbertus wrote in Latin: "Lamia namque Hebraice Lilith dicitur. Quam quidam Hebreorum YNVN id est unam ex furiis suspicantur quae arcae dicuntur eo quod nulli parcant sicuti Scribae et Pharisei qui non solum proximis in populo uerum nec prophetis pepercerunt." Pascasius Radbertus, *Expositio in lamentationes Hieremiae: Libri quinque*, ed. Beda Paulus (Turnhout, Belgium: Brepols, 1988), lib. 4, 387–88 (CM 85).

But what kind of figures/demons are Sideros, Gellos, Lamia, and Lilith? To my mind, they personify woman herself. They are but alter egos of women who transfer and project their own anxieties onto mythological figures. The pre- and post-natal anxieties become images in the popular imagination which represent danger and relief at the same time. It is no coincidence that the same characteristics that are associated with Lilith – the bloodthirsty Lilith who is sexually obsessed, childless and yet the mother of the demons – also apply to the womb itself as an autonomous living entity. In *Timaios* 91b, Plato mentions for the first time the idea that a woman's infertility could lead to asphyxiation because of the womb's motility:

> And in women again, owing to the same causes [i.e., disobedience and "frenzied carnality" of the genital organs], whenever the matrix or womb, as it is called, – which is an indwelling creature desirous of child-bearing – remains without fruit long beyond the due season, it is vexed and takes it ill; and by straying all ways through the body and blocking up the passages of the breath and preventing respiration it casts the body into the uttermost distress, and causes, moreover, all kinds of maladies; until the desire and love of the two sexes unite them.[503]

We have already mentioned that the womb allegedly licked blood. Its murderous intentions are shown by its motility in its host's body. The idea is graphically illustrated in a German incantation from Urwegen, Transylvania, which was thought to help against uterine bleeding:

English Translation	**German**
Womb sat on a marbled rock,	Beermutter saß auf marmelnden Stein,
An old man came inside of her,	Kam ein alter Mann zu ihr herein,
"Womb, where do you want to go?"	"Beermutter, wohin willst Du gehen?"
"I want to go to N.N.	"Ich will zur N.N. gehen,
I want to see her blood,	Ich will ihr Blut sehen,
I want to eat up her heart,	Ich will ihr Herz verzehren,
I want to take her life."	Ich will ihr Leben nehmen."
"Womb, you shan't do that,	"Beermutter, das sollst Du nicht tun,
You shall rest in marbled stone,	Du sollst im marmelnden Steine ruhn,
The forest woman shall devour you!	Die Waldfrau soll Dich fressen!
As if you'd never existed!	Als wärst Du nie gewesen!
In the name of God, the Son and	Im Namen Gottes, des Sohnes und
the Holy Spirit."	des heiligen Geistes."[504]

---

[503] Plato, *Timaeus* vol. IX, trans. R. G. Bury (Cambridge, Mass.: Harvard University Press, 1989), 248–251.

[504] Heinrich Ploss, Max Bartels, and Paul Bartels, *Das Weib in der Natur- und Völkerkunde: Anthropologische Studien*, vol. 1 (Berlin: Neufeld und Henius Verlag, 1927), 428.

In conclusion, the alchemistic snake bites its own tail. The womb defends itself against the woman in whom it dwells. Do women suffer because of themselves? Or is the male imagination involved in these descriptions, incantations, *historiolae*, etc.? Perhaps. My exegetical and psychological thoughts are likewise speculative.

10 Evidence and Plausibility: on Magic and Ariel Toaff's *Pasque di Sangue*

Magic is a field of knowledge or the illusion of knowledge that goes beyond all barriers of time and culture. Magic has the ability of infusion, regardless of ethnicity and geography, and overcomes the obstacles posed by time, religion, or language. Proving the origin of a magical belief through using historical methods is difficult, since a text or a magical tradition cannot be precisely dated to a specific time. One might just make the plausibility test and rely on identifying "foreign" aspects of the magical text or tradition. We examined above the magical traditions of the famous codex *Hebr. 95*,[505] where the formulae against damage by water were integrated into the text of the Talmud: simply as a magical aid protecting the manuscript against the imminent danger of flood water in 1342. On the basis of this deduction, the conclusion is sound and methodologically consistent: having identified the underlying historical and geographical context, we can understand the purpose of the practice of magic.

However, the process that brought certain magical traditions into history is very difficult to identify in a scholarly way if there are no external proofs within the tradition that can identify a given magical practice with a precise time or location. This is one of the flaws of a book by Ariel Toaff, a well-known scholar of medieval and Renaissance history. The work caused a sensation and an outcry; was publically debated, both applauded and rejected. The book also sparked a discussion about the freedom(s) of the historian.

10.1 Ariel Toaff's *Pasque di Sangue*

The book, *Pasque di sangue: Ebrei d'Europa e omicidi rituali* ("Blood Passover: The Jews of Europe and Ritual Murder"), was published in Italian in February 2007.[506] It was removed from the bookshelves a week later, but reissued after

---

[505] See chapter 8 in this volume, pp. 173–183.
[506] Ariel Toaff, *Pasque di sangue: Ebrei d'Europa a omicidi rituali* (Bologna: Il Mulino, 2007). For an English translation, likely unauthorised, see http://www.revisionisthistory.org/page10/page10.html (accessed 4 November 2013). I do not wish here to enter into the polemic discussions which followed the book's publication. From a historical standpoint, it is important to see some of the statements discussed in Cristiana Facchini, "Dibattiti – Omicidi rituali: Morte della storia?," *Storicamente: Laboratorio di storia*, www.storicamente.org/02f.acchini.htm (accessed 16 February 2013). It is part of a forthcoming important article on Ashkenazic religiosity.

a year with a new introduction and some editing and omissions. The work is a perfect example of how historians should be careful in conducting their research. In an almost rhapsodic way, the author employs every source available to prove the accusations (or confessions) of ritual murder raised by the Inquisition against Jews in medieval Trent. The subject of the trial was the alleged ritual murder of Simon Unferdorben (Simon the Unspoilt), a child twenty-eight months old at the time of his death. According to Toaff, the sources prove that Ashkenazic Jews had indeed used magical practices involving blood as a haemostatic or homeopathic remedy or for other purposes.

In the book, Toaff assumes that some Christian children could indeed have been killed by a "minority of fundamentalist Jews of Ashkenazic origin." He quotes Kabbalistic descriptions of the therapeutic usage of blood. He also assumes that a "black market flourished on both sides of the Alps with Jewish intermediaries who sold human blood with rabbinic certification for the product – kosher blood."

On February 14, 2007, Toaff explained that he had asked the Italian publisher of his book to immediately halt its sale. He wished to "review passages which had caused the outcry, and the controversies which had been published in the mass media." In an interview with the Israeli daily *Haaretz*, Toaff stated: "Over many dozens of pages, I proved the centrality of blood on Passover." He went on: "Based on many sermons, I concluded that blood was used, especially by Ashkenazi Jews, and that there was a belief in the special curative powers of children's blood. It turns out that among the remedies of Ashkenazi Jews were powders made of blood." The article also states: "Although the use of blood is prohibited by Jewish law, Toaff says he found proof of rabbinic permission to use blood, even human blood." 'The rabbis permitted it both because the blood was already dried, and because in Ashkenazi communities it was an accepted custom that took on the force of law,' Toaff said."[507]

We cannot discuss all the issues the book raises. However, I wish to emphasise that Toaff does not understand the difference between the method of how the Inquisition accused suspects – the use of torture procured "evidence" which did not necessarily prove the charges – and the evidenced contemporary practice of magic, or rather the way it was documented in the sources. The "evidence" was merely a tool for the judge or the inquisitor to force a suspect

---

[507] See Ofri Ilani, "Bar-Ilan professor who claimed Jews used Christian blood in Passover ceremonies defends his book: 'I will fight for my truth, even if I am crucified,'" *Haaretz*, February 12 (2007), http://www.haaretz.com/print-edition/news/bar-ilan-professor-who-claimed-jews-used-christian-blood-in-passover-ceremonies-defends-his-book-i-will-fight-for-my-truth-even-if-i-am-crucified-1.212739 (accessed 16 February 2013).

to confess a crime. The crime, and the suspect, that is, the branded culprit, were clear and apparent before the eyes of the inquisitor. We can only conclude from our perspective that the prosecution employed the idea of ritual murder, or better, the construction of a fictional scenario thereof, to explain why the child's body was in the ghetto. Simon had been found near the ditch that ran through the ghetto on the morning of March 26, 1485. Building up a theory from inquisitorial accusations which are seen as historical fact, as Toaff does, is not only incorrect but moreover also deceptive. The practice of magic, on which Toaff relies heavily in his book, had a logic in itself. It cannot be confused with the "evidence" which was presented at the trial of the Inquisition. With his book, Toaff strayed in his scholarship because unfortunately he did not have adequate command of the instruments he needed for understanding his subject. I will not delve into a historical analysis of his hypotheses. This has been done well by historians such as Roni Weinstein, Kenneth Stow, Anna Foa, Christina Facchini and many others. I only wish here to refer to some of the principles on which his speculations rest.

When I speak of "historical analysis," I refer to Toaff's reconstruction of the case of Simoncino who was thought to have been ritually murdered by Jews. Toaff's sole "evidence" was the information collected during the Inquisition's trial of this case. As no other document has been published from the case, Toaff draws his speculations only from the already published documentation of the Inquisition's interrogation. He concludes that *what the Jews had confessed under torture was credible.* If this was so, it is also plausible that witches had sexual intercourse with demons just the way they reported it under torture! It is also known that the Inquisition did not record the questions but only the responses. This is indeed a grave mistake for a historian. The so-called confessions that are recorded in the protocols of the Inquisition factually are the questions the inquisitor plants into the mouth of the accused. The questions are planted in order to make him "confess" a crime through his own words, or through a repetition of the utterances accusing him. Medievalists and modern historians have identified this procedure sufficiently, and there is no need to repeat the arguments.

Toaff does not address any arguments which were posed by Willehad Paul Eckert, a historian of the trials.[508] He ignores recent publications on ritual murder which shed a light on the process of how "mythological machine" was formed.[509] This approach to the subject, which I will only summarise here,

---

508 Willehad Paul Eckert, "Aus den Akten des Trienter Judenprozesses," in *Das Judentum im Mittelalter*, ed. Paul Wilpert (Berlin: De Gruyter, 1966), 281–336.
509 See Ruggero Taradel, *L'accusa del sangue: storia politica di un mito antisemita* (Rome: Editori Riuniti, 2002).

was recently discussed by David Bidussa.⁵¹⁰ Based on the research of Furio Jesi, Bidussa refers to myth as being a narrative strategy which "offers the rational foundation of the past, and stipulates the rules for the future."⁵¹¹ Myth is thus understood as an unconsciously present relationship between the text and the reader. Myth is unsubstantial in itself, and can only induce "epiphanies" in the reader.⁵¹² The relationship is not between recipient and myth, but between recipient and the myth's manifestations, which are based on the several "demands" of myth and mythologies. This process is what Furio Jesi calls the "mythological machine."

In conclusion: although there is a methodological abridgement, it is helpful for the analysis of the myth and its functions, without de-mystifying it and thus exposing its inconsistencies. The myth does not represent the laboratory of the *individual's* imagination in regard to beliefs. In its analysis, however, the myth allows gathering in the "lived" language or languages of the political *community*, which are inexpressible in some instances. This element of the myth – whose importance goes far beyond the understanding of accusations of ritual crimes – is fundamental for the understanding of every aspect of the "mythological" universe, which always has an impact on the real world. Toaff does not seem to have understood this crucial aspect. He starts from the premise, which might be considered naïve, that the Christian sources are reliable. Toaff then pieces together a list of medieval and modern rabbinic sources which lack a relevant evidential function, but which he believes substantiate the Christian accusations.

Let us now turn to Toaff's two methodological errors:
1. the geographical limits of magic, and
2. the literal approach to the interpretation of sources.

10.2 The Geographic Limits of the Phenomenon "Magic"

In order to address the first point of criticism, we read in *Pasque di sangue* that

> We must bear in mind that in the German Jewish communities, the phenomenon is – as far as can be identified – generally limited to the popular traditions of groups. These

---

510 David Bidussa, "Macchina mitologica e indagine storica: A Proposito di Pasque di sangue e del 'mestiere di storico,'" in *Vero e falso*, ed. Marina Caffiero and Micaela Procaccia (Rome: Donzelli, 2008), 139–172.
511 *Ibidem*, 153.
512 I put the word in quotation marks, since even in the history of religions, there is no plural for the "sudden realisation of great truth."

groups had long since bypassed and replaced the ritual norms of the Jewish *Halakhah*. The ancient customs were infused with magical and alchemistic elements, and had created a harmful amalgamation which was infused with a violent and aggressive religious fundamentalism.[513]

According to Toaff, there were violent and aggressive fundamentalist groups in Ashkenaz – note the specific geographical and cultural emphasis. The Sefardic tradition is, of course, not addressed. These groups used magical and alchemical practices beyond the strictures of the Halakhah. This assertion is a polemic one targeted against the Jewish-German communities. It is a polemic assertion concerning the nature of something one can speculate about without understanding the historical reality. The polemic notion is present indirectly as well, as the hypothesis deals with one region only, one in which allegedly a religious and "violent" magic had developed. He does not mention the Sephardic communities. It is impossible from a scholarly standpoint to pose a hypothesis of such magnitude without even referring to the opposite side. It is widely accepted that magic did not know geographic borders. It has been shown in historical discourse that magical practices that had evolved in Egypt, for example, were found throughout the Mediterranean world, including Bulgaria, Romania, and Trent/South Tyrol. Those Egyption practices eventually broke down the barriers of the Alps and entered the Bavarian regions.

I do not wish here to go into detail, but I would contend that Toaff does not have a sound understanding of magical practices. To mention but one absent work in his bibliography, I daresay he has entirely ignored *Sabba* by Carlo Ginzburg.[514] There, the question is raised about the paths of magical practices which cannot be readily charted except perhaps through linguistic traces, flawed translations, and lists of ingredients from a specific historical region, etc. The conclusion is self-evident: there are no geographical, religious, or cultural barriers for magic, since it is a practice unrelated to religious affiliation or geographic location. I have already discussed the "conjuration of the uterus" which appeared for the first time in Gnostic texts, and lived on in Greek, Aramaic, Hebrew and German texts.[515] The womb was believed to lick blood.

---

513 Toaff, *Pasque di sangue*, 13.
514 Carlo Ginzburg, *Storia notturna. una decifrazione del sabba* (Turin: Enaudi, 1989). It has appeared in several editions, and in English translation: *Ecstasies: Deciphering the Witches' Sabbath*, trans. Raymond Rosenthal (New York: Pantheon, 1991). See Ginzburg's remarks on *Pasque di sangue* in an interview with the *Corriere della Sera*, February 23, 2007.
515 See Veltri, "Zur Überlieferung medizinisch-magischer Traditionen: Das metrea-Motiv in den Payri Magicae und der Kairoer Geniza," *Henoch* 18 (1996): 157–175 and chapter 9 in this volume.

It was also believed to have murderous intentions, since it moves in its host's body. This was graphically illustrated in a German incantation from Urwegen, Transylvania, which was thought to help against uterine bleeding, as described above.[516]

10.3 The Use of "Blood" – The Word and the Code

The mistake of the geographic limits of magic, as discussed above, is secondary to a graver one if considering the quite bizarre and formally wrong hypotheses on the use of blood in Jewish magic. The use of the substance "blood" in magical-medical and therapeutic practices is not of recent origin. It is necessary, however, not to jump to hasty and historically incorrect conclusions concerning a practice whose rules are largely unknown. Some plants are referred to by the most fantastic names, such as *Harpagophytum*, known in Germany as *Teufelskralle*, in Italy as *artiglio del diavolo*, in France as *griffe du diable*, and in the English-speaking world as *devil's claw*, all meaning the same.

Other names include the component of English "blood," German "Blut," or French "sang." The following can serve as examples: *Sanguisorba* (family of the rosaceae, the English *burnet*), *Blutkraut* and *Blutwurz* (*Hypericum perforatum* and *Potentilla erecta*; the English *St John's wort* and *tormentil*), and *bloodwort* which is also known as *devil's nettle* (*Achillea millefolium*, or *yarrow*).[517]

The scholarly classification of Carl von Linné often mentions the common name of plants as well, although their origins have over the centuries been forgotten. Products of the laboratory or the magic kitchen are often referred in a coded language in order to guard the recipes against unauthorised usage. To hide the true nature of the products through coded language which was known only to a small number of people was a practice already familiar from the magical medicine of the Akkadian recipes.[518] It can be seen in Egypt with the great physicians of the Hellenistic Mediterranean world and even in the Middle Ages. For example, the recipe for a remedy which was likely used against scurvy

---

516 See chapter 9 in this volume.
517 On *Blutkraut*, see, "Blutkraut, auch rot kol nennet, und sol seyn [ein] recht blutkraut sein. ... Neben disem blutkraut (welches inn userm landst das recht blutkraut ist), findt man noch mehs Blutkreütter," quoted in William Kurrelmeyer, "German Lexicography – Part IX," *Modern Language Notes* 60 (1945): 161.
518 See Margaret J. Geller, *Akkadian Healing Therapies in the Babylonian Talmud* (Berlin: Max-Planck-Institut für Wissenschaftsgeschichte, 2004). It is available online: http://www.mpiwg-berlin.mpg.de/Preprints/P259.PDF (accessed 7 June 2013).

called for a child's feces (the recipe has been transmitted through the Jerusalem Talmud in 'Avodah Zarah 2:2 [40d]).[519]

Also, the name simply revealed the remedy for which the plant was used. The German *Blutwurz* (literally blood root), for example, was used for bleeding control. It is impossible to know exactly and with certainty if it was indeed "blood" or "feces" in the Talmudic example. Was it a coded language which confused the content and composition of chemical products with blood, together with the inquisitor, an approving or malignant smile on his lips as he fed the questions?

This second error by Toaff reveals that he does not understand his subject, and has not looked at the history of magical practices because they cannot be treated like archival documents. Documents in an archive can be localised and inventoried; one can clearly see when it is unpublished. On the other hand, the sources on magic differ. Their originality does not rest in their materiality but in their context. Modern historians are eager to identify new documents, since this is the central point of modern research. Reading the documents, analysing them, organising, etc., is much simpler than to formulate new hypotheses on historic events.

The magic of Jews was very likely similar to the practices among Christians, barbarians, and Muslims. The peculiarity of magical practices is that they demand research on the context in which they were employed because they essentially are cultural "omnivores": the process of adopting everything that might be useful without regard to origin, not even the religious conception of the origin. When referring to the use of blood of murdered children for the preparation of *matzoth*, it should be understood that it was nothing but reviving old clichés. It was an accusation first targeted against the early Christians and then, from the Middle Ages until today, against the Jews. This was only the pretext for a more formal judicial action against a group which was voluntarily marginalised. It was also a brittle cliché, albeit useful at times for infamous purposes.

10.4 Defining "Magic"

The essential element in all magical conceptions lies not in the ingredients of the recipes, in the spells or charms, but in the dynamics with which the power is demonstrated, and the pretence to be more powerful as a magician than

---

[519] See Veltri, *Magie und Halakha* (Tübingen: Mohr Siebeck, 1997), 279–280.

anybody else. There are several examples from the New and Old Testament for this attitude: when Moses faces the Pharaoh's magician, when Elijah confronts the priests of Ba'al, but also when Jesus faces the magicians of his time, and when St. Peter confronts Simon Magus, known as Simon the Sorcerer.

To illustrate this, I would like to present a little story transmitted in Yiddish in a popular anthology. It is called the *Ma'ase bukh*, or *Maiśebuch* (*Ajn schojn maasebukh ... mit dreihundert un'etlihe maasim ... ojs di gemara* / A Nice Book of Stories ... with Three hundred and more Stories ... from the Gemara), and was first published in Basel in 1602.[520]

The *Ma'ase bukh* is an anthology of legends, stories, and quotations taken from the Talmud, the Haggadah, the world of legends and the sagas of the Occident. It is composed of three parts. The first includes the texts taken from the Talmud. The second part contains wondrous stories of the German/Ashkenazic rabbis. The third part includes the *Midrashim* and the fables from both Orient and Occident. The following story is included in the second part (the wondrous stories of the Ashkenazic rabbis). The excerpt is from the English translation published by Moses Gaster in 1934.

[Story] 160. R. Samuel Hasid Amazes the Priests with his Wonderworking:

> One day three priests from foreign lands came to see R. Samuel the Pious, for they had heard that he was a very remarkable man. Informing him that they were able to perform magic with the aid of evil spirits, they said to him: "We have heard much of your skill and wonderworking in all the countries through which we have passed. We, therefore, ask you to show us your clever tricks and we will show you our own, which are greater than yours. Do not refuse our request, for we have come specially to see you from very distant parts."
>
> Now there lived at that time in another place a great man called R. Jacob, who had in his possession a book belonging to R. Samuel. So he said to the priests: "If you can conjure an evil spirit to carry a letter from me to R. Jacob, asking him to send me the book, I will believe you to be great masters of the art." The priests replied: "We have come here to honor you, therefore we will show you a greater wonder than this." Then they said to him: "Come, let us go out into the open country to a secret place and there you will see

---

[520] Several other editions have appeared: in Amsterdam (in 1701), Frankfurt (1703), Amsterdam again (1723), Rödelheim near Frankfurt (1753), and in other anthologies. See the digitalised edition of Frankfurt (1702/1703) in the collection of Frankfurt University. "Maiśebuch: wo arinn fil wundrlichi šini maiśes oiz dem zohar un andri kabole sefer gitzogn zainn ... mit 354 andri maiśes zich kon ermaien ... oiz dem talmud ...," *Goethe Universität Frankfurt am Main: Jiddische Drucke der Universitätsbibliothek*, http://sammlungen.ub.uni-frankfurt.de/download/pdf/1766275?name=Mai%C5%9Bebuch (accessed 7 June 2013). See also the latest German edition: Ulf Diederichs, ed. and trans. *Das Ma'assebuch: Altjiddische Erzählkunst mit 37 Bildern – Vollständige Ausgabe ins Hochdeutsche übertragen, kommentiert und herausgegeben von Ulf Diederichs* (Munich: Deutscher Taschenbuchverlag, 2003).

a very wonderful thing. One of us will draw a circle and the other companions will conjure his soul to leave his body, take the letter from your hand, carry it to R. Jacob, and bring you his answer together with your book, just as you have requested us to do. The man whose soul has left him, will not leave the spot for three days, but will remain lying still within the circle until the three days are over, and then the soul will return to the body, which will become alive and healthy again." So the pious man went with the priests to the field, and they did exactly as they had promised.

As soon as the soul had left the body of the priest, the remaining two said: "Let us return to the town, for we have nothing further to do here. On the third day, at noon, we will come back when the soul will re-enter the body, after it has fulfilled the errand which you asked us to do." So they went back to the town, and on the third day the two priests said to R. Samuel: "Now let us go again to the field and there you will see how the soul will reenter the body of our companion." The pious man went with them to the field, but by his art made it so that the soul, when it came back, was not able to reenter the dead body.

When the two priests saw that the corpse would not rise again, but lay there like any other corpse, they raised a great lamentation for their companion and mourned bitterly for him. The pious man then said: "If you will acknowledge that I can do more than you, I will make the soul enter the body again as before." So they both fell at his feet and begged him in God's name to bring their companion to life again. They were glad, they said, to acknowledge that he was a greater master than they. Then the pious man conjured the evil spirit to cause the soul to reënter the body, and instantly the man stood up alive and gave the pious man the letter as well as the book which he had missed for a long time. The priests thanked the pious man and went their way, saying that his art was even greater than the reputation of it in foreign lands.[521]

One could analyse the different elements of this little story, its allusions, its underlying concepts, and parallels in the Christian literature. Yet, this would lead us away from the subject under discussion here. The legends and stories of magic and the wonders of the saints, the pious men and the hermits are topics for multifaceted fruitful research: they not only allow access to the world of imagination and imaginative ability of the storyteller but are also important, since the stories are also a fertile ground for identifying historical elements which are hidden in what is told. That Jews *always* had the reputation of being magicians is one of the common yet false concepts in circulation. However, the accusation of using magic is just one of many charges hurled against Jews during the Middle Ages (at least from the 13th and the 14th century onward). Joshua Trachtenberg has analysed some of these constants on the basis of the accusations of demonic magic during the Black Death epidemics in southern

---

[521] "160. R. Samuel Hasid Amazes the Priests with his Wonderworking," in Moses Gaster, ed. and trans., *Ma'aseh Book: Book of Jewish Tales and Legends* vol. 2 (Philadelphia: Jewish Publication Society of America, 1934), 320–323.

France.[522] The "so-and-sos," always had been "strangers." They were persons "not from around here," who poisoned the water of the wells in order to cause poor Christians to die. Just in Ashkenaz alone, thousands of Jews were tortured and executed because of this perverse and fateful accusation.

But let us return to our story: Rabbi Samuel puts the priests out of action. They are easily recognisable as Christians as they came "from foreign lands" and there were three of them. This, of course, evokes the story of the Three Wise Men or Magi which was very vivid in medieval Germany and especially associated with the cathedral in Cologne, where the supposed relics of the three Oriental magicians or kings are still kept today.

The subject of the soul that leaves the body and remains in the magic circle might be of Judea-Babylonian origin, if we consider the fact that the centre of all demonology was Baghdad. It is also a part of the Jewish tradition that the soul after death wanders for twelve months and finally returns to the corpse. According to *Shulḥan ʿArukh Oraḥ Ḥayyim* § 576, we light a candle in the home of the deceased so the soul may find its way back. It will recognise it if there is a sign of its presence. If we follow the logic of magic, Rabbi Samuel likely had moved the body or the magic circle. In this case, the soul was unable to find the body.[523]

The art of the rabbi's "magic" was in perfect harmony with the context where he was. There is also a point of irony: the rabbi basically makes fun of the wise men. He acts as a kind of spoilsport by interrupting the magical practice. He even has power over the demons. He has the better of the "priests," and they decide to leave. One might see the same attitude toward Jesus of Nazareth. The comparison is not an arbitrary one. It is not surprising that we can discern the parallels in the developments of the mendicant orders and the Ḥassidim in the Ashkenazic world. On the contrary. But the Ashkenazic Jewish world Toaff presents us with is, unfortunately, influenced by the Christian polemics against Jews. Research or new interpretations of the sources cannot

---

[522] See Joshua Trachtenberg, *Jewish Magic and Superstition: A Study in Folk Religion* (New York: Behrman's Jewish Book, 1939). Several reprints have appeared (New York, 1970, 1987; Philadelphia, 2004).

[523] It is also a Christian practice, or at least has left traces in Christianity as well. The Synod of Elvira (c. 305–306 CE) decreed in its canon 34, that "candles are not to be burned in a cemetery during the day. This practice is related to paganism and is harmful to Christians. Those who do this are to be denied the communion of the church." Or, in Latin: "Cereos per diem placuit in coemeterio non incendi, inquietandi enim, sanctorum spiritus non sunt. Qui haec non observaverint arceantur Ecclesiae communione." See the canons in Kenneth J. Pennington, "The Council of Elvira, ca. 306," *The Catholic University of America*, http://faculty.cua.edu/pennington/Canon%20Law/ElviraCanons.htm (accessed 16 February 2013).

spring from this erroneous point of view. Only theories can be derived which risk complicating rather than explaining historical reality.

10.5 Conclusion

Toaff's book has unsettled the historical research of the past fifty years, since it proceeds from one core hypothesis: the historicity of the inquisitorial accusations of ritual murder. It is based on some "magical" practices gathered from Jewish sources which are for the most part unknown to the general and the academic public. By assuming *a priori*, a trustworthiness of the sources both Christian and Jewish, Toaff bases his assumptions on a fundamental error: the *plausibility* of the historical proof. One could conclude that there was a historical basis for the accusation of ritual murders committed by the Ashkenazic community, which was particularly attracted by magic. That could be a seemingly convincing conclusion if
1. it were *plausible* that the Ashkenazic world used magical-therapeutic practices by utilizing blood; and if
2. it were *plausible* that the (actual) blood of children is considered an essential ingredient and medium of power in some sources.

I have attempted to demonstrate in this chapter that magic has no geographical and cultural limits. Not only from a rational standpoint, but also from a particular logical perspective inherent to magic, we must not take the stories and recipes (and how to collect the ingredients for them), the ingredients themselves, the magical beliefs, etc. literally. The "magician," the "priest" of the magical practice, has no interest in exposing the true nature of the magical act – often for reasons that are quite practical and pragmatic: to establish and maintain his own authority in the field, and to make his audience and clientele dependent, which also has economic consequences. Magic belief has no other aim but *to reveal nothing*; to only foster the demand for the "mythological machine." Its aim is political and economic: to make persons believe that the magician possesses a hidden knowledge which, depending on circumstances, reveals itself to the magician or is hidden from him. Without this element of magic, one cannot recreate the past or use it for the present. Magic is a shrewd construct based psychologically on a hermeneutical trap: succeeding in attracting the attention of the audience and/or clients, and making them believe that failure and betrayal are factually also an integral part of the magical act. In other words, failure is always the fault of the client, not the magician.

By believing in the factuality of the stories concerning ritual murders, it is likely that Toaff fell prey to the "mythological machine" and into the trap of magic. First, he did not comprehend that there was a political aim of magic. Second, he was fascinated by his "evidence of trustworthiness," which is to say, the evidence on which the wrong assumption is based must be found with the reader or client. In the end, Toaff was betrayed by his own sources.

Part IV: Reflecting on Languages and Texts

11 Reflecting on Languages and Texts

In the Babylonian Talmud, Rosh ha-Shanah 26a–26b, the rabbis confess their ignorance about some biblical and rabbinic expressions:[524]

> In a certain place which Levi happened to visit, a man came before him and said, So-and-so has *kabaʿed* (קבע) me. He did not know what he meant, so he went and enquired in the Beth Ha-Midrash. They said to him: He wanted to say to you, "has robbed me," as it is written, "Will man rob [יקבע] God?"[525] Raba from Barnish said to R. Ashi: Had I been there, I should have said to him, How did he *qabaʿ* you, in what did he *qabaʿ* you, why did he *qabaʿ* you, and so I should have found out [from his answers]. The other [Levi], however, thought that he meant some kind of offence. The Rabbis did not know what was meant by סירוגין[526] till one day they heard the maidservant of Rabbi's household, on seeing the Rabbis enter at intervals, say to them, How long are you going to come in by סירוגין? The Rabbis did not know what was meant by חלוגלוגות[527] till one day they heard the handmaid of the household of Rabbi, on seeing a man peeling portulaks, say to him, How long will you be peeling your חלוגלוגות? The Rabbis did not know what was meant by סלסלה[528] and it shall exalt thee. One day they heard the handmaid of the household of Rabbi say to a man who was "curling" his hair, How long will you be מסלסל with your hair? The Rabbis did not know what was meant by וטאטאתיה במטאטא of destruction,[529] till one day they heard the handmaid of the household of Rabbi say to her companion, Take the טאטיתא [broom] and וטאטי [sweep] the house. The Rabbis did not know what was meant by "Cast upon the Lord thy יהב" and he shall sustain thee."[530] Said Rabbah b. Bar Hanah: One day I was travelling with an Arab and was carrying a load, and he said to me, Lift up your יהב and put it on [one of] the camels.[531]

The Talmudic composition challenges the scholar who wants to establish the historical background of the listing of unknown words in the rabbinic language and in the Bible. To explain the recourse to the lexical help of the maid concerning וטאטאתיה במטאטא השמד, Louis Finkelstein conjectured "that in 2nd century Palestine, there were a few towns where Hebrew was still the primary language, and that the woman was a native of such a town, hired by R. Judah

---

524 The translation follows Isidore Epstein, ed. and trans., *The Babylonian Talmud* (London: Soncino Press, 1935–1948). All quotations from the Babylonian Talmud are from this edition, unless I note my own translation. Slight variants in the translation are not expressly noted.
525 Maleachi 3:8.
526 See Babylonian Talmud, Megillah 17a.
527 Babylonian Talmud, Yoma 18a.
528 Proverbs 4:8.
529 Isaiah 14:23.
530 Psalms 55:23.
531 Babylonian Talmud, Megillah 18a.

for that reason."⁵³² Following the same logic, we can infer that Hebrew has been transmitted primarily among Arabian caravan merchants (טייעא) who better understood Psalms 55:23 than the Rabbis.⁵³³ Or, should we rather believe that the Rabbis had *ante litteram* a feeling for Semitic philology? We should at least consider a consciousness for the proximity of Hebrew and Aramaic as well as of Arabic.⁵³⁴ The story of the ignorant Rabbanan shows some very intriguing peculiarities: the special role of "common" people in transmitting texts, words, and traditions and the question of "gaps of understanding."

I do not wish to specifically emphasise the first point here. I would only like to stress that the rabbis tried to find the meaning of difficult words by basing their understanding of the term on the philological feeling of the allegedly unlearned people (in this case called maids). The procedure is known as referring to the "people" to have a term explained, and *vox populi vox traditionis* could be the better explanation without referring to any sociological and political evaluation of "classes" in rabbinic Judaism.⁵³⁵ Alternatively, the entire listing could be a fictitious story to emphasise the role of everyday life in explaining the texts and the words of the transmitted texts. Parallel compositions are the dicta of the mother of Abbaye who in the Babylonian Talmud, Shabbat 66b–67a transmitted an entire chapter of recipes based on popular medicine.⁵³⁶

Much more intriguing is, however, the fact that this text is an important testimony for a period in which at least the meaning of some Hebrew words was not understood. It is irrelevant whether the story is fact or fiction. The important point is that the rabbis are aware of their own ignorance of certain lexemes. I am not concerned with the topic of the *hapax legomena* and their treatment in Jewish texts at this point but rather with this awareness.

The history of the biblical text shows some gaps in lexicographic understanding. Acknowledging this fact is important for the students of ancient lit-

---

532 See his grandson's Ernie David, "Memories of my Grandfather, Louis Finkelstein," from http://www.cs.nyu.edu/faculty/davise/personal/lf/memories.html (accessed 7 June 2013). This source should, of course, be taken *cum grano salis*.
533 See Markus Jastrow, *A Dictionary of the Targumim, the Talmud Babli and Yerushalmi, and the Midrashic Literature* (London: Luzac, 1903), 531.
534 See Jasmin Henle and Johannes Thon, "Sprachkritik, Register- und Dialektvarianz sowie Sprachvergleich in der rabbinischen Literatur," in *Sprachbewusstsein und Sprachkonzepte im Alten Orient, Alten Testament und rabbinischen Judentum*, ed. Johannes Thon, Giuseppe Veltri and Ernst-Joachim Waschke (Halle: Zentrum für Interdisziplinäre Regionalstudien – Vorderer Orient, Afrika, Asien, 2012).
535 See also Shemaryahu Talmon, "The Judean *'am ha'areṣ* in Historical Perspective," *Fourth World Congress of Jewish Studies* vol. 1 (1967): 71–76.
536 See Veltri, *Magie und Halakha* (Tubingen: Mohr Siebeck, 1997), 230 et seq.

erature, so that they might have a better understanding of the crystallisation, standardisation, and transmission of the text. Knowledge and ignorance are two very important vectors of tradition: knowledge for interpreting and changing texts, and ignorance for preserving every form of them. We can perhaps move a step further: only those who comprehend a text and a tradition could have the intention of changing it, be they scholars or scribes. The temptation of mending and adapting texts is inherent to the process of adaptation of the past via the present. The student/teacher who transmits the text without understanding it is ignorant of the meaning, as Babylonian Talmud, Soṭa 22a says: "What is the difference between a *magus* and a *tanna*? There is none. The *tanna* repeats what he does not understand; the *magus* whispers what he does not comprehend."

I can remember what my learned teacher Roger Le Déaut told us in his famous lectures on the inspiration of the Septuagint by referring to the Church Father Epiphanius of Salamis: "Ephiphanius was a learned, but also stupid scholar, and thus he could transmit *fideliter* some ancient traditions on the Bible text which are only peculiar to him. If he had been more intelligent, he would have changed them."[537] The so-called stupidity – I would rather call it "unreflected memorisation" – guaranteed the rabbis the survival of texts and traditions, but also their meaning in cases where scholarship lacks the means to interpret it.

The main aspect of this chapter, as I will try to prove here, is that the crystallisation of texts (the so-called canonisation process) also requires the canonisation of linguistic elements and parallel or supplementary editorial intervention. Every transmission is inclined to mend the text, to adapt it to the exigencies of the present, unless the edition of such texts is too scattered in every corner of the world to properly and definitively mend it. The development of stories on successive "editions" of the biblical text in different periods points up the tendency of some schools to arrogate a version of the biblical text as the supposedly "better" redaction. The versions reveal at the same time the intention to advertise for schools and academies. Canonisation is thus also a question of advertising and depends on numerous elements which cannot be understood solely as *traditum* and *traditio*, as Michael Fishbane defines it.[538]

It is also an assumption of the present chapter that the awareness of the development of language, which is the first step in building and organising grammar and lexis, and thus establishing a text, is a later development in rab-

---

[537] The quote is, of course, *ad sensum* and not *ad literam*.
[538] See Michael Fishbane, *Biblical Interpretation in Ancient Israel* (Oxford: Oxford University Press, 1985).

binic academies. It can explain why an attempted standardisation of the biblical text took place at a later stage. The Masoretic text is a result of a long process which presupposes both the conception of languages and the constitution of a mainstream in the exegesis. That does not mean that every variant reading has to be supported by an exegetical process, although every exegetical process could have left its traces in variant readings. In the first section of this chapter, I sketch the development of the linguistic conception, and then quote two variant readings from the Torah to illustrate the idea of a confirmation of a textual variant reading, and of exegesis without a variant reading.

11.1 Holy, Rabbinic and Common language

Rabbinic Judaism does not have a special theory of language, its origins and development. The only text concerned with this is the story of the Tower of Babel in Genesis 11: the origin of language accordingly is nothing but a political decision to avoid the "dawn of divinity," as Isaac Abravanel interpreted it, or perhaps better to explain a status quo, namely the multiplicity of languages.

Like the Hellenistic scholarship of the author of the Greek Prologue to Ben Sira or Philo of Alexandria, rabbinic academies are a mirror of the tendencies in contemporary speculations on the origin of language and texts. Every language is the vector of communication; nevertheless, there is the acknowledged supremacy of the Greek idiom because of historical and cultural-historical reasons, i.e., the spread of Greek erudite literature all over the ancient world.

Rabbis thus reveal a necessary tolerance toward other cultures and languages by acknowledging the different functions of language in world history.[539] In the parallel contemporary Greek literary tradition, there are some attempts to conceptualise language and correspondent expressions of it, and the Jewish Hellenistic world adopted them – above all in the tradition of the translation of the Torah in Alexandria. Ancient language theories, however, did not go further than a quite naïve theory of the transmission of language, which presupposes the identity between the act of thinking, the thought, and the expression of it.

Rabbinic literature transmits the perception of three levels of the language they used: the so-called holy language or language of the holy (*leshon ha-qodesh*), the language of the Rabbis (*Leshon ḥakhamim*), and the common language. A peculiar case is the pronunciation of ancient Hebrew, which raised the question of dialects.

---

[539] See Jerusalem Talmud, Megillah 11:1 (8) 71b (63–69).

11.1.1 Leshon ha-qodesh

A glance at the semantic development of the expression *leshon ha-qodesh* suggests that the special stress on the Hebrew language as a sacred tongue was not possible until a certain point in Jewish history: when this language was no longer a spoken vernacular, and was acknowledged only for its liturgical role. The expression *leshon ha-qodesh* or *hiera glotta* with reference to Hebrew is unknown in either Jewish-Hellenistic literature or the New Testament. It appears in the Mishnah, Soṭa 7:2–4.[540] In this passage, distinction is made between the biblical *Parashat Soṭa*, which should be recited in all languages, and other *parashot* listed there, which have to be recited only in the holy language.[541] In this case, the understanding of the text does not have priority, but rather the precise rendition of its letters. It is difficult to ascertain whether the theurgy of the spoken word played a role in this ruling or only exegetical reasons, according to the discursive principle *ko tomar* "so you have to say." The Mekhilta Baḥodesh 2 illustrates this principle: "You have to recite in this way, in the holy language, in the same order, in the same situation, in the same way, without adding and without subtracting something."

The problem of the Midrash is to adapt these *parashot* to other legal and exegetical cases or situations. The obvious intention is to consider these texts as legally unique, i.e., applicable only to these cases. There is no doubt that at a certain time in connection with the rabbinic story, theurgic elements were also introduced to explain the nature of the Hebrew language, which is also interconnected with the very creation of the world.

How can one reconcile the theurgic value of the Hebrew with the rather free method which the Rabbis used in dealing with the biblical text? One an-

---

[540] The question of when this expression appears is vividly discussed among modern scholars. Often, the two scattered records in Qumran and Jubilees are – in my eyes – over-emphasised, so that the term is considered to be of a very early date. As one protagonist of this position, I wish to refer to my friend and former colleague Stefan Schorch, who assumes a dating of the prologue to Ben Sira in the 2nd century BCE. In my view, there are neologisms and special expressions of the 1st century CE which contradict this theory. Moreover, the dating of the emergence of the term says nearly nothing about its conceptual use. The early rabbinic records of it indicate that first it was a more technical term to denote the language of the Temple. See Stefan Schorch, "The Pre-eminence of the Hebrew Language and the Emerging Concept of the 'Ideal Text' in Late Temple Judaism," in *Studies in the Book of Ben Sira: Papers of the Third International Conference on the Deuterocanonical Books, Pápa, Ungarn, 2006*, ed. Gèza G. Xeravits and Józef Zsengellér (Leiden: Brill, 2008); Avigdor Shinan, "lishan bet qudsha," *bet miqra* 66 (1976): 472–474.

[541] Deuteronomy 26:3–10; 25:7–9; 27:15–26; Numbers 24–26; Deuteronomy 17,14–20; 21:7 et seq.; 20:2–7.

swer is to consider the crucial difference between the liturgical and non-liturgical use of Hebrew. Only the liturgical use which can be fulfilled solely under special conditions has certain theurgic consequences; one need but recall the sacerdotal benediction of Yom Kippur. More than anything else, this pertains to the divine name. The discussion about a "permitted use" of the Jewish name of God, the *tetragramma*, dates back to the rabbinic period. Then, the halakhic importance of God's name was emphasised in connection with written material to be concealed in the Genizah or to be saved from fire. We read in Midrash Sifre Numeri 16:

> Do we not find here the use (of the hermeneutic rule) of the *qal va-ḥomer?*, regarding the reconciliation of a man and his wife, if God says: The book which was written in holiness is to be erased by water, *a maiori* the books of the Minim should be removed from the world because they cause hostility, hatred, jealousy and war.
> R. Yishmaʻel (says): *sifre minim:* What about them? The name of God has to be cut out and the rest must be burnt. R. Aqiva says: They are to be completely burnt because they have not been written in holiness.[542]

The status of the name was entirely altered because it was not written according to the biblical and rabbinic laws of purity. There is no doubt that the redactor of Sifre modernised the Halakhah from Numbers 5 by mentioning the similarity between the act of a priest writing curses on the parchment/book and the rabbinic laws about writing a Torah scroll which "renders the hands impure." This comparison would be incomprehensible if we did not bear in mind that writing on parchment was also considered the precondition for the theurgic value of a written text. Only *tefillin* or *mezuzot*, written according to the Halakhah, have the power to protect (Mishnah, Megillah 1:8). It is not the characters of the *tetragramma* and other divine names which have theurgic energy, but only those written according to the Halakhah of purity.

We could also note at this point a certain anti-theurgic tendency in rabbinic Judaism: the mere characters of the *tetragramma* have no intrinsic power *per se*. Only if produced in terms of rules for what is permitted can the text be considered theurgic in its effect. If compared to the theurgic conception of the hermeneutic tradition of Iamblichus, Clemens, and Origen, we can conclude that the rabbis do not like to let the text act beyond its original authority. Moreover, the power of the divine name cannot act without a rabbinic premise (or authority). A sacramental *ex opere operato* cannot exist if the circumstances in

---

[542] [Chaim] Saul Horovitz, *Siphre d'be Rab* (Leipzig: Fock 1917), 21. On this Halakhah and its parallels, see Johann Maier, *Jüdische Auseinandersetzung mit dem Christentum in der Antike* (Darmstadt: Wissenschaftliche Buchgesellschaft, 1982), 26–33 and *passim*.

which this happens are not permitted by the Halakhah, as of course decided by rabbinic academies.

The conception of the sacral dimension of the entire Hebrew language emerged in the Amoraic era, above all in Babylonia (Babylonian Talmud, Sanhedrin 21b). We read in the already above (p. 35) mentioned text:

> Mar Zutra or, as some say, Mar 'Ukba said: Originally the Torah was given to Israel in Hebrew characters and in the sacred language (בתחילה ניתנה תורה לישראל בכתב עברי ולשון הקודש); later, in the times of Ezra, the Torah was given in Ashshurith script and Aramaic language (וחזר וניתנה להם בימי עזרא בכתב אשורית ולשון ארמית). [Finally], they selected for Israel the Ashshurith script and Hebrew language (ביררו להן לישראל כתב אשורית ולשון הקודש), leaving the Hebrew characters and Aramaic language for the hedyototh (והניחו להדיוטות כתב עברית ולשון ארמי). Who are meant by the hedyototh? – R. Ḥisda answers: The Cutheans. And what is meant by Hebrew characters? – R. Ḥisda said: The libuna'ah script.

This text is very important because it indicates a time process during which the text of the Torah was transmitted only in square characters (*Ashshurit*). The Aramaic language and Hebrew script are attributed to the tradition of the Samaritans. The text supports the opinion that the language of the rabbinic tradition is Hebrew and not Aramaic.

11.1.2 Leshon ḥakhamim

The perception of a different level of language is likewise no novelty in Tannaitic Judaism. Important are the references, above all in the Babylonian Talmud, 'Avodah Zarah 58b:

> R. Assi asked R. Joḥanan: How is it when wine is mixed by a heathen? – He said to him: Use the verb מזג! [R. Assi] replied: I used the Scriptural word as in, She hath killed her beasts, she hath mingled (מסכה) her wine.[543] He said to him: The language of the Torah is distinct and so is the language of the Sages. How is it, then, [if a heathen mixes it with water]? – [R. Johanan] answered: It is prohibited on the principle, "Keep off, we say to a Nazirite; go round the vineyard and come not near it!"

The difference is not only a problem of lexicography, but also of grammatical development, as Babylonian Talmud, Ḥullin 137b states (רחלים instead of רחלות in Genesis 32:15). In the Sifra Be-ḥuqqotay 11:1 (266a), we find the note that *sadeh* is masculine in the *leshon ha-qodesh*. The sources are too few to

---

[543] Proverbs 9:2.

identify a grammatical interest in rabbinic Judaism. We can only state that the rabbis noted the difference between their grammatical use and that of the Torah.

11.1.3 Common language

The Talmudic academies show a vivid interest in defining what the common language in Palestine and in Babylonia is: We read in Babylonian Talmud, Bava Qama (82b-)83a (see the parallel tradition in Babylonian Talmud, Soṭa 49b):

> But was Grecian Wisdom proscribed? Was it not taught that Rabbi stated: Why use the Syriac language in Eretz Yisrael [where] either the Holy Tongue or the Greek language [could be employed]? And R. Jose said: Why use the Aramaic language in Babylon [where] the Holy Tongue or the Persian language [could be used]? It may, however, be said that the Greek language is one thing and Grecian Wisdom is another.

Rabbinic Babylonian academies assert that the common languages in Palestine could only be Greek and Hebrew, while they (only) speak Syriac. Perhaps they speak of the common language (Syriac) and the elevated literary style of elitists who know Hebrew and Greek. The same can be applied to the Babylonian Diaspora, which commonly spoke Aramaic while the elevated languages were Persian and Hebrew. For the Babylonian redactor, there is no difference between the Hebrew of the Torah and the Hebrew language of the *ḥakhamim*.

11.2 Dialect or different pronunciation?

A very important element in text transmission, as is well-known, are the mistakes attributed to the pronunciation of the text. The tradition of the so-called "three scrolls of Torah found in the Temple court" (Sifre Devarim 356; Jerusalem Talmud, Ta'anit 4:2 68a; Soferim 6:4; Avot de Rabbi Natan B 46) perhaps also refers to this phenomenon, if the rabbis stated:

> In one scroll the words *me'on 'elohe qedem* (Deuteronomy 33:27) were found (written), in two others the words *me'onah 'elohe qedem*; the Sages declared the first to be invalid, the second valid.

The tradition might mirror a problem of pronunciation. We also read in Jerusalem Talmud, Megillah 1:11 (71d) that:

> R. Simon and R. Samuel bar Naḥman both say: The men of Jerusalem would write "Jerusalem" (ירושלים) as "to Jerusalem" (ירושלימה) and [Sages] had no scruple in this regard. Along these same lines, "north" (צפון) as written "to the north" (צפונה) and "south" (תימן) was written "to the south" (תימנה).

In my opinion, this tradition does not mirror any variant reading of the Torah, but the dialectal pronunciation of Jerusalem, which is much closer to the Greek one: *Hierosolyma*. The rabbis noted the changes in the pronunciation of similar consonants. Here are some examples regarding the pronunciation of *alef* and *ʿayin* and the consequences for the exegesis:

Babylonian Talmud, Megillah 24b

> R. Assi said: A priest from Haifa or Beth Shean should not lift up his hands. It has been taught to the same effect: We do not allow to pass before the ark either men from Beth Shean or from Haifa or of the Tibonin, because they pronounce *alef*s as *ʿayin*s and *ʿayin*s as *alef*s.

Babylonian Talmud, Berakhot 32a

> R. Eleazar also said: Moses spoke insolently towards heaven, as it says: "And Moses prayed unto the Lord (ויתפלל משה אל ה')" (Numeri 11:2). Read not *'el* [unto] the Lord, but *'al* [upon] the Lord, for so in the school of R. Eliezer *alef*s were pronounced like *ʿayin*s and *ʿayin*s like *alef*s.

Babylonian Talmud, Eruvin 53a

> Rab and Samuel are at variance. One learned מעברין and the other learned מאברין. He who learned מאברין explains it as 'adding a wing,' and he who learned מעברין explains it in the same sense as that of 'a pregnant woman' (Genesis 23:9).

To conclude this point: we have sources which testify to a clear difference between the language of the liturgy (*leshon ha-qodesh*) and the language of the sages. On the other hand, we also have sources which do not differentiate between them and consider rabbinic Hebrew the language of the Torah. This position is primarily found in Babylonian academies, where the rabbi played the role of Moses, and a *meturgeman* traduced the *derashah* into Aramaic, the language of the people.[544] This may clarify why the Babylonian teachers explain that the language of Babylon can only be Hebrew or Persian, the Jewish language and the local language of the environment.

---

[544] See Veltri, *Eine Tora für den König Talmai* (Tubingen: Mohr Siebeck, 1994).

The rabbis were also aware of language processes, e.g., of changes in pronunciation that could also be a hermeneutic method. Some alleged that variant readings which are transmitted in the rabbinic literature could have originated from such changes.

11.3 Language, text transmission and exegesis

As discussed above, to search for ancient language conceptions in Judaism and in contemporary literary traditions is a very difficult and daring undertaking because it is based on very few sources. The biblical authors did not seem to show much interest in speculations about transmission, changes of languages, distinctions between everyday and sacred idiom, etc. There are of course references to spoken languages and also to difficulties in understanding local idioms in the environment. Yet, the ancient biblical tradition proceeds from the assumption of a unity of language, and divine punishment for the arrogance of man by means of the multiplicity of languages. Little is known from the biblical texts about the perception of classical and common languages, and the conscious or unconscious periodisation of their own idioms. Even the revolution of the 5th (or better 4th) century BCE, with the adoption of a foreign *lingua franca*, Aramaic, has not been explicitly focused on in the biblical text.

However, it was specifically in the period of Ezra and Nehemiah that a characterisation or perhaps canonisation of the corpus of ancient Jewish literature took place, and a first conceptualisation developed which distinguished the ancient from the contemporary languages. Reading and explaining the Torah in front of the liturgical assembly is like the modern concept of canonisation by publishing an accepted text. The change in language, likely from Hebrew to Aramaic, was one (or the sole) reason to canonise the ancient traditions. The other was, of course, the formation of a concurrent tradition of the Samaritans. A later development which influenced the text tradition is the translation of the Torah into Greek. It was a venture of the Jewish community of Alexandria, which, to a considerable extent, canonised some form of texts. It is significant that the so-called Letter of Aristeas on the origin of Greek Torah uses frames and vocabulary in the description of the proclamation of the Greek Torah which automatically (and of course deliberately) call to mind the scene of Ezra before the Water Gate.

It is thus not the case that some rabbinic traditions focused on the aspect of mythical reference to the theory of the similar dignity of Ezra to Moses to receive the Torah. That is the Palestinian version. The Babylonian tradition is something different:

When the Torah in ancient times was forgotten from Israel, Ezra came up from Babylon and rebuilt it. It was again forgotten and Hillel, the Babylonian, came up and rebuilt it. Yet, again was it forgotten, and R. Ḥiyya and his sons came up and rebuilt it.[545]

The re-formation, or re-establishment, of the Torah's text under the leadership of Ezra is of course also reflected in the legend of Ezra in the so-called 4th book of Ezra and other very similar stories, which testify to and justify editorial work on established texts. The Babylonian tradition reports Ezra's return trip from the Babylonian deportation to stress the origin of the father of Judaism's wisdom. The same procedure is narrated in regard to Hillel, the Babylonian, and R. Ḥiyya, who in several traditions recognise the subordination of the Palestinian Patriarchate to the Babylonian Exilarchate.[546] In the rendition of the Palestinian tradition of the Torah's rebuilding, the Babylonian teachers overemphasised the function of their academic centres, according to the logic of the tradition's later canonisation: Babylonian Judaism was successful in imposing their own halakhic traditions, the Targum, the liturgy, and the Halakhah.

The choice of some technical terms in the above quoted text is also not casual: to rebuild the Torah (le-yassed torah). In Babylonian Talmud, Shabbat 104a, R. Ḥiyya bar Abba reports the tradition that the final or middle form of the letters – כ|ך, מ|ם, נ|ן, פ|ף, צ|ץ – were taught by the prophets, not because they were innovative, but because the letters were forgotten and they restored them: שְׁכָחוּם וְחָזְרוּ וְיִסְּדוּם. In the Palestinian Talmud, the Eastern Gate of the Temple was named Foundation Gate because they restored/established the decisions of Halakhah (Jerusalem Talmud, Eruvin 5:1 [22c]: שער היסוד ששם היו מייסדין את ההלכה).

What is the meaning of this tradition? The terminology is clear enough to refer to editorial work on the text in order to create an "updated" text of the Bible. It also insinuates a consciousness of being the guarantee of the tradition – not only in reference to the hermeneutic of the text, but also and above all in relation to the transmission of the text. The leading community arrogates for itself the privilege of having the best tradition of the biblical text. We have a Midrash which teaches:

> Wherefore are the dots (in the biblical text)? Nay, thus said Ezra: If Elijah will come and say, why didst thou write them? I shall say unto him: I have already put dots over them. And if he will say: Thou hast written well, I shall remove the dots from over them.[547]

---

545 Babylonian Talmud, Sukka 20a.
546 Jacob Neusner, *A History of the Jews in Babylonia: The Parthian Period* (Chico: California Scholars Press, 1984), 1:110 et seq.
547 Ba-Midbar Rabbah 3 in the English translation of Moses H. Segal, "The Promulgation of the Authoritative Text of the Hebrew Bible," *Journal of Biblical Literature* 72 (1953): 42. It also

Ezra, the perfect scribe, did not hesitate to change the text of the Torah if the prophet Elijah praised him for his work. Prophecy is clearly seen here as opposed to transmission. In other words: scribal authority is based authoritatively only on itself. The interaction of text and exegesis of the text, also present in the text itself, reveals the existence of other texts not included in the "final" directory of the *miqra*.

We have evidence that hermeneutic and text traditions are two different things, although the first attempted to standardise the second. The famous text Bereshit Rabbah 12:6 transmits a very precious commentary on *plene* et *defective*:[548]

> All *toledoth* found in Scripture are defective, except two, viz. *These are the toledoth* (generations) of Perez (Ruth 4:18), and the present instance. And why are they defective? R. Judan said in R. Abun's name: The six [which the lack] correspond to the six things which were taken away from Adam, viz., his lustre, his immortality [literally 'life'], his height, the fruit of the earth, the fruit of trees, and the luminaries. [...]
>
> R. Berekiah said in the name of R. Samuel b. Naḥman: Though these things where created in their fullness, yet when Adam sinned they were spoiled, and they will not again return to their perfection until the son of Perez [viz. Messiah] comes; [for in the verse] '*These are the toledoth* (generations) *of Perez*' *toledoth* is spelled fully, with *waw*. These are they: his lustre, his immortality, his height, the fruit of the earth and the fruit of trees, and the luminaries.

The Masorah does agree at first glance that the word *toledot* appears *defective* of the *waw* in the other verses, while the *waw* is present only in two verses: Genesis 2:4 and Ruth 4:18.[549] The tradition of the missing *waw* is widely accepted in rabbinic literature and is quoted by numerous Midrashim and both Talmudim.[550]

---

includes a commentary on the text. On the medieval and early modern discussion on this topic, see David Weiss Halivni, *Peshat and Derash: Plain and Applied Meaning in Rabbinic Exegesis* (New York: Oxford University Press, 1991), 140; Stephen D. Benin, "Jews, Christians, and the Authority to Interpret," in *With Reverence for the Word: Medieval Scriptural Exegesis in Judaism, Christianity, and Islam*, ed. Jane Dammen McAuliffe, Barry D. Walfish, and Joseph W. Goering (New York: Oxford University Press, 2003), 19.

548 *Midrash Rabbah*, Genesis, vol. 1, translated by H. Freedman (London: Soncino Press, 1983), 91–92.

549 See, for instance, the Sephardic MS Hebr. 790, of the Jerusalem National University Library, or the Codex Leningradensis 19A. Many thanks to Elvira Martín Contreras for her important annotations to an earlier version of this chapter. On the Midrash, see Elvira Martín Contreras, *La interpretación de la Creación. Técnicas exegéticas en el midrás Génesis Rabbâ* (Estella: Verbo Divino, 2002), 192.

550 See the footnotes in *Midrash Bereshit Rabba: Critical Edition with Notes and Commentary*, ed. J. Theodor and Chanoch Albeck, (Jerusalem: Shalem, 1996), 1:102–103.

Yet, a more precise analysis of the missing *waw* shows that the Midrash is very enigmatic: which *waw* is meant? The first, the second, or both of them?⁵⁵¹ The Midrash must consequently refer to both *wawim*, as Yedidyah Norzi concludes.⁵⁵² The Sephardic R. Meir ben Todros ha-Levi Abulafia (c. 1170–1244) quoted here testifies to the tradition of the (double) *waw* with reference to the Midrash Rabbah only in reference to Genesis 2:4 and Ruth 4:18. However, this is but a reference to a reference.

So this is one case in which we have evidence for influences between Midrash and Masorah. Is there a consistency of this *plene* writing among the MSS beside the codices, which could have motivated this Midrash? Unfortunately, there are only two biblical text records of the word *toledot* in Qumran and none of them of Genesis 2:4 or Ruth 4:18. So we cannot identify any significance, but in correspondence with the Midrash none of them is written with double *wawim*.⁵⁵³ The Samaritan MSS seem to have systematically been standardised, transmitting the first Holem *plene* and the second *defective*.⁵⁵⁴ The Masoretic tradition could only be fixed in the context of rabbinic exegesis. But, the medieval biblical MSS also show a wide range of orthographic variants.⁵⁵⁵ There was no need to adjust the texts to the Masoretic and Midrashic tradition.

We also have evidence that in some cases, the appearance of the text is rejected by creating pseudo-grammatical solutions to determine the meaning. A relatively young collection of Midrashim transmits the following meaningful exegesis of the verse:

> And Moses took his wife and sons, let them ride on a donkey. In *w-yrkbm* the consonant *yod* is lacking. In *ḥmr*, a *waw* is lacking. The verse teaches us that he had only one donkey. He let only his two sons ride on the donkey, but not his wife. That is one of the (biblical) verses which the elders of Israel changed for the king Ptolemy. They wrote for him: he let them ride on a draught animal for man. (They did this) because of Moses' honour.⁵⁵⁶

---

551 See also Daniel Mynatt, Timothy Crawford and Page H. Kelley, ed., *The Masorah of Biblia Hebraica Stuttgartensia* (Grand Rapids: William B. Eerdmans Publishing Company, 1998), 189.
552 In *Minḥat Shay* on Gen 2:4.
553 4QGen-Exodᵃ fr.4 to Genesis 36:9: תולדת. 4QLev-Numᵃ fr. 29 zu Numeri 1,38: תולדתם. See Eugene Ulrich, ed. *The Biblical Qumran Scrollss: Transcriptions and Textual Variants* (Leiden and Boston: Brill, 2010), 12, 138.
554 I am grateful to Stefan Schorch for having pointed out this fact.
555 Benjamin Kennicott, *Dissertation generalis in Vetus Testamentum Hebraicum: Cum Variis Lectionibus, ex Codicibus Manuscriptis et Impressis*, vol. I–II (Oxford, 1776–1780, several new editions). Random inspection to אלה תולדות: In Genesis 10 to 30 of the 97, constant examples differ from the Leningrad Codex. In all cases, there are also MSS with double *plene* orthography.
556 Sekhel Tov to Exodus 4:20 (Buber 28).

The absence of the consonants *waw* and *yod* refers to the *plene* and *defective* of the Hebrew text which the Masorah also shows. Here the text tradition, as reported by Kennicott, also displays a multifarious world of variant readings.

The very peculiar interpretation of the Midrash which let only the two children ride the donkey refers back not only problem of "three persons on a donkey" but also to the violation of the honor of Moses, who is to the forced to walk. How can such an interpretation be justified? Simply with a pause: "And Moses took his wife. And his sons, he let ride them on the donkey." The medieval chronographer and philosopher Abraham Ibn Daud (1110–1180) construed the difficulty of this verse as lying in a purely physical aspect, although he also alludes to the ancient theory of honor:

> "[The Elders changed this verse] so that the king did not despise our teacher, because he rode on a donkey and also did not have to object: How could *one* donkey transport *a* woman and *two* children?"[557]

This observation is not illogical and can perfectly explain the plural of the Greek Septuagint and of the rabbinic Torah for King Ptolemy, regardless of whether the rabbis had *really* seen the text of the Septuagint and its variant reading.

It seems that the Midrash combines the already given statement of Babylonian Talmud Megillah 9a that for Ptolemy, the sages changed the donkey to a "pack animal," but interprets this with the intention that this was only for one person (or two children). Now the Midrash connects this with the observations of plene and defective writing and seems to suppose that the positions of *yod* and *waw* are discussed: The sages transferred the *waw* before *yrkbm* to *ḥmwr* to denote the fact of *one* animal. Likewise, the lacking yod in *yrkbm* seems to refer to the problem of carrying only one person: It could denote the reading as a *qal* form (Moses himself riding), even if the suffix in the text is then superfluous.

Speaking of missing *plene* and a *defective* variant reading, we have to be careful. Rabbinic exegesis clearly shows that the teachers were perfectly aware of the manuscript condition of "fluidity," perhaps much more in some details than in others. However, the imperative of the exegesis, as Barry Levi stresses quoting Mishnah Avot 5:23, is to investigate the Torah "from every angle," perhaps also when the angle is multidimensional, or even virtual. For "all of it is in you, and all of you is in it."[558]

---

[557] *Divre Malkhe Isra'el* 50b.
[558] B. Barry Levy, *Fixing God's Torah: The Accuracy of the Hebrew Bible Text in Jewish Law* (New York: Oxford University Press, 2001), 6.

11.4 Conclusion

In Babylonian Talmud Eruvin 13a, Rabbi Aqiva gave advice to the scribe to be careful in writing the biblical text: "... for if you omit a sign, you will destroy the entire world." The history of the biblical text did not agree with the famous rabbi: the world has not been destroyed until now, although (or perhaps because) a myriad of scribes added, omitted, changed and mended a great many verses of the Bible. However, the Rabbi is very right to some extent. Perhaps a change in the text would not destroy the cosmological order of world, but without any doubt it would destroy the world of the rabbinic exegesis. And that is, of course, an instance of unforgivable damage.

12 On Editing Rabbinic Texts

Editing a text belongs to the oldest of scholarly activities, since scholarship functions not only through the modality of transmission by memorisation but also by writing down and publishing ideas, traditions, and useful texts.[559] That was the activity of ancient libraries, which were privileged centres of learning, teaching and research, academies comparable to modern universities and research centres.[560] The first edition of Homer's verse in the Alexandrian library offered clear-cut criteria to scholarship in defining what is an author's reading and what can be deemed spurious text. The same or similar criteria were adopted when producing the Christian edition of the Bible in Origen's Hexapla and editions made in Christian medieval centres like abbeys, monasteries, and church libraries. The humanist renaissance of ancient literature was nothing but a philological movement of editing and translating texts, and commenting on them. Finally, German enlightened research on Greek, Roman and subsequently "Oriental" literature started by putting together criteria and rules to render ancient texts readable for contemporary audiences.

12.1 The Quest for the Ur-Text

A fertile boom in editing Jewish texts can be seen in the 15th and 16th centuries in various centres of learning, above all Italy. Basically, the nature of such editions is an attempt to give a *vulgate* – a common readable text – of some manuscripts, mostly by an eclectic method. Not until the 19th century, and following the major trends of the new academic sciences, did the scholars developing the *Wissenschaft des Judentums* consider it of utmost importance to reach standards in editing texts of rabbinic and medieval literature. Leopold Zunz, the "founder" of the science of Judaism, critically noted that the "so-called *editiones principes*, as soon as they accomplish more then a reproduction of manuscripts (...) can rightly raise the claim of being literary preliminary studies."[561] A significant number of editions were completed in this key period

---

559 An excellent presentation of the *status quaestionis* on editing ancient text is in G. Thomas Tanselle, "Classical, Biblical, and Medieval Textual Criticism and Modern Editing," *Studies in Bibliography* 36 (1983): 21–68.
560 See my study *Libraries, Translations, and "Canonic Text": The Septuagint, Aquila, and Ben Sira in the Jewish and Christian Traditions* (Leiden and Boston: Brill, 2006), 26–99.
561 German: "Die sogenannten editiones principes, sobald sie mehr leisten als Vervielfältigung des Manuscriptes, desgleichen gute Uebersetzungen, richtige Handbücher, Biographien und ähnliches mehr, können auf den Namen litterarischer Vorarbeiten mit Recht Anspruch

and remain an indispensable tool on the desk of every scholar of rabbinic, medieval and early modern literature.

Yet there has been a change in the history of scholarship on text editing and textual commentary: the principle of searching for, creating or re-creating the *best* possible text, *re-covering it,* has been supplanted by the quest for the *original* text by criticising, analysing and commenting on the manuscript tradition. The "original text," created by intuition, reflection and supposition, became the hypothetical beginning of the tradition and/or of the author's intention. The search for the original text was also the prime question in the final decades of the 20th century and will doubtless also concern us in the future. I will attempt here to give some outlines of this field of research, offering some general considerations gleaned from modern editing activity as *status quaestionis.*

The edition of ancient, medieval and sometimes modern texts is a titanic task. Provided the text was produced by *one* author, the main question is whether to record all the different versions of the textual creation, if extant,[562] or to single out the "original" text seen either as the absolute beginning of the creative process or its final redaction. In regard to the final redaction by the author, it is necessary to distinguish between his/her former manuscript and the corrections of the text in print and after first print.

This aspect is faced by Theodor Kiesel's critique of the complete works (*Gesamtausgabe*), of Heidegger. Kiesel found numerous errors in translating the lecture course *History of the Concept of Time*, which had to be corrected on the basis of the original manuscript.[563] Kiesel took the redactors sharply to task because they demonstrate "contempt for philology" and "still have not mastered and truly 'overseen' their holdings to the degree needed to manage the publication of an archive with some degree of scholarly competence."[564] For example: the occurrences of the term *"Existenz"* in the typescript of 1925 were interpolated by Heidegger himself some time later. There is no mention

---

machen." Leopold Zunz, "Etwas über die rabbinische Litteratur [1821]," in *Zunz Gesammelte Schriften*, vol. 1 (Berlin: Louis Gerschel Verlagsbuchhandlung, 1875): 3–31.

[562] As in the synoptic edition of Joyce's *Ulysses*, concentrated on the genesis of the text; James Joyce. *Ulysses. A Critical and Synoptic Edition.* ed. Hans Walter Gabler (New York: Garland, 1984). See the criticism of this edition in John Kidd, "The Scandal of Ulysses," *New York Review of Books* (June 30, 1988): 32–39.

[563] Theodore Kiesel, *Heidegger's Way of Thought: Critical and Interpretive Signposts*, edited by Alfred Denker and Marion Heinz (London: Continuum, 2002), 203. I find myself in total agreement with the online review of Richard Polt in *Notre Dame Philosophical Reviews*, February 7, 2003, http://goo.gl/TCHxI (accessed 7June 2013).

[564] Kiesel, *Heidegger's Way*, 6, 8.

of this fact in the *Gesamtausgabe*, because its editors insist on producing a "final edition," a so-called *Ausgabe letzter Hand*, i.e. with no distinction between the original text and later emendations, and an "edition without interpretation." Kiesel condemns these principles as "devastating fictions totally at odds with Heidegger's lifelong thought."[565] Reviewing Kiesel's criticism, Richard Polt concludes: "A philosopher who insisted that existence itself is essentially hermeneutic could hardly endorse the ideal of an edition free of all interpretation."[566] So the first question a student of philology should answer is whether a manuscript edition can be achieved without any interpretation of the text itself.

A similar debate can be detected in other fields of research, for instance the edition of musical texts. What is an original text of a modern or contemporary composer? In musicology, an original text, if anything, is principally not the text issued by the author but the reconstruction of a fictive text by taking into consideration all the elements which should lead us to the author's intention.[567] However, even on the assumption that we can successfully reconstruct the original text, can we safely infer that we (re-)cover the author's real intention? By no means! Gustav Mahler changed the score after every performance. The conductor's experience led him every time to correct and implement his understanding of his own musical idea.

Therefore a second question to be answered by our virtual student of text editing is the following: should we construct/re-construct a text every time *after* interpreting it? The question is not so far off the mark as it might seem to be at first glance. Looking at the edition of fragments of lost works, every scholar would agree that every interpretation presupposes a new edition, as recent scholarship on the fragmentary documents of Qumran and of the Cairo and "Italian" Genizah sufficiently proves. A typical recent example is the edition of the so-called "Wisdom Text from the Cairo Genizah," a fragmentary gnomic text which probably dates back to the 11th century.[568] Within the short span of four years (1989 to 1993), it was edited four times. The new editions were justified because the text was supposed to be a creation of 1. New Testament times; 2. the 6th century; 3. the 8th century; or 4. the 10th century. Every supposition implies the need to deposit a new edition.

---

565 *Ibidem*, 150.
566 See Veltri, *Libraries, Translations, and "Canonic Text,"* 26–99.
567 See Peter Gülke, "Nachruf auf den Urtext?," *Die Musikforschung* 57 (2004): 383–388.
568 See the *status quaestionis* in Veltri, "Letteratura etico-sapienziale del primo medioevo: Alcuni frammenti dalla geniza del Cairo," *Henoch* 20 (1997): 349–366; Veltri, *Gegenwart der Tradition* (Leiden and Boston: Brill, 2003), 234–263.

If we look at Jewish literature as an object of edition, the situation is certainly not easier than in other branches, but rather exceedingly complicated. Looking first at literature by and ascribed to a single author, so-called authored literature, we have to face not only the question of different manuscripts and fragments, but also that of different text versions, perhaps consciously created by the author, or at least by scribes and schools on the basis of reasons difficult to reconstruct. Furthermore, centuries of Church censorship, of voluntary or forced expurgation of allegedly anti-Christian variant readings and texts, of public burning of manuscripts and prints of Talmud and Midrash as well as authored tractates, render modern edition-making no easier.

A typical example is the *status quaestionis* of manuscripts, fragments, and versions of Josippon, a Hebrew reworking of Josephus. How can we edit a book existing in at least three different versions, a great many manuscripts and fragments, and translations into Arabic and Ethiopic to boot?[569] Some excerpts transmitted by the *Chronicle of Yerahmeel* and fragments from the Cairo Genizah were not included in the edition of David Flusser.[570] The editor's rather naïve conviction to have discovered the original text was very short-lived. In his edition, he produced an eclectic text avoiding every discussion of the other configurations of the tradition.[571]

The editing of rabbinic texts is much more complicated. The documents which have come down to us in the multifarious forms of Mishnayot, Midrashim, Halakhot, Aggadot, Targumin, and Talmudim cannot be considered to be authored literature. It is only a kind of snapshot from a world of exegesis and school opinions. I recently read the Mishnah, tractate *Soṭah* and Midrash Sifre ba-Midbar with my students. In our work, we had to answer the question of variant readings in *parashat soṭah* with reference to the warning of the witnesses in case of adultery or suspicion of such. One student asked in some surprise: do the manuscripts of one treatise also testify to different schools of opinion? Such indeed is the everyday experience we have in studying a rabbinic text using manuscripts and the subsequent tradition more or less based on manuscripts. A third question should therefore be addressed by the virtual student of text editions: is the original text what we imagine as being such, or perhaps the beginning of a tradition, or indeed both?

---

[569] For the *status quaestionis*, see David Flusser, ed., *The Josippon (Josephus Gorionides)* (Jerusalem: The Bialik Institute, 1980–1981).
[570] Saskia Dönitz from the Institute of Jewish Studies in Berlin is preparing a study on the tradition of Josippon: already published: Überlieferung und Rezeption des Sefer Yosippon (Texts and Studies in Medieval and Early Modern Judaism 29). Tübingen: Mohr Siebeck, 2013.
[571] See my critique in *Gegenwart der Tradition*, 122–131.

I shall now attempt to address the three questions raised by way of commenting on the following three propositions:
1. ancient editions are a product of the time of authority;
2. editing a text is nothing but interpreting it;
3. an edition should be pragmatically heuristic without pretending to answer the difficult questions on the text's transmission.

12.2 Editions are a Product of Time and Authority

In order to explain what I mean by "a product of the time," I would like to quote an ancient Christian controversy: Jerome's defense of his new Latin translation of the Bible against the Septuagint, which was also called *ekdosis*, in English "edition" or "publication." Augustine's argument against the new translation is known: whatever the Seventy (translators) wrote can either be obvious or obscure. If obscure, you could be fallible too in translating the same passage; if obvious, one cannot believe *they* were fallible.[572] Answering *ad hominem*, Jerome introduces the hermeutic argument of the necessity of commentaries. He argues that when some ancient writers wrote commentaries on the whole Bible, they either commented on it in a perfect way and therefore there is no need for further commentaries, or they did not. But how can one hope to solve what they could not yet decipher? In Jerome's words: *tu quomodo post eos ausus es disserere, quod illi explanare non potuerunt*. And he concludes in his *Apology against Rufinus*:

> Some interpret the passage in this sense, some in that; some try to support their opinion and understanding of it by such and such evidence or reasons: so that the wise reader, after reading these different explanations, and having many brought before his mind for acceptance or rejection, may judge which is the truest, and, like a good banker, may reject the money of spurious mintage.[573]

We are dealing here with "canonical" texts, and consequently we cannot draw a general conclusion on all editions from the ancient period. However, the position of Jerome, endorsing the authoritative function of the reader, who like a good banker rejects money of spurious mintage, cannot hide the fact that

---

[572] In Latin: "... aut obscura fuerunt quae interpretati sunt septuaginta, aut manifesta. si obscura, te quoque in eis falli potuisse credendum est. si manifesta, illos in eis falli non potuisse perspicuum est." The text is likewise mentioned by Jerome in letter CXII (*Corpus Christianorum Series Latina* 55): 389.
[573] *Corpus Christianorum Series Latina* 79: 14–15.

every publication, *ekdosis*, represents more or less a canonisation of meaning. If accepted, the new version or publication crystallises a fleeting moment in the tradition, and in so doing makes further commentaries possible. It depends on the authority of the writer if his composition is to be considered a step forward in the tradition. If we consider a piece of traditional literature like the Mishnah, the situation is similar but not precisely the same. For we can imagine various attempts to publish Mishnayot (orally or in writing) to canonise a particular school's tradition. That is, in my view, the main reason for the differences between the Mishnayot of the corpus of the Mishnah, the Tosefta and the Halakhic Midrashim as well as the Mishnayot presupposed in Yerushalmi and Bavli. However, we have to be careful because ancient and medieval manuscript composers and writers could have had different "quotations" of the Mishnah before them, and the successive copyists could have harmonised their quotations according to the "vulgate," namely according to the commonly used text in the academies.

This aspect can be clarified further by the unique story of redactional activity transmitted in Talmud and Midrash, in particular around the Aggadah of the "three scrolls of Torah found in the Temple court,"[574] already mentioned above in another context. According to this tradition, three scrolls were found in the Temple court: one of the *meonim*, the second of the *hi' hi'* and the third of the *za'aṭuṭim*.

> In one scroll the words *me'ona elohe qedem* (Deuteronomy 32:27,) were found (written), in two others the words *me'onah elohe qedem*; the Sages declared the first to be invalid,

---

[574] Recorded in Sifre Devarim 356, Jerusalem Talmud, Taanit 4:2 (68a), Soferim 6:4 and Avot de-Rabbi Natan 46. See Azaria de' Rossi, *Me'or Enayim: Imre Birna* 6, ed. Dawîd Qassel vol. 1 (Vilnius: Romm, 1864–1866, repr. Jerusalem: Makor, 1970), 131; Alexander Kohut, "Correction d'une erreur de copiste plusieurs fois séculaire," *Revue des Études Juives* 22 (1891): 210–212; Christian D. Ginsburg, *Introduction to the Masoreticretico-Critical Editions of the Hebrew Bible* (London: Trinitarian Bible Society, 1894), 408–409; Ludwig Blau, *Studien zum althebräischen Buchwesen und zur biblischen Litteratur- und Textgeschichte* (Straßburg: Trübner, 1902), 102–106; Jacob Z. Lauterbach, "The Three Books Found in the Temple at Jerusalem," *Jewish Quarterly Review* NS 8 (1917–1918): 385–423; *Massekhet Soferim*, ed. Michael Higger (New York: Hotsa'at De-ve-Rabanan 1937), 169–170, note 17; Elias J. Bickerman, "Some Notes on the Transmission of the Septuagint," in *Alexander Marx Jubilee Volume*, Engl. Section, ed. Saul Lieberman (New York: The Jewish Theological Seminary of America, 1950): 167–168; Lieberman, *Hellenism in Jewish Palestine: Studies in the literary transmission beliefs and manners of Palestine in the 1 I century B.C.E.–IV century C.E.* (New York: Jewish Theological Seminary, 1962), 22–27; Shemaryahu Talmon, "The Three Scrolls of the Law that were Found in the Temple Court," *Textus* 2 (1962), 14–27; Veltri, *Eine Tora für den König Talmai*, 82–86; Solomon Zeitlin, "Were There Three Torah-Scrolls in the Azarah?," *Jewish Quarterly Review* 56 (1965–66): 269–272.

the second valid. In one scroll nine *hi'* were found (written), in the other two eleven; the Sages declared the first to be invalid, the second one valid. In one scroll it was written: *wa-yishlaḥ et za'aṭuṭe bne isra'el* (Exodus 24:5 and *we-el za'aṭuṭim bne Israel* (Exodus 24:11) In the other two *wa-yishlaḥ et na'are bne isra'el* and *we-el aṣile bne Israel*. the Sages declared the first to be invalid, the second one valid.[575]

The terminology here is very similar to the Alexandrian grammarians: "They found written", *maṣe'u katuv*, corresponds to *heuromen gegrammenon*.[576] According to Lieberman, a specimen copy of the Torah was stored in the Temple as an authoritative text, an idea he based on the Midrash Deuteronomy Rabbah. According to him, the aggadah does not deal with a correction of the original text of the Bible, stored in the Temple, but rather with the revision of the "common text," the vulgata.[577] I would argue, on the contrary, that here the aggadah suggests or tells about a comprehensible correction of the stored manuscripts on the basis of a chosen pre-existing text (*Vorlage*). That the text declared valid is always identical with our Masoretic text is a testimony to the accurate work of the "commission," regardless of whether this aggadah refers to a unique work or to continuous assiduous care to ensure accurate copies of the Torah. We thus have precisely the text they wished to be handed down. This is not a matter of orthodoxy or heterodoxy, as Shemaryahu Talmon puts it, because the Jerusalem Talmud attributes a very similar discussion on grammatical peculiarities, a non-Masoretic variant reading or pronunciation of letters, to the people of Jerusalem, without noting that they are *minim*! [578]

---

[575] Sifre Devarim 356. For the other versions of this Midrash, see Veltri, *Eine Tora für den König Talmai*, 81–82.

[576] Lieberman, *Hellenism in Jewish Palestine*, 21.

[577] Frank M. Cross rightly argues that "The distinction 'official versus vulgata' must be abandoned, however, as anachronistic. Official and vulgar text do exist, but after official definition, that is precisely after the promulgation of an official text." See Frank M. Cross, "The History of the Biblical Text in the Light of the Discoveries in the Judean Desert," *Harvard Theological Review* 57 (1964): 298.

[578] While the first two variant readings found in the Temple scroll are concerned with Masorah (the text as written and pronounced), the third is not a variant reading (and therefore not to be included here) but a problem of pure exegesis, which nonetheless denotes a change in the understanding of the authority on the biblical texts. According to the rabbinic literature, the young people who made burnt offerings and sacrificed young bulls as fellowship offerings have no precise identity as priests or Levites. According to Mishnah Zevaim 14:4, they are the first-born who practiced the sacerdotal service before the Levites. A sign of a radical change are Targum Onkelos, Mishnah Kallah 1:17. and Seder Eliyahu Rabbah (ed. Friedman, 52), for they interpreted them purely as common Israelites ("Even Israel is capable of offer offerings on the altar"). Targum Onkelos offers the same translation in Exodus 24:5 and Exodus 24:11 in reference to the *aṣile bne Israel*. Here was a radical change in leadership and a new shift in understanding. For the first time, as testified by Josephus, the storage of the biblical books

This story provides exemplary testimony as to how ancient Judaism published and preserved text. By entrusting a book/scroll or a simple document to the Temple, an ancient scholar or group of scholars sought to give it a two-fold function, intrinsically conjoined: to publish it as well as to have a guaranteed controlled preservation of the author's text. In the Temple, the scrolls were preserved in order to have an authorised copy in the frequent case of controversy or if arguments should arise about legal, historical, liturgical documents, customs and traditions. There, a college or advisory board was instituted to keep an eagle eye on the texts and scrolls to safeguard the literary past and its present actualisation for future generations.

This historical background regarding ancient libraries can shed light on the historical frames of Deuteronomy 31:9–13, where the Torah of Moses is handed over to the priests, to the sons of Levi and to the Elders with the duty of reading it "at the end of every seven years ... before them in their hearing ..." The procedure, also followed in the book of Ezra 7:12–26 and in the proclamation of the Greek Torah in the so-called Letter of Aristeas, is intended to be a publication of the Torah's text, and an official proclamation of the observance of the commandments, both of which meant as means to educate the people.[579] However, the procedure can also be interpreted as checking the text and actualizing it *before* a public audience: the act of reading before an audience then would be a guarantee that the text would be safeguarded against arbitrary changes. Moreover, the story of the scrolls, "discovered" by Josiah in II Kings 22–23 follows a similar logic, i.e., to illustrate fictively the event of "reading" the word of the book found in the Temple in the "hearing" of the elders, priests and prophets. Reading and hearing was the ancient way to propose and accept the authoritative actualisation of the effective tradition.[580]

A first conclusion is that the principle of the oral Torah let the rabbis have full control over the transmission and actualisation of texts considered important for the community. If the rabbis were not afraid to change the text of the written Torah, if possible, that did not deter them either from expurgating every other text not in agreement with their teaching. Yet, rabbinic Judaism

---

was a sacerdotal task (*Contra Apionem* 1:35, et seq.). The priests were entrusted with the correction of the Torah for the king (*Sifre Devarim* 160), a task passed on to the Sanhedrin in *Jerusalem Talmud*, Sanhedrin 2:4 (20c). The list of the three scrolls testify to this radical change in leadership, stressing that the people chosen to see God without suffering death are not priests or Levites, but the young Israelites.

579 See above, pp. 29–30.

580 A very interesting late parallel is the procedure of the listening to texts as described by Stefan Leder, *Spoken Word and Written Text: Meaning and Social Significance of the Institution of Riwāya* (Tokyo: Islamic Area Studies Project, 2002).

lacked a central authority and orthodoxy capable of suppressing other opinions. We are facing a most diverse approach by the rabbis to the written and oral Torah, which also explains the sea of variant readings in the manuscripts and of tractates being interlaced with the most divergent literary forms of transmission down to the period of authored literature in the Middle Ages. The edition of these texts is therefore a truly titanic task for scholars who intend to establish the pure, original text. For the word "origin" is not identical with the idea of a tradition born in the world of authority, and authority can also be a plural attribute of a tradition over the course of the time. And that is likewise the premise to understand the contemporary discussion on text redaction.

12.3 Editions as Interpretations of Texts

Turning now to recent decades of scholarly editing of rabbinic texts, I would like to discuss some controversial aspects. That concerns the *status quaestionis* of scholarship on rabbinic literature as raised by Peter Schäfer, who was the first to speak of the "fluidity" of text transmission. Consistent with his theory, he offered a "neutral" text tradition synoptically edited either in columns or in lines – a so-called "score" or *Partiturtext*. The word "interpretation" is avoided for the most part by the Berlin edition school he initiated and followed, among others, by Hans-Jürgen Becker in his edition of *Avot de-Rabbi Natan*. Rivka Ulmer, herself active in text editing,[581] is amused by the "cottage industry" of Rabbinic texts[582] produced in Germany, where, in her opinion, the paradise of fund-raising serves to "place(s) the scholar in the position of a managing editor in charge of financial and personnel management as well providing academic oversight". I remain very skeptical about the question of whether the success in Berlin in editing has something to do with an ability to manage, probably Ms Ulmer is indirectly referring to Daniel Bomberg's redactional activity. Bomberg, a skilled printer of editions of Hebrew texts, who, born in Antwerp and settled in Venice in the 16th century, published under the auspices of Pope Leo X. the first complete editions of the Babylonian and the Jerusalem Talmud. He was a man with superb managerial and business skills. Yet, these were other times, when every Jewish or Christian, Protestant or Catholic librarian was

---

[581] See *Pesiqta rabbati: A Synoptic Edition of Pesiqta Rabbati Based upon all Extant Manuscripts and the Editio Princeps*, ed. Rivka Ulmer, 3 vols. (Lanham, Oxford: University Press of America, 1997–2002).
[582] See her review of "*Geniza-Fragmente zu Avot de-Rabbi Natan*," ed. Hans-Jürgen Becker, *Review of Biblical Literature*, February 5, 2005, http://goo.gl/kMmxY (accessed 7 June 2013).

keen on buying manuscripts and editions of Jewish texts, with little care for cost or sacrifice. The present-day situation is different: very few libraries in the world are today ready to buy editions of Rabbinic texts, something comparable to the humanistic and renaissance period.

The success of the Berlin school is but an attempt to find another methodological paradigm in editing rabbinic literature. That was the real reason which convinced the referees of the German Research Society to fund Schäfer's projects (Hekhalot, Yerushalmi etc.). Schäfer was of the opinion that the texts of mystical and rabbinic academies were transmitted in a constant process of interpretation in schools, similar to the Heraclitean principle of pan-metabolism: *panta rei*, "all things are in constant flux." In this way, he tried to contrast the current procedure of editing text by searching out the supposed original text, or at least the text imagined as close to the original as possible. His pessimism with reference to the textual manuscript tradition resulted in the skeptical conclusion that indeed there is no original text at all.

Schäfer started his project with the edition of the so-called *sifrut hekhalot*, the mystical literature of the "descenders to the Chariot" (*yorde merkavah*). With reference to the manuscript composition and the variety of the variant readings, he preferred to edit all of them without giving preference to any as original text. He did not view his task in choosing the better readings for his readers, for "the so-called better variant reading is too frequently at the mercy of the chance or intuition of the editor. Thus, we cannot see in such a 'critical' edition a real alternative."[583] Schäfer presented the results of the fluidity of the text, the manuscripts in a synoptic format as a precautionary measure to avoid speculation on the better reading as intuited by the editor. It goes without saying that the translation of the corpus differs consistently from this theoretical approach: the team did not translate all the testimonies synoptically, but only those texts which substantially differed from each other. Beginning thus, from the theoretical system of Jerome of a text as an open work and of the reader as a 'good banker' – or to use Umberto Eco's intriguing terminology, as a *lupus in fabula* – Schäfer ended up in the position of the scribes, correcting the manuscripts to offer a coherent text.

My observations on Schäfer's conception of redaction are not at all a criticism of the synoptic method as such, for his theory of the text remains a challenge for every student of Jewish mysticism. Yet, a translation cannot *copy* the

---

[583] German: "Die sog. bessere Lesart ist zu häufig dem Zufall oder der Intuition des Herausgebers ausgeliefert, als daß wir in einer derart 'kritischen' Edition eine echte Alternative sehen können." Peter Schäfer et al., ed., *Synopse zur Hekhalot-Literatur* (Tübingen: Mohr Siebeck, 1981), V.

tradition, it must be a commentary. On the other hand, in the view of Peter Schäfer, every edition also *is* a commentary, as Schäfer at least had to subdivide the manuscript texts into some units, and this involves a difficult task of interpretation. Only if the text is given in the form of a facsimile is the "reader" synonymous with the editor. Very similar is the position of Sussmann's edition of the Talmud Yerushalmi, because he published one manuscript with restoration and correction.[584]

In his often quoted and much-discussed article on the "Status Quaestionis" of the research into rabbinic literature, Schäfer outlines the major trends of scholarly inquiry into ancient Jewish literature. He took as a point of departure the very fluid situation of the variant readings in all forms of rabbinic writings, and ended with the statement: "The terms with which we usually work – text, '*Urtext*,' recension, tradition, citation, redaction, final redaction, and work – prove to be fragile and hasty definitions that must be subsequently questioned."[585] His conclusion is clear and unmistakable: we must concentrate on the manuscripts while avoiding creating new eclectic or so-called critical editions. Only the manuscripts can be (more or less) dated and the historical and social context of scribes and copyists established. "That means," he concludes, "that it is not 'the' text as such that is to be fixed in time and space, but rather the history of the text as reflected in the transmission of its manuscript traditions."[586]

In his response to Schäfer, Chaim Milikowsky sharply criticised this approach, deeming it programmatic rather than analytic. The number of minor variant readings in rabbinic texts is immense, but, in his view, irrelevant to any discussion of redactional identity.[587] He is thus of the opinion that "we have barely begun the groundwork which will let us decide if recensional variants exist." In his optimistic view, an *Urtext* of almost every rabbinic text can be reconstructed. His first answer on the delimitation of redactional entities of early rabbinic texts is clearly positive, attributing the variants to the history of transmission. In his opinion, the situation of later Midrashic works such as

---

584 Yaacov Sussmann, ed., *Talmud Yerushalmi According to MS Or. 4720 (Sal. 3) of the Leiden University Library with Restoration and Correction*, new printing (Jerusalem: The Academy of the Hebrew Language, 2005).
585 Peter Schäfer, "Research into Rabbinic Literature: An Attempt to Define the Status Quaestionis," *Journal of Jewish Studies* 37 (1986): 150. See also a commentary on it in Piero Capelli, "Sullo *Status Quaestionis* nella ricerca sulla 'letteratura' rabbinica. Riflessioni metodologiche in margine ad una polemica recente," *Henoch* 13 (1991): 349–363.
586 Schäfer, "Research into Rabbinic Literature," 152.
587 Chaim Milikowsky, "The Status Quaestionis of Research in Rabbinic Literature," *Journal of Jewish Studies* 39 (1988): 201–211, see especially 203.

Tanḥuma-Yelamdenu is different because of the lack of any earlier redactional work. Milikowsky's argument does not stand close scrutiny, however, because it is circular: we cannot draw any conclusion on the redactional identity of *early* rabbinic writings because we still have not examined all the manuscript testimonies. However, if the analysis leads us to suspect that at the beginning there was no clear redactional unity, the tractate is *later*. But: what is the reason to date Yelamdenu as a *later* homiletic work? The absence of an initial redaction? The reference to the quotations of early midrashic texts in Yelamdenu is likewise not convincing. I have tried to prove elsewhere that the negative tradition on the Septuagint in the tractate Sefer Torah is a quote from the Jerusalem Talmud, while negatively changing its wording. In *this* case, I can only say that this tradition is later than the text of Yerushalmi. No other conclusion can be safely drawn about Yerushalmi and Sefer Torah as tractate or redactional unity.

However, I think that Milikowsky is right when he states that the redacting of Rabbinic texts is in its infancy and we need far more work on this field of research before we can draw any conclusion about the nature of Rabbinic literature. Without going into details of the very peculiar theme of scholarship concerned with the dating of redactional entities, I would propose my model of edition based on the consideration that, with reference to the analysis of manuscripts and early prints, we can establish some relationship between them constituting what we may call a "family" (to speak with Milikowsky). However, the members of this "family" are often not monogamist; moreover, they do not go back to one founder. The pragmatic solution is not to find or create but rather to collect the major testimonies of the tradition in a synoptic edition, though not all of them. The reader is not the editor, but he can recognize the most important, but he can recognise branches of this "family" without being overburdened with the numerous but unimportant variant readings. That is our experience in editing the Midrash Tehillim.

12.4 The Pragmatic Edition: Midrash Tehillim

The edition of Midrash Tehillim is a joint project of the Department of Old Testament Studies at the University of Münster, and the Department of Jewish Studies at the University of Halle-Wittenberg. Salomon Buber offered the first scientific edition in 1891, utilizing eight manuscripts and the prints of Constantinople (1512), and Venice (1546).[588] He took as his basis the text of the manu-

---

588 *Midrasch Tehillim (Schocher Tob): Sammlung agadischer Abhandlungen über die 150 Psalmen*. Herausgegeben nach einer Handschrift aus der Bibliothek zu Parma cod. 1332 [1232], mit

script of Parma 2552, with collations of other manuscripts. Like other editions of Buber, his edition of Midrash Tehillim does not excel in accuracy.

While distinguishing three recensions of the text, Buber's basic intuition regarding the manuscripts to be used was correct. Nevertheless, a new edition is indispensable, because he could not take into consideration all the manuscript testimonies and the fragments of the Cairo Genizah known to us today and, above all, because he created an eclectic text which does not do justice to the composition of the material.[589]

In his edition of 1891, Buber related the testimonies known to him to three "recensions" (*mahadurot*).[590] His first criterion to delimit these was the presence (or absence) of the partly extensive additions in some of the manuscripts. While this criterion for distinguishing different versions of the text has proven itself to be reliable at least in most cases, the manuscript he collated as a base-text (Ms Parma, Biblioteca Palatina Cod. 2552 / de Rossi 1232) seems, in the light of the new manuscripts taken into consideration, to belong to an already extended version of Midrash Tehillim. Creating a new eclectic text, as Buber did, or selecting a single manuscript as a base text in combination with one extensive critical apparatus, would blur even the most eminent differences between the versions – or the most distant branches of the "family," to speak with Milikowsky. If we aim at a printed edition, presenting all manuscripts as a score text is practically impossible in view of the great number of extant text-witnesses and of the extent of this work.

Also, it hardly seems reasonable since the mass of minor differences between the witnesses of one version may adequately be represented as a list of variants in a separate critical apparatus for each "recension." For these reasons, a synoptic edition of a small number of columns, each of which contains the text of a manuscript representing one "family" will be the better solution, presenting the reader with textual entities not present in Buber, and at the same time avoiding overburdening the reader with the innumerable errors of the scribes. That can then be called a pragmatic edition.

Vergleichungen der Lesarten anderer sieben Handschriften, ed. Salomon Buber (Wilna: Wittwe & Gebruder, 1891).
589 Esther M. Menn, "Praying King and Sanctuary of Prayer, Part I: David and the Temple's Origins in Rabbinic Psalms Commentary (Midrash Tehillim)," *Journal of Jewish Studies* 52,1 (2001): 1–26, 1, footnote 1: "The absence of a modern critical edition, which would not only take into account additional manuscripts including those found in the Cairo Geniza but also adequately present the diversity of the earliest manuscripts, continues to hamper research on *Midrash Tehillim*." In comparison to the Buber Edition, The Halle-Münster project will take into account six additional comprehensive manuscripts and about 15 important fragments, mostly of the Cairo Genizah, which promise to be highly informative in regard to the history of the text.
590 *Midrasch Tehillim*, ed. Buber, 81 et seq.

12.5 Conclusion

In view of the immense work of text editing still ahead of us, every theory is good if it gives a sufficient reason to students of Jewish studies to engage in this field of research. I must confess that I remain very skeptical about the 19th century aim to create the "perfect edition," or the 20th century endeavor to gather together a collection of evidence on the "original text." However, I am also very hesitant to agree with Umberto Eco when he supposes the openness of the artistic work, although it remains a fascinating theory. The reason has to do with our tendency when faced with multiple variety to prefer choosing *one* way of interpretation. We cannot just offer to the reader technical tools, merely editing manuscripts and avoiding any other way of presenting our interpretation of the text. When editing all the variant readings of the text, we overtax the reader with a task he or she cannot fulfill without becoming a specialist. This can discourage readers from taking our scholarship seriously. Any edition cannot be but an interpretation to be added to the mosaic of tradition. As Rivka Ulmer rightly observes, paraphrasing Ernst Cassirer, "The synthesis obtained from the data that one experiences adds a new attribute to the subject that one investigates."[591]

Moreover, text editing is a necessary hermeneutic tool for students and scholars of Jewish studies. Every student should be introduced to the world of text-critical analysis and avoid considering any edition as a revelation from Sinai. Or rather, he or she should consider the text as written revelation, as *Torah she-bikhtav*, and apply to it the same rules applicable to the written tradition, namely that the text can be meaningful only by the intervention of a reader/interpreter. As the Midrash Sifra states it with an ironic dictum of Rabbi Yishmael, quoting Rabbi Eliezer:

> Rabbi Yishmaʻel says: You say to the text (*katuv*): be silent until I explain you!
> (א"ל רבי ישמעאל הרי את אומר לכתוב שתוק עד שאדרוש!)[592].

The silence of the text is the indispensable premise for revelation to happen through the commentary.

---

[591] Rivka Ulmer, "Creating Rabbinic texts: Moving from a Synoptic to a Critical Edition of Pesiqta Rabbati," in *Recent Developments in Midrash Research: Proceedings of the 2002 and 2003 SBL Consultation on Midrash*, ed. Lieve M. Teugels and Rivka Ulmer (New Jersey: Gorgias, 2005): 132.

[592] Sifra, Tazria, par. 5 Negaim 13:2. On the irony of this dictum, see Günter Stemberger, *Der Talmud. Einführung, Texte, Erläuterungen* (Munich: Beck, 1982): 67.

13 On Some Greek Loanwords in Aquila's Translation of the Bible

In the words of Lester Grabbe, Aquila's translation is a veritable mirror of rabbinic exegesis.[593] This mirror reflects Aquila of Sinope (2nd century CE) translation, not only according to Origen's *Hexapla* (3rd century CE) and other testimonies, but most particularly according to the rabbinic exegetical literature. For it is the hermeneutic task of his "translations," transmitted in rabbinic literature with the formula *tirgem 'aqilas*, "as Aquilas translates," to render a difficult term, name, expression in the language of Japheth, meaning Greek. That is also the origin of Aquila's translations in rabbinic transmission. These *targumim* can be divided into three groups, Greek, Hebrew and Aramaic. I will deal here solely with some of Aquila's Greek "targumata," without dwelling on the philological and text-critical analysis, readily available elsewhere.[594]

13.1 Leviticus 23:24 and the Feast of Tabernacles

In the context of the Feast of Tabernacles (*Sukkot*), the biblical text speaks of *peri 'eṣ hadar* (Leviticus 23:24: "... and you shall take on the first day the *fruit of a splendid tree*, branches of palm trees and boughs of leafy trees ..." The problem of the Midrash is the identification of the vague description of the *fruit of a splendid tree*. To make the text more precise, Aquila translated the word *hadar* with the Greek word *hydōr*. As noted in the Jerusalem Talmud, Sukka 3:5 [53d]):

> Rabbi Tanuma said: Aquila translated *hadar* (with the Greek word) *hydōr* [water]. [It means] a tree which grows at waters [or, on the surface of waters, *al pene mayim*].

The Yerushalmi Gemara transmits a detailed discussion on the meaning of *hadar*, referring to possible identifications with pomegranate (and carob tree). According to the redactor of the text, only the *etrog* (*citrus fruits*) has a chance of acceptance because the tree and the fruit are beautiful (*hadar* as magnificent). The tradition of the translation of Aquila in this context cannot be interpreted as a confirmation of the rabbinic discussion, because the *etrog* does not grow at or on the surface of water. According to Josephus, it was called "the

---

593 Lester L. Grabbe, "Aquila's Translation and Rabbinic Exegesis," *Journal of Jewish Studies* 33 (1982): 527–536.
594 See especially Veltri, *Gegenwart der Tradition* (Leiden: Brill, 2002), 83–92.

fruit of the Persian-tree," and probably should be identified with Theophrastus' (c. 371–c. 287 BCE) botanic definition of a plant which grew in Persia and Media, identified by botanists as *citrus medica*.[595] This botanical discussion on the origin and spreading of citrus fruits cannot resolve the question as to why Aquila and some other Midrashic texts speak of water.

In my view, the translation of Aquila has nothing to do with *etrog*, which does not grow near water ("willow" would be preferable!). But it is a typical Midrashic method to extract meaning from an apparently meaningless or indistinct and ambiguous text. To refer to water means only to stress a very important element of the Feast of Tabernacles, the water in the ceremony of water-drawing, which according to Tosefta, Sukkah 3:3–13 should be associated with the primeval waters of Creation, and especially the miraculous well that accompanied the Israelites in their wanderings (*dar*) in the desert.[596] The tree which dwells on the surface of the water is nothing other than Israel itself. In this exegetical conclusion, Aquila uses a Talmudic procedure of an implicit *al tiqre* ("do not read in that way but rather in this way"), gaining the meaning from a foreign language, likewise a widespread philological practice. In contradistinction to Aquila of the rabbinic schools, the Aquila of the Hexapla translated the term *hadar* without exegetical mastery as *diaprepeia*, meaning "magnificence."

13.2 Ezekiel 16:10 on Dressing

Rabbinic exegesis sees a difficulty in Ezekiel 16:10: We read in Shir ha-Shirim Rabbah 4:11:

> "I clothed you with an embroidered dress (*riqmah*)" (Ezekiel 16:10). Rabbi Simay said: *porfyra*. Aquila translated: *ipliqt'*.

The first interpretation, transmitted in the name of Rabbi Simay is clear: *riqmah* means "purple." Aquila's translation is obscure in the transcription into Greek. Some authors try to interpret '*ipliqt*' as *poikilta* ("variegated, embroidered"), because this is Aquila's translation in the Hexapla. The Septuagint always translated the root *rqm* with the root *poikilt* (see Exodus 35:35; 37:21; and Judges 5:30). According to the parallel tradition in Ekha Rabbati 1:1 (ed. Buber 21b),

---

[595] *Historia plantarum* IV,4:2 f., quoted in this context by Håkan Ulfgard, *The Story of Sukkot* (Tübingen: Mohr, 1998), 85.
[596] Note also *al pne ha-mayim* in Genesis. Ulfgard, *The Story*, p. 273.

we have to read *piquliṭ*. Ekha Rabbati 1:1 (first edition) reads '*pqlṭurin pliqṭ*', although attributing the translation to Onkelos. I do not think that Aquila took his translation from the Septuagint, although Aquila of the Hexapla likely used that source. I prefer to identify '*pqlṭurin pliqṭ*' simply as *epikalyptērion plēkton*, a plaited covering. As Samuel Krauss noted,[597] a peculiarity of Aquila is to give difficult terms a double possibility, an option Aquila likely chose here as well. The interesting question therefore is why Rabbi Simay is introduced by "say" (*amar*), Aquila on the other hand by *tirgem*, although both of them translated the word into Greek. The language is not important when a pupil renders the teaching of a rabbi into the Targum, or when a student thus mediates the teaching of a master.

13.3 Ezekiel 23:43 on Prostitution

We read in Wa-yiqra Rabbah 33:6:

> And I said about the one worn out by adultery (Ezekiel 23:43). What is the meaning of *lblh*? Aquila translated: "*palaiai pornēi*" which means "worn-out adulteress."[598]

The word *lblh* is very difficult for modern exegesis as well. Aquila derives it from *blh*, in the meaning of "worn," translating correspondingly. A similar tradition can also be found in the Targum to Ezekiel. However, the Hexapla fragment of Aquila reads quite differently in lexical terms, although semantically similar: *tou katatripsai moicheias* ("of the worn-out prostitute"). Alec Silverstone's explanation, according to which Aquila's reading from the Hexapla was really composed by his contemporaries Symmachus or Theodotion, seems rather far-fetched.[599] Silverstone tries to solve a problem by creating another. The interesting point here is that the Midrash translates the Greek translation back into Aramaic as if the redactor did not think his readers could understand Greek. It is my supposition here that in mentioning the Greek translations of Aquila, the redactor seeks to refer to an authority from a past tradition.

---

[597] Samuel Krauss, "Akylas, der Proselyt," in *Festschrift zum achtzigsten Geburtstage Moritz Steinschneider's* (Leipzig: Harrassowitz, 1896), 148–163.
[598] The explanation is in Aramaic.
[599] Alec Eli Silverstone, *Aquila and Onkelos* (Manchester: Manchester University Press, 1931), 44.

13.4 Psalm 48 (47):15 and the Eternal World

A further difficult word from the Psalms is addressed in the Palestinian Talmud: '*lmt*

> For this is God our God for ever and ever: he will be our guide 'lmwt (Psalm 48:15). (The expression has to be understood) with *alimut*, skilfullness; '*lmwt* (means) like young women ('*alamot*). Aquila translated *athanasia*, a world in which there is no death. And the righteous point with the finger and say: *For this God is our God for ever and ever. He will he will be our guide* in the worlds. He will guide us in this world and he will guide us in the future world.[600]

That is a beautiful example of a Talmudic academy with different approaches for explaining a difficult expression from the biblical text. The first interpretation vocalises the text in contrast with the Masoretic reading '*alimut*, from '*elem* (vigorous, skillful), the second opinion prefers the vocalisation '*alamot*, from '*almah* (young girl), perhaps indirectly referring to Psalms 68:26 (Hebrew): "with them are the maidens playing tambourines." Aquila interprets it as '*al mawet*, a world in which there is no death." The *ṣaddiqim* opt for the other solution, to read '*olamot*, the two worlds. Friedman argues that Aquila must have read '*l mwt* ("Do not die!").[601] Silverstone considers the change unnecessary, and adds that "Aquila's rendering is compatible with either ['*alimut*, for him, "youthfulness," and '*olamot*, "worlds"], for immortality may be taken to mean perpetual youth, or may refer to the immortality in the next world."[602] Here we have four different interpretations, all possible. Aquila chooses to break the word into two segments, '*al mawet*' which literally means "over the death," that is, *a*-thanasia: *he will be our guide over/beside the death*.

An intriguing question that arises here is why does the redactor explain the Greek word? The reason could be that the reader does not understand what *a-thanasia* is, meaning immortality. If so, there is no reason to mention and explain what no one can understand immediately – for this contradicts the logic of understanding in translating. I believe the real reason lies elsewhere: *a-thanasia*, (im-mortality) offers the same play with words also presumed for '*lmwt*, or vice versa. This confirms the philological tendency of his method of translation.

---

[600] Jerusalem Talmud, Megillah 2:4 (73b); see also Jerusalem Talmud, Moed Qatan 3:7 (83b). English translation from Silverstone, *Aquila*, 45 with some changes of mine.
[601] Meir Friedmann, *Onkelos und Akylas* (Vienna: Lippe, 1896), 44.
[602] Silverstone, *Aquila*, 45.

13.5 Proverbs 18:21 and Rhetorical Figures

The Midrash Wa-yiqra Rabbah 33:1 transmits another Greek interpretation of Aquila in reference to Proverbs 18:21:

> *Death and life are in the power of the tongue* (Proverbs 18:2). Aquila translated: *mystrw mkirin*, death on the one side and life on the other".

The usual interpretation of these two Greek words is *mystron machairion*, "spoon and knife," which, in the opinion of Friderichus Field, are nonsensical (or, in the original Latin, "absurda et ridicula").[603] Silverstone tries to justify it by arguing that the "spoon and knife as symbolical of life and death is based on some midrash current in his day."[604] These attempts to explain the Greek words do not take into consideration the Hebrew text which follows the Hebrew letters: death on the one side (*mi-kan*) and life on the other (*mi-kan*). As I see it, the local preposition *mi-kan* presupposes *one* object and not two. Thus, the composition can be identified as *meso/mesaiteriō (tēs) machairas /* in the middle point of a sword. The pictures call to mind the rhetorical figure of the word as a sword with two tasks: to put to death or to produce life (see, for example, *Revelation* 1:16: "In his right hand he held seven stars, and out of his mouth came a sharp double-edged sword"). The first sword is used for war, the second by the surgeon.

13.6 Proverbs 25:11 on Rhetoric

The Midrash Bereshit Rabbah 93:3 transmits an interpretation of Aquila in relation to Proverbs 25:11:

> A word aptly spoken is like apples of gold in *maskiyyot* of silver (Proverbs 25:11). Aquila translated: apples of gold in a vessel/cup (*diskarion*) of silver.

The entire translation by Aquila is in Aramaic except for the one Greek word. The translation of Aquila *diskarion* as "cup, vessel" raises some problems because that is not the equivalent of *maskiyyot*, which means an object (for example, the wall) embellished with pictures or of engraved metal (see, for example,

---

603 Friderichus Field, ed., *Origenis Hexaplorum quae supersunt sive veterum interpretum Graecorum in totum vetus testamentum fragmenta*, vol. 1–2 (Oxford: Clarendom, 1875, reprint Hildesheim: Olms, 1964): *Prolegomena*, xvii.
604 Silverstone, *Aquila*, 47.

Ezekiel 8:12). Silverstone is right to stress that "ornamental object" is the meaning of *maskit*, but by no means the explanation of *diskarion*, probably coined based on Latin discus. According to Epiphanius of Salamis, *diskarion* was the common word for "cup" and not an engraved cup.[605] The more simple explanation is that *diskarion* was a common word for cup in Latin and Greek, but probably not for Jews who associated something else with an engraved cup. We read in several rabbinic texts that a *diskarion* (or Lat. *discus*) was rejected as a gift by rabbis due to the danger of idolatry.[606] This is only possible if the image of a divinity or an idolatrous motto, etc. was engraved on the disk. With his translation, Aquila explains to his reader (hearer) what the biblical text means: apples of gold in an engraved cup of silver, and that is probably also the meaning of Proverbs 25:11.

13.7 Esther 1:6 on Colours

In reference to Esther 1:6, Aquila addresses two difficult words, which are *hapax legomena* in the Bible, in Midrash Esther Rabbah 2:7:

> The garden had hangings of white and blue linen (Esther 1:6).[607] Aquila translated *aerinon karpasinon* [light blue, fine linen or flax]. Rabbi Bini said: *iantinon* [violet-coloured].

The difficulty of a *hapax legomenon* obviously lies in the nature of it, i.e., its uniqueness in the vocabulary or literary corpus. The common tool also in use today is to arrive at the meaning by proceeding from linguistically and semantically related lexemes in other languages, or to change one letter as a possible aid. And such is the case with *ḥur/ḥor* the biblical text interpreted by Aquila as or. Therefore, he reads *ḥor* in the Greek language as *aer* (air). For the second word, there is no difficulty because the Greek equivalent is of Semitic origin.[608] Rabbi Bini's bid to translate is difficult to follow because there is no definite manuscript tradition and it remains solely an attempt.

---

[605] Epiphanius, *De Mensuris et Ponderibus* 86:8: *toublion to en tē synetēiai legomenon diskarion*.
[606] Bereshit Rabba 78:12; Jerusalem Talmud, 'Avodah Zarah 1:1 (39b); see Saul Lieberman, *Texts and Studies* (New York: Ktav, 1974), 143; Gerald Blidstein, "A Roman Gift of Strenae to the Patriarch Judah II," *Israel Exploration Journal* 22 (1972): 150–152. See above, p. 77.
[607] This is the new common International English translation without regard to the Midrash.
[608] This in accordance with the common Hebrew vocabulary.

14 The Septuagint in Disgrace[609]

According to ancient Christian sources, the Greek translation of the Torah, the so-called *Septuagint*, was a bone of contention between the Church fathers and the rabbis. Christian authors believed that the Septuagint was divinely inspired, just as God had inspired Moses to write down the Torah on Mt. Sinai. In a similar way, seventy-two or seventy translators (depending on the source) assembled near the library in Alexandria, and provided a perfect reproduction of the Hebrew biblical text.[610] Rabbinic Judaism mentions only some *Hebrew* "translations" or texts of the "Torah for the King Ptolemy" (*Talmai* in Hebrew) and a story on these translations transmitted by Babylonian sources. In the post-Talmudic tractates *Sefer Torah* and *Soferim*, we have the earliest attestation of direct criticism of the Septuagint. In this chapter, I shall analyse the Talmudic stories about the Septuagint and the medieval sources, seeking to ascertain their source and context.

14.1 Talmudic Stories and Post-Talmudic Developments

Babylonian rabbinic authorities show some familiarity with the legend of the Septuagint in the story of the translation in Babylonian Talmud, Megillah 9a–b (see also Soferim 1:7):[611]

---

[609] This chapter is based on my studies on the traditions and the legend of the Septuagint in rabbinic and medieval Judaism, incorporating some changes. Many of the sources and the arguments are to be found in Veltri, *Eine Tora für den König Talmai* (Tübingen: Mohr Siebeck 1994). On the stories of the Septuagint in the Middle Ages, see my earlier studies: "Tolomeo Filadelfo, emulo di Pisistrato. Alcune note su leggende antiche di biblioteche, edizioni e traduzioni," Laurentianum 32 (1991): 146–166; "Der Fasttag in Erinnerung an die Entstehung der Septuaginta und die Megillat Taanit Batra," Frankfurter Judaistische Beiträge 19 (1991–1992), 63–71; "Die Entstehung der LXX in der jüdisch-mittelalterlichen Historiographie. Rezeption des Josephus und Einfluß christlicher Quellen," *Laurentianum* 33 (1992): 89–116.

[610] Sources of the legend and commentary now in G. Veltri, *Libraries, Translations, and "Canonic" Texts: The Septuagint, Aquila, and Ben Sira in Jewish and Christian Tradition* (Leiden and Boston: Brill, 2006). See especially the first chapter for the Jewish-Hellenistic and Christian sources. In 2006, David J. Wasserstein published his father's posthumous work: Abraham Wasserstein, *The Legend of the Septuagint: From Classical Antiquity to Today* (Cambridge: Cambridge University Press, 2006).

[611] Soferim is a later tractate which depends on Talmudic material existing at the time of the writer; see Veltri, *Eine Tora*, 236–239.

> The permission of our teachers to write in Greek is extended only to the Pentateuch because of the events with the King Ptolemy. It is taught there: It so came to pass that King Ptolemy summoned seventy-two Elders and put them in seventy-two houses without communicating to them why he had summoned them. He went to everyone separately, saying to them: write out for me the Torah of Moses, our teacher. The Holy one, blessed be He, granted knowledge to the heart of every one and they agreed with each other in their judgement. They wrote for him: [here the changed verses follow].

The number and the separation of the Elders, the houses (or cells) and the intervention of God to inspire either the "writing" or the translation of the Pentateuch, the royal attempt to avoid direct agreement arranged among the elders/translators, are all basic elements in the *Christian* version of the legend of the Septuagint. Although this tradition is transmitted as a *baraita* (implying a Mishnah-like Palestinian origin), there is no doubt that it is a product of the Babylonian academies, since no Palestinian source before the Babylonian Talmud is concerned with the story of the Seventy-two or Seventy. They speak only of "changes for King Ptolemy/Talmai" in the form of lists or individual verses, but no mention is made of the circumstances of the translation. It can be supposed that Babylonian teachers read the legend of the Septuagint in the edition of Epiphanius of Salamis (c. 310/20–403 CE). This is the only patristic source which collected all the elements the rabbis needed, with the notable exception of the number, because he speaks of 36 cells, not 72. The fact that the Babylonian rabbis privileged the number 72 is fully understandable because of the gematria of the Hebrew name of Greece: יוון/Yewwan, *yud + waw + waw + nun*, or, 10 + 6 + 6 + 50 = 72. Epiphanius is of the opinion that divine "inspiration" produced the agreement among the translators in making *changes* in the text, precisely the changes of the Babylonian teachers. At any rate, a Christian influence on the Gemara is undeniable.

The sources examined so far are either positive or neutral in regard to the evaluation of the circumstances of the translation of the Torah into Greek. However, there are two other rabbinic sources which are definitely negative in judging the process of translation of the Septuagint and its aftermath. We read in the Talmudic minor tractate Soferim 1:7:

> The text of the Torah must not be written in [Old] Hebrew or in Aramaic, or in Median or Greek. The Scripture [*ktav*] in every language and every writing may only be recited if it was written in Assyrian script.
>
> It came to pass that five elders wrote the Torah for the King Ptolemy. This day was as ominous for Israel as the day when the golden calf was made. For the Torah could not be adequately translated.
>
> Once again it happened that the King Ptolemy summoned seventy-two Elders and put them in seventy-two houses without communicating to them why he had summoned them. He went to everyone separately, saying to them: write out for me the Torah of

Moses, our teacher. The Holy one, blessed be He, granted knowledge to the heart of every one and they agreed with each other in their judgement. Each person wrote a Torah for him in which they changed thirteen passages [here the changed verses follow].

A very similar tradition is transmitted in Sefer Torah 1:6:

> The text of the scroll of the Torah must not be written in [old] Hebrew, or in Elamitic, or in Median, or Greek. Seventy elders wrote the whole Torah in Greek for King Ptolemy and that day was as ominous for Israel as the day when the Israelites made the golden calf. For the Torah could not be adequately translated. They changed thirteen passages [here the changed verses follow].

There is no doubt that Soferim, Sefer Torah and Babylonian Talmud Megillah follow the same tradition, only the accents are different, although they seem to speak of two different translations. The negative aspects of translating are emphasised only by the Soferim (first translation) and Sefer Torah. The Babylonian Talmud is openly positive in following the Halakhah of the Mishnah, which permits the Greek letters (and language).

The story of the two translations reported by tractate Soferim has occupied the attention of Jewish scholars since the Renaissance. According to the Italian humanist Azariah de' Rossi (1513/14–1578), the negative report refers to the translation of Aquila, Symmachus and Theodotion.[612] Abraham Geiger was of the opinion that the editor of *Soferim* was confused and fused the positive report of the Babylonian Talmud with the negative story of Sefer Torah.[613] Joel Müller (1827–1895), the editor of Massekhet Soferim, considers both translations as referring to one and the same translation; however, the negative report on the Torah of the five translators goes back in his opinion to a later period under the negative influence of Megillat Ta'anit Batra (see below).[614] Manuel Joël (1826–1890) distinguishes between a first translation of the seventy-two and a later translation by the five translators at the time of Trajan or Hadrian

---

612 Azariah de' Rossi, *Sefer Me'or 'Enayim*, ed. Dawîd Cassel, 3 vols. (Vilnius: Romm, 1864–1866, reprint, Jerusalem: Makor, 1970), chapt. 8, vol. 1:136. See the translation in Azariah de' Rossi, *The Light of the Eyes*, translated by Joanna Weinberg (New Haven and London: Yale University Press, 2001), 172.
613 Abraham Geiger, *Urschrift und Uebersetzungen der Bibel in ihrer Abhängigkeit von der innern Entwickelung des Judenthums* (Breslau: Hainauer, 1857), 419–420 and 441. According to Frankel, the report of the five translators is fictitious. See Zacharias Frankel, *Vorstudien zu der Septuaginta* (Leipzig: Vogel, 1841), 61, note k.
614 Joel Müller, ed., *Masechet Soferim: Der Tractat der Schreiber, eine Einleitung in das Studium der althebräischen Graphik, der Masora und der altjüdischen Liturgie, nach Handschriften herausgegeben und kommentiert* (Leipzig: Hinrichs, 1878), 12.

(2nd century CE), since the first was considered a danger for Israel equal to that provoked by the episode of the golden calf.[615]

The thesis of a translation made by five translators had no lasting influence in modern scholarship. The number five can be explained on the basis of other considerations: a mistake in the manuscript (Berliner), an indirect or direct reference to the five books of the Torah (Frankel, Graetz, Aptowitzer, Hadas), or as an allusion to the fifth column of the Hexapla of Origen (Joël).[616]

The number of translators oscillates in Jewish and Christian sources between seventy (*Sefer Torah* and *Soferim*, manuscript Halberstamm), seventy-two (Babylonian Talmud, Megillah 9a–b), and five (Sefer Torah, Soferim and Avot de-Rabbi Natan, ed. B 37).[617] An explanation for Aristeas's report is surely the number of the tribes, while Josephus gives seventy beside the traditional seventy-two. I think that gematria may also have played a role. The number seventy refers to the elders of Exodus. The number five can also be explained on the basis of the following reasons: influence of Avot de-Rabbi Natan (version B, 37), provided that this does not depend on the same source; allusion to the "five Elders" in Mishnah Eruvim 3:4, Babylonian Talmud, Rosh Ha-Shanah 15a and Tosefta Sheviit 4:21;[618] and finally a reference to the tradition of the five sages charged by Moses to restore the Bible after its destruction by fire (4 Ezra 14), a very intriguing reference if we suppose that the legend of Ezra influenced the legend of the Septuagint.[619] In my opinion, the number five is

---

615 Manuel Joël, *Blicke in die Religionsgeschichte zu Anfang des zweiten christlichen Jahrhunderts* vol. 1 (Breslau: Schottlaender, 1880), 3.

616 Abraham Berliner, *Targum Onkelos: Einleitung und Register* (Frankfurt am Main: Kauffmann, 1884), 79; Zacharias Frankel, *Über den Einfluß der palästinischen Exegese auf die alexandrinische Hermeneuthik* (Leipzig: Barth, 1851), 228–231; Heinrich Graetz, *Geschichte der Juden von den ältesten Zeiten bis auf die Gegenwart*, vol. 3/2 (Leipzig: Leiner, 1906), 579; Avigdor/Viktor Aptowitzer, "Die rabbinischen Berichte über die Entstehung der Septuaginta," *Ha-Kedem* 2 (1908): 120; Moses Hadas, *Aristeas to Philocrates* (New York: Harper, 1951), 81; Joël, *Blicke in die Religionsgeschichte*, vol. 1, 4.

617 The number of translators was also discussed in Jewish-Hellenistic and Christian literature. See Moritz Steinschneider, "Die kanonische Zahl der muhammedanischen Secten und die Symbolik der Zahl 70–73, aus jüdischen und muhammedanisch Quellen nachgewiesen," *Zeitschrift der deutschen morgenländischen Gesellschaft* 4 (1850): 145–170; Steinschneider, "Nachtrag," *Zeitschrift der deutschen morgenländischen Gesellschaft* 57 (1903): 474–507; Bruce M. Metzger, "Seventy or seventy-two disciples," *New Testament Studies* 6 (1959–60): 319–321; Gilles Dorival, "La Bible de la Septante: 70 ou 72 traducteurs?" in *Tradition of the text: Studies offered to D[ominique]. Barthélemy in celebration of his seventieth birthday*, ed. G. J. Norton, S. Pisano (Fribourg, Göttingen, 1991), 45–62.

618 See Berliner, *Targum Okelos*, vol. 2: 78, note 2.

619 See chapter 1.3 of Veltri, *Libraries, Translations, and "Canonic" Texts*.

not a historical reference to a new translation different from the Torah for King Ptolemy but only a literary clue for distinguishing two different traditions, one negative and the other positive.

The only constant in reports on the "Septuagint" is the information about the aim of the translation: *for* Ptolemy according to rabbinic sources, *for* the royal library of Alexandria according to Jewish-Hellenistic and Christian literature. In Jewish-Hellenistic tradition, the king plays a role as a patron and lover of Jewish wisdom, while in the Christian tradition he emerges rather as an unwilling initiator of the Christian religion. In the Jewish tradition, in the main Palestinian in origin, King Ptolemy is neither the initiator nor the mentor/patron, but rather the addressee of the Torah, and that is an intriguing peculiarity. For the tradition of a Torah for the king is not new in rabbinic sources, but refers to Deuteronomy 17:18: "When he takes the throne of his kingdom, he is to write for himself on a scroll a copy of this law, taken from that of the priests, who are Levites." *Katav lo* (so the Masoretic text) can either mean that he should write it for himself, or that someone else should write it out for him.[620] That is also the explanation of the Jerusalem Talmud, Sanhedrin 2:4 (20c): "they wrote for him (means) in his name." According to Sifre Devarim, the priests correct the copy of the king, while the Jerusalem Talmud, Sanhedrin 2:4 (20c) quoted above adds that the Sanhedrin should correct the copy on the basis of the scroll of the Temple court. In this context, it is obvious that the text of Deuteronomy 17:18 is read in a different way: instead of *mishneh torah*, they understand *meshanneh torah* ("he changes the Torah") or even *meshunnah torah* ("an altered Torah"). And this tradition is also present in rabbinic tradition, expressing a change in the Torah (perhaps in the messianic era). It is a possible reference to the changes in the Torah beginning in Ezra's time.[621]

If interpreted in terms of this logic, the rabbinic interpretation of the Septuagint as Torah for King Ptolemy suggests a deconstruction of meaning in the history of hermeneutics: the high value of this translation lies in its nature as a *written* (*ketav*) alteration of the Torah of Moses, an alteration implemented by the Priests or by the Sanhedrin. This is only the copy for royal needs. Of course, in this view the Septuagint cannot be a liturgical and didactical document: it is solely a Torah for the king's use, so that he may learn from it.

Returning to the relation of Sefer Torah and Soferim (first report) to the mishnaic and Talmudic Halakhah, it is important to note that both tractates

---

620 See M. A. Friedman, "u-katevu lo, ose lo ktav [Hebrew, He writes, He makes a Writ]," *Sinai* 84 (1979): 177–179.
621 See Jerusalem Talmu , Megillah 11 (71b); Tosefta, Sanhedrin 4:7–8; Babylonian Talmud, Sanhedrin 21b–22a.

should be dated to a time *after* the Talmudic period, because they prohibit what the Talmud allows, via the literary distortion of the meaning taken from the Talmud. Neither the Soferim nor Sefer Torah distinguish clearly between writing and language. They confuse the Halakkah they are quoting. The redactor of Soferim affirms that it is prohibited to write in Old Ivrit (Hebrew), Median, or Greek. If a person has written in other languages, he could recite from them in the liturgy only if they are written in Assyrian script (called *ashshurit*).

What is the aim of this Halakhah, the script or the language? The question is relevant, because from the time of the Mishnah until at least Maimonides, there was a spirited discussion on whether other alphabets were suitable for liturgy.[622] In the Middle Ages, the opinion gained acceptance that in the time of the Mishnah, first only the Greek alphabet, not the Greek language, was allowed; later it was replaced by the Assyrian square characters.[623]

The clash between the premise (no other *alphabet* is permitted) and the conclusion (reading in other *languages*) is also confirmed by the sentence: "If one wrote it (*katav*) in every language and every form of writing one may recite it only if it was written (*ketuvah*) in Assyrian script." The feminine *ketuvah* is a valuable reference to the fact that the redactor of the scribe's tractate is quoting from earlier texts: the expression "only if it was written (*ketuvah!*) in Assyrian writing" originates from the reading of the Megillat Ester, which according to the Mishnah (Megillah 2:1; cf. Babylonian Talmud, Shabbat 115a; Megillah 18a) has to be written in Assyrian characters and recited in the Hebrew language. The redactor of Soferim deconstructs the original context and applies and extends a ban on other scripts for the Megillah to the Torah, although without specifying whether he opts for Assyrian characters or for the Hebrew language. This confusion proves that he collects texts but has little interest in really understanding them.

The distortion of earlier halakhot can also be observed in the case of *Sefer Torah* if the redactors maintain: "Seventy elders wrote (*katevu*) the whole Torah in Greek for the king Ptolemy and that day was as ominous for Israel as the day when the Israelites made the golden calf. For the Torah could not be adequately translated (*tirgem*)." The sentence *she-lo' hayetah ha-torah yekholah le-targem kol ṣorkhah* is a quotation from Jerusalem Talmud, Megillah 1:11 (71c)

---

[622] See Maimonides, Hilkot Tefillin 1:19, in *Mishneh Torah: The Book of Adoration*, ed. Moses Hyamson (Jerusalem: Boys Town, 1965), 121a.

[623] See the fragment published by Elkan N. Adler, "An Eleventh Century Introduction to the Hebrew Bible: Being a Fragment from the Sepher ha-Ittim of Rabi Judah ben Barzilai of Barcelona," *Jewish Quarterly Review* 9 (1897): 669–716 and Rabbi Me'iri, *Beyt ha-beḥiral 'al masekhet megillah*, ed. Moses Hersler (Jerusalem, 1967–1968), 35–36.

with the omission of *ella yevvanit* ("with the exception of Greek"). In the Jerusalem Talmud, the Halakhah states that only the Greek language is suitable for the translation (as targum), while the redactor of Sefer Torah omits the language and extrapolates an absolute ban on all languages from this sentence. The comparison with the golden calf is also a quotation from earlier rabbinic traditions, namely from the Jerusalem Talmud, Shabbat 1:4 (3c) and Babylonian Talmud, Shabbat 17a, where the comparison with the execrable day refers to the (historical?) dispute between the schools of the Hillelites and Shammaites, which ended in violence. The golden calf here symbolises the division between two rabbinic schools and the consequences of that division.

It is not clear what the redactor of Sefer Torah was aiming at when comparing the Septuagint translation to the golden calf. But if we think that according to Pesiqta Rabbati § 5 (see below), the written Torah is an example of a discussion between the nations of the world which translated the Torah and read it in Greek, and Israel, we can perhaps conclude that what is important here is the claim to possession of the written Torah. However, there too the texts are not clear enough to spell out the object of the controversy: the written or the oral Torah, the writing (*ketav*) or the liturgical, didactic translation (*targum*)? In any event, the negative stories and reports on the Septuagint should be placed in a later post-Talmudic period when a revival of Hebrew took place, accompanied by dangers to one's identity because of Christian or Gnostic adoption of the Jewish Torah.

The oft-quoted Midrash in the context of the adoption of the Septuagint is Pesikta Rabbati § 5 (ed. Friedman, 14b):

> Rabbi Judah, pupil of Rabbi Shalom said: Moses prayed [God] to have the Mishnah in writing. The Holy one, blessed be He, predicted that in the future the nations of the world would translate the Torah and recite it in Greek and make it known: 'They [the Jews] are not Israel.' The Holy one, blessed be He, said to him: "Oh Moses: one day the nations will say: 'We are the sons of God'. Israel will answer: 'We are the sons of God.' And this will hold the scales even.
>
> The Holy one, blessed be He, said to the nations: "Why do you claim that you are my sons? I know only that my son is the one who owns my secrets" [word in Greek: *misṭerin*]. The nations answer him: 'What are your secrets'? He says to him: 'The Mishnah.'

The message of the Midrash is unambiguous: The Mishnah constitutes the *discrimen*, the *only* difference, between Israel and the nations of the world. The historical circumstances into which this tradition should be placed remain unclear. The common opinion views this text in relation to the so-called Jewish-Christian controversy because of the Christian claim to be the *verus Israel*.[624]

---

[624] See the discussion in George F. Moore, *Judaism in the First Centuries of the Christian Era*, 3 vols. (Cambridge, Mass.: Harvard University Press, 1927–30), vol. 2:68, footnote 6; Dominique

Some scholars even see a discrediting of the Greek Torah in this text.[625] I cannot recognise any blame or reproof of the Septuagint here. On the contrary, look first at the liturgical terminology of the text: the nations of the world would translate (in the meaning of *targum*) and recite the text in Greek.[626] *Qara'* and *tirgem* are Jewish liturgical technical terms for the synagogue service (see Mishnah, Megillah 4). Second, after the appropriation of the written Torah by the nations of the world, the scales are even, meaning that the claim of the nations to base their right in the giving of the Torah is upheld. But that is not enough. It was solely the Mishnah as a secret doctrine[627] that authorised the Jewish people to claim the status of "son[s] of God." If we recall here what was stated with reference to Hilarius – according to whom the Seventy are "authorities" because they possess a particular hidden doctrine in addition to the written law (*praeter scientiam legis*) and incorporated in the written text – we can fully understand the focus of the Midrash. Moreover, the attempts to canonise the Septuagint as a *synolon* (the whole) of oral and written Torah do not give "the Gentiles" the right to consider themselves sons of God, because the specific difference lies in the Mishnah, transmitted orally.

To conclude the first part: although recent studies try to offer a different vision of the "negative" attitude toward the Septuagint in old rabbinic texts by

---

Barthélemy, "L'Ancien Testament a mûri à Alexandrie," *Theologische Zeitschrift* 21 (1965): 364–365; repr. in *Études d'histoire du texte de l'Ancien Testament* (Fribourg, Göttingen: Éditions universitaires; Vandenhoeck & Ruprecht, 1978), 133–134; see further Julius Bergmann, *Jüdische Apologetik* (Berlin: Reimer, 1908), 61; Ephraim E. Urbach, "Halakha we-nevu'a," *Tarbiz* 18 (1946–1947): 6–7, footnote 50; Urbach, *The Sages: Their Concepts and Beliefs* (Jerusalem: Magnes Press of the Hebrew University, 1979), 305–306; Marcel Simon, *Verus Israel: Étude sur les relations entre Chrétiens et Juifs dans l'empire romain (135–425)*, (Paris: Boccard, 1964), 225; Leo Baeck, "Haggadah and Christian doctrine," *Hebrew Union College Annual* 23/1 (1950–1951): 557–558; Marcel Simon, "La Bible dans les premières controverses entre Juifs et Chrétiens," in *Le monde grec ancien et la Bible*, ed. Claude Mondésert (Paris: Beauchesne, 1985), 111. But see also Johann Maier, *Jüdische Auseinandersetzung mit dem Christentum in der Antike* (Darmstadt: Buchgesellschaft, 1982), 184–185.

625 So Nicholas de Lange: "It is the purpose of such apologetic to discredit the Greek version of the Bible at the same time as bestowing a spurious respectability on the Rabbinic traditions. The Rabbis persistently deprecated the translation of the Bible into Greek." Nicholas de Lange, *Origen and the Jews: Studies in Jewish-Christian Relations in Third-Century Palestine* (Cambridge: Cambridge University Press, 1977), 50.

626 On the differerence between *likhtov bilshon* and *letargem*, see chapter 3 of Veltri, *Libraries, Translations, and "Canonic" Texts*.

627 Jerusalem Talmud, Pe'a 2:6 (17a/43–50) and Jerusalem Talmud, Hagiga 1:8 (76d/17–24). On this terminology, see Gerd A. Wewers, *Geheimnis und Geheimhaltung im rabbinischen Judentum* (Berlin and New York: De Gruyter, 1975), 87–90.

dating Sefer Torah and Soferim to the 3rd century,[628] both must in my view date from the post-Amoraic period, because they confused the material of the preceding tradition. We do not have any evidence of an Amoraic verdict against the translators and their product.

In addition to this, the rabbis contextualised the literary motif "Torah for King *Talmai*" in a favorable exegetical tradition, making the king a special *talmid*, as a later Midrash states: "This is one of the passages which the Elders of Israel changed for [K]ing Ptolemy. They wrote for him: *Elohim bara' bereshit* ("God created in the beginning"). For he [the King] did not have enough knowledge to reflect on the Midrash of the Torah (Leqaḥ Ṭov to Gen 1:1)."

Virtually no scholar has noted that the "changes for the king" are nothing but a rabbinic paradigm referent to the "changed Torah for the king" (*mishneh Torah*) of Deuteronomistic tradition and the main question in the evaluation of the Septuagint is the *written* character of the translation. The *written* translation could be interpreted as a substitute for the Hebrew original. This was the real problem.

14.2 Medieval reception and the Megillat Ta'anit Batra

Two opposite tendencies run through the Middle Ages: praise and contempt for the undertaking of the Septuagint. The positive attitude to the Greek Torah originates from Hellenistic Jewish sources (Josephus) as well as from Christian sources.[629]

The translation of the Greek Torah was praised in the Byzantine world. The anonymous translator or adaptor of Josephus in the *Sefer Yosippon* records the event of the translation without adding any negative connotation.[630] Its Arabic and Ethiopian versions, in a short summary of episodes, also display no negative attitude.[631] In addition to the *Yosippon* reception, there are also more direct

---

[628] The study by Moshe Simon-Shoshan offers only a summary of old opinions based on already known texts. The Amoraic, or even Tannaitic, origin of *Sefer Torah* and *Soferim* is only claimed but not proved. In particular, I find what is lacking is a discussion of *ketav* and *letargem*. See Moshe Simon-Shoshan, "The Task of the Translators: the Rabbis, the Septuagint, and the Cultural Politics of Translation," *Prooftexts* 27 (2007): 1–39.

[629] On this part, see also the work of Wasserstein, quoted above.

[630] There is ample literature on the topic. See G. Veltri, *Gegenwart der Tradition* (Leiden: Brill, 2002), 122 et seq. On the edition of Yosippon, see Saskia Dönitz, *Überlieferung und Rezeption des Sefer Yosippon* (Tübingen: Mohr, 2013).

[631] See Julius Wellhausen, *Der arabische Josippus*, in *Abhandlungen der Königlichen Gesellschaft der Wissenschaft zu Göttingen*, vol. 1 (Berlin: Weidmann 1897); Murad Kamil, ed. *Des*

readings of Josephus in the thirteenth century: evidence for that are the *Sefer ha-Zikhronot* of El'azar b. Asher ha-Levi (13ᵗʰ–14ᵗʰ centuries), and the so-called *Chronicles of Jerahmeel* (MS Bodley, Neubauer and Cowley 2797), published in part by Adolf Neubauer and Moses Gaster, and recently by E. Yassif.[632] Of interest is the fact that the Chronicle also transmits some "histories" of the Hebrew translations which were probably translated from Christian *catenae* in a Latin version, as I have tried to show elsewhere.[633]

Also subordinate to the Christian tradition are the Karaite notices on the Septuagint. As Abū Yūsuf Ya'qub al-Qirqisāni puts it:

> They[634] surpass the Christians in nonsense and falsehood, for the Christians rely in many of their teachings on nonsense and obstinacy for they recognise and admit the truth of the Jewish religion and at the same time renounce it. When it became clear to them that alterations and changes had been introduced into the translations of our books, impudence led them to claim Syriac as the primaeval language. Cyprian and his like are the authorities for this. Many of them argue that no alteration or change has been introduced into the translation because King Ptolemy, having assembled seventy elders of the Jews, divided them up and placed every pair in a separate place and then he ordered them to translate for him the twenty-four books; which they did, and when their translations were compared, no difference was found between them. This is what they call the Edition of the Seventy. The Rabbanites confirm this story, giving the king in question the name of "Talmai," but claim that the great and glorious Creator dictated to them so that they wrote the same thing; but they changed ten things in the Scripture, and wrote them not as they are in the original.[635]

Josef ben Gorion (Josippon) Geschichte der Juden, Zēna Āihŭd, (Hamburg and New York: Augustin, 1937).

[632] See Adolf Neubauer, *Mediaeval Jewish Chronicles*, vol. 2 (Oxford: Clarendon, 1895); Moses Gaster, "The Unknown Aramaic Original of Theodotion's Additions to the Book of Daniel," in Gaster, *Studies and Texts in Folklore, Magic, Medieval Romance, Hebrew Apocrypha and Samaritan Archaeology*, vol. 3 (London: Maggs, 1928), 16. Translation and commentary in vol. 1, 42 (39–68); Eli Yassif, ed. *Sefer ha-Zikhronot hu' Divrey ha-Yamim le-Yeraḥme'el*, ed. (Tel Aviv: Tel Aviv University, 2001).

[633] Veltri, *Gegenwart der Tradition*, 132–138. These traditions indicate the depth of knowledge of Christian sources among Jews in the twelfth and thirteenth centuries.

[634] The Rabbanites.

[635] Abraham Harkavy, "Remarks of the Qaraite Abū Yūsuf Ya'qub al-Qirqisāni on the Jewish Sects" [Russian], *Memoirs of the Oriental Department of the Imperial Russian Archeological Society* 8 (1894): 247–278. New edition by Leon Nemoy, ed. *Kitāb al-Anwār wal-Marāqib. Code of Caraite Law by Ya'qub al-Qirqisāni*, vol. 1 (New York: Kohut, 1939), 37–38; Nemoy, "Al-Qirqisāni's Account of the Jewish Sects and Christianity," *Hebrew Union College Annual* 7 (1930), 358–359. The quoted English translation is Wilfrid Lockwood's. See Bruno Chiesa and Wilfrid Lockwood, ed. and trans., *Ya'qūb al-Qirqisānī on Jewish Sects and Christianity: A Translation of "Kitāb al-anwār"* (Frankfurt am Main: Lang, 1984), 130–131.

In his report on the Septuagint, Qirqisāni probably follows Epiphanius (and *not* Cyprian) by reading the Syriac version of his *De Mensuris and Ponderibus*,[636] a text which was also well received among Muslim sources.[637]

A first negative notice on the LXX is transmitted by Abraham Ibn Daud (c. 1110–c. 1180), in his *Divre Malkhe Yisra'el ba-Bayit ha-Sheni* (Chronicle of the Kings of Israel during the Second Temple), where we also find a mixture of Christian and Jewish sources.[638] The story of the Septuagint translation in the cells, the precise agreement in the translated text, the miracle and finally the changes in the texts are rabbinic and Christian in origin. The literary aim of the story, however, is Christian. Ibn Daud writes: "(Talmai) looked for an argument against Israel and for a pretext in their teaching to expel them from society." Yet his plan did not work out. The translation was a success and the translators were praised and honored at the king's court, according to Ibn Daud following the story of Josephus-Josippon.

The motif of fear against the king is already present in the report of the Latin Church father Jerome.[639] Yet the first to speak of a pretext is the Arabic writer Muhammad Ibn Ahmad Al-Birūni, who may also be Ibn Daud's source:

> The Jews, however, give quite a different account, viz., that they made the translation under compulsion and that they yielded to the king's demand only from fear of violence and maltreatment and not before having agreed upon inverting and confounding the text of the book.[640]

Al-Birūni refers to a negative tradition, i.e., that the traduction was a product of compulsion. No source of the Tannaitic and Amoraic period reports compulsive

---

636 James E. Dean, ed., *Epiphanius' Treatise on Weights and Measures: The Syriac Version* (Chicago: The University of Chicago Press, 1935). See also Paul J. Bruns, "Syrische Nachrichten von den griechischen Übersetzungen aus Manuscripten gesammlet," *Eichhorn's Repertorium für biblische und morgenländische Litteratur 14* (1784): 39–59.
637 See George Vajda, "La version des LXX dans la litterature musulmane," *Revue des Études Juives* 89 (1929–1930): 65–70; Wasserstein, *The Legend*, 174 et seq.
638 Abraham ben David Ibn Daud/Halevi, *Seder 'olam raba ve-seder 'olam zuṭa : u-Megilat Ta'anit : ve-Sefer ha-Ḳabalah leha-Ra'avad : ve-Divre malkhe Bayit Sheni* (Amsterdam: Bi-defus uve-vet Shelomoh ben Yosef Kats Props, Mokher sefarim, 5471 [1710/1711]), 50a–b.
639 Latin: "Iudaei prudenti factum dicunt esse consilio, ne Ptolomeus, unius dei cultor, etiam apud Hebraeos duplicem divinitatem deprehenderet, quos maximi idcirco faciebat, quia in Platonis dogma cadere videbantur" See *Prologus in Pentateuchum, Patrologia Latina* 28, 121. See also Robert Weber, ed. *Biblia sacra iuxta Vulgatam versionem* (Stuttgart: Württembergische Bibelanstalt, 1975), 3–4.
640 English translation by C. Edward Sachau, ed. and trans., *The Chronology of Ancient Nations* (London: Allen, 1879), 23–24; see the Arabic text in *Chronologie orientalischer Völker von Albêrūnī*, ed. C. Edward Sachau (Leipzig: Brockhaus, 1878).

measures by King Ptolemy when looking for a pretext. The origin of the tradition of a "compulsion" may once more be Epiphanius of Salamis, who, according to the Greek-Syriac version, mentions a letter of Ptolemy to the rulers ("principibus") of Jerusalem asking for the prophetic books on God and the creation of the world: "sine invidia et dolo mittite mihi."[641] An indirect threat and compulsion cannot be overlooked.

Al-Birūni is likewise a very important testimony, because he also transmits a list of Jewish fasts. Under the entry for Tevet he writes:

> 5. First appearance of darkness. Ptolemy, the king of the Greeks, had asked them for the Torah, compelled them to translate it into Greek, and deposited it in his treasury. They [the Jews] maintain that this is the version of the Seventy. In consequence darkness spread over the world during three days and nights.
> 8. A fast-day, the last of the three Dark Days, so called for the reason just mentioned.[642]

Al-Birūni is reading the so-called *Megillat Ta'anit Batra* (Additions to the Scroll of the Fasts), which with the exception the rabbinic tractates *Soferim* and *Sefer Torah* is the only gaonic source with a very negative attitude toward the Septuagint. We read in it:

> On the eighth of Tevet, the Torah was translated into Greek at the time of King Ptolemy. For three days, darkness descended upon the world.[643]

I do not intend to go into detail here on the complicated origins of this Gaonic tractate,[644] which some scholars have antedated (as usual for this genre) to the first centuries C.E. But important to note is the fact that the manuscript transmission on the fast offers no option for its dating to a pre-Gaonic period. Even the date given, 8 Tevet, is uncertain: some manuscripts transmit the date of the fast as 7 Tevet;[645] in the *Sefer Orḥot Ḥayyim*, the date is the first of

---

641 See the Latin version in Michel van Esbroeck, "Une forme inédite de la lettre du roi Ptolémée pour la traduction des LXX," *Biblica* 57 (1976): 547.
642 Sachau, *The Chronology*, 272.
643 On the scroll, see Sid Z. Leiman, "The Scroll of Fasts: the Ninth of Teveth," *Jewish Quarterly Review* 74 (1983): 174–195. On the text of the scroll, see Hans Lichtenstein, "Die Fastenrolle: eine Untersuchung zur jüdisch-hellenistischen Geschichte," *Hebrew Union College Annual* 8–9 (1931–1932): 318–351.
644 On the fast of 8 Tevet, see Shulamit Elizur, *Wherefore Have We Fasted? Megillat Taanit Batra and Similar lists of Fast* [Hebrew] (Jerusalem: World Union of Jewish Studies, 2007), 197–199.
645 MS Bodley, Opp. Add. fol., 55 (Neubauer 2421), fol. 69; Neubauer, *Mediaeval Jewish Chronicles*, vii–viii, 24.

Tevet.⁶⁴⁶ In *Sefer Kol Bo* § 63, there is no special day. The earliest text is a *piyyuṭ* of the eighth century, attributed to R. Pinḥas ben Yaʿaqov ha-Cohen, which reads: צום כתב תורה יוונית בשמונה בו.⁶⁴⁷ There is no mention of the darkness, while the Genizah fragment T-S H11.32, published by Menachem Zulay, commented; תורה יוונית נכתבה חשכו לכוכביו כוכבי נפשו.⁶⁴⁸

Alongside very positive or at least neutral traditions on the Septuagint, a negative vision of the event of the Septuagint's translation has also been transmitted. There is, however, no proof that it was in the mainstream before the liturgy of Tevet⁶⁴⁹ fomented or expanded criticism against the Greek Torah. The three days of darkness unequivocally refers to the Exodus tradition (Exodus 10:21–3) and its Midrashic developments, according to which the darkness was employed by God to dispose of those Israelites who refused to leave Egypt.⁶⁵⁰ If we follow this tradition, we can understand the fast of Tevet as a reproach to the Jews of Egypt, the great diaspora, who abandoned Hebrew traditions and embraced Greek culture and customs.

Yet Alexandria of Egypt was but a pale idea in Jewish memory when the first Jewish poets of the rabbinic period composed the first *piyyuṭim* transmitted to us. Other troubles and compulsions were on the agenda of the Christian ruling power. In Byzantine times, Emperor Justinian (482–565) prohibited reading and commenting on the Torah (by sermon or targum) in Hebrew or Aramaic.⁶⁵¹ It is not by chance that the first negative attitude to the Septuagint is not in the Midrashic exegesis, but in liturgical texts or those with liturgical connections (such as Soferim, Sefer Torah or the *piyyuṭim*). R. Yehudai Gaon, contemporaneous to the author or collector of the *Megillat Taʿanit Batra*, reports a Byzantine prohibition of studying and teaching the Torah:

---

646 Aaron ha-Kohen of Lunel, *Sefer Orhot Hayyim*, vol. 1 (Jerusalem: n.p., 1956), 214.
647 Arthur Marmorstein, "Qiddush Yeraḥim de-Rabbi Pinhas," in *ha-Zopheh le-Hokhmat Israel* 5 (1921): 249. See a new edition in Shulamit Elizur, ed., *The Liturgical Poems of Rabbi Pinhas ha-Cohen* [Hebrew] (Jerusalem: World Union of Jewish Studies, 2004), 715.
648 *Sinai* 28 (1950–1951), 167. See also MS Vatican 360; and see Leon J. Weinberger, "Shirim Ḥadashim Meha-Tekufah Ha-Bizantinit," *Hebrew Union College Annual* 39 (1968): 10; and the *piyyut* of Yosef ben Shmuel (ca. 1040), "The Fast of Tebeth," translated by Nina Davis in *Jewish Quartely Review* 11 (1899): 409–10.
649 There is no evidence that such a fast was observed at all. Yet the list of fasts is very popular from the eighth-ninth century up until the *Arbaʿa urim* and beyond.
650 Sources of the legend in Louis Ginzberg, *The legends of the Jews* vol. 2 (Philadelphia: Jewish Publication Society of America, 1968), 345; *Ibidem* vol. 5, 431–432.
651 Giuseppe Veltri, "Die Novelle 146 Perì Hebraion: Das Verbot des Targumvortrags in Justinians Politik," in *Die Septuaginta zwischen Judentum und Christentum*, ed. Martin Hengel, Anna. M. Schwemer (Tübingen: Mohr Siebeck, 1994), 116–130; now also in Veltri, *Gegenwart der Tradition*, 104–119.

> We have heard that the evil government prescribed that the Torah cannot be read and translated. Thus, the sages of that generation decided to read and translate the whole of Psalm 20, Isaiah 6,3 and Ezekiel 3,12 (Qedushah).[652]

We do not have enough evidence to ascertain whether a change in the liturgy (*piyyut* instead of sermon) took place on the basis of a new historical situation.[653] It is certain, however, that the negative attitude to the experience of the Septuagint was accompanied by the revival of the Hebrew language and the beginning of liturgical poetry. The darkness of Tevet shelters the seeds of a new creativity.

---

[652] Solomon Halberstamm, ed. "Shte tshuvot 'im hearot," *Jeschurun* 6 (1868): 126–127, quoted in Jacob Mann, "Changes in the divine service of the Synagogue due to religious persecution," *Hebrew Union College Annual* 4 (1927): 268, note 54.

[653] On this aspect, see Saul Libermann, "Ḥazanut Yannai," *Sinai* 4 (1939): 225 et seq. Jefim Shirman, "Hebrew Liturgical Poetry and Christian Hymnology," *Jewish Quarterly Review* 44 (1953–1954), 141 et seq.; Zvi M. Rabinowitz, *The Liturgical Poems of Rabbi Yannai According to the Triennal Cycle of the Pentateuch* [Hebrew], vol. 1 (Jerusalem: Bialik Institute, 1985), 14 et seq.; Ezra Fleischer, "Studies in the Problems Relating to the Liturgical Function of the Types of Early Piyyut" [Hebrew], *Tarbiz* 40 (1970–1971): 41–63.

15 In Lieu of a Conclusion: Pleasure and Desire of Learning

The Song of Songs/Song of Solomon[654] שיר השירים

1:2
Let him kiss me with the kisses of his mouth – for thy love is better than wine.

יִשָּׁקֵנִי מִנְּשִׁיקוֹת פִּיהוּ, כִּי-טוֹבִים דֹּדֶיךָ מִיָּיִן 1.2

4:1
Behold, thou art fair, my love;
Behold, thou art fair;
Thine eyes are as doves behind thy veil;
Thy hair is as a flock of goats,
That trail down from mount Gilead.

הִנָּךְ יָפָה רַעְיָתִי, הִנָּךְ יָפָה--עֵינַיִךְ יוֹנִים, מִבַּעַד 4.1
לְצַמָּתֵךְ; שַׂעְרֵךְ כְּעֵדֶר הָעִזִּים, שֶׁגָּלְשׁוּ מֵהַר
גִּלְעָד

7:2
How beautiful are thy steps in sandals,
O prince's daughter!
The roundings of thy thighs are like the links of a chain,
The work of the hands of a skilled workman.

מַה-יָּפוּ פְעָמַיִךְ בַּנְּעָלִים, בַּת-נָדִיב חַמּוּקֵי 7.2
יְרֵכַיִךְ חֲלָאִים, מַעֲשֵׂה יְדֵי אָמָּן

7:3
Thy navel is like a round goblet,
Wherein no mingled wine is wanting;
Thy belly is like a heap of wheat
Set about with lilies.

שָׁרְרֵךְ אַגַּן הַסַּהַר, אַל-יֶחְסַר הַמָּזֶג; בִּטְנֵךְ עֲרֵמַת 7.3
חִטִּים, סוּגָה בַּשּׁוֹשַׁנִּים

7:4
Thy two breasts are like two fawns
That are twins of a gazelle.

שְׁנֵי שָׁדַיִךְ כִּשְׁנֵי עֳפָרִים, תָּאֳמֵי צְבִיָּה 7.4

7:7
How fair and how pleasant art thou,
O love, for delights!

מַה-יָּפִית, וּמַה-נָּעַמְתְּ--אַהֲבָה, בַּתַּעֲנוּגִים 7.7

7:13
Let us get up early to the vineyards;
Let us see whether the vine hath budded,
Whether the vine-blossom be opened,
And the pomegranates be in flower;
There will I give thee my love

נַשְׁכִּימָה, לַכְּרָמִים--נִרְאֶה אִם-פָּרְחָה הַגֶּפֶן פִּתַּח 7.13
הַסְּמָדַר, הֵנֵצוּ הָרִמּוֹנִים; שָׁם אֶתֵּן אֶת-דֹּדַי, לָךְ

---

654 Translation based on the "Jewish Publication Society of America Version 1917".

15.1 The Song of Songs in Discussions

Readers of these verses will always be under the impression that the poem describes a love which is both sublime and passionate. The poet attempts to find the most beautiful and captivating images in order to describe contemplation in verse form: the fruit of a relation between man and woman. Perhaps it is but a figment of his imagination, or the creation of an artist molding it through vibrant and intense images. The images describe the pleasure in delights, the beauties of the female and male body, through the description of every part of this artwork of God. The description is apt to awaken emotions. It emphasises, ignores, and alludes to the details of an act intertwining love and sex. It seeks to arouse the reader, not necessarily sexually, through a series of images and emotions. It calls on Eros, that feeling originating in the intellect, or better, the brain. That feeling is supposed to spread quickly through the fibres of the body, and to shift the attention from the author to the reader/listener; from the images of the mind to images of reality. This sensation is Eros. It is this feeling which involves and overwhelms human beings in their entirety, creating the paradoxical longing for the eternal moment.

The prudent reader knows that we are not discussing Ovid's love poems, but a text that has been and still is considered sacred. Does the text describe sacred or profane love? And is there a difference between them? The Hebrew Bible is not a cold, piously religious tractate aimed at directing man towards God through worldly asceticism and ceaseless prayer (although this is at times erroneously assumed). The Bible is a literary text about the past of one people, establishing it essentially and historically on the basis of an experience which is historically accurate or believed mythically to be as such. In the experience of this people there is a basic founding moment (the exodus from Egypt). There is a tragic experience (life in the desert), and there is the precarious existence in the Promised Land, which largely plays out in an unreal dimension strung between myth and obligation to God.

Taking possession of the land, the construction of the Temple, and the mythical reign of the kings David and Solomon form the background of the Song of Songs, also known as Song of Solomon. It is a poem inherent in which is the flavour of spring and summer. It creates a notion of that particular land's fragrance, that particular time's eternity.

It was, nevertheless, precisely during the classical period of Hebrew language that this extraordinary example of the love poem was created. Its Hebrew language is polished to high perfection. It is metaphorical, vivid, and concise. It has repetitions, in the same way that the endless ocean of insatiable love is repeated. If we were unaware of the song's mythical age (ca. 2,500 years),[655] we would scarcely doubt its contemporary origin: The images, and most particularly the emotions they evoke, are too familiar to be covered over with the dust of millennia.

At the end of the 18th century, the German Protestant biblical scholar Johann David Michaelis (1717–1791) believed that the Song of Songs spoke of a love too profane, too sensual. It was consequently unfit to be included in the canon of sacred scriptures. Mercilessly, Michaelis expurgated it from his German translation of the Hebrew bible. In explaining his decision, he wrote:

> I only omitted [from the canon the translation and the inclusion of] the Song of Songs, because it seemed to me too grossly indecent, at times too seductive, to place before readers of the Bible, let alone young people and children, thus familarizing them with notions that become even more indecent and dangerous the more faithfully they are translated by those more knowledgeable in the languages of the Orient.[656]

From this perspective then, it is a scandalous text, a divine indecency even though divinely inspired. Did Michaelis perceive it as such because it was deemed inappropriate for the religious morality of the Germans at the time? He was neither the first nor probably the last to express shock. It was precisely at the beginning of the 19th century, the era of idealism and romanticism, when the question was also raised within German Jewry. A common and perplexing question was: why had the compilers of sacred literature included this specific erotic text? Leopold Zunz (1794–1886) opined, with intuition and in almost cryptic style, why the rabbis' later theological interest in the poem had led them to retain the erotic text within the biblical canon of *Tanakh*. In his view, the post-biblical theologians had deprived this profane song of its context, turning it into a theological metaphor of love between God and Israel which was universally valid.[657] Thus, profane love had been "castrated," so to speak,

---

[655] There is no precise reference in the book as to when this poem was composed. We can only speculate about the age in which such a poetic masterpiece could have been composed; on the current state of research, see Anselm C. Hagedorn, ed., *Perspectives on the Song of Songs. Perspektiven der Hoheliedauslegung* (Berlin: de Gruyter, 2005). This volume, with eighteen contributions in English, French and German, also contains a copious bibliography on the parallel culture and possible similarity to Egyptian love literature.

[656] Johann David Michaelis, *Deutsche Übersetzung des Alten Testaments, mit Anmerkungen für Ungelehrte*, vol. 1 (Göttingen and Gotha: Dieterich, 1773), 9: "Nur das Hohe Lied ... habe ich ausgelassen ... weil es mir zu anstössig, bisweilen zu verführerisch vorkam, als das ich den Leser der Bibel, sogar Jünglichen und Kindern vorlegen, und sie gleich mit solchen Vorstellungen bekannt machen möchte, noch dazu immer anstössiger und gefährlicher, je treuer und den morgenländischen Sprachen kundiger es übersetzt wird."

[657] Zunz wrote: "ªLänger als ein und ein halbes Jahrtausend hat man in weiter Ferne des hohen Liedes Sinn und Bedeutung, und in mancherlei menschlichen Erkenntnissen und nationalen Beziehungen die Lösung des vermeintlichen Räthsels gesucht. Dieses Räthsel bot

so as to become divine love.⁶⁵⁸ Or perhaps it had not. We cannot ask this question, taking into consideration all of its hermeneutic implications for the (de)canonisation of Hebrew Scripture. I shall not address this topic here.⁶⁵⁹ Nonetheless, I will return to it briefly below since it involves an essential aspect.

Zunz knew the basic aspects for making a text canonical: decontextualisation and its disentanglement from the text's historical and cultural context. The aim was clear: turning a thought or an expression into universal truth.⁶⁶⁰ Decontextualisation is connected with a new element: a text might be inspired by and infused with another context. Yet the original context will never be truly eliminated since eventually it will be reconstructed by philological methods.

Another discussion concerning the Song of Songs had occurred many centuries before Zunz or Michaelis. It was equally as lively and passionate as the later commentary. The discussion took place in the rabbinic schools, focused on two texts, the so-called Qohelet (Ecclesiastes) and the Song of Songs. We read in Mishnah, Yadayim 3:5:

> The Song of Songs and Ecclesiastes render the hands unclean. R. Yehudah says: the Song of Songs renders the hands unclean, but there is a dispute about Ecclesiastes. R. Yose says: Ecclesiastes does not render the hands unclean, but there is a dispute about the Song of Songs. R. Shimʻon says: [the ruling about] Ecclesiastes is one of the leniencies of Bet Shammai and one of the stringencies of Beth Hillel. R. Shimʻon b. ʻAzzai said: I received a tradition from the seventy-two elders on the day when they appointed R. Eleʻazar b. ʻAzaryah, head of the academy, that the Song of Songs and Ecclesiastes render the

---

nicht der Inhalt der Dichtung dar, sondern ihr Platz unter den heiligen Schriften, deren ein Wettgesang zärtlicher Liebe nicht würdig schien. Aber als der Dichter sang, war die Sprache noch nicht den schmerzhaften Tod der heiligen gestorben, und die ersten, die sich an dem Liede ergötzten, wussten noch nichts von sinnbildlicher Deutung kanonischer Bücher. Man musste endlich aus dem Traum, der theologische Lehrsätze unter jenen Versen sah, zur ächter Hermeneutik erwachen." Leopold Zunz, *Gesammelte Schriften* vol. 1 (Berlin: Louis Gerschel Verlagsbuchhandlung, 1875), 142.

658 I follow here the perhaps awkward yet expressive formulation of an unpublished semiotic exercise by Daniel Barbieri, Renato Giovannoli and Ettore Panizon, "Come castrarsi col rasoio di Ockham" (How to castrate oneself with Ockham's razor), mentioned favorably by Umberto Eco in his *Lector in Fabula* (Milan: Bompiani, 1979), 9; see the original manuscript by Barbieri et al. http://goo.gl/6tVrN (accessed 7 June 2013), and U. Eco, *The Role of the Reader; Explorations in the Semiotics of Texts* (Bloomington, Indiana University Press, 1984), 257.

659 See, for instance, David M. Carr, "The Song of Songs as a Mirror of the Canonization and Decanonization Process," in *Canonization and Decanonization*, ed. Arie van der Kooij and Karel van der Toorn (Leiden: Brill, 1998), 173–189.

660 See Giuseppe Veltri, *Libraries, Translations, and 'Canonic' Texts: The Septuagint, Aquila, and Ben Sira in the Jewish and Christian Traditions* (Leiden: Brill, 2006), 20–22. See also the Hebrew translation of the first chapter "Dekanonizatziah we-deqonstruqtziah," *Teʻudah* 23 (2008): 99–121.

hands unclean. R. Aqiva said: Far from it! None in Israel disputed about the Song of Songs [by saying] that it does not render the hands unclean. For the whole world is not as worthy as the day on which the Song of Songs was given to Israel. For all the writings are holy, but the Song of Songs is the holy of holies. So that if they had a dispute, they had a dispute only about Ecclesiastes.[661]

The status of Ecclesiastes (Qohelet) and Song of Solomon (Shir ha-Shirim) was questioned because of certain theological problems which led some rabbis to consider them unsuitable for liturgical use (it "renders the hands unclean"). We can largely imagine the key points of the discussion: The book of Qohelet/Ecclesiastes has been considered far too removed from God, or in other words, too skeptical a discourse, even God or the divine name is not mentioned there. The Song does not speak of the salvation-oriented history of God's holy covenant with His people of Israel. It does not speak of sin or expiation, the Temple or its offerings, prophecy or the Messiah, purity or impurity. In essence, it does not speak of any of the favored subjects of rabbinic academies. Indeed, what was deemed worse: neither the Song of Songs nor Qohelet mention God.

What the Song of Songs speaks of abundantly is human experience. Was it then too human a text, too worldly? Is this a reason for hiding or even burning the text? Rabbi Aqiva saved what could be saved although nobody knows really why, as Amos Luzzatto states.[662] Rabbi Aqiva only explained himself stating: "All the books are *sifre-haqodesh*, books of Holiness. The *shir ha-shirim* is the Holy of Holiness, the innermost part of the Temple, [the] *qodesh-ha-qodashim*." In *qodesh ha-qodashim* were preserved the Torah scroll and Aharon's rod (which he used to smite the rock in the desert). Essentially speaking, the Song of Songs is the Temple of the Holy One itself!

Rabbi Aqiva locutus causa soluta? Of course not. The discussion continued. The Tosefta *Sanhedrin* 12:5 refers to Rabbi Aqiva's opinion to excommunicate those who sang the Song of Songs with an undulating and languid voice (מגעגע בקול), as though it were a song in a tavern (כמין זמר), from eternal life. This threat was reserved for the worst "sinners" – in fact, like those who denied the resurrection of the dead, eternal life, and that the Torah was received from God at Sinai (see Mishnah, Sanhedrin 10:1). Rabbi Aqiva hence regarded the Song of Songs as the *summa summarum* of Jewish knowledge and behaviour.

---

661 I follow here, with small changes, Isidore Epstein et al., ed. and trans. *The Soncino Babylonian Talmud* (London:Soncino Press, 35 Bde., London 1935–1952).
662 Amos Luzzatto, *Una lettura ebraica del Cantico die Cantici* (Florence: La Giuntina, 1997), 21.

The Babylonian Talmud, Sanhedrin 101a, speaks at another point of such an idea, where Rabbi Aqiva is noticeably absent in the discussion, while it softens the punishment but nevertheless keeps it valid:

> Our Rabbis taught: He who recites a verse of the Song of Songs and treats it as a [secular] air, and one who recites a verse at the banqueting table unseasonably, brings evil upon the world. Because the Torah girds itself in sackcloth, and stands before the Holy One, blessed be He, and laments before Him, "Sovereign of the Universe! Thy children have made me as a harp upon which they frivolously play." He replies, "My daughter, when they are eating and drinking, wherewith shall they occupy themselves?" To which she rejoins, "Sovereign of the Universe! If they possess Scriptural knowledge, let them occupy themselves with the Torah, the Prophets, and the Writings; if they are students of the Mishnah, with Mishnah, Halachoth, and Haggadoth; if students of the Talmud, let them engage in the laws of Passover, Pentecost and Tabernacles on the respective Festivals.
> R. Shim'on b. Ele'azar testified on the authority of R. Shim'on b. Ḥanina: He who reads a verse in season [defined as just] brings good to the world, as it is written, and a word spoken in season, how good is it (Proverbs 15:23).[663]

The fact that the punishment is softened to a generalised "brings evil into the world" or "wickedness" suggests that the song was still in common use as a lustful discourse, its usage widespread to such a degree that the author of *Sanhedrin* slyly has the Most High utter the most popular opinion: "When they are eating and drinking, wherewith shall they occupy themselves?"

The Torah is angry because it appears as if it was used for amusement, as if it were a musical instrument like a harp. Mentioning of the *kinnor* is not accidental: according to the Mishnah *Qinnim* 3:6, body's parts (of an offered animal) are equated to musical instruments. The thighs are flutes, the horns are trumpets, the skin is the tympanum. בני מעיו לכינורות / the "sons of the spring" (colon and private parts) are the *kinnor*.[664] The *kinnor* is a metaphor for the genitalia, especially exemplifying the comparison of the body with music. It will later also become the foundation of the mysticism of the limbs of the perfect man. The perfect man's geometrical structure is reminiscent of divine perfection.

However, more interesting for us at this point is the fact that God Himself does not seem to be too disconcerted about the euphoria induced by wine and

---

[663] The English translation is taken from *Sanhedrin*, translated by Jacob Shachter and H. Freedman in Isidore Epstein et al., ed. and trans. *The Soncino Babylonian Talmud* (London: Soncino Press, 1948). http://www.come-and-hear.com/sanhedrin/sanhedrin_0.html (accessed 7 June 2013).
[664] I am grateful to Professor Don Harrán, Hebrew University in Jerusalem, for his immeasurable help in interpreting the *kinnor* in rabbinic literature.

food, which in festive turn induces humans to intone the Song of Songs. God does not seem to be too upset about handling the Torah as if it was a harp. Quite the contrary: God's "daughter," the Torah, wants to educate, excluding idleness which does not bring any good to the world. This moralizing aspect will eventually prevail, since the pleasure of sin and the feeling of guilt because of this pleasure will always be present.

The history of the Song of Songs is a hermeneutic sign; it becomes here the legendary Golden Fleece of the Argonauts, explaining why erotic love almost always has had the (positive) connotation of guilt. The more one fantasises about this guilt without carrying it out as action, the more attractive it becomes. In order to understand this implication, we need to travel back to Babylonia. There a very educated Jewish community existed until the 11th century. This community created the Babylonian Talmud, which established Judaism in a form still vital and valid to the present. Debating sexuality and the body plays a certain role there. For example, the men in the Babylonian academies also discussed the issue of sexual abstinence in marriage during the period of menstruation and a week thereafter. The tractate Niddah 31b notes:

> It was taught: R. Me'ir used to say: Why did the Torah ordain that the uncleanness of menstruation should continue for seven days? Because being in constant contact with his wife [a husband might] develop a loathing towards her. The Torah, therefore, ordained: Let her be unclean for seven days in order that she shall be beloved by her husband as at the time of her first entry into the bridal chamber (כדי שתהא חביבה על בעלה כשעת כניסתה לחופה).

Babylonian rabbis who always showed an open or rather pragmatic turn of mind, trying to explain a Biblical regulation by means of experience: the sexual act is better performed after a pause in the beloved woman's desire. Desire of union is part of lovemaking. It is, indeed, the most luring aspect and is, for instance, most present in the young lovers who await the first night of sex with a strong desire that most of us have forgotten later in life. Desire is an essential aspect of the sexual act, a fact of adult life.

In order to access the Song of Songs properly, and to understand it in its hermeneutic implications, we should note that Halakhah has an explanatory dimension springing from the experience of reality. The absolute divine will is presented as the guarantee of justice and wisdom of a commandment. We need the reference to reality to understand the biblical text. It is not important whether the sacred author has seen this in its full dimension, but the importance of reality is the key to understanding and accepting the regulations. This is the positive aspect of the commandments.

Judaism in antiquity and the Middle Ages is almost always presented under the seemingly evident and possibly conscious thin layer of passivity towards the lawgiver. Laws were allegedly adhered to without criticism. Judaism is understood according to the criticism of the evangelist Matthew and in particular Paul of Tarsus as blind obedience to the law. It supposedly was obedience later deemed stubborn and supine in the Christian attacks on Judaism. Some experienced in the field would notice that Judaism has many fathers and mothers, depending on the culture and the environment where Jews settled, a form of historical ecology. We must always take into consideration that the starting point of the authors we study is their environment and its ecology. This is a basic element for understanding their texts. There is a monolithic Judaism but it only exists in the minds of those looking for certainties, not for the evolution of reality on the ground.

It was precisely in the wake of the relations with Hellenistic culture, later in its Oriental version, that the medieval *paideia*, a form of the Arab *adab* continued the love for eros and the body as such. Not only were the synagogues decorated with mosaics whose artists did not shy away from depicting naked bodies, but the novel discussing love was also born. The novel of Joseph and Aseneth appeared. It tells the story of the love between the Egyptian priest's daughter and the Jew Joseph and her conversion to the Jewish God. The crucial scene of their meeting is well-known (chapter 19, 1–4):

> And Aseneth said to him, "Come, my lord, come into my house;" and she took his right hand and brought him inside her house. 2. And Joseph sat down on her father Pentephres's seat, and she brought water to wash his feet; and Joseph said to her, "Let one of your virgins come, and let her wash my feet." 3. And Aseneth said to him, "No, my lord, for my hands are your hands, and your feet my feet, and no one else shall wash your feet;" and so she had her way and washed his feet. 4. And Joseph took her by the right hand and kissed it, and Aseneth kissed his head.[665]

The skilled reader will surely identify the eros implied in the meeting. Its symbolic meaning is clear when the writer, conscious of the reader's reaction, adds:

> And Joseph stayed that day with Pentephres; and he did not sleep with Aseneth, for he said, "It is not right for a man who worships God to have intercourse with his wife before their marriage."[666]

Eros is present, but in a rather sublime way of a meeting and detached from actual sexual intercourse. On the contrary, the sexual act must take place in

---

665 This translation is from Hedley F. D. Sparks, ed. *The Apocryphal Old Testament* (Oxford: Oxford University Press, 1984), 473–503. See Mark Goodacre, ed. *The Asenet Home Page*, http://markgoodacre.org/aseneth/translat.htm (accessed 7 June 2013).
666 Ibidem.

the frame of a structure. Eros is present through postponements, suspensions and subliminal references. The reader must not think that sex is not part of Jewish thought and culture. Quite the contrary, since Jewish culture had been thoroughly infused by the surrounding environment. Hellenism not only introduced the thermal bathing culture, the palaces and sport games, but also theatre, mime and pantomime. I have already discussed this above at length.[667] Thus, let me repeat here that the passages are sufficiently clear: through the impact of Hellenistic culture, Jewish culture came to have a circus on Shabbat, and theatre stages with mime. These were not far removed from the sphere of activity in brothels. The Church Father Aurelius Augustine scorned Jews since in his opinion, they should work on the Shabbat instead of attending such shows. The same remarks can be found in a response by the African church reproaching the clergy because they had attended such shows. Rabbinic literature explicitly states that it is harmful for the daughters of Israel to attend the theatre. The mime artists also continued their art in the Arab period, and at least until the onset of the Middle Ages.[668]

Without denying the attraction of sex and pornographic art (which we cannot demonstrate with reliable evidence but only can assume indirectly), there remains the rabbinic obligation toward a relationship with one's own wife (or husband) as the only commandment requested by God. Sexual intercourse in marriage, however, is not necessarily an act of erotic love. It is a requirement, a *mitzvah*. There is no tradition of celibacy in Judaism "more sacred" than marriage, with the noteworthy exception of Philo of Alexandria's therapeutic community where love in marriage played no role. Philo's own mentor, Plato of the Symposium, saw love positively, even as a powerful force (if not *the* force that drives the spinning spheres beyond the visible world). Yet, it was precisely the idea of a negativity here that, at least in the Mediterranean cultures, exercised a crucial impact, likewise because it was implemented by anthropological theories.

According to Philo's anthropology, the body is the element that connects humans with animals. Therefore it is the source of evil, the prison that locks away our spirit. Sensuality is a sin by definition, and sin consequently is inherent to human beings. Hence, the basic principle of ethics is the renunciation of sensuality, and the eradication of desire and passion. This negative thought

---

667 See pp. 51–53 and my article, "Magic, Sex and Politics: The Media Power of Theatre Amusements in the Mirror of Rabbinic Literature," in *The Words of a Wise Mouth are Gracious: Divre Pi-Hakam Hen – Festschrift for Günter Stemberger in his 65th Birthday*, ed. Mauro Perani (Berlin: De Gruyter, 2005), 243–256.
668 For the sources, see my article quoted in the footnote above.

about the body re-entered Judaism in the late Hellenistic period through neo-Platonism. It was shaped into the philosophical matrix of mystic attitudes, also in some branches of the literature of the Hekhalot and of the Kabbalah. According to the *Midrash Yeşirat ha-Walad*, the soul revolts against God because it does not want to enter the "stinking drop" of spermata. But God, unlike the neo-Platonic viewpoint, has a positive approach to the sexual act. We read in Midrash *Yeşirat ha-Walad*:[669]

> [The soul says]: Master of the world, I am happy in this (divine) world where I have lived since the time I was created. Why do you want me to go into this smelly drop? I am pure and holy and I have been drawn from the material that forms the throne of magnificence. The Holy, may He be blessed, said: The world into which thou shalt pass on is better than the world where you are. Moreover, when I created you, I did so precisely in view of this drop.[670]

This positive approach to sexual intercourse must not lure us away from the fact that the sexual union in Judaism, at least according to the interpretation of some Ashkenazic circles, has nothing at all to do with the emotional love between husband and wife. On the contrary, there are warnings against it. Elhanan Hendel Kirchhahn (1666–1757), author of the book of moral ethics *Simḥat ha-Nefesh* denies any value in worldly matters for the benefit of future expectations. Ruth Berger called it a baroque example of a tractate against the world.[671]

In Kirchhahn's *Simhat ha-Nefesh*, we read:

> Blessed is he who leads with his wife a good life und with her he serves God. These have advantages in this and in the other world. However, he who loves his wife and his sons ... is as if he would eat honey, which contains deadly poison. It has a sweet taste, but it will cause his death: That is like all other joys of this world: they have a sweet taste, yet they are bitter in the end.[672]

Following the biblical regulations, Elkhanan considers family relationships nothing more than a *mitzvah*: there is no love for the *mitzvah*, because the

---

669 "Midrash Yetsirat ha-Walad," in Adolf Jellinek, ed. *Bet ha-Midrasch: Sammlung kleiner Midraschim und vermischter Abhandlungen aus der älteren jüdischen Literatur*, 6 vols. (Leipzig: Nies, 1853–1877), I. 153–158. See also J. H. Laenen, *Frederik Weinreb en de joodse mystiek* (Den Haag: Quintessentia:, 2003), 126 et seq.; Karl-Erich Grözinger, *Jüdisches Denken: Theologie – Philosophie – Mystik*, vol. 1 (Darmstadt: Wissenschaftliche Buchgesellschaft, 2004), 265.
670 Translation by the author.
671 See Ruth Berger, *Sexualität, Ehe und Familienleben in der jüdischen Moralliteratur (900–1900)* (Wiesbaden: Harassowitz, 2003).
672 Translation by the author. Elhanan Hendel Kirchhahn, *Simhat ha-Nefesh* (Frankfurt am Main: Matthias Andreae, 1707), 86.

mitzvah is only a *mitzvah*. This attitude can be found in another work, the likely pseudo-epigraphic testament of Rabbi Ismael Ba'al Shem Tov, a collection of Ḥassidic sayings difficult to date. There it reads:

> One has to love his wife as man loves the tefillin (phylacteries), because the tefillin come from a divine commandment. This means that we must not think of the woman the way that can be deduced from this example that I have given for you. A man who wants to go to the market can do so only by means of a horse that takes him there. Does the man, therefore, have to love the horse? It is difficult to imagine a stupidity greater than this one. For the same reason, a man needs a woman in this world for the divine office; in order to achieve the world to come. Those who stop their (moral) activities and guzzle thoughts on her instead [do not fulfill the commandments], because there is no stupidity greater than this.[673]

Modern European readers will, of course, not have a generous view of the evident misogyny of the anonymous author of this passage. It does, however, emphasise an implication that is important from a certain perspective: the sexual act is only a mitzvah, a commandment with a certain purpose.

Should we be satisfied with this idea? Should we thus be reconciliatory toward contemporary conservative Christian literature that openly displays the same notion? Is the act of sex only a duty and not a pleasure? Is there a pleasure in the sin of having impure thoughts which are not considered a miṣwah by the Torah? I daresay, reducing sexuality to a commandment, and thus stripping it of its sensuality, does injustice to both reality and tradition.

15.2 The Pleasure of Sin

Monogamy is an answer to the problem of the cohesion of lineage. In the beginning it, may have had only a material grounding: to ensure a viable and enjoyable retirement with support from one's children. The idea was to live life at an advanced age without the fear of being forced to beg for bread. The name (in other words, the lineage continuation) was the only element that helped man to die "full of years" (Job 42:17). The romantic approach to love belongs to a modern, even contemporary period. In the main, it is difficult to identify the concept for realities in the ancient world. In Christianity as well, *agapao/* to love dearly is mentioned regarding one's wife. Eros as an essential feature of sexuality does not appear.

---

673 *Sawwa'at ha-RIVA*, 3:51; see Berger, *Sexualität, Ehe und Familienleben*, 192. My translation.

Paul the Apostle speaks in his letter to the Ephesians about a specific kind of love: "And walk in love, as Christ also hath loved us" (Ephesians 5:2). Paul referred to an a-septic love one may feel for anybody, not only for one's wife. It seems that eros is not part of Christianity: Jesus of Nazareth forbade even the gaze and the adulterous intention. We must make clear that while seemingly following an ideal directed *against* eros, Christianity also rediscovers this dimension of love later in mysticism. Rather ironically, it has a neo-Platonic element to it. Whatever erotic facet of the (hetero- and homo-) sexual act cannot be mentioned resurfaces *tel quel* in mysticism. This is a decisive point. We are not discussing here what psychologists call sublimation, but rather an intimate experience of the mystic, expressing through imagination what is forbidden in practice. If we investigate mystic language, whether Jewish, Christian or Muslim, we will notice the use of an outspokenly erotic dimension in such discourse. Therefore, it is not a contradiction that Rabbi Aqiva spoke in defense of the Song of Songs as a rabbi may speak in defense of the Torah. The mystic is described during his/her experience as a sexual being or organ whose purpose is the union with the deity. Penetration into the mystery of mysteries is referenced and we must welcome divine seeds (God's seed) into the flesh. We speak about enthusiasm making a human being quiver in every cord of his or her soul and body. We look for intimate contact with divinity. Love and sexual language are used to describe the divinity. We speak about kissing, touching, lovesickness and desire. Thus, the conclusion is the union knowing no other language but one of fusion, and in the end the soul is inseminated and peace returns.

The unsatisfied libido of sexual castration builds for itself a corner in imagination and asks for freedom. It is a desire that must be fulfilled and cannot be subdued for good. We can indeed speak about a basic principle: the more one achieves a systematic abstinence, the more one speaks against human relationships that involve love and eros, the more one seems to idealise the mysticism springing from that very eros a person was striving to avoid. Leaving aside examples from Christian mysticism, which is not my focus here, I refer to David Biale's work on Jewish eros.[674]

However, I must point out that attraction to erotic literature is not only a feature of mysticism but is hidden in the poetic works of the 11th century as well. At the beginning of the influence of Arab culture on the Jewish world, a new literary genre was born in Sephardic Judaism. Poems were written about wine and love: *shire yayin we-ahava*. The authors are known to us, among them

---

[674] David Biale, *Eros and the Jews: From Biblical Israel to Contemporary America* (Berkeley and Los Angeles: University of California Press, 1997).

were the statesman Shmuel ha-Naggid (993–1056) and the poet Shlomo ibn Gavirol (c. 1021–1058). Examples are Moshe ibn Esra's *diwān* and anonymous texts found in the Cairo Geniza.

We also can refer to Immanuel Romano's (1261–1328) poems.[675] Romano's poems display a very peculiar feature: while speaking of love in general, they often actually describe homosexual love. There is a tendency among religious scholars of Jewish poetry to make clear that when male sex is mentioned, it does not necessarily imply that the author is speaking about homosexuality, not the least because the bible speaks out against such relationships.

Others have already noticed that homosexuality and the sexual desire connected with it is not clearly and openly forbidden in the Hebrew Bible. This fact is very different from the writings of the New Testament. During the Muslim Middle Ages, the *shariʿa* did not forbid male homosexual desire as such but only its practice. We now have reached the point of defining the pleasure in sin. According to a Talmudic tradition, there are cases when the fulfilling of a principle demands its own transgression: מצוה הבאה בעברה, as written in the Babylonian Talmud, Sukka 29b–30a.[676]

The pleasure (eros), the huge range of what the body is capable of offering, and the guilt that is generated through a certain Western education, will always be one focus in historical, psychological, cultural, social, and religious studies. This is inherent to the sciences, since the sexual and sensual emotions induced by eros, sensual love, have always been related to the pleasure of guilt, at least in Western world. After all, it is a masterly idea to relegate such unrealised desire to the sphere of religion. In this way, one appropriates an alibi to emphasise the subordination of the ego and to set free the libido one wished to suppress. This is a constant in the law of human evolution, while religious aspects differ. Although human experience is the constant element, love does not fulfill what the beautiful sonnet by Immanuel Romano proclaims:[677]

---

[675] On Manuello Romano, see the literature in G. Veltri, *Renaissance Philosophy in Jewish Garb* (Boston, Leiden: Brill, 2009), 39–59.

[676] *Kneset* 2 (1936–37): 347–392.

[677] The English translation is taken from http://www.oocities.org/ImmanuelloRomano/sonnets.html (accessed 7 June 2013), with some in part significant changes. The Italian original is edited by Mario Marti, ed., *Poeti giocosi del tempo di Dante* (Milan: Rizzoli, 1956), 313–321.

English Translation	Italian Original
Love never read the Ave Maria;	Amor non lesse mai l' avemaria;
Love never adhered to a religious law or faith;	Amor non tenne mai legge né fede;
Love is a heart, which neither hears nor sees,	Amor è un cor, che non ode né vede
And never knows what measure it is.	e non sa mai che misura si sia.
Love is a pure lordship	Amor è una pura signoria,
Which only stops in wanting that which it asks for;	che sol si ferma in voler ciò che chiede;
And always withdraws itself through every way.	Amor fa com' pianeto, che provvede, e sempre retra sé per ogni via.
Love never leaves, neither for pater-nosters	Amor non lassò mai, per paternostri
Nor for incantations, its gentle pride;	né per incanti, suo gentil orgoglio;
Nor has it separated for fair, so that I joust	né per téma digiunt' è, per ch' i' giostri.
Love does that which grieves me most:	Amor fa quello, di che più mi doglio:
That it does not attain those things which I may show it,	ché non s'attène a cosa ch' io li mostri,
But is always able to say to me: "That's how I want it too."	ma sempre mi sa dir: – Pur così voglio.

Selected Bibliography

Aaron ha-Kohen of Lunel, *Sefer Orhot Hayyim*, Jerusalem: n.p., 1956.
Abarbanel, Nitzah. Ḥavah we-Lilit. Bene-Brak: Bar-Ilan University Press, 1994.
Abt, Adam. *Die Apologie des Apuleius von Madaura: Beiträge zur Erläuterung der Schrift De Magia.* Gießen: Töpelmann, 1908.
Adler, Ada. Ed. *Suidae Lexicon.* Munich: Saur, 2001.
Adler, Marcus. Ed. *The Itinerary of Benjamin of Tudela: Critical Text, Translation and Commentary.* London: Henry Frowde, 1907.
Ahrens, Wilhelm. *Hebräische Amulette mit magischen Zahlenquadraten.* Berlin: Lamm, 1916.
Alexander of Tralles. *Original-Text und Übersetzung nebst einer einleitenden Abhandlung: Ein Beitrag zur Geschichte der Medicin.* 2 Vols. Ed. and trans. by Theodor Puschmann. Amsterdam: Hakkert, 1878.
Alexander, Philip S. "Bavli Berakhot 55a–57b: The Talmudic Dreambook on Context." *Journal of Jewish Studies* 45 (1995): 230–248.
André, Jean-Marie. *Griechische Feste, römische Spiele: Die Freizeitkultur der Antike.* Stuttgart: Reclam, 1994.
Apocalypsis Henochi graece: Fragmenta pseudepigraphorum quae supersunt graeca una cum historicorum et auctorum judaeorum hellinistarum fragmentis [PVTG 3], edited by Albert-Marie Denis and Matthew Black. Leiden: Brill, 1970.
Aptowitzer, Avigdor/Victor. "Issur shetiyat mayim be-sha'at ha-tequfa." *Ha-Zofeh me-Erez Hagar* 2 (1912): 122–126
Aptowitzer, Avigdor/Victor. "Die rabbinischen Berichte über die Entstehung der Septuaginta." *Ha-Kedem* 2 (1908): 11–27, 102–122.
Apuleius, Lucius. *La magia*, edited and translated by. Claudio Moreschini. Milan: Biblioteca Universale Rizzoli, 1990.
Avemarie, Friedrich. "Esaus Hände, Jakobs Stimme: Edom als Sinnbild Roms in der frühen rabbinischen Literatur." In *Die Heiden: Juden, Christen und das Problem des Fremden.* Edited by Reinhard Feldmeier and Ulrich Heckel, 177–208. Tübingen: Mohr Siebeck, 1994.
Avishur, Yitzhak. "Darkhe ha-emori. Ha-reqa' ha-kena'ani-bavli we-ha-mivne ha-sifruti." In *Studies in the Bible and the Hebrew Languague offered to Meir Wallenstein on the Occasion of his Seventy-Fifth Birthday.* Edited by Chaim Rabin, et al. 17–47. Jerusalem: Jewish Society for Bible Research in Israel and the Tarbut Society, 1979.
Bacher, Wilhelm. "Lilith, Königin von Smargad." *Monatsschrift für die Geschichte und Wissenschaft des Judentums* 19 (1870): 187–189.
Barb, Alfons A. "Diva Matrix: A Faked Gnostic Intaglio in the Possession of P. P. Rubens and the Iconology of a Symbol." *Journal of the Warburg and Courtauld Institutes* 16 (1953): 193–238.
Bäumer, Änne. "Die Macht des Wortes in Religion und Magie, Plinius Naturalis Historia 28: 4–29." *Hermes* 112 (1984): 84–99.
Beagon, Mary. *Roman Nature: The Thought of Pliny the Elder.* Oxford: Clarendon, 1992.
Berliner, Abraham. *Targum Onkelos: Einleitung und Register.* Frankfurt am Main: Kauffmann, 1884.
Ben-Sasson, Ḥaim H. "The Reformation in Contemporary Jewish Eyes." *Proceedings of the Israel Academy of Sciences and Humanities* 4 (1971): 239–327.
Berger, Ruth. *Sexualität, Ehe und Familienleben in der jüdischen Moralliteratur (900–1900).* Wiesbaden: Harassowitz, 2003.

Bergmann, Jehuda. "Zur Geschichte religiöser Bräuche." *Monatsschrift für die Geschichte und Wissenschaft des Judentums* 71 (1927): 161–171.

Bergmann, Jehuda. "Die Schicksalserforschung der römischen Kaiser in der Agada." *Monatsschrift für Geschichte und Wissenschaft des Judentums* 81 (1937): 478–479.

Bezold, Carl, ed. *Die Schatzhöhle aus dem syrischen Texte dreier unedirten Handschriften in's Deutsche übersetzt und mit Anmerkungen versehen von Carl Bezold*. Leipzig: J. C. Hinrisch'sche Buchhandlung, 1883.

Biale, David. *Eros and the Jews: From Biblical Israel to Contemporary America*. New York: Basic Books, 1992.

Bidussa, David. "Macchina mitologica e indagine storica: A Proposito di Pasque di sangue e del 'mestiere di storico.'" In *Vero e falso*. Edited by Marina Caffiero and Micaela Procaccia, 139–172. Rome: Donzelli, 2008.

Blau, Ludwig. *Studien zum althebräischen Buchwesen und zur biblischen Litteratur- und Textgeschichte*. Straßburg: Trübner, 1902.

Blaufuss, Hans. *Römische Feste und Feiertage nach den Traktaten über fremden Dienst (Aboda zara) in Mischna, Tosefta, Jerusalemer und babylonischem Talmud*. Nuremberg: Stich, 1909.

Blidstein, Gerald. "A Roman Gift of Strenae to the Patriarch Judah II." *Israel Exploration Journal* 22 (1972): 150–152

Brown, Peter. *Macht und Rhetorik in der Spätantike: Der Weg zu einem "christlichen Imperium."* Munich: DTV, 1995.

Bruns, Paul J. "Syrische Nachrichten von den griechischen Übersetzungen aus Manuscripten gesammelt." *Eichorn's Repertorium für biblische und morgenländische Litteratur* 14 (1784): 39–59.

Buber, Salomon, ed. *Midrasch Tehillim (Schocher Tob): Sammlung agadischer Abhandlungen über die 150 Psalmen. Herausgegeben nach einer Handschrift aus der Bibliothek zu Parma cod. 1332 [1232], mit Vergleichungen der Lesarten anderer sieben Handschriften*. Edited by Salomon Buber. Wilna: Wittwe & Gebruder, 1891.

Castiglioni, Arturo. "The Contribution of the Jews to Medicine." In *The Jews: Their History, Culture, and Religion*. Edited by Louis Finkelstein, vol. 2, 1358–1359. New York: Harper & Row 1960.

Chiesa, Bruno and Wilfrid Lockwood, ed. and trans. *Ya'qūb al-Qirqisānī on Jewish Sects and Christianity: A Translation of "Kitāb al-anwār."* Frankfurt am Main: Lang, 1984.

Cohen, Gerson D. "Esau as Symbol in Early Medieval Thought." In *Jewish Medieval and Renaissance Studies*. Edited by Alexander Altman, 19–48. Cambridge, Mass.: Harvard University Press, 1967.

Cohen, Gerson D., Shaye J. D. "Anti-Semitism in Antiquity: the Problem of Definition." In *History and Hate. The Dimension of Anti-Semitism*. Edited by David Berger, 43–47. Philadelphia, New York, and Jerusalem: Jewish Publication Society, 1986.

Columella, *On Agriculture*. Vol. 2, translated by E. S. Forster and Edward H. Heffner. Cambridge, Mass.: Harvard University Press, 1941–1955.

Chronicles (The) of Jerahmeel. Translated by Moses Gaster, and revised by Haim Schwarzbaum. New York: Ktav 1971.

Cross, Frank M. "The History of the Biblical Text in the Light of the Discoveries in the Judean Desert." *Harvard Theological Review* 57 (1964): 281–299.

D'Alverny, Marie-Thérèse. "Survivance de la magie antique." in *Antike und Orient im Mittelalter: Vorträge der Kölner Mediaevistentagungen, 1956–1959*. Edited by Paul Wilpert, 154–178. Berlin: De Gruyter, 1962.

Dan, Joseph. "Samael, Lillith and the Concept of Evil in the Early Kabbalah." *AJS Review* 5 (1980): 17–40.
David, Ernie. "Memories of my Grandfather, Louis Finkelstein." http://www.cs.nyu.edu/faculty/davise/personal/lf/memories.html, accessed August 31, 2010.
de Lange, Nicholas. *Origen and the Jews: Studies in Jewish-Christian Relations in Third-Century Palestine*. Cambridge: Cambridge University Press, 1977.
De' Rossi, Azariah. *Me'or 'Enayim*. Edited by Dawîd Qassel. Vilnius: Romm, 1864–1866. Repr. Jerusalem: Makor, 1970.
Dean, James E. Ed. *Epiphanius' Treatise on Weights and Measures: The Syriac Version*. Chicago: The University of Chicago Press, 1935.
Dibelius, Martin. *Die Formgeschichte des Evangeliums*. Tübingen: Mohr, 1933.
Dio Cassius: *Dio's Roman History*. Translated by Earnest Cary and Herbert B. Foster. Cambridge, Mass.: Harvard University Press, 1914.
Dittenberger, Wilhelm, ed. *Sylloge Inscriptionum Graecorum* vol. 1. Leipzig: Hirzelium, 1915.
Diodorus: Diodorus Siculus, edited and translated by Charles H. Oldfather. Cambridge, Mass., and London: Harvard University Press, 1946.
Dupont-Sommer, André. "Deux lamelles d'argent à inscription hébréo-araméenne trouvées à Agabeyli (Turquie)." *Jahrbuch für Kleinasiatische Forschung* 1 (1950/51): 1403–1413.
Eckert, Willehad Paul. "Aus den Akten des Trienter Judenprozesses." In *Das Judentum im Mittelalter*. Edited by Paul Wilpert, 281–336. Berlin: De Gruyter, 1966.
Edelstein, Ludwig. *Ancient Medicine: Selected Papers of Ludwig Edelstein*, edited by Owsei Temkin and C. Lilian Temkin. Baltimore: The Johns Hopkins University Press, 1967.
Ehrlich, Ernst L. "Luther und die Juden." In *Antisemitismus: Von der Judenfeindschaft zum Holocaust*. Edited by Herbert A. Strauss and Norbert Kampe, 47–66. Frankfurt am Main: Campus, 1988.
Elizur, Shulamit, ed., *The Liturgical Poems of Rabbi Pinhas ha-Cohen* [Hebrew]. Jerusalem: World Union of Jewish Studies, 2004.
Enelow, Hyman G., ed. *The Mishna of Rabbi Eliezer or The Midrash of the Thirty-Two Hermeneutic Rules*. New York: Bloch, 1933.
Ernout, Alfred. "La magie chez Pline l'Ancien." In *Hommages à Jean Bayet*. Edited by Marcel Renard and Robert Schilling, 190–195. Brussels-Berchem: Latomus Revue d'Études Latines, 1964.
Evans-Pritchard, Edward P. *Theories of Primitive Religion*. Oxford: Clarendon Press, 1965.
Feldman, Louis H. *Jew and Gentile in the Ancient World: Attitudes and Interactions from Alexander to Justinian*. Princeton: Princeton University Press, 1993.
Field, Friderichus, ed., *Origenis Hexaplorum quae supersunt sive veterum interpretum Graecorum in totum vetus testamentum fragmenta* vol. 1–2. Oxford: Clarendom, 1875, reprint Hildesheim: Olms, 1964.
Fink, Robert O., Allan Hoey, and Walther F. Snyder, "The Feriale Duranum." *Yale Classical Studies* 7 (1940): 1–222.
Fishbane, Michael. *Biblical Interpretation in Ancient Israel*. Oxford: Oxford University Press, 1985.
Flusser, David, ed. *The Josippon (Josephus Gorionides)*. Jerusalem: The Bialik Institute, 1980–1981.
Fögen, Marie-Theres. *Die Enteignung der Wahrsager: Studien zum kaiserlichen Wissensmonopol in der Spätantike*. Frankfurt am Main: Suhrkamp, 1993.
Frankel, Zacharias. *Über den Einfluß der palästinischen Exegese auf die alexandrinische Hermeneuthik*. Leipzig: Barth, 1851.

Frankel, Zacharias. *Vorstudien zu der Septuaginta*. Leipzig: Vogel, 1841.
Freedman, Harry and Maurice Simon, trans. *Midrash Rabbah in Ten Volumes*. Vol. 1: *Genesis 1*. London: Soncino Press, 1961.
Friedheim, Emmanuel. *Rabbinism et Paganism en Palestine romaine. Étude historique de Realia talmudiques (Ier–IVème siècles)*. Leiden, Boston: Brill, 2006.
Friedmann, Meir. *Onkelos und Akylas*. Wien: Lippe, 1896.
Friedman, M. A. "u-katevu lo, 'ose lo ktav." *Sinai* 84 (1979): 177–179.
Gager, John G. *Curse Tablets and Binding Spells from the Ancient World*. New York: Oxford University Press, 1999.
Ganschinietz, Richard. *Hippolytos' Capitel gengen die Magier, Refut. haer. IV 28–42*. Leipzig: Hinrichs, 1913.
Gaster, Moses. "Beiträge zur vergleichende Sagen- und Märchenkunde: X. Lilith und die drei Ängel." *Monatsschrift für die Geschichte und Wissenschaft des Judentums* 29 (1880): 553–565.
Gaster, Moses. "Two Thousand Years of a Charm against the Child-Stealing Witch." *Folk-Lore* 11 (1900): 129–161.
Gaster, Moses. *Studies and Texts in Folklore, Magic, Medieval Romance, Hebrew Apocrypha and Samaritan Archaeology*. Vol. 3. London: Maggs, 1928.
Gaster, Moses. Ed. and trans. *Ma'aseh Book: Book of Jewish Tales and Legends* vol. 2. Philadelphia: Jewish Publication Society of America, 1934.
Geiger, Abraham. *Urschrift und Uebersetzungen der Bibel in ihrer Abhängigkeit von der innern Entwickelung des Judenthums*. Breslau: Hainauer, 1857.
Geiger, Joseph. "Latin in Roman Palestine." *Cathedra* 74 (1994): 3–35.
Ginsburg, Christian D. *Introduction to the Masoreticretico-Critical Editions of the Hebrew Bible*. London: Trinitarian Bible Society, 1894.
Ginzberg, Louis. *The Legends of the Jews*. Philadelphia: Jewish Publication Society of America, 1968.
Goldberger, Isidor. "Der Talmid Chacham." *Monatsschrift für Geschichte und Wissenschaft des Judentums* 68 (1924): 211–225; 291–307.
Goldin, Judah. "The Magic of Magic and Superstition." In *Aspects of Religious Propaganda in Judaism and Early Christianity*, ed. Elisabeth Schüssler Fiorenza, 115–147. Notre Dame, Ind.: University of Notre Dame Press, 1976.
Goldziher, Ignaz. "Wasser als Dämonen abwehrendes Mittel." *Archiv für Religionswissenschaft* 13 (1910): 20–46
Gordon, Cyrus H. "Aramaic Incantation Bowls." *Orientalia* NS 10 (1941): 116–141.
Grabbe, Lester L. "Aquila's Translation and Rabbinic Exegesis." *Journal of Jewish Studies* 33 (1982): 527–536.
Graetz, Heinrich. *Geschichte der Juden von den ältesten Zeiten bis auf die Gegenwart*, vol. 3/2. Leipzig: Leiner, 1906.
Greenfield, Jonas. "raten magusha." In *Joshua Finkel Festschrift: In Honor of Joshua Finkel*, edited by Sidney Benjamin Hoenig and Leon D. Stitskin, 63–69. New York: Yeshiva University Press, 1974.
Grimm, Jakob. *Deutsche Mythologie* vol. 3. Göttingen: Dieterische Buchhandlung, 1854 [reprint Berlin: Ullstein 1981].
Grünbaum, Max. "Beiträge zur vergleichenden Mythologie aus der Hagada." *Zeitschrift der deutschen Morgenländischen Gesellschaft* 31 (1877): 183–359.
Grünwald, Max. "Kleine Beiträge zur jüdischen Volkskunde: Aus Hausapotheke und Hexenküche II." *Monatsschrift der jüdischen Volkskunde* NF 3 (1907): 118–145.

Güdeman, Moritz. "Vermischungen von Jüdischen und Heidnischem aus neuer und alter Zeit." *Monatsschrift für die Geschichte und Wissenschaft des Judentums* 24 (1875): 269–273.
Gülke, Peter. "Nachruf auf den Urtext?" *Die Musikforschung* 57 (2004): 383–388.
Hadas, Moses. *Aristeas to Philocrates*. New York: Harper, 1951.
Hadas-Lebel, Mireille. *Le Paganisme à travers les sources rabbiniques des IIe et IIIe siécles: contribution à l'étude du syncrétisme dans l'empire romain*. Berlin and New York: De Gruyter, 1979.
Halbertal, Moshe. *People of the Book: Canon, Meaning, and Authority*. Cambridge, Mass.: Harvard University Press, 1997.
Hallewy, E. E. "Concerning the Ban of Greek Wisdom [Hebrew]." *Tarbiz* 41 (1971): 269–274.
Hayman, Peter. "Monotheism – A Misused word in Jewish Studies?" *Journal of Jewish Studies* 42 (1991): 1–15.
Heitsch, Ernst. *Gesammelte Schriften*. Vol. 1: *Zum frühgriechischen Epos*. Munich and Leipzig: Saur, 2001.
Herr, Moshe D. "The Historical Significance of the Dialogues Between Jewish Sages and Roman Dignitaries." *Scripta Hierosolymitana* 22 (1971): 123–150
Herz, Peter. "Herrscherverehrung und lokale Festkultur im Osten des römischen Reiches (Kaiser/Agone)." In *Römische Reichsreligion und Provinzialreligion*, edited by Hubert Cancik and Jörg Rüpke. Tübingen: Mohr Siebeck, 1997.
Heim, Ricardus. *Incantamenta Magica Graeca Latina*. Leipzig: Teubner, 1892.
Heszer, Catherine. "Social Fragmentation, Plurality of Opinion, and Nonobservance of Halakha: Rabbis and Community in Late Roman Palestine." *Jewish Studies Quarterly* 1 (1993–1994): 234–251.
Heszer, Catherine. Ed. *The Oxford Handbook of Jewish Daily Life in Roman Palestine*. Oxford: Oxford University Press, 2010.
Himmelfarb, Martha. Review of *Jew and Gentile in the Ancient World: Attitudes and Interactions from Alexander to Justinian* by Louis H. Feldman. *Judaism* 43 (1994): 328–334.
Hody, Humphrey. "Contra historiam LXX interpretum Aeristeae nomine inscriptum dissertation." In Hody, *De Bibliorum textibus originalibus versionibus graecis et latina vulgata*, 1–89. Oxonii: Scheldoniano, 1705.
Hogan, Larry O. *Healing in the Second Temple Period*. Fribourg and Göttingen: Vandenhoeck & Ruprecht, 1992.
Horace. *The Odes of Horace: Translated into English Verse with a Life and Notes by Theodore Martin*. Boston: Ticknor and Fields, 1861.
Ibn Daud, Abraham ben David/Halevi. *Seder 'olam rabbah we-seder 'olam zuṭa u-Megillat Ta'anit: we-Sefer ha-Qabbalah leha-Ra'avad: we-Divre malkhe Bayit Sheni*. Amsterdam: Bi-defus uve-vet Shelomoh ben Yosef Kats Props, Mokher sefarim, 5471 [1710/1711].
Idel, Moshe. *Golem: Jewish Magical und Mystical Traditions on the Artificial Anthropoid,*. Albany, N.Y.: State University of New York Press, 1990.
Isaac, Benjamin H. *The Limits of Empire: The Roman Army in the East*. New York: Oxford University Press, 1990.
Jacobs, Louis. *A Tree of Life: Diversity, Flexibility and Creativity in Jewish Law*. Oxford: The Littman Library and Oxford University Press, 1984.
Jacobs, Martin. *Die Institution des jüdischen Patriarchen: Eine quellen- und traditionskritische Studie zur Geschichte der Juden in der Spätantike*. Tübingen: Mohr Siebeck, 1995.

Jacobs, Martin. *Islamische Geschichte in jüdischen Chroniken*. Tübingen: Mohr Siebeck, 2004.
Jastrow, Markus. *A Dictionary of the Targumim, the Talmud Babli and Yerushalmi, and the Midrashic Literature*. London: Luzac, 1903.
Jellinek, Adolf, ed. *Bet ha-Midrasch: Sammlung kleiner Midraschim und vermischter Abhandlungen aus der älteren jüdischen Literatur*. 6 vols. Leipzig: Nies, 1853–1877.
Joël, Manuel. *Blicke in die Religionsgeschichte zu Anfang des zweiten christlichen Jahrhunderts*. Vol. 1. Breslau: Schottlaender, 1880.
Kamil, Murad, ed. *Des Josef ben Gorion (Josippon) Geschichte der Juden, Zēna Āihŭd*. Hamburg and New York: Augustin, 1937.
Kidd, John. "The Scandal of Ulysses." *New York Review of Books* (June 30, 1988): 32–39.
Kirchhahn, Elhanan Hendel. *Simḥat ha-nefesh*. Frankfurt am Main: Matthias Andreae, 1707.
Kohut, Alexander. "Correction d'une erreur de copiste plusieurs fois séculaire." *Revue des Études Juives* 22 (1891): 210–212.
Köves-Zulauf, Thomas. *Reden und Schweigen: Römische Religion bei Plinius Maior*. Munich: Fink, 1972.
Krauss, Samuel. "Akylas, der Proselyt." In *Festschrift zum achtzigsten Geburtstage Moritz Steinschneider's*, 148–163. Leipzig: Harrassowitz, 1896.
Krauss, Samuel. *Griechische und lateinische Lehnwörter im Talmud, Midrasch und Targum*. 2 Vols. Berlin: Calvary, 1899; repr. Hildesheim: Olms, 1964.
Kriss, Rudolf. *Das Gebärmuttermotiv: Ein Beitrag zur Volkskunde nebst einer Einleitung über Arten und Bedeutung der deutschen Opfergebräuche der Gegenwart*. Augsburg: Filser, 1929.
Kurrelmeyer, William. "German Lexicography – Part IX," *Modern Language Notes* 60 (1945): 157–166.
Laertes, Diogenes. *Lives of Eminent Philosophers*. 2 Vols., translated by Robert D. Hicks. Cambridge: Mass.: Harvard University Press, 1972 = 1925.
Lauterbach, Jacob Z. "The Three Books Found in the Temple at Jerusalem." *Jewish Quarterly Review* NS 8 (1917–1918): 385–423.
Leder, Stefan. *Spoken Word and Written Text: Meaning and Social Significance of the Institution of Riwāya*. Tokyo: Islamic Area Studies Project, 2002.
Lemprière, John, Lorenzo da Ponte, and John David Ogilby. *Bibliotheca classica: Or a Dictionary of all the Principal Names and Terms Relating to the Geography, Topography, History, Literature, and Mythology of Antiquy and of the Ancients*. New York: W. C. Dean, 1851.
Lewy, Heinrich. "Philologische Streifzüge in dem Talmud." *Philologus* 52 (1898): 567–572.
Lewy, Israel. "Über die Spuren des griechischen und römischen Alterthums im talmudischen Schriftthum." In *Verhandlungen der 33. Versammlung Deutscher Philologen und Schulmänner*. Leipzig: Teubner, 1878.
Levine, Baruch E. "The Language of the Magical Bowls." In Jacob Neusner, *A History of the Jews in Babylonia*, vol. 5: *Later Sasanian Times*, 343–375. Leiden: Brill, 1970.
Levine, Lee I. *Caesarea under Roman Rule*. Leiden: Brill, 1975.
Levy, B. Barry. *Fixing God's Torah: The Accuracy of the Hebrew Bible Text in Jewish Law*. New York: Oxford University Press, 2001.
Lieberman, Saul. *Greek in Jewish Palestine*. New York: Jewish Theological Seminary, 1965.
Lieberman, Saul. *Hellenism in Jewish Palestine: Studies in the literary transmission beliefs and manners of Palestine in the I century BCE–IV century CE* New York: Jewish Theological Seminary, 1962.

Lieberman, Saul. "The Martyrs of Caesarea." *Annuaire de l'Institute de Philologie et d'Histoire Orientales et Slaves* 7 (1939–1944): 395–446.
Lieberman, Saul. "Redifat dat Israel." In *Salo Wittmayer Baron Jubilee Volume on the Occasion of his Eightieth Birthday*. Vol. 3 [Hebr. Section]. Jerusalem: American Academy for Jewish Research, 1974.
Lieberman, Saul. *Texts and Studies*. New York: Ktav, 1974.
Lieberman, Saul. *Tosefta Ki-Fshutah: A Comprehensive Commentary on the Tosefta* [Hebr.]. Vol. 3. New York: Jewish Theological Seminary of America, 1962.
Linder, Amnon. *The Jews in Roman Imperial Legislation* [Hebrew]. Jerusalem: The Israel Academy of Sciences and Humanities, 1983; English Detroit: Wayne State University Press, 1987.
Linder, Amnon. *The Jews in the Legal Sources of the Early Middle Ages*. Detroit and Jerusalem: Wayne State University Press 1997.
Lloyd, Geoffrey E. R. *Magic, Reason and Experience: Studies in the Origin and Development of Greek Science*. Cambridge: Cambridge University Press, 1979.
Luther: D. *Martin Luthers Werke: Kritische Gesamtausgabe*, vol. 51. Weimar: Böhlau, 1914.
Luzzatto, Amos. *Una lettura ebraica del Cantico die Cantici*. Florence: La Giuntina, 1997.
Magie, David, ed. and trans. *Scriptores historiae Augustae*. Vol. 1. Cambridge, Mass.: Harvard University Press, 1921.
Maier, Johann. *Jesus von Nazareth in der talmudischen Überlieferung*. Darmstadt: Wissenschaftliche Buchgesellschaft, 1978.
Maier, Johann. *Jüdische Auseinandersetzung mit dem Christentum in der Antike*. Darmstadt: Buchgesellschaft, 1982.
Maier, Johann. "Magisch-theurgische Überlieferungen im mittelalterlichen Judentum: Beobachtungen zu 'Terafim' und 'Golem'." In *Die Juden in ihrer mittelalterlichen Umwelt: Protokolle einer Ring-Vorlesung gehalten im Sommersemester 1989 an der Universität Wien*, edited by Helmut Birkhan, 249–287. Bern: Lang, 1992.
Maimonides, Moses. *Mishneh Torah: The Book of Adoration*. Edited by Moses Hyamson. Jerusalem: Boys Town, 1965.
Mann, Jacob. "Changes in the divine service of the Synagogue due to religious persecution." *Hebrew Union College Annual* 4 (1927): 241–310.
Marchetti, Valerio. "The Lutheran Discovery of Karaite Hermeneutics." In *Una Manna Buona per Mantova: Man tov le-Man Tovah – Studi in onore di Vittore Colorni per il suo 92° compleanno*. Edited by Mauro Perani, 433–459. Florence: Olschki, 2004.
Marmorstein, Arthur. "Beiträge zur Religionsgeschichte und Volkskunde." *Jahrbuch für jüdische Volkskunde* 1 (1923): 280–319.
Marmorstein, Arthur. "Comparisons between Greek and Jewish Religious Customs and Popular Usages." In *Occident and Orient: Being Studies in Semitic Philology and Literature, Jewish History and Philosophy and Folklore in the Widest Sense – In Honour of Haham Dr. M. Gaster's 80th Birthday*. Edited by Bruno Schindler. London: Taylor's Foreign Press, 1936.
Menn, Esther M. "Praying King and Sanctuary of Prayer, Part I: David and the Temple's Origins in Rabbinic Psalms Commentary (Midrash Tehillim)." *Journal of Jewish Studies* 52,1 (2001): 1–26.
Michaelis, Johann David. *Deutsche Übersetzung des Alten Testaments, mit Anmerkungen für Ungelehrte*, vol. 1. Göttingen and Gotha: Dieterich, 1773.
Mieses, Matitjahu. "Die Dämonisierung fremder Feiertage: Die Umkehrung heidnischer Dekadenendtage durch die Hebräer." *Jahrbuch für jüdische Volkskunde* 26/27 (1925): 292–306.

Milikowsky, Chaim. "The Status Quaestionis of Research in Rabbinic Literature." *Journal of Jewish Studies* 39 (1988): 201–211.
Müller, Joel, ed. *Masechet Sopherim: Der Tractat der Schreiber, eine Einleitung in das Studium der althebräischen Graphik, der Masora und der altjüdischen Liturgie, nach Handschriften herausgegeben und kommentiert.* Leipzig: Hinrichs, 1878.
Müller-Kessler, Christa. *Die Zauberschalentexte in der Hilprecht-Sammlung, Jena, und weitere Nippur-Texte anderer Sammlungen.* Wiesbaden: Harrassowitz, 2005.
Naveh, Joseph and Shaked, Shaul. *Amulets and Magic Bowls: Aramaic Incantation of Late Antiquity.* Jerusalem and Leiden: Magnes, 1985.
Naveh, Joseph. *Magic Spells and Formulae: Aramaic Incantations of Late Antiquity.* Jerusalem: The Hebrew University Magnes Press, 1993.
Neubauer, Adolf. *Mediaeval Jewish Chronicles*, vol. 2. Oxford: Clarendon, 1895.
Neudecker, Reinhard. "Meister und Jünger im rabbinischen Judentum." *Dialog der Religionen* 6 (1997): 42–53.
Neusner, Jacob. *A History of the Jews in Babylonia: The Parthian Period.* Chico: California Scholars Press, 1984.
Neusner, Jacob. *The Making of the Mind of Judaism: The Formative Age.* Atlanta, Ga.: Scholars Press, 1987.
Neusner, Jacob. *The Talmud of the Land of Israel: A Preliminary Translation and Explanation*, vol. 11: Shabbat. Chicago and London: University of Chicago Press 1991.
Neusner, Jacob, trans. *The Tosefta.* 6 Volumes. New York: Ktav, 1977–1986 (reprint in 2 vols., Peabody, MA, 2002.
Nilsson, Martin P. "Studien zur Vorgeschichte des Weihnachtsfestes." *Archiv für Religionswissenschaft* 19 (1916/19): 50–150.
Noethlichs, Karl L. *Das Judentum und der römische Staat.* Darmstadt: Wissenschaftliche Buchgesellschaft, 1996.
Önnerfors, Alf, ed. *Antike Zaubersprüche* [Greek/Latin and German] (Stuttgart: Reclam, 1991)
Orlinsky, Harry M. "The Septuagint as Holy Writ and the Philosophy of the Translators." *Hebrew Union College Annual* 46 (1975): 89–114.
Patai, Raphael. "The 'Control of Rain' in Ancient Palestine: A Study in Comparative Religion." *Hebrew Union College Annual* 14 (1939): 251–286.
Paulys Real-Encyclopädie der classischen Alterthumswissenschaften. Several Volumes.
Pennington, Kenneth J. "The Council of Elvira, ca. 306." *The Catholic University of America*, http://faculty.cua.edu/pennington/Canon%20Law/ElviraCanons.htm (accessed February 16, 2013).
Perles, Felix. "Notes sur les Apocryphes et les Pseudépigraphes." *Revue des Etudes Juives* 73 (1921): 173–185.
Petronius: *Petronius*, translated by William H. D. Rouse. New York: Putnam's Sons, 1913.
Plato. *Laws*: trans. Benjamin Jowett. Available online at http://classics.mit.edu//Plato/laws.html (accessed October 2014)
Plato. *Timaeus* vol. IX, translated by R. G. Bury. Cambridge, Mass.: Harvard University Press, 1989.
Pliny the Elder, *The Natural History*, trans. John Bostock, vol. XXVIII,5, *Perseus Digital Library of Tufts University*, www.perseus.tufts.edu/hopper/text?doc=Plin.+Nat.+toc (accessed January 12, 2013).
C. Plinii Secundi Naturalis Historiae Libri XXVIII/C. Plinius Secundus d. Ä. Naturkunde. Buch XXVIII: Lateinisch-Deutsch. Edited and translated by Roderich König and Gerard Winkler. Munich and Zürich: Artemis, 1988.

Ploss, Heinrich, Max Bartels, and Paul Bartels. *Das Weib in der Natur- und Völkerkunde: Anthopologische Studien*. Vol. 1. Berlin: Neufeld und Henius Verlag, 1927.
Porton, Gary G. "Forbidden Transactions: Prohibited Commerce with Gentiles in Earliest Rabbinism." In *"To see Ourselves as Others See Us": Christian, Jews, "Others" in Late Antiquity*, edited by Jacob Neusner et al., 317–335. Chico, Calif.: Scholars Press, 1985.
Porton, Gary G. *Goyim: Gentiles and Israelites in Mishna-Tosefta*. Atlanta, Ga.: Scholars Press, 1988.
Preisendanz, Karl. "Ein Wiener Papyrusfragment zum Testamentum Salomonis." *Eos* 48 (1956): 161–167.
Ptolemaeus, Claudius. *Tetrabiblos*, edited and translated by Frank E. Robbins. Cambridge, Mass. and London: Harvard University Press, 1948.
Radbertus, Pascasius. *Expositio in lamentationes Hieremiae: Libri quinque*. Turnhout, Belgium: Brepols, 1988.
Rafal, Dov. *Sheva' ha-ḥokhmot: Ha-wikuaḥ 'al limmude ḥol be-sifrut ha-ḥinnukh ha-yahadut 'ad ha-haskala*. Jerusalem: Misrad ha-ḥinnukh we-ha-tarbut, 1989.
Raspe, Lucia. "Manetho on the Exodus: A Reappraisal." *Jewish Studies Quarterly* 5 (1998): 124–155
Rebiger, Bill. Ed. *Sefer Shimmush Tehillim: Buch vom magischen Gebrauch der Psalmen; Edition, Übersetzung und Kommentar* (TSAJ 137). Tübingen: Mohr Siebeck, 2010.
Reeg, Gottfried. *Die Ortsnamen Israels nach der rabbinischen Literatur*. Wiesbaden: Reichert, 1989.
Reichmann, Ronen. *Mishna und Sifra: Ein literarkritischer Vergleich paralleler Überlieferungen*. Tübingen: Mohr Siebeck, 1998.
Rohde, Erwin. *Psyche: Seelencult und Unsterblichkeitsglaube der Griechen*. Tübingen and Leipzig: Mohr, 1903.
Roueché, Charlotte, and Joyce Maire Reynolds, *Aphrodisias in Late Antiquity: The Late Roman and Byzantine Inscriptions Including Texts from the Excavations at Aphrodisias Cconducted by Kenan T. Erim*. London: Society for the Promotion of Roman Studies, 1989.
Ruderman, David B. *Jewish Thought and Scientific Discovery in Early Modern Europe*. New Haven, Conn: Yale University Press, 1995.
Sachau, C. Edward, ed. and trans. *The Chronology of Ancient Nations*. London: Allen, 1879.
Sacks, Nissin, Ed. *Mishna Zeraim* [Hebrew]. Vol. 1. Jerusalem: Institute of the Complete Israeli Talmud 1972.
Safrai, Ze'ev. "The Roman Army in the Galilee." In *The Galilee in Late Antiquity*. Edited by Lee I. Levine. New York: Jewish Theological Seminary of America, 1992.
Sammons, Benjamin. *The Art and Rhetoric of the Homeric Catalogue*. Oxford: Oxford University Press, 2010.
Scaliger, Justus. "Animadversiones in chronologia Eusebii" In *Thesaurus Temporum Eusebii Pamphili Caesareae Palaestinae Episcopi*, edited by Scaliger, 122–125. Leiden, 1606.
Schäfer, Peter, ed. *Synopse zur Hekhalot-Literatur*. Tübingen: Mohr Siebeck, 1981.
Schäfer, Peter. "Research into Rabbinic Literature: An Attempt to Define the Status Quaestionis." *Journal of Jewish Studies* 37 (1986): 139–152.
Schäfer, Peter. "Merkavah Mysticism and Magic." In *Gershom Scholem's Major Trends in Jewish Mysticism*, edited by Peter Schäfer and J. Dan, 59–78. Tübingen: Mohr-Siebeck, 1993.
Schäfer, Peter. *Judeophobia: Attitudes Toward the Jews in the Ancient World*. Cambridge and London: Harvard University Press, 1997.

Schäfer, Peter, ed. *The Talmud Yerushalmi and Graeco-Roman culture*. Vol. 1. Tübingen: Mohr Siebeck 1998.
Schäfer, Peter et al., ed. *Magische Texte aus der Kairoer Geniza* vol. 3. Tübingen: Mohr Siebeck, 1999.
Schäfer, Peter and Catherine Hezser, eds. *The Talmud Yerushalmi and Graeco-Roman culture*. Vol. 2. Tübingen: Mohr Siebeck, 2000.
Schäfer, Peter and Shaul Shaked. *Magische Texte aus der Kairoer Geniza III*. Tübingen: Mohr, 2000.
Schäfer, Peter, ed. *The Talmud Yerushalmi and Graeco-Roman Culture*. Vol. 3. Tübingen: Mohr Siebeck, 2002.
Scheftelowitz, Isidor. *Alt-Palästinensischer Bauernglaube in religionsvergleichender Beleuchtung*. Hannover: Lafaire, 1925.
Scholem, Gershom. *Jewish Gnosticism, Merkabah Mysticism, and Talmudic Tradition*. New York: Jewish Theological Seminary, 1965.
Scholem, Gershom. "New Chapters in the Story of Ashmedai and Lilith [Hebrew]." *Tarbiz* 19 (1948): 160–175.
Scholem, Gershom. *Zur Kabbala und ihrer Symbolik,*. Zürich: Rhein-Verlag 1960.
Schorch, Stefan. "The Pre-eminence of the Hebrew Language and the Emerging Concept of the 'Ideal Text' in Late Temple Judaism." In *Studies in the Book of Ben Sira: Papers of the Third International Conference on the Deuterocanonical Books, Pápa, Ungarn, 2006*. Edited by Géza G. Xeravits and József Zsengellér, 43–54. Leiden: Brill, 2008.
Segal, Alan F. *Two Powers in Heaven: Early Rabbinic Reports about Christianity and Gnosticism*. Leiden: Brill, 1977.
Segal, Alan F., Moses H. "The Promulgation of the Authoritative Text of the Hebrew Bible." *Journal of Biblical Literature* 72 (1953): 35–47.
Sicker, Martin. *The Moral Maxims of the Sages of Israel: Pirkei Avot*. Lincoln, NE: iUniverse, 2004.
Silverstone, Alec Eli. *Aquila and Onkelos*. Manchester: Manchester University Press, 1931.
Smallwood, E. Mary. *Documents Illustrating the Principates of Nerva, Trajan, and Hadrian*. Cambridge: Cambridge University Press, 1966.
Sparks, Hedley F. D., ed. *The Apocryphal Old Testament*. Oxford: Oxford University Press, 1984.
Sperber, Daniel. *Minhagei Yisra'el: Meqorot we-telodot*. 2 vols. Jerusalem: Mossad harav Kook, 1990–1991.
Sperber, Daniel. *Roman Palestine, 200–400*. Vol 1: *Money and Prices*. Ramat-Gan: Bar-Ilan University, 1974.
Stein, Siegfried. "The Influence of Symposia Literature on the Literary Form of the Pesa Haggadah." *Journal of Jewish Studies* 7 (1957): 13–44
Steinschneider, Moritz. *Die hebräischen Handschriften der K. Hof- und Staatsbibliothek in München*. München: Palm'sche Hofbuchhandlung, 1895.
Stemberger, Günter. *Das klassische Judentum*. Munich: Beck, 1979.
Stemberger, Günter. *Die römische Herrschaft im Urteil der Juden*. Darmstadt: Wissenschaftliche Buchgesellschaft, 1983.
Stemberger, Günter. *Juden und Christen im Heiligen Land: Palästina unter Konstantin und Theodosius*. Munich: Beck, 1987.
Stern, Menahem. Ed. and trans. *Greek and Latin Authors on Jews and Judaism* vol. 1–2. Jerusalem: The Israel Academy of Sciences and Humanities, 1974–1980
Stern, Sacha. *Jewish Identity in Early Rabbinic Writings*. Leiden and New York: Brill, 1994.

Strack, Hermann L., ed. *Talmud Babylonicum codicis Hebraici Monacensis 95: Der Babylonische Talmud nach der Münchener Handschrift Cod. Hebr. 95* [Faksimile]. Leiden: A. W. Sijthoff's Uitgevers Maatschappij, 1912.
Sussmann, Yaacov, ed. *Talmud Yerushalmi According to Ms. Or. 4720 (Sal. 3) of the Leiden University Library with Restoration and Correction, new printing*. Jerusalem: The Academy of the Hebrew Language, 2005.
Talmon, Shemaryahu. "The Judean 'am ha'areṣ in Historical Perspective." *Fourth World Congress of Jewish Studies* vol. 1 (1967): 71–76.
Thon, Johannes, Giuseppe Veltri and Ernst-Joachim Waschke. Eds. *Sprachbewusstsein und Sprachkonzepte im Alten Orient, Alten Testament und rabbinischen Judentum*. Halle: Zentrum für Interdisziplinäre Regionalstudien – Vorderer Orient, Afrika, Asien, 2012.
Toaff, Ariel. *Pasque di sangue: Ebrei d'Europa a omicidi rituali*. Bologna: Il Mulino, 2007.
Trachtenberg, Joshua. *Jewish Magic and Superstition: A Study in Folk Religion*. New York: Behrman's Jewish Book House, 1939 (repr. Philadelphia: University of Pennsylvania Press, 2004).
Trinkaus, Charles. *In our Image and Likeness: Humanity and Divinity in Italiaen Humanist Thought*, vol. 2. Chicago: Constable, 1970.
Ulfgard, Håkan. *The Story of Sukkot*. Tübingen: Mohr, 1998.
Ulmer, Rivka. "Creating Rabbinic texts: Moving from a Synoptic to a Critical Edition of Pesiqta Rabbati." In *Recent Developments in Midrash Research: Proceedings of the 2002 and 2003 SBL Consultation on Midrash*. Edited by Lieve M. Teugels and Rivka Ulmer, 117–136. New Jersey: Gorgias, 2005.
Ulmer, Rivka. Review of *"Geniza-Fragmente zu Avot de-Rabbi Natan,"* edited by Hans-Jürgen Becker. *Review of Biblical Literature*, February 5, 2005, http://www.bookreviews.org/bookdetail.asp?TitleId=4426&CodePage=4426 (accessed February 26, 2013).
Ulrich, Eugene, ed. *The Biblical Qumran Scrolls: Transcriptions and Textual Variants*. Leiden and Boston: Brill, 2010.
Urbach, Ephraim E. *The Sages: Their Concepts and Beliefs*. Cambridge, Mass. and London: Harvard University Press, 1975.
Urbach, Ephraim E. "The Rabbinical Laws of Idolatry in the Second and Third Centuries in the Light of Archaeological and Historical Facts." *Israel Exploration Journal* 9 (1959): 229–245.
Vajda, Georges. "La version des LXX dans la litterature musulmane." *Revue des Études Juives* 89 (1929–1930): 65–70.
Vana, Liliane. "Les relations sociales entre juifs et païens à l'époque de la Mishna: la question du banquet privé," *Revue des Sciences Religieuses* 71 (1997): 147–170.
van der Horst, Pieter. "Two Notes on Hellenistic Lore in Early Rabbinic Literature." *Jewish Studies Quarterly* 1 (1993–1994): 255–262.
van Esbroeck, Michel. "Une forme inédite de la lettre du roi Ptolémée pour la traduction des LXX." *Biblica* 57 (1976): 542–549
Veltri, Giuseppe. "Enteignung des Landes oder pax romana? Zur politischen Geschichte der Juden nach 70 (Josephus, Bell 7, 216–218)." *Frankfurter judaistische Beiträge* 16 (1988): 1–22.
Veltri, Giuseppe. "Defining Forbidden Foreign Customs: Some Remarks on the Rabbinic Halakha of Magic to the "Chapters of the Amorite.'" In *Proceedings of the Eleventh World Congress of Jewish Studies*. Div. C. Vol. 1: *Rabbinic and Talmudic Literature*, 25–32. Jerusalem: World Union of Jewish Studies, 1994.

Veltri, Giuseppe. "Die Novelle 146 Perì Hebraion: Das Verbot des Targumvortrags in Justinians Politik." In *Die Septuaginta zwischen Judentum und Christentum*. Edited by Martin Hengel and Anna. M. Schwemer, 116–130. Tübingen: Mohr Siebeck, 1994.

Veltri, Giuseppe. "Jewish Traditions in Greek Amulets." *Bulletin of Judaeo-Greek Studies* 18 (1996): 37–39.

Veltri, Giuseppe. "Zur Überlieferung medizinisch-magischer Traditionen: Das màtra-Motiv in den Papyri Magicae und der Kairoer Geniza." *Henoch* 18 (1996): 157–175.

Veltri, Giuseppe. *Eine Tora für den König Talmai: Untersuchungen zum Übersetzungsverständnis in der jüdisch-hellenistischen und rabbinischen Literatur*. Tübingen: Mohr, 1994.

Veltri, Giuseppe. "Letteratura etico-sapienziale del primo medioevo: Alcuni frammenti dalla geniza del Cairo." *Henoch* 20 (1997): 349–366.

Veltri, Giuseppe. *Magie und Halakhah*. Tübingen: Mohr-Siebeck, 1997.

Veltri, Giuseppe. "On the Influence of 'Greek Wisdom': Rabbinic Attitudes to Theoretical and Empirical Sciences," *Jewish Studies Quarterly* 5 (1998): 300–317.

Veltri, Giuseppe. "The Rabbis and Pliny the Elder: Jewish and Greco-Roman Attitudes to Magic and Empirical Knowledge." *Poetics Today* 19 (1998): 63–89.

Veltri, Giuseppe. "The 'Other' Physicians: the 'Amorites' of the Rabbis and the Magi of Pliny." *Koroth* 13 (1998-1999): 37–54.

Veltri, Giuseppe. "Der Magier im antiken Judentum: Von empirischer Wissenschaft zur Theologie," in *Der Magus: Seine Ursprünge und seine Geschichte in verschiedenen Kulturen*. Edited by Anthony Grafton and Moshe Idel, 147–167. Berlin: Oldenbourg, 2001.

Veltri, Giuseppe. *Gegenwart der Tradition*. Leiden: Brill 2002.

Veltri, Giuseppe. "'… in einigen Glaubensartikeln neigt die jüdische Nation eher zur römischen Kirche': Jüdische Gelehrte über Reformation und Gegenreformation." In *Katholizismus und Judentum: Gemeinsamkeiten und Verwerfungen vom 16. bis zum 20. Jahrhundert*. Edited by Hubert Wolf and Giuseppe Veltri, 15–29. Regensburg: Pustet, 2005.

Veltri, Giuseppe. "Magic, Sex and Politics: The Media Power of Theatre Amusements in the Mirror of Rabbinic Literature." In *The Words of a Wise Mouth are Gracious: Divre Pi-Hakam Hen – Festschrift for Günter Stemberger in his 65th Birthday*. Edited by Mauro Perani, 243–256. Berlin: De Gruyter, 2005.

Veltri, Giuseppe. *Libraries, Translations, and "Canonic" Texts: The Septuagint, Aquila, and Ben Sira in Jewish and Christian Tradition*. Leiden and Boston: Brill, 2006.

Versnel, Hendrik S. *Inconsistencies in Greek and Roman Religion*. Vol. 2: *Transition and Reversal in Myth and Ritual*. Leiden: Brill, 1993.

Wandrey, Irina. *"Das Buch des Gewandes" und "Das Buch des Aufrechten": Dokumente eines magischen spätantiken Rituals*. Tübingen: Mohr Siebeck, 2003.

Weber, Robert, ed. *Biblia sacra iuxta Vulgatam versionem*. Stuttgart: Württembergische Bibelanstalt, 1975.

Weinstock, Stefan. "Saturnalien und Neujahrsfest in den Märtyreracten." In *Mullus: Festschrift Theodor Klauser*. Edited by Alfred Hermann and Alfred Stuiber, 391–400. Münster in Westfalen: Aschendorff, 1964.

Weismann, Werner. *Kirche und Schauspiele: Die Schauspiele im Urteil der lateinischen Kirchenväter unter besonderer Berücksichtigung von Augustin*. Würzburg: Augustinus-Verlag 1972.

Wellhausen, Julius. *Der arabische Josippus*, in *Abhandlungen der Königlichen Gesellschaft der Wissenschaft zu Göttingen*. Vol. 1. Berlin: Weidmann 1897.

Wewers, Gerd A., trans. *Avoda Zara: Götzendienst*. Tübingen: Mohr, 1980.
Wewers, Gerd A. *Geheimnis und Geheimhaltung im rabbinischen Judentum*. Berlin and New York: De Gruyter, 1975.
Yassif, Eli, ed. *Sefer ha-Zikhronot hu' Divre ha-Yamim le-Yeraḥme'el*. Tel Aviv: Tel Aviv University, 2001.
Zeitlin, Solomon. "Were There Three Torah-Scrolls in the Azarah?" *Jewish Quarterly Review* 56 (1965–66): 269–272.
Ziegler, Konrat, and Walther Sontheimer, ed. *Der Kleine Pauly: Lexikon der Antike in fünf Bänden*. Munich: DTV, 1979.
Zilsel, Edgar. "The Sociological Roots of Science." *American Journal of Sociology* 57 (1942): 245–279.
Zingsem, Vera. *Lilith: Adams erste Frau*. Tübingen: Klöpfer & Meyer, 1999.
Zimmels, Hirsch J. *Magicians, Theologians, and Doctors: Studies in Folk Medicine and Folklore as Reflected in the Rabbinical Responsa*. London: E. Goldston, 1952.
Zunz, Leopold. "Etwas über die rabbinische Litteratur [1821]." In *Zunz Gesammelte Schriften*, vol. 1, 3–31. Berlin: Louis Gerschel Verlagsbuchhandlung, 1875.
Zunz, Leopold. *Gesammelte Schriften*. Berlin: Louis Gerschel Verlagsbuchhandlung, 1875.

Index of Primary Sources

Tanakh – The Hebrew Bible

Genesis
1:1	178, 181
1:9	175, 178, 181, 183
1:26	21
1:27	21
2:4	228, 229
3:15	79
3:24	167
10:16	132
11	220
18:12	56
23:9	225
27:41	86
31:19	181
32:15	223
36:9	229

Exodus
4:20	229
7:11	166
7:14	87
7:22	166
8:17	132
10:21–3	265
10:22	181
14:20	181
14:19	180
15:26	104, 143
24:5	239
24:11	239
30:34	177
35:35	248
37:21	248

Numeri
1:38	229
5:11–31	171
16	222
24–26	221
11:2	225

Leviticus
13:42–43	133
18:3	58, 93, 94, 132–134
19:27	134
20:23	133
23:24	247–248

Deuteronomy
4:2	30
4:35	167
6:4–9	169
10:12–11:21	169
11:13–21	169
13:1	30
17:14–20	221
17:18	35, 257
18:9	58
18:11	58
18:22	166
20:2	221
20:17	132
21:7	221
24:6	138
26:3	221
31:9	29
31:9–13	240
31:12	29
32:27	238
33:27	224

2 Kings
23:3	29, 31
23	31
22–23	240

Isaiah
6:3	266
14:23	217
29:10	170
29:11	170

Jeremiah
34:5	92, 93, 134

Ezekiel
3:12	266
8:12	252
16:10	248
21:29	132
23:43	249

Psalms

1	56
1:2	56, 60
20	266
21	198
23:1	178, 180
47:15	250
48:15	250
55:23	217, 218
58:9	170
68:26	250
69:24	170
107:23	180
107:25	176
139:11	79
149:6	102

Proverbs

4:8	217
9:2	223
15:23	272
18:2	251
18:21	251
25:11	251, 252

Job

31:10	56
37:3	79
42:17	277

Judges

5:30	248
11:40	87

Ruth

4:18	228, 229

I Samuel

31:12	93
32:12	93, 134

Esther

1:6	252
2:22	20

Daniel

5:8	35

Ezra

4	227
4:7	35
4:14	32, 256
7	31
7:12	240
7:12–26	29
7:14	29

Nehemiah

8:8	36, 37

Maleachi

3:8	217

Mishnah

Avodah Zarah

1:1	69, 72
1:2	81
1:3	65
1:4	89
4:4	73

Avot

1:1	2, 18
2:1	19
5:32	230
6:4	17
6:6	17, 19

Eruvim

3:4	256

Kallah

1:17	239

Megillah

1:8	169, 222
2:1	258
4	260

Nega'im

13:2	246

Qinnim

3:6	272

Sanhedrin

7:4	165
10:1	143
10:1	271

Shabbat

6:2	107
6:10	132, 135, 165

Soṭah

7:2–4	221
9:14	102

Ta'anit
   3:9   74
   4   87

Yadayim
   3:5   270

Yoma
   5:3–4   182

Midrashim

Ba-Midbar Rabbah
   3   227
   3:3   37
   16:25   199

Bereshit Rabbah
   8:9   20
   12:6   228
   12:16   228
   16:4   49
   48:17   56
   78:12   252
   93:3   251

Esther Rabbah
   2:7   252

Leqaḥ Ṭov Bereshit
   1:1   35; 261

Leqaḥ Ṭov on shemot
   8:10   87

Rut Rabbah
   2:23   51

Sekhel Tov (acc. to Buber 28)   229

Shemot Rabbah
   9:11   166, 167
   42:8   50

Shoḥer Ṭov on Psalms
   117   74

Sifre ba-Midbar
   16   169, 222

Tanḥuma, Ṣaw
   14   198

Wa-yiqra Rabbah
   33:1   251
   33:6   249

Yalqut toledot
   §110   84

Babylonian Talmud

Avodah Zarah
   6a   78, 81
   8a   81, 86, 87
   8b   90
   10a   92
   11a–11b 133
   55a   136
   58b   223

Baba Batra
   16b   84
   134a   19

Bava Meṣia
   59b   20, 21

Bava Qama
   82b–83a 224

Berakhot
   17a   19
   24b   176

   32a   225
   55a–57b 129
   62a   21

Eruvin
   13a   231
   22ab   88
   24b   176
   53a   225

Ḥagiga
   16a   191

Ḥullin
   105b   137
   137b   223

Ketubbot
   5a   110
   15b   110
   19a   110

Megillah
- 3a — 36
- 9a — 230
- 9a–b — 253, 256
- 16a — 114
- 17a — 217
- 18a — 217, 258
- 24b — 225

Menaḥot
- 32b — 169

Nedarim
- 62a — 19
- 37b–38a — 36, 37

Niddah
- 31b — 273
- 48b — 177

Pesaḥim
- 8b — 63
- 11b — 137
- 25a–b — 74

Qiddushin
- 49a — 18, 160

Rosh Ha-Shanah
- 15a — 256
- 26a–26b — 6, 217

Sanhedrin
- 17b — 62
- 19b — 196
- 21b — 223
- 21b–22a — 35, 257
- 52b — 93
- 67a — 167
- 67b — 63, 165, 166, 183
- 101a — 272

Shabbat
- 17a — 259
- 53b — 107
- 63a — 19
- 65b — 176
- 66b — 176
- 66b–67a — 218
- 67a — 135, 142
- 67b — 157
- 75a — 161
- 104a — 227
- 129a — 87
- 115a — 258

Soṭah
- 22a — 16, 161, 219
- 49b — 224

Sukkah
- 20a — 227
- 28a — 19
- 29b–30a — 279

Yoma
- 18a — 217
- 35b — 23
- 84a — 110

Zevaḥim
- 37b — 36

Tosefta

Avodah Zarah
- 1:1 — 72
- 1:3 — 77
- 1:4 — 68, 89
- 2:6 — 54
- 2:7 — 54

Eruvin
- 6:13 — 88

Ḥullin
- 1:22 — 168
- 2:22 — 168

Megillah
- 4:41 — 18

Sanhedrin
- 4:2 — 93
- 4:7–8 — 257
- 12:5 — 271

Shabbat
- 4(5):10 — 107
- 6:1 — 58, 133
- 6:2 — 136
- 6:2a — 155, 157
- 6:2b — 155
- 6:3 — 156
- 6:4 — 145
- 6:4a — 191

6:5	156	7:7	157
6:8	146	7:12	146
6:9	138	7:13	59, 156
6:10	146	7:14	156
6:11	138	7:18	92
6:12	147	7:21	109, 142
6:13	147	7:23	143
6:14	147	7:25	132, 164
6:17	139	12:5	271
6:18	154	**Shevi'it**	
6:19	140	4:21	256
6–7	58	**Sukkah**	
7:5	140, 155, 156	3:3–13	248
7:6	154		

Jerusalem Talmud

Avodah Zarah		2:4(73b)	250
1:1(39b)	78, 252	11:1(71b)	257
1:2(39c)	68, 79, 81,84	**Moed Qatan**	
1:3(39c)	88	3:7(38b)	250
1,7(40a)	53, 60	**Pe'a**	
2:1(40c)	108, 148	2:6(17a)	260
2:2(40b)	168	**Sanhedrin**	
2:2(40d)	74, 209	2:4(20c)	257, 240
Berachot		2:8(20c)	93
8:5(12b)	79	**Shabbat**	
Demai		1:4(3c)	259
2:1(22c)	72	6,1(7d)	161
4,6(24a)	88	6:2(8b)	107
Eruvin		6:10(8c)	135, 148
5:1(22a)	68	6:10(8d)	108, 112, 168
5:1(22c)	227	14:4(14d)	168
5:1(22d)	88	**Sheqalim**	
Ḥagiga		5,1(48b)	62
1:1(87a)	176	**Sukkah**	
Megillah		3:5(53d)	247
1:11(71b)	50, 102, 220	**Ta'anit**	
1:11(71c)	258	1:4(64b)	74
1:11(71d)	224	4:2(68a)	224, 238

Apocrypha & Non-Canonical Texts

Joseph and Aseneth (Apocryphal Novel of)		**Sirach**	
19:1–4	274	36(33):6	55

Aggadic Midrashim

Shir ha-Shirim (Rabbah)
  4:11   248
Bereshit Rabbah
  8:9   20
  12:6   228
  16:4   49
  48:17   56
  66:14   84
  67:8   86
  78:12   78, 252
  93:3   251
Ba-Midbar Rabbah
  3   227
  3:3   37
Devarim Rabbah
  7:7   73
Ekha Rabbati
  1:1   248, 249
Pesiqta Rabbati
  §5   15, 259

Qohelet Rabba
  10:5   168
Shemot Rabbah
  9:11   166, 167
  15:27   49
  42:8   50
Halakhic Midrashim
Sifra aḥare
  Pereq 13   58, 59; 133
Sifra Beḥuqqotay
  11:1   223
Sifre Devarim
  §34   18
  §161   19
  §356   224, 238, 239
  §160   240
Mekhilta de rabbi Yishma'el
  Baḥodesh 2   221
  petiḥta   180
  pisqa 18   20, 132

Minor Tractates/posttalmudic texts

Avot de-Rabbi
  Natan   241
  3:3   37
  46   238

Massekhet
  Soferim   238, 255
  1:7   253
  6:4   224, 238
Sefer Torah
  1:6   255

Magic Medieval Texts

'Inyan Soṭa   123, 171
  See also Geniza Manuscripts
Chronicles of
  Yerahmeel   164, 236, 262
Havdalah de
  Rabbi Aqiva   123

Ma'ase bukh
  (Maiśebuch)   210, 211
Sefer
  ha-Malbush   123, 183
Shimmushe
  Tehillim   180
Sword of Moses   123

Medieval Texts and Authors

Alpha Beta de-ben
   Sira   117
Arba'a Turim   265
Beyt ha-beḥirah 'al masekhet
   megillah   258
Divre Malkhe Yisra'el ba-Bayit
   ha-Sheni   263
   50b   230
Megillat Ta'anit
   Batra   38, 255, 261, 264, 265
Minḥat Shay   229
Sawwa'at
   ha-RIVA   277
Seder 'olam raba we-seder
   'olam zuta   263
Sefer ha-Ittim of Rabi Judah ben Barzilai of Barcelona   258
Sefer ha-Yashar   183
Sefer ha-Zikhronot hu' Divrey ha-Yamim le-Yeraḥme'el   262
Sefer Kol Bo
   §63   265
Sefer Orhot
   Hayyim   264, 265
Sefer Yeṣira   181
Sefer Yosippon   261
Sefer 'Alilot
   Devarim   196
Sepher ha-Ittim   258
Shulḥan 'Arukh
   §576   212
Simḥat
   ha-Nefesh   276
Yeṣirat ha-Walad   276

Responsa/Medieval Texts

R.Shelomo b. Adret
   1,413   63

R.Shelomo ben Yeḥiel Luria
   §3   63

Christian Bible

Luke
   9:49–50   167
Mark
   6:21   92
Matthew
   5:13   17
Ephesians
   5:2   278
Revelation
   1:16   251

Ancient and Pre-modern Texts

Ambrose of Milan
De Officiis
    2.2.21   57
De Elia et ieiunio
    13:42   62
Apuleius Madaurensis
Apologia
    26–27   161
Aretaeus of Cappadocia
De causis et signis acutorum morborum
    2,11.1–3   193
Aristeas
    (Letter of)   30, 31, 226, 240, 256
Augustine of Hippo
    Sermo IX   51
Canons of the Synod of Elvira
Canon 34   212
Cassius Dio
Historia romana
    X   83
    XLVII:18   91
    LI:19,6   89
    LVII:15   62
Cicero
Ad Familiares
    IX:16   55
De Divinatione
    1:23,46   162
Clement of Alexandria
Stromata
    5:14–97,7   103
Codex Theodosianus
    IX.16.3,
    a321/4   150
    IX,16,4   161
    IX,16,6a   161
Columella
De re rustica
    VIII:5,12   141
    X:357–361   139, 164
Corpus Hermeticum
    16:2   168
Diodorus Siculus
Diodori bibliotheca historica
    II, 29:1–3   111
    II, 30:1   111

Diogenes Laertius
Vitae philosophorum
    VIII,8,34   137
Dioscurides
De Materia Medica
    II,126   135
Eligius
Paganae consuetudines
    156
Ephraim the Syrian
Spelunca Thesaurorum
    32
Epiphanius
De Mensuris et Ponderibus
    86:8   252
Eusebius of Caesarea
Praeparatio Evangelica
    IX:7,1   162
    XIII:12,2   103
Fulgentius Mythographus
Mitologiarum libri tres
    1:7,20   189
Herodotus
Historiae
    IV:26,7   91
Historia Augusta
Didius Julianus
    VII:9–11   1, 61
Hadrian
    XVII:3   86
Tacitus
    IX:5   85
Horace
Carmina
    3,27,1–12   59
Satirae
    II,7   86
Isidorus of Sevilla (Hispalensis)
Etymologiae
    11   199
Jerome
Apologia contra Rufinum
    79: 14–15   237
Commentarius in Isaiam
    10:34,8   200

Epistulae
    CXII:389   237
Prologus in Pentateuchum
    263

Josephus
Antiquitates
    XI,5   38, 44
De bello Judaico
    5,407   44

Livy
Ab urbe condita
    10.23.9–10   72

Lucian of Samosata
Philopseudes
    9   165

Lucretius
De rerum natura
    V,975   80

Macrobius
Saturnalia
    I:9,16   82
    I:10   86
    I:10,18   85
    I:10,24   85, 86
    I:12,2–16,37   66
    I:13,3   82
    I:16,5   66
    I:16,6   67
    I:16,7   67
    I:16,8   67
    I:16,9   70
    I:16,10   70
    I:16,14   70
    I:16,22   82

Marcellus Empiricus
De Medicamentis
    VIII:172   109, 143
    XV:108   109, 143
    XXI:3   190
    XXVIII:74   190

Maurus Servius Honoratus
Aeneis
    1.22.8   189
    10:76   190
Eclogae
    4:62   191

Numenios of Apamea
De Bono   162

Origen
Epistula ad Africanum
    20   130, 160

Ovid
Fasti
    I:175   76
Tristia
    II:497   52

Papyri Graecae Magicae
    108, 119,134, 168
    IV:665   198
    V:2345   198

Paschasius Radbertus
Expositio in lamentationes Hieremiae
    200

Paulinus of Nola
Epistulae
    13:16   57

Petronius
Satyricon
    74   139

Philo of Alexandria
Ad Gaium
    368   55
Contra Apionem
    I:41   32
    I:35   240
De Iosepho
    97:3   92
De Vita contemplativa
    50   62

Plato
Nomoi
    933d–e   159
Timaios
    91b   201

Pliny the Elder
Naturalis Historia
    X:75,152   140
    XX:49,126   140
    XXI:83,143   140
    XXI:104,176   140
    XXII:24,50   140
    XXVI:9,18–20   136, 150, 153
    XXVI:60,93   140
    XXVIII   150
    XXVIII:3,10   149

XXVIII:4,19–
20 144
XXVIII:4–29 154
XXVIII:5,22 76, 149
XXVIII:5,23 142
XXVIII:5,26 139
XXVIII:5,27 137
XXVIII:5,29 149
XXVIII:7,59 138
XXVIII:11,46 136
XXVIII:12,49 109,142
XXVIII:23,78 139
XXVIII:23,85 163
XXVIII:27,95 136
XXVIII:64,
127 147
XXVIII:78,
257 135
XXX:1,1 162
XXX:1,2 162, 163
XXX:4,13 163

Pliny the Younger
Epistulae
X:35 76
X:36 76

Porphyrios
De Abstinentia
IV:16 164

Prudentius
Contra Orationem Symmachi
I:237–244 76

Seneca
Apocolocyntosis
12.2–3 87

Sextus Empiricus
Pyrrhoneioi Hypotyposeis
III:205 162

Soranus
Gynaekologie
4,36,4 194

Statius
Silvae
1.6.82 87

Suetonius
Caligula
17 85

Suida
Lexicon 162

Symmachus
I:44 75
X:27 75

Tacitus
Annales
IV:70,1 76

Tertullian
De Spectaculis
XVII 53
XX 56
Exhortatio Castitatis
12 71

Testament of Solomon
18:34–40 109, 142

Theophrastus
Historia plantarum
IV, 4:2 248

Varro
De lingua latina
VI:12 67

Arabic Texts

Kitāb al-Anwār wal-Marāqib
262

Qu'ran 38

Manuscripts

Tosefta Manuscripts
Editio Princeps (First edition) 133
Manuscript Vienna 133

Cairo Genizah and other Manuscripts
T.S: Misc. 9.57,
fol. 1a/1 170
T.S.K 1.37 170

JTSL ENA 3635,
    fol.17a-d   171
T.-S. AS 142.13,
    fol. 1a/7–11   180
T.-S. AS 143.340,
    fol. 1a–2b   182
T.-S. 12.41   182
ENA 3635, 17a/1–17b/4 = T.S.K 1.56,
    fol. 1a/3–19   171
MS Oxford Michael 9,
    fol. 183b/19   180
MS New York JTSL 1878,
    fol. 81a/7   180
MS London Wellcome Institute Hebr. 34,
    fol. 7a/15   180
Qumran
    8Q(DJD III)   169
Manuscript Munich Hebr. 95
    fol.157b   173, 182, 203
MS Hebr. 790 (Jerusalem National University
    Library)   228
Codex Leningradensis
    19a   228

www.ingramcontent.com/pod-product-compliance
Lightning Source LLC
Chambersburg PA
CBHW062021180426
43200CB00030B/2612